Studien zum ausländischen und internationalen Privatrecht

253

Herausgegeben vom

Max-Planck-Institut für ausländisches und internationales Privatrecht

Direktoren:

Jürgen Basedow, Holger Fleischer und Reinhard Zimmermann

AF767682

Almudena de la Mata Muñoz

Typical Personal Security Rights in the EU

Comparative Law and Economics in Italy, Spain and other EU Countries in the Light of EU Law, Basel II and the Financial Crisis

Mohr Siebeck

Almudena de la Mata Muñoz, PhD (Universität Hamburg); Law and Business Law Degrees (Universidad Pontificia Comillas-ICADE, Madrid); Postgraduates in European Law (Europa Institut, Universität des Saarlandes) and in Business Administration (Haute École de Commerce (HEC)-Université de Liège and University of Reading). Currently Legal Counsel (European Affairs Coordinator) at the Spanish Central Bank and since 2000 Lecturer at the Humboldt Universität zu Berlin, Bucerius Law School and Universität Hamburg.
Previous positions include: Scientific Researcher at the Max-Planck-Institut (Hamburg) and at the Centre for European Policy Studies (Brussels) where she also acted as head of the European Credit Research Institute; and Management positions in leading EU and US Financial Institutions. She has been Advisor to the Deutsche Bundesbank and the European Commission; Member of the Study Group for a European Civil Code and appointed Scientific Committee Member of the European Credit Research Institute.

ISBN 978-3-16-150662-8
ISSN 0720-1141 (Studien zum ausländischen und internationalen Privatrecht)

Die Deutsche Nationalbibliothek verzeichnet diese Publikation in der Deutschen Nationalbibliographie; detaillierte bibliographische Daten sind im Internet über *http://dnb.d-nb.de* abrufbar.

© 2010 Mohr Siebeck Tübingen.

Das Werk einschließlich aller seiner Teile ist urheberrechtlich geschützt. Jede Verwertung außerhalb der engen Grenzen des Urheberrechtsgesetzes ist ohne Zustimmung des Verlags unzulässig und strafbar. Das gilt insbesondere für Vervielfältigungen, Übersetzungen, Mikroverfilmungen und die Einspeicherung und Verarbeitung in elektronischen Systemen.

Das Buch wurde von Gulde-Druck in Tübingen auf alterungsbeständiges Werkdruckpapier gedruckt und von der Buchbinderei Nädele in Nehren gebunden.

A mis padres y a mi hermana Guadalupe.
A los míos.

Preface

This volume was mainly written during the years I spent working as a scientific researcher at the *Max-Planck-Institut für ausländisches und internationales Privatrecht* in Hamburg. During that time, I had the opportunity to experience the immense value of comparative law as a source of creative legal thinking. The years spent in the financial industry also allowed me to complement the academic approach with pragmatic elements and a business perspective. I am grateful to all those who contributed to these exciting experiences.

This dissertation as well as the work performed as a member of the Study Group for a European Civil Code (Draft Common Frame of Reference) would not have been possible without the fabulous library of the *Max-Planck-Institute*. I wish to thank the Institute for treasuring the greatest international academic legacy for the benefit of researchers and visitors. I also thank my colleagues at the *Max-Planck-Institut* for their inspiring company and shared moments of academic work. I especially thank Nicole Monleón for her friendship and essential contribution to the PhD process and to Christoph Steck for his encouragement during the final phase.

I am deeply grateful to my supervisor, Prof. Dr. Mankowski, for his vision, profound trust and outstanding support. His generous words in his assessment's vote will remain source of encouragement. I further thank Prof. Dr. Freitag, for his also heartening second vote.

A warm and very special thanks to my parents and my sister Guadalupe for being my constant source of support and inspiration; and also to those key persons whose affection and care have provided me with balance and strength in life.

Die nachfolgende Arbeit wurde im April 2010 als Dissertation vom Fachbereich Rechtswissenschaft der Universität Hamburg angenommen.

Overview

Table of Contents

Abbreviations

ADC	Anuario de Derecho Civil
AGBG	Gesetz zur Regelung des Rechts der Allgemeine Geschäftsbedingungen
AC	Actualidad Civil
App.	Corte d'Appello
Arch. civ.	Archivio civile
Arch. ziv. Praxis	Archiv für die zivilistische Praxis
art.	article
arts.	articles
BBTC	Banca, Borsa e Titoli di Credito
BMIJ	Boletim do Ministério da Justiça
BGH	Bundesgerichtshof
BGHZ	Entscheidungen des Bundesgerichtshofes in Zivilsachen
Bull.civ.	Bulletin des arrêts des chambres civiles de la Cour de cassation
Cass.	Cassazione
Cass. s.u.	Cassazione sezione unite
Cass.civ	Cour de cassation, chambre civile
CC	Civil Code
CCJC	Cuadernos Cívitas de Jurisprudencia Civil
Comm.C.	Commercial Code
c.p.c.	Codice di Procedura Civile
D.	Recueil Dalloz
Dig. It.	Digesto Italiano
DNotZ	Deutsche Notar-Zeitschrift
ECR	European Court Reports
EU	European Union
f.	et sequentia
ff.	et sequentias
FI	Foro Italiano
FS	Festschrift
GI	Giustizia Italiana
GC	Giustizia Civile

ICC	International Chamber of Commerce
i.e.	id est
JCP	Juris-classeur périodique
JBl	Juristische Blätter
LC	Legge Cambiaria
LCC	Ley Cambiaria y del Cheque
LCS	Ley del Contrato de Seguros
LECiv	Ley de Enjuiciamiento Civil
LH	Ley hipotecaria
lit.	litera
LOE	ley de Ordenación de la Edificación
Law Q. Rev.	Law Quarterly Review
Nov. Dig. It.	Novissimo Digesto Italiano
NJW	Neue Juristische Wochenschrift
NJW-RR	Neue Juristische Wochenschrift-Rechtsprechungs-Report
no.	number
nos	numbers
OGH	Oberster Gerichtshof (Austria)
OJ	Official Journal
ÖJZ	Österreichische Juristen-Zeitung
OLG	Oberlandesgericht
p.	page
par.	paragraph
QB	Queen's Bench Division Law Reports (1891–) Queen's Bench Reports (Adolphus and Ellis New Series) (1841–1852) = ER 113–118
QBD	Queen's Bench Division Queens Bench Division Law Reports (1875–1890)
RA	Repertorio Aranzadi
RCDI	Revista Crítica de Derecho Inmobiliario
RDBB	Revista de Derecho Bancario y Bursátil
RDM	Revista de Derecho Mercantil
RDP	Revista de Derecho Privado
Rep.	Repertorio (FI Rep=Repertorio del Foro Italiano)
RGD	Revista General del Derecho
Riv. Dir. Civ.	Rivista di diritto civile
Riv. Dir. Comm.	Rivista di Diritto Commerciale
Riv. Dir. Domm.	Rivista di Diritto Domminicale
Riv. Not.	Rivista del notariato
RJC	Rules of Personal Security
RJN	Revista jurídica del notariado
RPS	Rules on Personal Securities

SAP	Sentencia de la Audiencia Provincial
SAT	Sentencia de la Audiencia Territorial
spec.	specially
STS	Sentencia del Tribunal Supremo
SSTS	Sentencias del Tribunal Supremo
Stan. L. Rev.	Stanford Law Review
Trib.	Tribunale
Tul. L. Review	Tulane Law Review
U. Chi. L. Rev	University of Chicago Law Review
US	United States
v.	volume
Vit. Not.	Vita notarile
Vorbem	Vorbemerkung
WM	Wertpapier-Mitteilungen
ZIP	Zeitschrift für Wirtschaftsrecht

Introduction

Over the last few decades, a growing credit-based culture has boosted the grant of credit and with it also the use of security rights. Particularly in recent times, the demand for personal security has expanded both in business as well as in the private sphere. Being less costly and burdensome than real security rights, personal security has become increasingly used in the context of small and medium sized enterprises, as well as for exports and investments in foreign countries. The significant increase of households´ indebtedness in the last several years has also boosted the use of personal guarantees, giving rise to a number of interesting legal issues, specifically related to consumer protection. In the context of Real Estate, guarantees "on first demand" have also been increasingly used as a protection for claims against building companies.

In terms of future trends, personal security rights are expected to play a key role in the coming years. The 2008 financial crisis has resulted in credit constraints so credit enhancers will likely be more required. Moreover, the recent downturn of the housing prices is reducing the appetite for mortgaged lending which may reflect into a greater use of personal security rights, especially as mortgages (and remortgages) were increasingly used to secure consumer loans in the last few years. The recent regulatory treatment of personal security rights as "credit risk mitigators" in the Basel II Accord and the Capital Requirements Directive will likely promote their use in the business context, as professional lenders will benefit from capital relief.

In view of this practical relevance, it seemed worth offering an in-depth access to the current status of the law and legal practice of personal security in several jurisdictions. With a focus on Italy and Spain and extensive references to EU law and other legislations, this comparative study aims at nurturing reflection on the different regulations as well as alternative ways to deal with the needs in commercial practice.

Beyond this practical approach, this thesis also aims at contributing to the works performed in the context of EU law harmonisation. The political will to unify EU Contract Law may soon turn into reality as a voluntary regime of common legislation (the so called Common Frame of Reference). Against this background, comparative studies provide the necessary basis to identify the implications and challenges of harmonising EU Contract Law. In particular, in the field of personal security, it is sensible to compare Italian and Spanish Law. In both countries the legal treatment of the guarantee contract is based upon the French codification (ultimately built on the Roman *fideiussio*). The Spanish regulation on the guarantee (including the local civil legislations ("foral laws"[1])), has remained mainly unchanged while the natural evolution due to social and economic needs has been reflected in the contractual practice and case law. By contrast, in Italy, the original codification of the guarantee was revised in the Civil Code of 1942. The result of the long drafting process for this new Code (starting 1922) is a highly elaborated codification which represents, beyond the introduction of modern elements, a synthesis between the two dominating models in European continental law: the French and the German. All this makes the Italian Civil Code a good basis for comparison between different EU legal systems.

Current practice and future legislation also need to take into account the most recent developments in contractual practice as well as in case law within the EU. For instance, the protection of private guarantors has been a rather recent development done mainly by courts on the basis of national and EU consumer protection legislation. Indeed, personal security rights are often granted by family members or friends in favour of their loved ones, normally in rather critical financial situations. Private guarantors are also often the directors of companies with limited liability for the financing of company debts. Such private guarantors provide security for emotional reasons, without being economically rewarded and are often not aware of the risk assumed.

These and other matters are extensively treated in this volume along the following six Chapters:

Chapter one refers globally to the system of security rights[2] both in Italy and Spain. It provides the framework and context to correctly place the personal security rights within the respective systems. The concept of se-

---

[1] Within the Spanish jurisdiction different civil law regulations (foral laws) coexist with the Spanish Civil Code. These regulations also partly include a number of provisions on the guarantee, which are also considered.

[2] With regard to terminology, within the English speaking context, the basic form of personal dependent security right ("fideiussione"/"fianza") is generally referred to as "guarantee" or "suretyship" in the US context. In this volume the term "guarantee" contract is used. The general form of independent personal security rights ("Garanzia" as compared to "Fideiussione" in Italy, "Garantie" as compared to "Bürgschaft" in Germany; "Garantie indépendante" and compared to "Cautionnement" in France) is referred to in the English-speaking literature as "indemnity" or "independent personal security right", which is the term used in this book.

curity right, the classification of these rights and their practical uses and functions are analysed in this Chapter.

Chapter two entails the bulk of the document and regards the full analysis of the guarantee contract as the basic form among the dependent personal security rights. The guarantee is still strongly used in commercial practice and provides the legal basis for the creation of a number of "atypical personal security rights" which are not regulated. A thorough knowledge of the guarantee is therefore essential to understand the evolution of personal security rights and contribute to further developments in this context.

Chapter three contains the study of other dependent personal security rights regulated in Italy and Spain such as the "aval", etc. The independent guarantee is left outside this chapter as it is not regulated in the Spanish Civil Code.

Chapter four studies the different possibilities and implications of combining a plurality of security rights, both personal and proprietary, for one debt.

Chapter five analyses the impact of the Basel II Accord and the EU Capital Requirements Directive on the contract of guarantee for the purpose of minimum capital requirements.

Chapter six reviews security rights in the context of the European Union. Specifically, it takes note of the recent attempts to develop European private law and the impact that this may have on security rights. Special reference is made to the policy and law making decisions taken in the context of the current financial crisis.

Chapter 1

The system of security rights in Italy and Spain

A. Delimitation of the concept of security right

I. The concept of security right in a broad sense

"The concept of security is easy to understand but difficult to define"[1]. Terminologically as well as conceptually a significant level of confusion has existed regarding the matter of security rights. Because the notion of security is present in many different spheres of human activity, it is difficult to offer an overarching, purely legal definition of the term absent of moral, social or economic connotations[2]. In both the Italian[3] and Spanish legal systems the word security ("garanzia"/"garantía") is used as a general term to describe a number of very different concepts, all of which are based on the idea of ensuring/securing a legitimate interest. Such functional approach combined with the variety of interests that are due to be protected, render it difficult to precisely define the concept of "security in this broad sense"[4]. Depending on the use and the interests protected, a different meaning will be given to the term. A basic distinction can be found between the use of security in public[5] and private law and also within Private Law, depending on the specific field[6].

II. The concept of security right in Private Law. The need for a flexible legal framework

A legal definition of security right does not exist within private law in either Italy or Spain. However, it is traditionally considered by legal writers

---

[1] *Cabrillac* and *Mouly*, 2; *Piazza*, 1.

[2] *Piazza*, 1; *Mastropaolo*, 23.

[3] *Thietz-Bartram*, 25–26; *Petti*, 506.

[4] Term used by *Cabrillac* and *Mouly*, 2.

[5] Constitutional Law, Administrative Law, Procedural Law.

[6] Also within Private Law there are different meanings and contents regarding the term „garanzia"/"garantía". This is patent within Italian Civil Code which art. 1266, art. 1267, art. 1490, art. 1512, art. 1575, art. 1585, art. 1667, art. 1668 contain the term garanzia referring to the obligation of a party to fulfil contractual duties. The legal formulation in Spain avoids the term garantía in these cases but it is commonly found in the theory.

to be any measure, which aims at securing the performance of an obligation owed by a person i.e. a credit.[7] Any discussion of the concept of security thus requires the consideration of some basic aspects of the concept of credit[8]. In many languages the term credit ("crédito", "crédito", "Kredit", "credit") finds its origins in the Latin word "credere", meaning trust or confidence[9]. Depending on the creditor's trust on recovery, security rights will be used to reinforce repayment chances and/or to improve the lending conditions[10]. All EU legal systems recognise the use of security rights within their contract law provisions. As contracts, they are governed by the principle of freedom of contract, which reflects twofold within the sphere of security rights. First and obviously, the parties to a typical contract of security right (as regulated by law) may agree on the terms of their contractual relationship. Second, new forms of contractual security rights might be developed beyond the standard (typical) forms. This has been the case in practice and especially in the field of personal security rights, with the use of so called atypical guarantees such as binding comfort letters, co-debtorship for security purpose or independent guarantees[11]

One lesson learnt from this recent expansion of personal security is that any rule-making in the field, be it by legislation or by informal means such as a restatement, must be flexible, so as to leave room for new developments, i.e. must not be mandatory[12]. An exception to this general principle can be drawn for the case of consumers[13] providing personal security. The high level of risk assumed by the guarantor (who, in application of general law of obligations, remains responsible for the guaranteeing obligation with the full patrimony until repayment) and the, in practice proven, lack

---

[7] *Petti*, 506; *Díez-Picazo*, Fundamentos, 395.

[8] Security rights are directly linked with the credit. "Le suretés sont les filles du crédit", *Cabrillac* and *Mouly*, 5. That is why the expansion of credit granted under the II World War brought also the expansion of security rights.

[9] The concept of credit is very old – historians have found that ancient civilizations had complex systems of lending and repayment. Very early banking systems even created regulation of debt, interest and credit extension. The historic philosophy on lending and debt was that individuals in debt would work hard to repay what they owed – the crop yields of farmers with debt were found to be significantly higher than those without debt", *Dyke*, 1. It is said that credit was defined as "a state of mind that all will honor their obligations", *Rhode*, 1.

[10] See below under: C. The practiacal functions of security rithts, 14.

[11] See within this Chapter, B. under: d) Different kinds of personal security rights (typical and atypical), 11.

[12] *Drobnig*, 2007, 80.

[13] The concept of consumer in this regard might be understood in defferent ways; either stricto sensu, as a private person contracting with a professional or more generally as a non-professional surety, private or legal person, dealing with a professional and being therefore the weakest part of the relationship.

of awareness on the possible effects of such risk justifies the mandatory application of protection rules to this type of weaker contractors. This has been the approach taken in the Dutch Civil Code of 1992, one of the more modern civil law codifications in the EU. The Book regulating personal security rights (Book 7, arts. 7:850-7:870) includes specific mandatory rules on dependent personal security rights agreed by consumers (arts. 7:857-7:864). Also in the context of academic work towards harmonisation of EU private law, the need to protect consumer guarantors has been particularly considered. In the Principles of European Contract Law (PECL) [14], the Book on Personal Securities has included a specific chapter (Chapter IV), entailing special rules for personal security for consumers[15/16].

III. The concept of security and the debtor's general liability

The central principle underlying the Italian and Spanish law of civil obligations is the principle of liability affecting one's own property (so called debtor's general liability) (art. 2740 Italian CC[17] and art. 1911 Spanish CC[18]). The creditor is thereby ensured that the present and future property of the debtor will be by law primarily allocated to perform the obligation owed. Since this principle contributes to assuring the performance of an obligation, it has been considered[19] as the most basic form of security for civil obligations. According to this theory, the primary security for a creditor is provided by the debtor himself[20]. This concept of "full liability" has been defined as "general security",[21] in contrast to so-called "specific security". It is a basic security provided to every single creditor, whom in case of non-performance will compete for payment with all other creditors of his debtor, under the principle of par conditio creditorum (equality of all

---

[14] The Principles of European Contract Law have been developed by a team of researchers in the framework of the Study Group on a European Civil Code. A special team of researchers of which I had the honour to be a member, developed a set of harmonised rules on Personal Security Rights. The result of the work was published in 2007. See, *Drobnig* et al.

[15] See, *Drobnig* et al., 379.

[16] The term 'consumer' must be understood in this context in a broader sense than is usual in European law. It refers to the weak party of the relationship. See *Drobnig* et al., 99.

[17] Art. 2740 Italian CC: "Liability affecting one's own property. A debtor is liable with all his present and future property for the performance of his obligations".

[18] Art. 1911 Spanish CC: "A debtor is liable for the performance of his obligations with all his present and future property".

[19] In Italy: *Torrente*, 368 f. For extensive references see: *Piazza*, 2. In Spain: *Guilarte*, 6 f.

[20] According to art. 1949 former Italian CC of 1865: "The goods of the debtor are a common security for his creditors [...]".

[21] *Petti*, 509; *Roca/Nieto*, 138.

creditors). By contrast, the idea of "specific security", i.e. a supplementary security over and above the debtor's general liability, is aimed at giving preference to those specifically secured creditors.

Certainly, the creditor's right vis-à-vis the debtor is also protected by the full liability principle. However, this principle is essentially inherent to every principal obligation while a security right means a new obligation is created in order to protect the creditor. Moreover, the full liability principle does not result in any supplementary reduction of the creditor's risk, hence, not fulfilling the basic function of a securitydo not agree[22]. Having thoroughly analysed the principle of full liability of the debtor, prestigious legal writers[23] prefer to use a more restrictive concept of security right, based on the fact that any such specific security enlarges the protection of the obligation above the automatic, general liability established in the Italian and Spanish Civil Codes.

In any case, whether the principle of full liability can be considered a security right, remains a theoretical discussion, with no practical implications.

B. Classification of security rights

I. Dichotomy between personal and real security rights

1. In general

Security rights (negozi giuridici di garanzia/negocios jurídicos de garantía) may be classified according to a number of different criteria, the main being the distinction between personal and real security rights. This distinction is clearly drawn in the Law of security rights in Italy and Spain[24].

2. Personal security rights

a) Concept of personal security right

The essence of a personal security is the personal undertaking assumed by a third party (the surety) to be answerable for the payment of another person's debt or the fulfilment of another party's contractual obligation. The surety assumes his own liability[25], known as the "guarantee obligation"[26].

---

[22] For an overview see *Petti*, 506.

[23] *Messineo*, 74 f.; *Díez-Picazo*, Fundamentos, 395 f. See also: *Montés/Valpuesa*, 235; *Lalaguna*, 397; *Díez-Picazo*, Fundamentos, 395 f.; *Montés/Valpuesa*, 235; *Lalaguna*, 397.

[24] *Ravazzoni*, 22; *Roca/Nieto*, 132.

[25] About the evolution of theories on the distinction of the guarantor's obligation from the principal debt, see *Giusti*, 7.

According to the principle of full liability for one's debts, the surety is liable for this guarantee obligation with his total present and future assets (patrimony). As a result, a new obligation is created and another patrimony serves to ensure performance of the original debt. The creditor assumes the risks of negative changes in the sureties' patrimony.

b) *Personal security rights granted by private or by professional sureties*

The traditional and most basic form of personal security is that granted by a private person. In modern practice, the importance of private guarantees has been complemented by an increase of personal securities provided by professional guarantors[27]. However, private guarantees are still regularly used and in certain situations almost automatically required. For example in Spain it is common to demand a mutual guarantee by spouses, so that not only the conjugal estate[28] (the community of goods) but also the property belonging to each of the individual spouses[29] secures the fulfilment of

---

[26] The liability of the guarantor derives from his own obligation to be answerable for the debt of another person. The guarantee obligation is therefore to be distinguished from the principal debt. The obligation of the guarantor must be valid according to the general rules on Civil Law: it must be validly assumed by the guarantor, on a valid object and with a causa of guarantee, which clearly differentiate it from the principal debt. "Il fideiussore assume un'obbligazione propria accessoria della principale [...], dalla quale può differire per contenuto e modalità, ma sempre un'obbligazione che serve di base alla pura responsabilità", *Ferrara*, 311.

[27] *Hémard*, 40.

[28] By virtue of the conjugal partnership the profits obtained by either of the spouses during the marriage shall belong to the husband and the wife, share and share alike, upon the dissolution of the marriage (art 1347 of Spanish CC). Art. 1347 Spanish CC: Community property consists of: 1) Things obtained through the work or industry of any of the spouses. 2) Fruits, rents or interest produced by both separate and community property. 3) Things acquired by onerous title at the expense of the community property, whether the acquisition is made for the community or for one of the spouses only. 4) Things acquired by a right of return, of a community nature, even where the acquisition is made with separate funds, in which case the partnership shall become a debtor of the spouse for the sum disbursed. 5) Enterprises and establishments founded during the existence of the partnership by any of the spouses at the expense of the community property. If both separate and community capital is used in the formation of the enterprise or establishment, the provisions of art. 1354 shall govern".

[29] See art. 1346 Spanish CC: "Separate property of the each of the spouses consists of: 1) Things and rights belonging to each of them at the beginning of the partnership. 2) Those acquired thereafter by each of them under gratuitous title. 3) Those acquired on account or in substitution of separate property. 4) Those acquired on account or in substitution of separate property. 4) Those acquired by the right of return belonging to one of the spouses only. 5) Stictly personal things and patrimonial rights and rights that are not transferable inter vivos. 6) Awards for damages caused to the person of one of the spouses or to his separate property. 7) Clothing and objects of personal use that are of no ex-

the debt assumed by one of the spouses[30]. Another example is that of limited liability companies. As the minimum capital required to create a limited liability company[31] is often considerably smaller than the large number of obligations and debts usually incurred by the company, the shareholders are often requested to assume personal liability for credit granted to the company[32]. Furthermore, subsidiaries frequently guarantee the debts of their parent company in practice.

In all these cases, the patrimony of the surety can drastically change, thus reducing or eliminating its security function[33]. It is a matter of risk management for the creditor to value the security and accept it as sufficient to cover the principal obligation in case of debtor's default. Non-professional guarantors are required to be more solvent than the principal debtor[34]. As professional sureties, such as banks or insurance companies[35] offer a lower risk of insolvency[36], a great number of personal security rights (especially in business practice) are granted by this kind of sureties. As a result, in the context of the modern credit economy[37], the personal guarantee has changed its assisting role to become a substantial element of commercial activity[38] and therefore of economic development.

c) State guarantees: and their particular role in the context of 2008/2009 financial crisis

The State or public entities may also act as sureties of certain types of credit. Usually, state guarantees are provided in order to enhance sectors of

---

traordinary value. 8) Instrumets necessary for the exercise of profession or trade, except when they are a part of, or belong to, an establishment or industry that is community property. The assets mentioned in numbers 4 and 8 shall not lose the status of separate property by virtue of the fact that they were acquired with community funds; but, in such a case, the partnership shall be a creditor of the owner spouse for the sum disbursed".

[30] See: *Rubio/Paquau*, on arts. 1821–1856, spec. chapter II, V. 5.

[31] 3000 Euro, art. 4 Law of limited liability company (Ley 2/1995, de Sociedades de Responsabilidad Limitada (LSRL)).

[32] *Cabrillac* and *Mouly*, 6.

[33] *Cano*, 588.

[34] Non professional guarantors need to have the necessary legal capacity to assume liability and also sufficient assets to provide security (art. 1828 Spanish CC). See *Llebot*, 26.

[35] "L'Octroi de sûretés et principalement de cautionnements [...] est le fait des banquiers", *Hémard*, 40.

[36] The solvency of professional sureties is partly secured by law.

[37] See *Schlessinger*, 485 ff cited by *Giusti, 7*.

[38] "Le code civil avait conçu le cautionnement comme un service de parent ou d'ami. Cette conception est évidement dépassée du fait que le cautionnement est devenu un instrument de crédit très répandu dans les droit des affaires", *Jestaz*, 1; *Lepach*, 18–20.

specific public interest, such as export finance (through export credit insurance).

In the context of the 2008 financial crisis, special state guarantee programs have been applied in particular to the financial sector. The fear of a sectorial collapse with a possible systemic risk impact has increased the general willingness to support this sector. This aid has been partly instrumentalised through State guarantee programs. The state aid nature of these guarantees justifies the application of state aid legislation. EU law (art. 86 and 87 EC Treaty) has hence covered a particular importance in view of the impact that such state aid could and would obviously have in the normal functioning of the single market. It is worth mentioning the special measures[39] taken by the EU institutions in view of protecting competition standards within the EU and on the basis of art. 96 and 97 EC Treaty. The Commission issued the EU Commission Notice on the application of art.87 and 88 of the EC Treaty to State aid in the form of guarantees[40]. This Notice updates the Commission's approach to State aid granted in the form of guarantees and aims to give Member States more detailed guidance about the principles on which the Commission intends to base its interpretation of Articles 87 and 88 and their application to State guarantees[41].

d) Different kinds of personal security rights (typical and atypical)

The contracts of personal security are not numerus clausus. Those personal security rights which are regulated in the law are "typical personal security rights". The contract of guarantee (the most important form of personal security) is regulated in Spanish and Italian Civil Codes, and the contract of mandate to provide credit (m.p.c.), is regulated in Italian CC[42]. The de-

---

[39] For a full overview of EU approach in the matter see the website of the EU Commission: (http://ec.europa.eu/competition/state_aid/overview/index_en.html) In particular on state aid to financial crisis see following Communications: a) Communication from the Commission on the treatment of impaired assets in the Community banking sector, O.J. C. 72, 26.3.2009, 1–22; (http://eur-lex.europa.eu/LexUriServ/LexUriServ.do?uri=CELEX:52009XC0326(01):EN:NOT); b) Communication from the Commission, The recapitalisation of financial institutions in the current financial crisis: limitation of aid to the minimum necessary and safeguards against undue distortions of competition, OJ C 10, 15.1.2009, 2–10 (http://eur-lex.europa.eu/LexUriServ/LexUriServ.do?uri=CELEX:52009XC0115(01):EN:NOT) and c) Communication from the Commission, The application of State aid rules to measures taken in relation to financial institutions in the context of the current global financial crisis, OJ C 270, 25.10.2008, 8–14, (http://eur-lex.europa.eu/LexUriServ/LexUriServ.do?uri=CELEX:52008XC1025(01):EN:NOT).

[40] OJ C 155, 20.6.2008, 10–22.

[41] See reasoning of the Commission's Notice.

[42] In Spain the contract of m.p.c. has been recognised in case law, STS 22 December 1941 [RA 1941 no. 1400].

mand for security in today's business relations has stimulated the creation of new forms of personal security rights ("atypical personal security rights"[43]), over and above those forms regulated by the law. Thus, a number of different kinds of personal security contracts have been developed in practice to provide the various effects and services which are required in particular areas of business practice[44], being a clear expression of living law[45].

3. *Real security rights*

Real (proprietory) securities grant the creditor rights over an asset (movable or immovable) or over a right of the debtor or of a third party, or usually both. The person granting real security does not assume a personal obligation himself. In most cases where it is the debtor itself, who furnishes real (proprietary) security this debtor is already liable with all its assets, including those, which it encumbers with a proprietary security right. The main function of proprietary security in these cases is different: it conveys, with respect to the assets encumbered by a security right, a right of preferential satisfaction to the secured creditor as against other unsecured creditors of the debtor[46].

A proprietary security may also be furnished by a person other than the debtor. In this situation, proprietary and personal security are combined. For the secured creditor this is proprietary security. However, the bilateral relationship between the third party who has furnished the proprietary security in favour of the debtor, and the latter is to be regarded as one equivalent to a personal security[47].

The basic real security contracts are the mortgage, the non-possessory mortgage, the pledge and the non-possessory pledge[48/49].

---

[43] Italy: *De Nictolis*, Nuove garanzie personali e reali, Padova, 1998; *Bozzi*, L'autonomia negoziale nel sistema delle garanzie personali, Napoli, 1990; *Briganti*, Garanzie personali atipiche, in Rapporti atipici nell'esperienza negoziale, Milano, 1988, 33 ff.; *Salanitro*, Le fideiussioni bancarie, BBTC, 1984, I, 135 ff.; Spain: *Ballarín Cuñat*, Fianza bancaria y suspensión de pagos, Estudios sobre jurisprudencia bancaria, 2000, 409 ff.; *De Angulo* 9–32; *Reyes*, Fianza y nuevas modalidades de garantía, Valencia, 1996.

[44] See unter Chapter 3, 186.

[45] „Nel settore delle garanzie personali è riscontrabile una particolare "ricchezza inventiva" dell'autonomia privata"; *Giusti*, 9.

[46] *Drobnig*, Conference report, not published 1 and 2.

[47] *Drobnig*, Conference report, not published 1 and 2.

[48] *Garrido*, Preferenza 43–61; *Garrido*, Garantías reales, 25–66; *Rojo*, 718–811.

[49] However it is controversial as to whether the list of real security contracts is *numerus clausus* or *apertus*; there is a tendency to consider it *numerus clausus* (*Bouza*, 17 f.; *Roca*, Regulación en materia de negocios de garantía, 162).

4. Personal vs. Real security rights

There is one fundamental difference between personal and real security rights: while a personal surety is fully liable with all its assets as against the creditor for the unpaid debts of the debtor towards the creditor, in the case of proprietary security the security provider is liable only with the encumbered assets.

Each kind of security right is adequate for a certain case, in view of the characteristics of the secured credit and the attributes and personal situation of the principal debtor. Therefore, real and personal security rights are more likely complementary and not opposed or competing instruments as they have been often considered by the scholars[50].

The real character of proprietary security rights provides numerous advantages. They are not affected by the debtor's (or the surety's) insolvency, as they are enforceable against the world at large. Moreover, the creditor's right over the encumbered asset has priority against all other creditors[51]. The additional certainty that is given to the creditor regarding the performance of the secured debt is probably the main advantage of this type of security. The creditor is not, as in case of personal security rights, exposed to the risk of change in the debtor or the surety's patrimony. Moreover, real securities do not necessarily imply the transfer of possession of the encumbered assets to the creditor. The development of new forms of non-possessory real securities has increased the possibility of obtaining credit in many cases, thus contributing to the development of credit finance and a rational economic use of property[52].

These advantages explain and justify the success of real security rights in the practice. However, some disadvantages have also been identified. The formal requirements for creation and publicity of such security rights are often complex and expensive; enforcement, especially in case of bankruptcy of the debtor, is laborious and presents difficulties in practice[53]. This gives rise to an increase in costs. Regarding simplicity of creation, personal securities do not have any complex formal requirements, which often also means a reduction of the costs. They offer a high level of flexibility, as certain personal security rights are conceived to adapt to possible changes in the credit relationship (which is not the case within real security

---

[50] *Dagot*, 93; *Mouilliart*, 906; *Cabrillac* and *Mouly*, 8.

[51] For a complete overview of the Italian and Spanish legal basis for these rights, see for Italy: *Bussani*, 165 ff.; *Gabrielli*, 643 ff. and for Spain: *Llebot*, 32.

[52] The economic function of non-possessory real securities on movables is extremely important especially for small and medium enterprises. These organisations' access to personal security is usually limited and their production machinery is the only property they can give as security.

[53] *Blanco/Sánchez-Calero/Sánchez-Calero Guilarte*, 170.

rights). Moreover, execution is simple and at lower-cost. If the surety is a professional institution, execution usually takes place upon the first demand. The creditor is not required to be involved in insolvency proceedings in the instance of the debtor's bankruptcy. In the case of real security rights, execution is generally subject to complex procedures; the asset might be lost or damaged and its value generally diminishes at that point of execution[54]. These reasons justify a change in the appraisal of security rights as a whole, the so-called "powerlessness of the real security rights"[55] and the increase of the use of personal security rights for certain transactions[56].

In terms of future trend, after years of constant increase of market prices (the so called housing bubble)[57], starting in 2007, mainly in the US, the housing market has experienced a significant price downturn, which reflected in the EU during 2008[58]. Italy but very strongly also Spain, are suffering from a stronger decline of the housing prices, which is foreseen to continue in 2009. Such downturn of the worldwide housing prices is reducing the appetite for mortgaged lending which should naturally reflect on a greater use of personal security rights[59].

Moreover and in any case, personal securities may always be reinforced[60] by real security[61].

C. The practical functions of security rights: Law, economics and social implications

Security rights play a supporting role in the granting of credit. Their auxiliary character does, however, not limit their importance within business practice as they directly affect the credit relationship, contributing thereby to the economic development of a society.

---

[54] See *Cabrillac* and *Mouly*, 9.

[55] *Barbiera*, Autonomia, 843.

[56] *Blanco/Sánchez-Calero/Sánchez-Calero Guilarte*, 170; *Sánchez-Calero Guilarte/Sánchez-Calero*, 455. See also *Cabrillac* and *Mouly*, 10.

[57] Bank for International Settelments, Housing finance in the global financial markets, 2006.

[58] See charts, 3/7 f.

[59] In this regard, it should be also considered that in the last years, mortgages (and remortgage) were increasingly applied as security for consumer lending.

[60] *Roca/Nieto*, 143; Goode, Consumer, Binder 1, IC [37.2]/1892.

[61] See below under Chapter 4, 227.

I. Security protects the creditor against debtor's default

1. Assessing the need or security

The most basic function of any kind of security is the protection of the creditor against default by the debtor. If such default is due to insolvency, a creditor with security will be considered a "secured creditor", and therefore is often not involved in any insolvency proceedings. For this reason secured creditors are often called super-prioritised creditors. In contrast, unsecured creditors often receive little or nothing through the rateable process of distribution[62] employed in such proceedings[63].

Economic literature[64] has identified two main reasons why security is beneficial for creditors and debtors: the first rests on the assumption that creditors cannot identify the riskiness of a potential borrower – resulting in adverse selection, the second is based on the idea that borrowers might default strategically – referred to as moral hazard.

In order to grant a loan, the creditor needs to have confidence in the regular repayment of the money lent[65]. Since the debtor is primarily liable for the repayment of the loan, the creditor can rely firstly on the debtor's integrity and ability to repay on the agreed terms[66]. If the reputation or record of a debtor sufficiently assures proper repayment, the creditor may be prepared to grant the loan without security[67].or increase it volume of risk towards that debtor (extend more credit). Such assurance would come from: a) subjective aspects of the debtor's personality such as his honesty and integrity[68], as well as b) his current and/or prospective patrimony, solvency and/or liquidity at the point of enforceability[69]. These factors will determine the debtor's ability to perform his obligation[70/71]. A debtor is

---

[62] About the rules of distribution in insolvency proceedings under Spanish Law see: *Llebot*, 22.

[63] *Goode*, Principles, 143–144 and 151–161; *Fletcher*, 613–616.

[64] *Lehmbecker*, 10.

[65] *Brink/Bärmann*, 24.

[66] *Abeyratne*, 71.

[67] In economic literature it has been noted that the existence of security in credit contracts is due to a lack of information on the part of creditors since security is irrelevant in a perfect neoclassical world. See *Bigus/Langer/Schiereck*, 2005 and *Lehmbecker*, 2008.

[68] "L'habilité, la prudence et la bonne foi sont les sûretés personnelles qu'apporte l'emprunter", *Petit-Dutaillis* and *Bernard*, 16.

[69] The analysis of the evolution of *solvability* must consider not only the ability to perform the debt owed (liquidity) but also the ability to perform an equivalent in case the agreed performance cannot be fulfilled. All this is to subsist at the moment the agreement has been reached and must endure until the moment of performance, *Llebot*, 27.

[70] See *Brink/Bärmann*, 24.

[71] The creditor must demonstrate his skills and judgement on assessing the risk of default. Credit scoring techniques are applied and the so-called "five C's" in credit assess-

considered to be solvent when the value of his assets exceeds the amount of his debt, and liquid when he has sufficient cash available to perform payment[72].

Creditors used to be, and to a certain extent still are, faced with the so-called "asymmetry of information"[73] – i.e. a debtor knows more about his ability and willingness to perform than the creditor himself. Today, the assessment of future solvency and liquidity is performed with a greater number of sophisticated methods based on the access that (professional) lenders commonly have to information on their potential borrowers. In first place, the relationship between the lender and the borrower impacts credit decision. Empirical data shows that housebanks, i.e. banks, which have developed a long-term relationship with their clients, provide more credit to their clients and more security rights[74]. Beyond, credit bureaux provide an overview on the clients' global level of indebtedness and general behaviour with regard to borrowing. The increasing trend in financial regulation to impose duties on financial institution to know well their customers (so called "Know Your Customer" due diligences (KYC))[75], mainly in view of preventing financial crime[76] and money laundering[77], also provides a good insight on the customers, generally used to assess the clients ability to perform.

All these new means have increased the ability of financial institutions to provide credit without security, as it is the case of credit card lending. Also other new forms of lending without security have developed, where the ability to repay is mainly based on the mutual control by a group of

---

ment will be proved: Character, Capacity, Capital, Conditions and Collateral. Guide to Credit Scoring, Office of Fair Trading, London, 1993; *Abeyratne*, 72.

[72] *Abeyratne*, 110; *Piazza*, 2.

[73] *Levitzky* (http://www.the-financier.com).

[74] It indicates that a borrower with a housebank relationship has a higher percentage of his balance-sheet total as credit line with the housebank. Housebanks obtain more collateral and provide more finance. See: *Machauer/Weber*, 2 and 9 ff.

[75] The EU Markets in Financial Instruments Directive (MiFID) (Directive 2004/39/EC, of the European Parliament and of the Council of 21 April 2004) has introduced a large number of requirements in terms of KYC. The Directive and implementing measures entered into force 1 January 2008.

[76] See: Market Abuse Directive (Directive 2003/6/EC) and Directive 2004/72/EC of 29 April 2004 implementing Directive 2003/6/EC of the European Parliament and of the Council as regards accepted market practices, the definition of inside information in relation to derivatives on commodities, the drawing up of lists of insiders, the notification of managers' transactions and the notification of suspicious transactions.

[77] Directive 2005/60/EC of the European Parliament and of the Council of 26 October 2005 on the prevention of the use of the financial system for the purpose of money laundering and terrorist financing.

lenders. This is the so-called micro-finance, generally used in less developed countries.

These forms of lending without security represent still a minority of the overall lending activity worldwide and are mainly (except for micro-finance) directed at lending for consumption purposes.

In most cases, a lender will demand some form of security as a safeguard against the risk that the borrower may not be able to perform his obligations. As risk management is the key element for a successful lending activity, secured lending is always preferred by lenders[78] and also reflects in a lower price for the borrower.

Risks faced by lenders do not only come from circumstances related to the debtor. The present geopolitical situation is often characterised by widespread insecurity, due to social or economic disasters, which often affect the whole world[79]. The demand for security has therefore greatly increased over time. Moreover, our current society is marked by complexity, interconnection, uncertainty and risk[80]. The phenomenon of globalisation makes this situation more acute, with the consequence that the aforementioned personal reliance usually does not exist, even with regard to financially secure and trustworthy debtors[81]. The legal principle of full liability of the debtor for his debts is not considered sufficient to cover the risks assumed by a creditor on granting credit.

In almost every case, security rights are agreed between the creditor and the person providing them (either the debtor or the surety) as supplementary to the creditor's primary right to obtain performance from the debtor.

2. Assessing the value of security upon enforcement: recovery rate

Secured creditors only enjoy a privileged position if the security is sufficient to cover the secured debt and can be both, obtained and realised when required[82]. This is only possible if the mechanisms of enforcement of securities enable the creditors to recover their debts swiftly, without being forced to follow a cumbersome process. Therefore, the value of a security depends, a) on the creditor's ability to assess its worth at the moment of

---

[78] See: *Grunert*, 2009, 133. In this article, Grunert provides a study on the use of security and the recovery rates: "Dass seine hohe Besicherungsquote durch die Verwertung der zugrundeliegenden Kreditsicherheiten die Recovery Rate steigen last, gilt in der Literatur als unbestritten".

[79] A recent example being the subprime crisis in 2007. Starting in the United States, its effects have spread around the world, including Europe.

[80] *Mastropaolo*, 3.

[81] "No doubt banks are concerned with the security that a customer can offer for a loan but this ought not to be the first, or only consideration", *Weerasooria*, 554.

[82] Mather makes a comparison between securities and insurances: *Mather*, 1.

enforceability and b) on the efficiency and effectiveness of its enforceability[83]. While the first is based on the creditor's skills and tools to evaluate the risk entailed in the security, the second needs to be provided by the society through effective regulation and its correct application. As credit is directly impacted by security, if creditors' trust on the security system is undermined, their willingness to lend will likely be reduced, which will also have an impact on the complete credit system.

Assessing the value of the security at the moment of enforeceability is a difficult task. Each lender uses its own data and risk management tools for this purpose. Factors such as the economic global situation (macroeconomic factors) might also impact the effective value of the security right at the moment of enforcement.

Such value and the creditor's ability to evaluate it will reflect on the risk assumed and finally on the effective losses (Loss Given Default (LGD)).

In the case of personal security rights, the ability to assess the creditworthiness of the guarantor and its actual solvency at the moment of enforceability will be essential. The efficiency of credit bureaux, access to information and global assessment of the guarantor's creditworthiness will make the difference. Economic analysis has drawn general conclusions on how lenders consider security rights in view of their effective value upon the debtor's default. Thereby personal guarantees are highly ranked[84]. Among them, state guarantees and guarantees provided by public entities provide the greatest level of "safetiness" (ranked 92,19 %), while those provided by private persons are ranked 49, 45 % and guarantees provided by companies are ranked 38,91 % [85].

In the case of real securities, it will be key to evaluate the economic worth of the goods pledged or mortgaged. The ability to foresee market trends will also be decisive, as it has become obvious after the fall of housing prices in most western countries and certainly in Italy, Spain, UK and the US. Mortgaging a property was during the last decade probably one of the safest ways to secure a credit in the Italy or Spain. The housing market was profitable; as profitable as to create a so-called housing (prices) bubble, which started its end around 2006 with a fall of the market prices[86]. Those creditors that underestimated the risk of a price downturn either in

[83] *Abeyratne*, 110.

[84] "(…) der Wert von abgetretenen Forderungen aus Finanzprodukten sowie Bürgschaften im Rahmen von Förderungsdarlehen als externe Sicherheiten ist besonders hoch", *Grunert*, 2009, 134.

[85] See: *Grunert*, 2009, 132. These conclusions are drawn from an empirical analysis performed by the author. See *Grunert*, 2009, 128 for further information on the conditions under which the study was performed.

[86] See chart 1, 2 and 3 and EMF Hypostat, 2008, p. 66.

their valuation of the security or in their portfolio management are encountering serious solvency difficulties today.

The protective role of security becomes particularly clear in economic downturns when default rates increase[87]. This is already the case in Spain according to Spanish Central Bank and will likely continue to be within the EU in 2009[88].

3. *How personal and real security rights affect the principle of par conditio creditorum*

The principle of *par conditio creditorum* refers to the equal position of all creditors upon insolvency of the debtor[89]. Secured creditors are objectively privileged over the non-secured ones since they enjoy a supplementary assurance of repayment of the secured debt. However the constitution of a security does not necessarily contradict the principle of *par conditio creditorum*. The latter is only infringed insofar as one of the creditors has a preferential right over the debtor's patrimony[90]. This only happens within real securities over assets of the debtor. In all other cases (personal securities or real securities over assets of third persons) the position of all creditors regarding the debtor's patrimony is not altered.

II. Security enhances the grant of credit

Creditors are mostly professionals interested in carrying on a profitable business. They will only operate their business if the level of risk being assumed is reasonable in relation to the potential profit[91]. Since security reduces the risk upon default (so called "Loss Given Default")[92], the creditor will be more willing to grant credit if security is provided. The re-

---

[87] See below under: Chapter 1, C., VI. The role of security rights in the 2008 financial crisis, 23.

[88] See chart 4.

[89] The principle of *par conditio creditorum* is established in art. 2741 Italian CC. Although it cannot be specifically found in any provision of the Spanish Civil Code, it is generally considered as a natural consequence of art. 1911, which prescribes the full liability for one's debts.

[90] See *Ravazzoni*, 22, 23.

[91] A proof of it is the low level of security granted by banks to small and medium companies. This is due to the high risk usually inherent to them. This was the reason to create the Mutual Guarantee Societies (*Sociedades de garantía recíproca*), whose aim it is to grant security to small and medium companies. See: *Fahri de Montalbán*, 1 (http://www.societario.com/revista/1/doctrina/sgrdiana-i.htm). For a financial approach to different aspects of credit risk management see: *Caouette* et al., 2008.

[92] "Dass eine hohe Besicherungsquote durch die Verwertung der zugrunde liegenden Kreditsicherheiten die Recovery Rate steigen lässt, gilt in der Literatur als unbestritten", Gunert, 2009, 134.

quirement of security, the kind of security and the amount secured are directly related to the level of risk of the debtor's default, according to the credit appraisal. Empirical data[93] has shown that riskier borrowers rely more on bank loans. In view of basic credit risk management principles, security will play a greater role for riskier borrowers.

Security therefore enables the conduct of a business which otherwise would not function or would only have been operated under more difficult conditions, which benefits both the creditor and the debtor. In practice, security plays an important role in the economic activities carried out by large institutions (for instance, industrial activities operated by corporations, banks, insurance companies, etc.)[94]. For smaller creditors, like Small and Medium Enterprises selling on credit, security is vital to ensure business continuity.

As a result of the different needs of the many different players in the commercial world, a large number of security rights have developed, some of which are regulated ("typical security rights") while others are a result of the parties agreements as a consequence of the freedom of contract ("atypical security rights"). The type of security chosen depends on several factors. The nature and characteristics of the borrower will have an impact on the access to certain types of security rights. For instance Small and Medium Enterprises often pledge machinery or productive goods while private borrowers commonly mortgage their homes or find a personal guarantor. The likelihood to realise the value of the security right is of essence in order to evaluate the risk of lending which has a direct impact on the lender's decision whether to approve the credit or not.

III. Security enables the grant of credit at lower costs

In credit risk management a usual goal is to price loans according to their risk exposure[95]. Indeed, empirical data[96] has shown that riskier borrowers pay higher loan rate premiums and rely more on bank loans. The rational is clear; lenders should be compensated for the risk that borrowers do not repay their loans[97].

---

[93] *Machauer/Weber*, 2.

[94] See *Galbraith*, 310 f.

[95] *Saunders*, 583.

[96] *Machauer/Weber*, 2. The study is based on data collected from Small and Medium Enterprises. The result can be though generalized for all sorts of creditors, even if with a different impact on pricing.

[97] This idea will serve as a general principle. However, other elements will also affect the price calculation of loans. For instance, cross-selling cause banks to provide cheap loans in order to attract customers for other profitable business. Volume oriented wages might induce bank employees to increase volume by undertaking business with borrow-

If a debt has been secured, the creditor eliminates or at least reduces the effective risk on the credit as well as the cost of monitoring the solvency of the debtor. In the case of personal security, these costs are to a greater extent assumed by the guarantor[98]. In the case of a real security this outlay is less required. At the same time the conditions on which the credit is authorised will be more lenient for the debtor[99], since the creditor may be prepared to offer lower interest rates, extend longer periods for repayment of the loan and, if necessary, increase the amount of credit[100]. This is also because security is in some cases an indirect proof of the debtor's solvency[101]. The surety is supposed to either know and trust the debtor or have correctly studied the risk of non-performance. The grant of credit is thereby facilitated with less cost of information for the creditor[102]. This enables the debtor to obtain credit on better conditions[103], which encourages people to ask for credit and increases enterprise finance and movements of capital. This is especially true in those countries without (or with no trustworthy) credit scoring or ranking of debtors (which is not the case in Italy or Spain) or for those debtors that are unknown to the credit scoring[104] (for instance new created companies, young individuals for their first credits, etc).

Since the approval of the Basel II Accord and the EU Capital Requirements Directive[105], the use of security also impacts positively the capital requirements of lending financial institutions. The cost of lending is thereby reduced, which will likely reflect in the final cost for the borrower.

---

ers of bad quality. Another factor might be the phenomena of interest rate smoothing during a bank-borrower relationship. See: *Machauer/Weber*, 1.

[98] *Katz*, 62–74; *Llebot*, 30.

[99] This has been manifest within the Mutual Guarantee Societies (*Sociedades de Garantía Recíproca*) whose creation has not only allowed the grant of credit but also reduced its costs. See (http://www.econolink.com.ar/finanzas/finanza1.htm) and Fahri de Montalbán, 1 (http://www.societario.com/revista/1/doctrina/sgrdiana-i.htm).

[100] *Simpson/Rover/Norton/Andenas*, 143, 144; *Llebot*, 23.

[101] *Swartzt*, Security interests and bankruptcy priorities: a review of current theories. Legal Studies, 1981, 1–37; 14–21.

[102] In most cases, the surety is a financial institution so that the risk analysis for the creditor is easier or simply eliminated and hence, screening costs are reduced.

[103] *Llebot*, 37.

[104] For a practical economic analysis on credit scoring see: *Siddiqi*, Credit risk scorecards: developing and implementing intelligent credit scoring, 2006.

[105] See full explanation of the impact of the Basel II Accord and the Capital Requirements Directive on security rights in Part V.

IV. Security contributes to economic development

1. How security impacts economic development

Beyond the personal benefit that a trustworthy security system gains for the creditor, the debtor and the commercial guarantor, it also contributes to long-term economic development[106].

Credit plays an essential role regarding productive and consumptive activities[107]. This has been evidenced during the last decade in the western economies, where economic growth has been accompanied by an increased use of credit[108]. Modern business depends to a large extent on their access to lending facilities. Although the over-extension of credit is not to be encouraged[109], responsible lending[110] contributes to the economic development of a society[111]. It has been proved that the more developed the economy of a country is, the greater is the need for credit finance[112]. Where the use of security rights is limited or not efficient, the grant of credit is low or non-existent[113]. It can be consequently asserted that there is a direct and mutual relationship between the development of a security system and the

[106] On the credit economies, see Morales, Creditism: World Credit Economy (http://www.allacademic.com/meta/p110123_index.html). See also *Fleisig*, The Power (http://www.worldbank.org/fandd/english/pdfs/0696/0150696.pdf or http://www.worldbank.org/html/fpd/notes/43/43fleisig.html); *Fleisig*, The Right to Borrow, (http://www.worldbank.org/html/fpd/ notes/44/44summary.html).

[107] *Schlesinger*, Il "*primato*" del credito, 485 ff cited by *Giusti*, 7.

[108] For an extensive overview of the credit situation in Europe see European Credit Research Insititute Statistical Package 2008 (www.ecri.be). See chart 5.

[109] While indebtedness is positive and contributes to further economic development, "over-indebtedness" puts societies and individuals in danger of bankruptcy, particularly in case of financial instability or crisis. The understanding of over-indebtedness varies significantly. The EU Commission has made an attempt to unify the concept of over-indebtedness. See: EU Commission, Towards a common operational definition of over-indebtedness, February, 2008. See also de *la Mata*, Household's over-indebtedness in the EU today. CEPS Policy Brief for seminar, May 2005.

[110] See, Council of Europe – (ECRC) Principles of Responsible Credit identified in the Recommendation adopted by the Council of Europe on 20 June 200, Committee of Ministers adopt Recommendation on legal solutions to debt problems. First coherent political text for identifying legal and political measures that could be adopted by member States and lead the Implementation Process of the Consumer Credit Directive. Another Challenge for the ECRC Principles.

[111] "Credit markets are just as important as equity markets to financial development." *Dam*, 1.

[112] *Drobnig*, 9. For a comparative study see *Wood*, 10–26.

[113] See *Cabrillac* and *Mouly*, 5.

development of the credit economy it is serving[114]. Moreover, secured credits benefit from more favourable terms, which will inevitably result in a better flow of credit to the economy, leading to increased investment and growth rates[115]. Hence, despite its natural assisting role, security rights become essential for credit economies[116].

2. The EU policy action in view of enhancing credit and its impact on security interest

The positive impact of credit in terms of economic development has also been recognised in the European context by the EU institutions. Specific policy measures have been taken on in order to promote the use of credit within the EU. This issues has been treated in depth under Part Six "Security interest in the EU context: market implications and harmonization of EU private law.

V. The role of security rights in terms of financial stability

Macroeconomic literature has evidenced the important role of security for monetary policy and hence for financial stability[117]. More than two thirds of all credit contracts in developed countries are secured by collateral[118]. Yet, only in exceptional times does collateral make the headlines. However, if it does – as in the recent crisis in the international banking system – even central banks need to act vigorously to prevent the whole system from collapsing[119]. Beyond, a negative, robust and statistically significant correlation between inflation and the quality of eligible collateral is found, meaning that quality of eligible collateral is able to explain inflation. The result supports the theory that securitisation of central bank lending is crucial for price stability.

VI. The role of security rights in the 2008 financial crisis

The turmoil in financial markets originated from the 2007 subprime mortgage crisis in the United States, has made it clear again how important credit is for the maintenance of economic welfare in western economies.

---

[114] A proof of this principle is the correspondence between the development of the credit economy after the Second World War and the parallel increase in the use of securities as well as the development of different types.

[115] *Diamond*, 2.

[116] In the opinion of Giusti, security loses its assisting role, being an essential and necessary element of credit operations; see *Giusti*, 7.

[117] *Lehmbecker*, 2.

[118] *Bigus*, 465 ff.

[119] *Lehmbecker*, 2.

One of the major dangers of the 2008 crisis resulting from that turmoil is the credit constraint based, among other reasons, on a) the lack of liquidity in the banking system and b) the higher prudence of lenders in granting credit. Such constrains have a direct impact on key macroeconomic welfare parameters (such as default rates, employment rates, bankruptcy rates – especially SMEs bankruptcies). Beyond, economic research suggests that credit constraints are binding for some groups in the population, in particular for young and low-income households[120]. Governments seriously fear the lack of credit in the respective (and interlinked) economies, which justifies a number of exceptional governmental measures taken in all EU countries as well as in the US and several other western economies[121].

In a period of economic instability, security rights contribute to providing certainty of recovery to lenders, acting, hence as credit enhancers. Accordingly, security rights play a particularly important role in this period of limited credit availability.

---

[120] *Attanasio/Goldberg/Kyriazidou*, 1.

[121] For an overview of the governmental measures of all countries in the world see: Economic stabilization Advisory Group, Governmental Assistance to the Financial Sector: an Overview of the Global Responses (v.3) – December 19, 2008.

Chapter 2

The contract of guarantee in the Spanish and Italian legal systems (fideiussione/fianza)

Introduction

The contract of guarantee is the essential form of personal security. From a practical perspective, guarantees are among the most common forms of security in commercial transactions. In modern times, new, atypical forms of personal security have been developed and increasingly used due to the requirements of business practice. However, this has not resulted in a downgrading of the guarantee contract as the basic personal security right[1]. From a legal perspective, the guarantee regulation provides a legal framework for other kinds of personal security[2]. The provisions governing the guarantee are applicable mutatis mutandis to all the various contracts of personal security[3]. Hence, the guarantee can today still be seen as basic reference in the field of personal security rights[4].

This practical and legal relevance of the contract of guarantee is thus the underlying reason for the focus of this dissertation on the regulation and practical use of the guarantee.

A. Concept and legal nature of the guarantee contract

I. Notion of guarantee. The Roman law imprinting

By means of a guarantee, a third party (guarantor) undertakes a secondary obligation to answer for the due performance of the obligation of another person (principal debtor[5]) upon the contingency that the latter fails to perform his obligation as agreed.

---

[1] *Mc Guiness*, 1.

[2] *Giusti*, 6 ff.; *Díez-Picazo*, Fundamentos, 416.

[3] For an extensive study of this matter, see: *Carrasco*, Fianza, spec. "Aplicación generalizada de las normas de la fianza", 51–64.

[4] *Cabrilac* and *Mouly*, 36; *Giusti*, 6: "Il quadro delle garanzie personali, imperniato sullo schema codicistico della fideiussione [...]".

[5] Also referred to as "secured debtor" and as "debtor".

This basic notion derives from the Roman conception of guarantee and is valid in all modern common or civil law systems. In the classical period of the Roman Empire the guarantee (fideiussio) was the most widely used form of personal security[6]. In the time of Justinian, the fideiussio prevailed over the other two forms of personal security known by the Romans (sponsio and fideipromissio)[7/8] and became the regular way to secure credit[9]. It thus came to be regulated in the Corpus Iuris (Justinian's Law). The principles established in these rules became the basis for the modern regulations of the guarantee[10]. However, not all modern civil codes have received the Roman legacy in the same form and intensity[11]. The traditional codes follow more directly Roman principles as contained in the Justinian's Corpus Juris. However, as the Roman notion of guarantee does not always meet the requirements of today's legal and commercial practice, regulation in these systems has been construed by case law and theory as adapted to the needs of the modern use of the contract. This is the case in France and also in Spain and in Italy under the former Italian CC of 1865, as directly inspired by the French CC[12].

In the modern codes, the classical Roman principles are combined with the German consuetudinary rules and have been adapted to the requirements of current commercial practice[13]. That is the case of Italian CC of 1942, which offers a modern and practical regulation on the guarantee furnishing a more precise form of wording in many provisions. Examples include the regulation on future and conditional guarantees with a limit of the guaranteed amount (art. 1938 Italian CC)[14] or the guarantee granted by a plurality of guarantors (art. 1946 and art. 1954 Italian CC)[15]. Also the liability of the guarantor in Italy has been adapted to the current legal prac-

---

[6] *Kaser*, 457.

[7] *Phillipson*, 1230; *Petti*, 5–20.

[8] This is the reason why modern civil codes contain a regulation of the guarantee but not of forms inspired in the *sponsio* or *fideipromissio*. See *Jones*, 129–155.

[9] An analysis of the reasons is found in: *De Martino*, 271 ff; *Kaser*, 457.

[10] For Italy: *Petti*, 5; for Spain: *Guilarte*, 2; for France, *Malaury* and *Aynès*, no. 103; for Portugal, *Almeida Costa* 770; for the Netherlands: *Norman* [http://ials.sas.ac.uk/library/guides/research/res_neth.htm]. English law, by contrast, was developed from common law: *Philips* and *O'Donovan,* 3 ff.

[11] See: *Jones*, 129–155; *Phillipson*, 1230; Recueils de la société Jean Bodin, Les Sûretés Personnelles (Troisième partie, période contemporaine), Bruxelles, 1969. With regard to the linkage between roman law and modern private law, see: *Grossi*, 651 ff. and *Calderale*, 4.

[12] Also Belgian and Luxemburgian CC.

[13] *Calderale*, 3; *De Martino*, 271 ff.; *Giusti*, 4.

[14] See under Chapter 2, C., IV. The guarantee for future obligations, 69 and V. Guarantee for conditional obligations, 72.

[15] See under Chapter 4, Plurality of security rights, 227

tice. According to art. 1944 Italian CC the guarantor is joint and severally liable ex lege in contrast to the also ex lege secondary liability of the guarantor according to French CC (art. 2011 and 2021) and Spanish CC (art. 1822 par.1)[16] and to the former Italian CC. Such secondary liability of the guarantor is based in the Roman idea that the guarantee is a gratuitous contract, based in the friendship between debtor and guarantor. However, this conception of guarantee is not realistic in the modern times. Today almost every guarantee contract contains a clause that establishes the joint and several liability of the guarantor. This is an example of the adaptation of a modern regulation, such as that found in the new Italian CC, to the needs of commercial and civil law practice[17].

II. Legal notion of guarantee

1. In general

The guarantee is legally defined in art. 1936 Italian CC as well as in art. 1822 par. 1 Spanish CC and in art. 439 Spanish Comm.C. In Italy "a guarantor is a person who guarantees the performance of the obligation of another by binding himself personally to the creditor. A guarantee obligation is binding even if the debtor has no knowledge of it". This definition is very general, makes no express reference to the sources of the guarantee and is principally based on the obligation of the guarantor. The legal definition in art. 1822 Spanish CC is even vaguer: "by a guarantee a person obligates himself to pay or perform for another person in case the latter fails to do so". This definition refers neither to the sources of the obligation nor to its security function. In both countries the legal definition of guarantee is merely descriptive of the undertaking of the performance of another person's obligation. A functional and comprehensive definition requires the reflection of the complete regulation of the guarantee[18], from which three different characterising elements can be identified[19]: a) the

[16] Also in art. 2011 and art. 2021 Belgian and Luxembourgian CC; art. 1355 Austrian CC and § 771 German CC; § 3 Finnish Law of Guarantees (Lag om borgen och tredjemanspant (Law on Dependent Guarantees and Third Pledge Security) Law nr. 361, 19. March 1999); art. 855 par. 1 Dutch CC; art. 855 Greek CC and art. 638 Portuguese CC.

[17] Portuguese CC, approved by Decreto-Ley no. 47 344, of 25 November 1966 and Dutch CC, which entered into force in 1992 are also modern regulations. However they maintained the traditional secondary liability of the guarantor in their guarantee regulations.

[18] *Petti*, 37.

[19] The difficulty to find a comprehensive definition of the guarantee is evidenced by the various attepts done by the scholars. Each of them stresses certain characteristics but no definition is fully satisfactory. See an extensive study in *Petti*, 33–37.

guarantee is a contract, b) the guarantee is a security right and c) the guarantee is a personal form of security.

a) The guarantee is a contract

In both Italy and Spain the guarantee is systematically regulated within the wider sphere of the regulation on contracts. However, not every obligation to perform in the place of a different person has its origin in a contractual agreement. A guarantee can be legally or judicially required and it must not necessarily be a consequence of a contractual relationship. In any case, the guarantee as an obligation to perform on behalf of another person is always a consequence of the guarantor's declaration of his will to undertake such liability. This declaration, together with the acceptance of the creditor is called a contract of guarantee and it can also occur in the cases of the legal and judicial guarantees. The obligation to grant guarantee might derive from the law, a judicial decision or the freely consenting agreement of the parties, but in all these cases, the obligation to perform in case of the default of the debtor (guarantee obligation) is a direct consequence of the guarantor's declaration of will. Therefore the guarantee is always considered to be a contract[20].

b) The guarantee is a form of security right

The guarantee is a form of contractual security right. Like any other form of personal or real security, the guarantee reinforces the creditor above the general liability of the debtor.

The guarantee contract gives origin to a new obligation (the guarantee obligation) that serves to fulfill the creditor's interest in case the principal debtor does not perform. The guarantee obligation has the same purpose (satisfaction of the creditor's interest) but holds a different content and nature to that of the principal debt. The guarantor is therefore a "debtor" but his liability has its origin in a different title than that of the debtor; i.e the guarantee contract.

The guarantor owes his debt in his capacity as a surety and not as the principal debtor. Even if he has undertaken a joint and several guarantee[21], his liability will be secondary in the sense of being a reinforcing liability. That is the reason why the guarantor is also usually called reinforcing debtor, as opposed to principal debtor. The guarantor holds his right of reimbursement vis-à-vis the debtor if he performs his guarantee obligation because his liability is based on a security title. This is a key aspect which

---

[20] *Carrasco, Cordero and Marín*, 71.

[21] SAP Sevilla 18 June 2008 [008 no. 52887]: "(…) the general principle that teh joint and several liability is not presumed for the guarantee".

helps distinguishing the contract of guarantee from the co-debt or the so called co-debt for security purpose. In the co-debt and in the co-debt for security purpose two or more patrimonies are fully or partly liable for the same debt as principal debtors. Therefore both obligations have the same title.

The security function of the guarantee and the legal cause of the contract of guarantee are specifically mentioned in art. 1936 par. 1 Italian CC ("a guarantor is a person who guarantees the performance of the obligation of another")[22]. In contrast, these are not explicitly contained in the parallel art. 1822 Spanish CC. However they can be deduced from the guarantee regulation as a whole (especially art. 1825, art. 1828, art. 1829, art. 1835 and art. 1855 Spanish CC). Moreover, some important authors such as Puig Peña[23], Gullón[24] or Guilarte[25] have introduced this idea of security into their definitions of guarantee. The guarantee is therefore regarded as being a security measure for the debt of another person.

c) The guarantee is a personal security right

The contract of guarantee is a personal security right. In contrast to real securities, the guarantor assumes personally a new secondary obligation. The guarantor is liable for the undertaken obligation with his entire present and future patrimony. Since no one can be guarantor for his own debts, each of the two obligations (principal and guarantee) is to be fulfilled by a different person. Accordingly two different patrimonies may be subject to execution. This increases the creditor's confidence with regard to performance.

2. The guarantee obligation

The contract of guarantee gives rise to the obligation of the guarantor to perform in the case of the debtor failing to do so[26]. It was very controversial in the past as to whether this guarantee obligation should be considered as simple "liability for a third person" or as a new and different obligation (guarantee obligation). The wordings of art. 1822 par. 1 Spanish CC

---

[22] Art. 1936 par. 1 Italian CC: "è fideiussore colui che (...), garantisce l'adempimento di un'obbligazione altrui".

[23] *Puig Peña*, 479.

[24] *Gullón*, 1972, 425.

[25] *Guilarte*, 8.

[26] Again the guarantee is subject to a degree of terminological uncertainty. The term *guarantee* (*fideiussione/fianza*) usually refers to the contract of guarantee itself and also to the guarantee obligation originated by it, i.e. the obligation to perform for the principal. In order to avoid confusion this obligation will be called *guarantee obligation* hereinafter.

and of art. 1898 of the former Italian CC (both following art. 2011 of French CC) facilitated the identification of the guarantee obligation with the principal one. It was taken to be the case that the guarantor "obligates himself to pay or perform for a third person in the case of the latter failing to do so". According to this conception, in case of a guaranteed debt there is one unique obligation and two different debtors. This is the case as the guarantor is considered to be a subsidiary debtor for the same principal debt. Sánchez-Román described the guarantee as being a contract by means of which a third person, different to the creditor and the debtor, assumes the subsidiary performance of the principal debt without giving rise to a novation[27]. This conception was followed by a significant number of Spanish scholars[28]. However, the model of guarantee as a contract which gives rise to a new, separate obligation, different from that of the principal one[29], is now generally accepted by scholars and court decisions in both Italy[30] and Spain[31]. The matter was clarified in Italy after the Civil Code of 1942, which art. 1936 and 1944 par. 1 serve to infer this conception more directly. Thus, the guarantor performs instead of the original debtor. However the guarantor is himself considered to be a debtor by virtue of his own obligation. Two different obligatory relationships must therefore be distinguished: a) between creditor and debtor there is an obligation which is subject to the guarantee while b) between creditor and guarantor there is another obligation, which guarantees the principal relationship[32].

The introduction of a guarantee obligation does not modify the subjective elements of the principal relationship[33]. Moreover, this guarantee obligation, even if defined per relationem to the principal debt, has its own content, terms and conditions. Therefore, the eventual payment by the guarantor means the payment of his own debt, the content of which may be different to that of the principal obligation[34].

III. Structure of the contract of guarantee

1. The parties to the contract of guarantee

The guarantee contract only occurs between the guarantor and the creditor. Though, de facto there are three persons involved and impacted by it: the

---

[27] *Sánchez Román*, 911.

[28] *Castán*, 682; *Falcón*, 448. See longer references in *Guilarte*, 12.

[29] The general liability of the debtor for his own debts is established in art. 2740 Italian CC and 1911 Spanish CC (and art. 2092 French CC).

[30] *Petti*, 84; *Alpa*, 973; Cass. 27 February 1991 no. 2115 cited by *Giusti*, 24.

[31] *Puig Peña*, 479; *Cossio*, 480; *Guilarte*, 8; *Carrasco, Cordero and Marín*, 68.

[32] *Díez-Picazo*, Fundamentos, 415.

[33] *Reyes*, 54.

[34] See *Casanovas*, 151 f.

debtor; the creditor; and the guarantor. The guaranteeing function of the contract establishes a strong link between the secured obligation (debtor-creditor) and the guarantee obligation (creditor-guarantor). Furthermore, the effects generated by the contract also take place between the creditor, the guarantor and the debtor. In view of this factual structure, the guarantee has been regarded as being trilateral[35]. The lack of precision with regard to the term "guarantee" in Spain and Italy contributes to the uncertainty on this matter. The "guarantee" could refer to the factual trilateral relationship between debtor, creditor and guarantor, while "the contract of guarantee" would be a bilateral relationship between the creditor and the guarantor (art. 1823 par. 2 Spanish CC and art. 1940 Italian CC).

The contract of guarantee only exists between the guarantor and the creditor. The effects of the guarantee vis-à-vis the debtor and the rights of the guarantor vis-à-vis the latter in case of performance are legal rights[36]. The debtor remains outside the contract[37]. That is the reason why the guarantee remains valid even if the debtor is not aware of it[38] or even if he disapproves its constitution[39]. The fact that the guarantee is included in the contract that gives origin to the secured debt, or in any unique document which includes the participation of the debtor, does not result in the inclusion of the debtor in the guarantee relationship[40].

Very frequently in practice, the debtor looks for a person willing to guarantee his debt and introduces this potential guarantor to the creditor. But also in these cases, the guarantor is not a party to the guarantee contract[41]. Even if debtor and guarantor have previously signed a contract by which the latter compels himself to grant guarantee under certain circums-

---

[35] See references in *Guilarte*, 63. Guilarte considers it to be unacceptable to include the debtor as a party to the contract of guarantee, *Guilarte*, 64.

[36] *Guilarte*, 64.

[37] "Il negozio fideiussorio corre tra fideiussore e creditore, e il debitore nessuna influenza ha sul suo sorgere", Aru, 348. Cass. 18 Sept. 1974 no. 2502 cited by *Giusti*, 65.

[38] According to art. 1936 par. 2 Italian CC and art. 1823 par. 2 Spanish CC, based on the roman principle "fideiubere pro alio potest quisque, etiamsi promissory ignoret" (Digest 46, 1, 30) and more recently in art. 2014 French CC: "On peut se render caution sans ordre de celui pour lequel on s'oblige, e même a son insue".

[39] Art. 1823 par. 2 Spanish CC explicitly establishes the validity of the guarantee upon the disapproval of the debtor. This case is not provided for in the Italian CC but it has been recognised by case law and theory, based on the legal cause of the guarantee: *Ravazzoni*, La fideiussione, 146 ff; *Giusti*, 65. *Contra*: *Barbero*, Sistema istituzionale, 1958, 665.

[40] Cass. 5 March 1984 no. 1525, BBTC, 1985, II, 467; *Giusti*, 66.

[41] For France: *Marty* and *Rynaud*, 335: "dans la pratique c'est le débiteur qui a recherché la caution et lui a demandé son engagement, mais le rôle du débiteur est extérieur au contrat de cautionnement proprement dit". The same is valid for Italy or Spain.

tances, this agreement does not form part of the guarantee. The debtor remains outside the guarantee contract[42]. This situation is to be distinguished from the case of a contract in favour of a third party[43], agreed between a debtor and a guarantor, under which the latter compels himself with the debtor to grant a guarantee in favour of the creditor. The creditor is held to be the beneficiary of the contract agreed between the debtor and the guarantor.

The uncertainty or divergence of views with regard to the parties to the guarantee has not been definitely clarified by the European Court of Justice. While in Berliner Kindl Brauerei[44], Attorney-General Léger, considered the guarantee to be a unilateral contract, in the case TIARD[45], the Court regards the guarantee (suretyship) as a triangular process. Finally, in the case Frahuil, it seems that the Court considers the guarantee as a trilateral contract as there is no guarantee if the debtor is not a party to the contract. [46]

---

[42] *Fragali/Scialoja e Branca*, 348. Contra: *Ravazzoni*, La fideiussione, 147 ff.

[43] See art. 1411 Italian CC: "A stipulation in favour of a third person is valid when the stipulator has an interest therein. The third person acquires a right against the promisor as a result of such stipulation, unless otherwise agreed. The stipulation, however, can be revoked or modified by the stipulator until the third person declares to the promisor, that he intends to avail himself of the stipulation. In case of revocation of the stipulation or refusal of the third person to avail himself to it, the obligation of performance for the benefit of the stipulator remains, unless it appears otherwise from the intention of the parties or the nature of the contract" ("Contratto a favore di terzi. È valida la stipulazione a favore di un terzo, qualora lo stipulante vi abbia interesse. Salvo patto contrario, il terzo acquista el diritto contro el promittente per effetto della stipulazione. Questa però può essere revocata o modificata dallo stipulante, finché il terzo non abbia dichiarato, anche in confronto del promittente, di volerne profittare. In caso di revoca della stipulazione o di rifiuto del terzo di profittarne, la prestazione rimane a beneficio dello stipulante, salvo che diversamente risulti dalla volontà delle parti o dalla natura del contratto") and art. 1257 par. 2 Spanish CC: "If the contract contains a stipulation in favour of a third party, the third party may demand its fulfillment, provided that he makes his acceptance known to the obligor before the stipulation is revoked", ("Si el contrato contuviera alguna estipulación a favor de tercero, éste podrá exigir su cumplimiento, siempre que hubiese hecho saber su aceptación al obligado antes de que haya sido aquella revocada").

[44] Berliner Kindl Brauerei AG v. Siepert (case no. C-208/98) of 23 March 2000, ECR 2000 I 1741, p. 1752 nos. 36–37.

[45] Préservatrice Foncière TIARD SA v. Staat der Nederlanden (case no. C-26601) of 15 May 2003, ECR 2003 I 4867, p. 4891 no. 27.

[46] Frauhil SA v. Assitalia SpA (case no. C-26502) of 5 Feb. 2004, ECR 2004 I 1543, p. 1554, no 21 and no. 25.

2. The contract of guarantee as a source of obligations. Unilateral or bilateral obligations

a) In general

The contract of guarantee gives rise to the guarantee obligation, i.e. the obligation of the guarantor to perform upon the default of the debtor. This obligation might be assumed gratuitously (without being remunerated by the creditor), commonly due to a personal relationship between the guarantor and the debtor. Alternatively it may be assumed onerously with the guarantor being remunerated, which is the case in the context of professional guarantees (normally commission fees).

The contracts of guarantee which are assumed by the guarantor without remuneration only create obligations for one party (the guarantor). They are therefore held to be unilateral contracts[47/48]. In contrast, if the guarantor is remunerated for the granting of guarantee, the contract is considered to be bilateral. Hence, the contract of guarantee may be unilateral or bilateral depending on whether the creditor pays for the guarantee obligation. Art. 1823 Spanish CC explicitly states the possibility to constitute either remunerated or gratuitous guarantees, while in Italy this alternative is implicit in the general rules on contract law.

b) Natural gratuitousness of the typical guarantee

Since its origins in Roman Law, the concept of guarantee has been based on the kind of guarantees which were granted by relatives or friends on the basis of a wish to help a beloved person. The archetypal form of guarantee is hence not remunerated. Consequently, scholars now agree that the guarantee has a typical but not essential (i.e. natural) character of gratuitousness[49], i.e. unless a payment for the guarantor has been agreed, the guarantee will be granted without the guarantor being remunerated[50]. The Italian

---

[47] Some scholars have refused to accept the existence of unilateral guarantees. They base this view on the fact that the necessary acceptance of the guarantee by the creditor is a constitutive requirement for the contract (Cossio, 481). This must be considered to be a mistaken view on this matter. The unilateral or bilateral character of the guarantees refers to the mutual obligations of the parties derived from the terms of the contract and not to the requirements of constitution of the latter (i.e. offer and acceptance).

[48] Cass. 19 December 1987, no. 9468, GC, 1988, I, 971; Cass. 4 September 1984, no. 4751, GI, 1985, I, 1, 960; *Valenzuela/Nieto/Bonet*, 448.

[49] *Giusti*, 72: "La presenza degli elementi della unilateralità e della gratuità non è costante e neppure necessaria perché abbia vita il negozio fideiussorio"; *Carrasco, Cordero* and *Marín*, 72. For a broader treatment of the matter see: *De Marchi*, 637 ff; *Deiana*, 441 ff.; *Bo*, Sulla gratuità, 22 ff. In Germany see: *Horn/Staudinger* on §765 nos. 5–6. In France: *Tendler*, 8.

[50] See an extensive study in *Giusti*, 75.

Supreme Court has also agreed on the natural gratuitous character of the guarantee (with a consequent application of art. 1333 f. Italian CC on unilateral obligations)[51].

c) Onerous character of professional guarantees

In current commercial practice the proportion of guarantees which are granted by professionals in the course of business has increased. These are always remunerated and they are therefore bilateral. Accordingly there is a presumption of onerousity if the guarantor is a professional[52]. In Spain this presumption is legally established in art. 441 Spanish Comm.C. In Italy the contract of guarantee is presumed (iuris et de iure) to be onerous when the guarantee is conditio sine qua non for the granting of credit ("contestualità della garanzia"), i.e. when the credit would not have been granted or only under different conditions if the guarantee had not been provided[53].

Certain scholarly opinion and even case law have applied this presumption a sensu contrario. In the absence of this "contestualità" or direct link between the grant of the respective guarantee and the credit, the contract of guarantee is held to be gratuitous[54]. This application appears to be misguided. The fact that a credit would have been granted without the guarantee cannot be enough to consider gratuitous a guarantee which has been remunerated; for instance with a percentage of the credit[55].

Moreover, it is clear that the grant of credit, even if it indirectly benefits the guarantor, can in any case be considered as remuneration stricto sensu.

d) Concept of remuneration for a guarantee

"Remuneration" for the guarantee is any kind of compensation given by the creditor to the guarantor or a third party.

aa) Any kind of compensation

Compensation for guaranteeing does not need to be in relation to the benefit obtained. Neither must it be monetary. Any kind of compensation should be considered to be valid. Usually, remuneration is simply a percentage of the credit granted to the debtor. However, it can also be a reduction of the rights of the creditor vis-à-vis the guarantor. In contrast, the rights that are granted ex lege to the guarantor due to his payment (like the

---

[51] Cass. 19 December 1987 no. 9468, GC, 1988, I, 971; Cass. 4 September 1984, no. 4751, GI, 1985, I, 1, 952.

[52] STS 18 November 1988 [RA 1988 no. 8609].

[53] Cass. 5 Dec. 1992 no. 12948, FI 1994, I, 1126 ff.; *Giusti*, 76.

[54] Cass. 21 June 1974, Riv. Dir. Comm. 1975, II, 83; *Messineo*, 194.

[55] *Ferri*, 83 f.; *Giusti*, 77.

right of subrogation, the right to be refund, etc.) are not to be considered remuneration. They do not arise from the contract itself but rather by virtue of the law as legal consequences of the effective performance by the guarantor[56].

bb) Remuneration to the guarantor or to a third party

The remuneration in an onerous contract of guarantee does not necessarily have to be corresponding[57]. It does not have to be given to the guarantor himself as the counter-party in the guarantee relationship, but it can also be given to a third party. This third party is usually the debtor, who will thus gain a benefit in his relationship with the creditor. This benefit may take the form of improved credit conditions.

cc) Performed by the creditor

Even if the remuneration can benefit a person other than the guarantor, it occurs within the guarantee obligation to which only the creditor and the guarantor are parties. It is the creditor who obtains the benefit of being secured and therefore it is him the one who must compensate the guarantor.

If the debtor is the party who is remunerating the guarantor, the contract of guarantee is not onerous. There is an onerous relationship between the debtor and the guarantor but this is outside the guarantee. The structure of the guarantee contract is not altered thereby[58]. The creditor does not provide compensation for the right granted by the guarantor. Therefore the guarantee remains gratuitous and unilateral.

e) Effects of the gratuitous or onerous character of the guarantee

The gratuitous or onerous character of the guarantee also indirectly influences the regulation that is applicable to the contract. The rules of the guarantee which aim to protect the guarantor (in favor fideiussoris) are based on a concept of guarantee granted gratuitously by a private person. Hence, these rules of favor fideiussoris are not applicable to the professional guarantor, who makes profit out of the business of providing guarantee.

---

[56] *Giusti*, 69.

[57] *Sandulli*, 339 f., *Giusti*, 73 with long references. *Contra*: Cass. 5 December 1992, no. 12948 FI, 1994, I 1140 f. and Cass. 20 May 1987 no. 4608, GC, 1987, I, 2890.

[58] *Giusti*, 68.

IV. Constitutive characteristics of the guarantee contract (ancillarity and subsidiarity)

1. In general

The guarantee is by nature an ancillary obligation to the underlying debt. Its function only becomes meaningful in relation to this secured debt. As a consequence, the essential and typifying features of the contract of guarantee are the ancillary character of the guarantee obligation with regard to the principal debt (accessorietà/accesoriedad) and the secondary liability of the guarantor.

2. Ancillary character of the guarantee obligation: the principle of co-extensiveness

a) Definition and legal effect of the principle of co-extensiveness

The principle of co-extensiveness or ancillary character of the guarantee regards the structural and functional dependency of the guarantee vis-à-vis the principal debt[59]. The accessory character of the guarantee is derived directly from its securing or guaranteeing function (causa contracti)[60] and the way this function is conceived of within the regulation of the contract of guarantee. Hence, although the principle of co-extensiveness is not specifically defined in the law, it can be inferred from the regulation. The basic functional link between the guarantee obligation and the principal debt is expressed in art. 1939 Italian CC and 1824 par. 1 Spanish CC[61] by virtue of which there can be no guarantee unless there is a valid debt to be secured[62]. Apart from certain legal exceptions[63], there is no liability on the

[59] Cass. 5 March 1973 no. 609, GC, 1973, I, 937.

[60] *Petti*, 141; *Giusti*, 33 and 36: "Alla base del nesso di accessorietà sta la funzione di garanzia svolta dall'obbligazione fideiussoria, che mira ad un risultato pertinente al rapporto principale e che rinviene la propria giustificazione causale nel suo carattere ausiliario […] e nel riferimento […] ad altro rapporto al quale si pone in funzione strumentale".

[61] The ancillary character was first contained in the Roman concept of guarantee (Digest 45.2.19 and 46.1.1; *Buckland*, 445 f.). Correspondingly, art. 1941 Italian CC and art. 1847 Spanish CC: „The guarantor's obligation is extinguished at the moment of extinction of the principal debtor's obligation and upon the same legal causes as every other type of obligation". Both are based on art. 2012 French CC.

[62] The guarantee may be constituted in the course of the transaction by matters ex post facto. But there can be no guarantee until there is a principal debtor. Moreover, the obligation of the guarantor only falls due if the principal debt has been determined and has become due. See art. 1825 Spanish CC and STS 27 September 1993 [RA 1993 no. 6745]; STS 29 April 1992 [RA 1992 no. 4470]; STS 31 October1984 [RA 1984 no. 5153; STS 20 February 1987 [RA 1987 no.701]; STS 29 March 1979 [1979 no. 1235].

[63] See art. 1939 sent. 2 Italian CC and art. 1824 par. 2 Spanish CC.

part of the guarantor if the underlying obligation is void or unenforceable, or if that obligation ceases to exist.

The legal consequences of this ancillary character are reflected in the law. First, the extent of the guarantee is limited by reference to the principal debt. The guarantor's liability cannot be greater than that of the debtor, with respect to the amount, time of payment and terms under which the debtor is liable (art. 1941 Italian CC and art. 1826 Spanish CC).

Another effect of the accessory character of the guarantee can be found in art. 1945 Italian CC and art. 1853 Spanish CC[64] according to which the guarantor may raise against the creditor all the defenses which are inherent to the debt and are not personal to the debtor.

Moreover, unless otherwise agreed, the locus destinatae solutionis (jurisdiction) of the guarantee obligation will be that of the place in which the principal obligation will be performed (art. 1828 sent. 2 Spanish CC). The same is valid in Italy according to case law[65].

Other effects are not specified in the Law but are considered to be natural consequences of the accessory character[66]. For example, in case it has not been established in the contract, the limits of the guarantee obligation shall be construed with regard to the principal debt. Therefore, unless the guarantee is specifically limited, the extension of the guarantee will be identical to that of the debt[67]. Consequently, if there are obligations which are ex lege included in the principal debt the guarantor will be liable for them as well. This is for instance the case, if a guarantee has been agreed without limit for a debt of an employer with regard to an employment relationship. Such guarantee will also cover liability for damages linked to social rights as they are due ex lege by the debtor as a consequence of the principal obligation[68].

These are all legal consequences of the structural and functional dependency of the guarantee obligation with regard to the principal debt which is known in legal theory as principle of co-extensiveness (principio di accessorietà/principio de accesoriedad).

---

[64] See under: Chapter 2, D., III., 3. The right to set up defences (eccezioni/excepciones), 103.

[65] Cass. 22 January 1982 no. 422 cited by *Giusti*, 36.

[66] See *Moretti/Nicita/Visalli*, 82 ff.; *Marty/Reynaud*, 336 f.; *Tendler*, 8 f.

[67] Cass. 6 February 1975 no. 438, BBTC, 1975, II, 22.

[68] Cass. 22 May 1976 no. 1859 cited by *Giusti*, 36.

b) Principle of co-existensiveness as a typical characteristic of the contract of guarantee

There is unanimous agreement of the courts[69] and the academics[70] that the principle of co-extensiveness is a typifying element of the guarantee contract. This is also held to be the case with regard to joint and several guarantees[71]. The guarantee obligation is always functionally linked to the principal debt.

In a broad sense every personal security contract, including independent guarantees (indemnities), is accessory to the principal debt. Every personal security is based on the existence of a secured obligation and fulfils a security function (funzione di garanzia/ función de garantía) on which the ancillary character is based. However the meaning of the principle of co-extensiveness (accessory character) with regard to the contract of guarantee goes further than the basic, functional link between guarantee obligation and principal debt. The nature and the evolution of the guarantee from the moment it is constituted until its extinction[72] are dependent upon the debt. This kind of structural dependency does not exist within autonomous security rights[73]. These kinds of contracts are commonly used in practice specifically because of their lack of ancillarity vis-à-vis the secured debt. The principle of co-extensiveness thus actually serves to distinguish traditional guarantees from those independent (such as indemnity)[74]. In this

---

[69] STS 19 june 2008 [RA 2008 no. 4258], STS 5 February 1992 [RA 1992 no. 830]: "A guarantee even if it is joint and several [...] is always an accessory obligation"; also STS 27 June 1941, STS 6 February 1976 [RA 1976 no. 320], STS 19 November 1982 [RA 1982 no. 6550], STS 4 June 1984 [RA 1984 no. 3212], STS 11 June 1984 [RA 1984 no.3227], STS 31 October 1984 [RA 1984 no. 5153], STS 26 December 1986 [RA 1986 no. 7799], STS 2 December 1988 [RA 1988 no. 9287], STS 3 March 1990 [RA 1990 no. 1663], STS 4 May 1993 [RA 1993 no. 3403].

[70] *Bo*, Contributto, 43; *Valenzuela/Nieto* and *Bonet*, 437. For France, *Cabrillac* and *Mouly*, 36; for Germany: *Horn/Staudinger*, on § 765 no. 18; for The Netherlands: *Broekhuizen/Drobnig/Sagel-Grande/Snijders*, 92.

[71] *Bo*, Contributto, 43.

[72] SAP Zaragoza 20 April 2007 [AC 2007 no. 270988].

[73] On autonomous personal security rights see: *De Nictolis*, 1 ff.; *Nuñez*, 1 ff.

[74] The German *Abstraktionsprinzip* allowed for the creation of abstract or autonomous security rights beside the traditional accessory rights *(Garantievertrag/Bürgschaft)*. Therefore the distinction between these two kinds of securities came to receive extensive treatment by German authors. See as exemples: *Weth*, 303 ff.; *Boetius*, 18 ff. The advantages which are afforded by autonomous securities in certain situations in the practice caused these to become part of the law within non-abstract (causalist) legal systems such as Italy or Spain. In these systems a greater effort to provide theoretical justification was necessary. See a comparative analysis of the different civil law systems with regard to this matter in *Calderale*, 14 ff.; *Bo*, Contributo 43 ff. spec. 45; *Giusti*, 33; *Carrasco*,

sense, the principle of co-extensiveness is clearly a typifying element of the contract of guarantee[75] as it has also been recognised by the European Court of Justice[76].

c) Limitation of the principle of co-extensiveness

Although the guarantee is typically dependent of the secured debt (principle of co-extensiveness), a number of provisions within the guarantee regulation constrain the extent of such dependency. Also, the parties to the contract may limit the dependency between the guarantee and the principal obligation by excluding the application of certain legal provisions which typically stress the link between both obligations.[77]

aa) Legal exceptions to the principle of co-extensiveness

There are a number of established exceptions under which the guarantor may find himself to be liable to the creditor, notwithstanding the unenforceability[78] or nullity[79] of the principal obligation[80]. Moreover, the guarantee is not affected by changes in the secured debt that enlarge the guaran-

---

Fianza, 1 ff.; *Moralejo*, specially 685–687; *Valenzuela/Nieto* and *Bonet*, 439 ff.; *Reyes*, 54.

[75] Cass. 7 October 1967 no. 2334, BBTC, 1968, II, 244; Cass. 19 May 1969 no. 1744, FI, Rep. 1969, voce *Fideiussione e mandato di credito*, no. 6; Cass. 12 April 1984 no. 2356, FI, 1985, I, 2383; Cass. 23 April 1992 no. 4899, GC, 1993, I, 1293. In Spain: STS 6 February 1976 [RA 1976 no. 320]; STS 19 November 1982 [RA 1982 no. 6550]; STS 4 June1984 [RA 1984 no. 3212]; STS 11 June 1984 [RA 1984 no. 3227]; STS 31 October 1984 [RA 1984 no. 5153]; STS 26 December 1986 [RA 1986 no. 7799]; STS 2 December 1988 [RA 1988 no. 9287]; STS 3 March 1990 [RA 1990 no. 1663]; STS 4 May 1993 [RA 1993 no. 3403].

[76] See Bayerische Hypotheken- und Wechselbank AG v. Dietzinger (case no. C-45/96) of 17 March 1998, ECR 1998 I 1199 p. 1221 nos 18 and 20; Berliner Kindl Brauerei AG v. Siepert (case no. C-208/98) of 23 March 2000, ECR 2000 I 1741, p. 1744 no. 26; Préservatrice Foncière TIARD SA v. Staat der Nederlanden (case no. C-26601) of 15 May 2003, ECR 2003 I 4867, p. 4891 no. 29. All these cases regarded the application of certain EU Directives on Consumer protection or the Brussels Convention of 1968 on jurisdiction in civil and commercial matters were or not applicable to the contract of guarantee.

[77] See: *Díez-Picazo*, Fundamentos, 416; *Guilarte*, 18–20; *Reyes*, 156 and *Valenzuela/Nieto/Bonet*, 441. For Germany see *Horn/Stuadinger*, vorbem zu §§ 765 ff., no. 64: „Die Akzessorietät kann vertraglich in vieler Hinsicht eingeschränkt, freilich nicht grundsätzlich abbedungen werden“.

[78] As in case of bankruptcy of the debtor.

[79] See art. 1939 sent. 2 Italian CC and art.1824 par. 2 Spanish CC regarding the nullity of the principal debt by reason of the debtor's lack of capacity. See: *De Martini*, Obbligazione, 487; *Giusti*, 37; *Reyes*, 175 f.

[80] See under: Chapter 2, C., VII. Guarantee for an invalid obligation, 84.

tor's liability, either if they are due to modifications agreed between the debtor and the creditor or if the debt has become more onerous. This is also seen as a legal limitation of the guarantee's ancillary character[81].

bb) Derogation by the parties of provisions regarding the principle of co-extensiveness: the guarantees "on first demand"[82]

Since the ancillarity is a typifying element of the guarantee, the rule which underlies this principle (the need for a valid secured obligation in order to create a valid guarantee[83]) cannot be derogated without changing the nature of the contract into that of an autonomous security right[84]. However, the parties to the contract may derogate other provisions which imply the ancillarity of the guarantee. In many cases an "on first demand" clause is included in the guarantee contract. The guarantor thereby waives the right to raise those defenses based on the underlying obligation. The principle of co-extensiveness remains suspended until the moment at which the guarantor provides payment[85]. The validity of such a waiver has received theoretical discussion[86] and case law has accepted its validity on numerous occasions[87]. The guarantor retains his right of recourse and reimbursement. Therefore, if the debtor had already paid the value of the guarantee or if the guarantee is void or unenforceable, the guarantor may claim against the creditor for reimbursement on the basis of his guarantee contract. The possibility to agree first demand guarantees implies a limitation of the dependency between the guarantee and the principal debt. All these factors evi-

---

[81] See *Reyes*, 155 ff.

[82] See *infra* under Chapter 2, D., III., 3., b, dd) Waiver of the right to set up defenses, 106 and under Chapter 2, C., VII., 5. Validity of the waiver by the guarantor to set up the defence of nullity of the secured obligation. The case of guarantees on first demand, 87.

[83] Art. 1939 Italian CC and art. 1824 par. 2 Spanish CC.

[84] Relazione al Codice Civile Italiano, no. 759; *Valenzuela/Nieto* and *Bonet*, 438; *Petti*, 73. See *infra* under Chapter 2, C., VII., 5. Validity of the waiver by the guarantor to set up the defence of nullity of the secured obligation. The case of guarantees on first demand, 87.

[85] *Valenzuela/Nieto/Bonet*, 439. In Germany see BGH 23 January 1997, WM 1997, 656 ff.; BGH 24 November 1983, NJW 1984, 923 f.; BGH 2 May 1979, BGHZ 74, 244 ff. See also for Germany *Drobnig/Sagel-Grande/Snijders*, 13: "Alle eben erwähnten Einreden, die dem Bürgen bei seiner Inanspruchnahme zunächst verschlossen sind, kann er, nachdem er an den Gläubiger geleistet hat, gegen diesen nachträglich geltend machen".

[86] In a negative way *Petti*, 75. In a positive, see *Valenzuela/Nieto/Bonet*, 439.

[87] Cass. 21 April 1999 no. 3964, Riv. not., 1999, 1271. See also Cass. 19. March 1993 no. 3291 cited by *Petti*, 73. STS 31 May 2003 [RA 2003 no. 5217] with further references.

dence that the degree of dependency may be significantly limited without changing the nature of the contract[88].

3. The secondary nature of the guarantee

Another typifying feature of the guarantee in Italy and Spain is the secondary nature of the guarantee obligation vis-à-vis the principal debt (sussidiarietà/subsidiariedad). There has been a certain level of controversy regarding this concept. Some legal authors refer it to the securing function of the guarantee and consider it an essential feature of the contract while other scholars identify it with the benefit of discussion, which is a natural (not essential) feature of the guarantee.

The guarantee is a reinforcing contract to be answerable for the debtor's obligation. The liability of a guarantor is essentially an obligation to make good the deficiency or loss that results from the debtor's default to perform his obligation. In this sense, the liability of the guarantor is secondary to that of the debtor, who always remains primarily liable for the debt. The performing guarantor substitutes the debtor in giving satisfaction to the creditor and he has the right of reimbursement against the principal debtor. This places the guarantor in a secondary position either if the guarantee obligation is secondary (meaning the guarantor may raise the benefit of discussion) or if it is joint and several. In both cases the guarantee performs a back up function in relation to the debt. This phenomenon is known in academic theory as "principio di sussidiarietà"/"principio de subsidiariedad". It makes it possible to distinguish the joint and several guarantee from the joint and several co-debt. Co-debtors are liable to the same degree and for the same debt. In contrast, a guarantor performs his own guarantee obligation, which is clearly secondary with regard to the creditor. The secondary nature characterizes every guarantee irrespective of whether the guarantor's liability is joint and several or secondary. In this sense it is considered to be an essential distinguishing feature of the guarantee[89].

However, some legal authors[90] relate the guarantee's secondary nature directly to the benefit of discussion (the rank of payment assumed by the guarantor). A guarantee is secondary if the guarantor is liable only upon the default of the debtor. Consequently, joint and several guarantees are in their opinion not secondary, since the creditor may first require payment from the guarantor, who must perform his guarantee obligation also if the

---

[88] *Briganti*, 147 ff. STS 31 January 2005 [RA2005 no. 963].

[89] *Ravazzoni*, 181 ff.; *Fragali*, L'inerzia del creditore, 744; *Guilarte*, 23; *Lacruz*, 503.

[90] In Italy, on the former Civil Code: Campogrande, 40; Bo, Contributo, 46. In Spain: *Albadalejo*, 325; *Puig Peña*, 484; *Díez-Picazo*, Fundamentos, 415. In Germany: *Horn/Staudinger* on § 765 no. 17.

debtor has not been requested for payment and his goods are sufficient to cover the debt.

The guarantee is only secondary if the guarantor holds the benefit of discussion (ex lege in Spain and most other countries[91], or by agreement of the parties, in Italy[92]). According to this conception, the secondary character of the guarantee cannot be defined as being an essential feature of this contract. The term "secondary" is commonly used in this sense, as contrary to joint and several.

V. Similarities between the guarantee and other related legal instruments

1. Guarantee and assumption of debt

The assumption of debt is a general term which refers to the different cases in which one person assumes the debt of another person[93]. As the guarantor assumes[94] the debtor's liability vis-à-vis the creditor, the guarantee can be considered a type of intercession. There are other forms of assumption of debt, not all of which possess a guaranteeing function: a) "discharging assumption of debt", by means of which the debtor is substituted by a third person, and b) "cumulative or reinforcement assumption of debt", by which the original debt is not altered, but the creditor's right is re-ensured with a new debt[95].

The discharging assumption is not a form of liability for the debt of another person. The debtor is substituted by a new party, which becomes thereby the main debtor. There is a change in the subjective structure of the credit relationship.

---

[91] The guarantee was conceived as secondary (in the sense that the guarantor has *ex lege* the benefit of discussion) in Roman Law since the times of Justinian. The French CC, and subsequently also Spanish CC and the former Italian CC adopted this model, which was also followed by most other guarantee regulations: art. 2021–2024 French, Belgian and Luxembourgian CC, art. 1830 to art. 1833 Spanish CC; § 771 and § 772 German CC, art. 1355 Austrian CC, art. 7: 855 par. 1 Dutch CC; art. 1941–1944 Civil Code of Quebec, and art. 3045 and 3048 Civil Code of Lousiana; art. 638 Portuguese CC; art. 855 Greek CC. The parties may also agree to the joint and several liability of the guarantor and the debtor. This possibility is also explicitly established in art. 1822 par. 2 Spanish CC.

[92] In contrast to Spanish Law and to the Common and Civil Law traditions the Italian CC of 1942 renders the guarantor as being *ex lege* joint and severally liable with the debtor (art. 1944 par. 1). According to art. 1944 par. 2 Italian CC the parties can however agree that the guarantor shall not be bound to pay before the remedies against the principal debtor are exhausted.

[93] See 21 March 1996 [RA 1996 no. 2234].

[94] Also if the guarantee obligation is different from the debt, the guarantor assumes *de facto* the debtor's liability or a part of it.

[95] *Roca Puig*, 188 f.

By contrast, cumulative assumption refers to the case of one person assuming the liability for the debt of another person. The performance of the credit is guaranteed by adding a new obligation to the original one between the creditor and the debtor. In this respect, various legal instruments may be distinguished: 1. assumption of performance; 2. adherence to the debt; 3. guarantee; 4. mandate to provide credit. In all of these structures the principal debtor remains liable to the creditor. Certain of the similarities that exist between each one of them and the guarantee can result in a degree of confusion. A comparison may therefore be useful in this respect.

2. *Guarantee and assumption of performance*

a) *In general*

A third person may assume the obligation to perform the debtor's obligation vis-à-vis the creditor (assumption of performance). This might take place either by delegation of payment by the debtor (delegazione di pagamento/delegación cumulativa) or by initiative of the third person (espromissione/expromisión).

b) *Assumption of performance (delegazione di pagamento/asunción de cumplimiento)*

Art. 1269 Italian CC[96] regulates the case in which the debtor delegates the duty to make payment to a third person. In assuming the obligation, the third party agrees to perform the debt of another person (assumption of performance). This agreement only occurs between the original debtor and the third party. There is no contribution from the creditor. The relationship between the latter and the debtor is not altered[97].

This contract could easily be confused with the contract of guarantee. In both cases the principal obligation remains unaltered (regarding subject and object) and the creditor's position is secured by the agreement. But there are distinguishing features. First, in the assumption of performance the guarantor has agreed with the debtor to fulfill the obligation of the latter. Therefore in the event of the agreed contingency, the guarantor performs the debtor's obligation. By contrast, if a guarantee has been agreed the guarantor performs his own obligation, which is different to the principal debt.

---

[96] Art. 1269 Italian CC: "Delegation of payment. If the debtor has delegated a third person to make payment, such person can bind himself to the creditor, unless the debtor has forbidden it. The third person delegated to make payment is not bound to accept the obligation even if he is a debtor of the delegor. Usage to the contrary is accepted".

[97] *De Maria/Franzoni*, 868.

Second, since the assumption of performance is agreed by the debtor and the third party, they may modify the agreement at anytime in any way they wish. Such changes can occur without the participation of the creditor. Differently, the guarantee is directly agreed with the creditor. Since the debtor is not part of it, he cannot affect such agreement. The creditor has the right to commence an action against the guarantor without consulting the debtor.

The creditor may also give his conformity to the assumption of performance. In this case, since he has also entered the relationship, the agreement cannot be withdrawn or modified without his consent. This lessens the differences with the contract of guarantee. However, the main structural difference between both contracts is still present. In the case of assumption of performance, two different persons are liable for the performance of one unique obligation while in the contract of guarantee there are two differentiated obligations which have a common interest.

c) Expromission (espromissione/expromisión)

Expromission refers to the situation in which a third party assumes the debtor's obligation without delegation. It is regulated in art. 1272 Italian CC[98] and is found in Spanish commercial practice. It is an agreement between the debtor and a third party. The creditor remains outside the relationship unless he accepts the agreement. Both co-debtors are liable in solido for a unique obligation.

3. Guarantee and adherence to the debt (acollo/adhesión a la deuda)[99]

By means of a contract of adherence to the debt a third party enters the obligatory relation and becomes principal debtor alongside the original one. This case is also known as a "co-debt for security purpose"[100]. The legal structure of this relationship is that of a co-debt. The subjective structure of the contract is modified, so that the new debtor is now co-obliged,

---

[98] Art. 1272 Italian CC: "A third person who, without delegation by the debtor, assumes the obligation of the debtor to the creditor, is bound *in solido* with the original debtor unless the creditor expressly releases the latter. Unless otherwise agreed, the third person cannot set up against the creditor the defences connected with the third person's relationships with the original debtor. However, he can set up the defences which the principal original debtor could have set up against the original debtor or are derived from acts subsequent to the expromission. The third person cannot set up against the creditor the compensation which might have been set up by the original debtor, even if such compensation occurred before the expromission".

[99] *Petti*, 271; *Roca Puig*, 189; *Basozabal*, 83 ff.; *Adame Martinez*, 143 ff.

[100] In Germany Kumulative Schuldmitübernahme oder Schuldbeitritt. See a comparison with the contract of guarantee in *Horn/Staudinger* on § 765 no. 363.

together with the original one. There is only one obligation, for which both the original debtor and the new party are liable simultaneously, at the same rank and degree, and independently from each other[101]. This liability is joint and several, for the same obligation and interest. However, the exclusive intention of the new co-debtor is to secure the creditor against the non-performance of the original debtor. Consequently, the legal causa of the contract is that of a guarantee. This has allowed certain Spanish scholars[102] to sustain that the co-debt for security purpose is a guarantee with the only particularity that liability between the co-debtors is presumed to be joint and several.

In contrast to the guarantee, the co-debt for security purpose constitutes a second, different obligation, which is not ancillary (co-existent) and not secondary. The new debtor assumes his own principal obligation, which may have a different extent and which is not affected by changes in the original debt[103].

In Spain the liability of the guarantor is secondary and not joint and several like that of a co-debtor. But even if joint and several liability has been agreed for the guarantee, the liability of the guarantor is derived from his guarantee obligation. His position regarding the credit is secondary, in the sense that he performs instead of the debtor and also retains his rights against him. The rules of the guarantee on the relationship between the debtor and the guarantor are also observed in the case of a joint and several guarantee. By contrast, in the co-debt for security purpose, these rules do not apply[104]. In Italy this case is explicitly regulated in art. 1273 ff. Italian CC. The third party is joint and severally liable according to art. 1273 par. 3 Italian CC. By contrast, in Spain (as also in Germany) there is no specific regulation on this issue. The general rules on co-debt are applied (art. 1137 ff. Spanish CC[105]), together with the stipulations of the agreement of the parties. Co-debtors in Spain are not ex lege joint and several (art. 1137

---

[101] In Spain: STS 28 September 1960 [RA1960 no. 3150]; STS 17 June 1985 [RA 1985 no. 3277]; STS 24 February 1984 [RA 1984 no. 777]; STS 28 March 1985 [RA 1985 no. 1218]; STS 15 December 1989 [RA 1989 no. 8832]; STS 30 December 1994 [RA 1994 no. 10243] commented by Adame Martínez, CCJC 38 [1995] § 1028. In Germany see *Horn/Staudinger* on § 765 no. 363 with case law.

[102] *Carrasco, Cordero* and *Marín*, 128.

[103] BGHZ 6, 397 cited by *Horn/Staudinger*, on § 765, no. 363.

[104] *Contra*: *Carrasco*, *Cordero* and *Marín*, 128. These scholars believe that the new debt that is assumed is ancillary to the original one and that the cause or title of the new obligation is always that of a guarantee. They completely identify the adherence/assumption of debt with the contract of guarantee. The only difference is that in the case of the assumption it is presumed that the new debtor/guarantor assumes a joint and several liability.

[105] Co-debtors in Spain are not ex lege joint and several according to art. 1137 CC.

CC). However the co-debt for security purpose is generally understood as the agreement to be joint and severally liable, together with the original debtor. Also if the parties have not explicitly agreed the joint and several liability, it is presumed to be agreed upon, due to the security function of the contract[106].

4. Guarantee and mandate to provide credit (mandato di credito/ mandato de credito)[107]

The mandate to provide credit can be easily confused with the contract of guarantee, especially with the guarantee for future debts[108]. The mandator orders the creditor to grant credit to the debtor and compels him thereby to guarantee such credit. He has the same rights as the guarantor and his obligation is (ipso iure) extinguished as a result of the extinction of the principal debt.

However, essential differences distinguish the guarantee from the mandate to provide credit. While the guarantee can be constituted before or after the establishment of the principal obligation, the mandate has to be constituted before the secured debt. This allows for the possibility of withdrawal (revocación) for so long as the mandator has not granted the credit, which is obviously not possible in case of a guarantee. Moreover, the mandate does not need to be constituted in written form to be valid as is the case for the guarantee in all EU countries, with the exception of Spain. The rights and duties of the parties until the moment the credit has been granted are governed by the law on the mandate[109].

The affinity between the mandate to provide credit and the guarantee is clear in those legal systems which have a special regulation for both contracts (art. 1958 Italian CC, § 778 German CC and art. 408 to 411 Swiss Code of Obligations). In Germany § 778 CC is systematically included among the rules of the guarantee. But in all these countries the differences between these contracts are also clearly exhibited and accepted[110].

5. Guarantee and guarantee for a bill of exchange (avallo/aval)[111]

The guarantee and the guarantee for a bill of exchange they both share the same security function. The distinction between both contracts is found

---

[106] *Carrasco*, 128.

[107] See under: Chapter 3, A. The mandate to provide credit for a third party, 186.

[108] *Horn/Staudinger* on § 778 no. 8.

[109] *Horn/Staudinger* on § 778 no. 8 and 11.

[110] *Giusti*, 295; *Horn/Staudinger* on § 778 no. 8 and 11.

[111] See Chapter 3, B. The guarantee for a bill of exchange (l'avallo/el aval cambiario), 210.

with regard to their different legal nature. In Italy and Spain[112] the guarantee for a bill of exchange is conceived of as being an autonomous contract[113] (the obligation of the guarantor is valid even if the guaranteed obligation is invalid). It is thus different from the guarantee (ancillary to the secured debt).

In Spain the enactment of the Ley Cambiaria y del Cheque (LCC)[114] in 1985 does not seem to have completely solved the disagreement of the scholars in this area. Some authors continue to support the view that the nature of the guarantee for a bill of exchange is that of an ancillary contract[115]. However, the terms of the Law on this issue make the autonomous character of the bill of exchange absolutely clear[116].

B. Creation of the guarantee

I. The sources of the contract of guarantee

1. In general

The contract of guarantee may be created by the consensual agreement between creditor and debtor, by a statutory provision or by the decision of a judge or court. These are known as primary sources of the contract of guarantee and give origin to the obligation of furnishing with a contract of guarantee. They need to be distinguished from the source of the guarantee obligation, which is the free consent of the guarantor to be liable for the debt of another person[117].

---

[112] In Spain there is agreement on the autonomous character of the guarantee for bill of exchange only since the Ley Cambiaria y del Cheque of 1985. Previously, the confusing terms of art. 486 Spanish Comm.C. divided the opinion of scholars on this point. Some followed the Italian theories (autonomous character of the guarantee for a bill of exchange). Other legal writers were inspired by the French and considered it to be a special kind of guarantee, with the same ancillary nature. See under Capter 3, B. Gurantee for bill of exchange (l'avallo/el aval cambiario), 210.

[113] "L'avallo (…) si differenzia dalla fideiussione tipica in quanto esso esprime il principio della autonomia", *Petti*, 266.

[114] *Ley* 19/1985 Cambiaria y del Cheque (Law 19/1985 on bills of exchange, promissory notes and cheques) (see arts.35 to 37).

[115] *Guilarte*, 51.

[116] See Chapter 3, B. The guarantee for a bill of exchange (l'avallo/el aval cambiario), 210.

[117] *Santamaría*, 856; *Guilarte*, 62. STS 23 March 1988 [1988 no. 2422].

These three primary sources of the contract are expressly listed in art. 1823 Spanish CC[118] and have been widely recongised in Italy by legal writers and within case law[119].

a) Consensual guarantee

The consensual guarantee is the obligation assumed by the debtor to provide a guarantor for his debt. It is created by agreement between creditor and debtor, by unilateral promise or by testamentary clause of the debtor[120] under the form of a separate agreement previous to the conclusion of the principal contract or as a clause inserted in it. The non-performance of the obligation to provide guarantee gives the creditor a right to resign the contract and recover compensation for the damages suffered. The debtor is compelled by this agreement. Therefore, no guarantee is constituted by the consensual guarantee unless the guarantor accepts the conditions established thereby. The consensual guarantee can so clearly be distinguished from the contract of guarantee which takes place between the guarantor and the creditor. Moreover, as no guarantee is actually created by the consensual guarantee agreement, the requirements for the formal constitution and validity of a guarantee do not need to be fulfilled at this stage[121].

The consensual guarantee is not necessary for the valid constitution of the guarantee. It is in fact rather unusual in the practice.

b) Statutory guarantee

The obligation to furnish a transaction with a guarantee may also arise from a legal provision. In Italy the statutory guarantee is not explicitly mentioned as a source of the guarantee contract as it is in art. 1823 Spanish CC. However, a number of Italian legal provisions prescribe the constitution of a guarantee in specific cases in order to secure the performance of obligations or preserve certain legal rights and prerogatives. Therefore, the statutory guarantee is also a primary source of the guarantee in Italy. In certain cases the legal requirement is the grant of any kind of security right in favour of a third person (art. 492, art. 639, art. 640, art. 647, art. 1608 Italian CC). This obligation would be fulfilled with the grant of a guaran-

---

[118] Art. 1823 Spanish CC: "The guarantee may be conventional, legal or judicial, gratuitous or under onerous title. It may be constituted, not only in favour of the principal debtor, but also of another guarantor, whether with the consent of the latter, without his knowledge, or even in spite of his opposition thereto".

[119] *Ravazzoni*, Le garanzie, 49; *Giusti*, 56; *Petti*, 30. About it and a list of examples relating to the former Italian CC in Dig. It., v. XI, Parte seconda, 1892–1898, 162.

[120] *Moretti/Bigiavi*, Fideiussione, Giurisprudenza sistematica civile, 124; *Ravazzoni*, Fideiussione, Nov. Dig. It., 276. *Guilarte*, 61.

[121] *Carrasco, Cordero* and *Marín*, 97.

tee or any other security right. Other provisions specifically foresee the need to grant a guarantee contract. This is the case of those special Italian laws that impose the creation of State guarantees[122]. Moreover, those situations in which the law establishes the joint and several liability of one person for the debt of another are generally considered "fideiussione ex lege" by courts and scholars. This is the case of certain managers, liable for the obligation undertaken by them in the name and for the account of the association they are representing (art. 38 Italian CC[123]). Other cases of legal guarantees are established in the law for private individuals (art. 50, art. 515, art. 1319, art. 1416 to art.1418 Italian CC)[124].

c) *Judicial guarantee*

The contract of guarantee can also be originated by a court decision; judicial guarantee. In this case the court imposes the obligation to provide a guarantee on the ground of a legal provision in order to maintain a right or privilege set by law (see art. 119 Italian c.p.c.; art. 167, art. 260, art. 261, art. 491 Spanish CC or art. 64, art. 529 LECiv)[125]. It can therefore be assumed that a judicial guarantee is a particular type of legal guarantee which requires by law the intervention of the court. Every judicial guarantee is a legal guarantee but not all legal guarantees are dependent on the courts to decide on their creation.

---

[122] *Moscati*, 94 ff; *Bozzi/Rescigno*, 209. For a deep study and list of explained examples of statutory guarantees see: *Giusti*, 56 ff. and *Petti*, 37–46.

[123] Art. 38 Italian CC: "Third persons can enforce their rights against the common assets of the association for obligations undertaken by the person representing it. Persons who have acted in the name and for the account of the association are also personally liable *in solido* for such obligations". ("Per le obbligazioni assunte dalle persone che rappresentano l'associazione i terzi possono far valere i loro diritti sul fondo comune. Delle obbligazioni stesse rispondono anche personalmente e solidalmente le persone che hanno agito in nome e per conto dell'associazione"). See *Giusti*, 58; *Piazza* 1985, 726. Court decisions: Cass. 25 October 1969 no. 3502, FI, 1970, I, 2536:"La responsabilità personale assunta ope legis per il fatto stesso di avere operato e contratto con terzi nell'esercizio di una funzione rappresentativa e, comunque, in nome e per conto di un'associazione, va concepita come una forma di fideiussione ex lege, avente una funzione di garanzia per i terzi contraenti estranei all'associazione"; Cass. 19 April 1973 no. 1138, FI, 1973, I, 2054; Cass. 26 Feb. 1985 no. 1655 FI, 1985, I, 672: "la responsabilità personale, e solidale con quella dell'associazione non riconosciuta, della persona o delle persone che hanno agito in nome e per conto dell'associazione medesima si configura come una forma di fideiussione ex lege".

[124] For longer explanations see: *Giusti*, 64.

[125] *Petti*, 46; *Bozzi*, La fideiussione, 1995, 31; *Guilarte*, 62 ff.; *Santamaría*, 858; *Castán*, 668; *Carrasco*, *Cordero* and *Marín*, 98.

2. *Legal regulation on consensual, statutory and judicial guarantees*

Conventional, statutory and judicial guarantees all give origin to an obligation to provide a guarantee. This obligation will only be considered fulfilled provided certain conditions are observed. The specific requirements and legal effects for the validity of this obligation are clearly established in Italian and Spanish civil codes. First, art. 1943 Italian CC[126] and art. 1828[127] Spanish CC set up the main requirements that the presented guarantor must fulfil in order to consider the obligation as performed. Moreover, a more specific regulation on the legal and judicial guarantees is contained in arts. 1854–1856 Spanish CC.

a) Requirements regarding the guarantor

The debtor must present a guarantor who is of full capacity and has sufficient assets to eventually fulfill the obligation he secures (art. 1943 par. 1 Italian CC and art. 1828 par. 1 Spanish CC). If the creditor does not accept a guarantor that objectively covers the requirements, the debtor is discharged of his obligation to provide a guarantor. In that case, if the guarantor has not revoked his offer and the debtor defaults on payment, then the creditor shall not afterwards be entitled to demand payment from the guarantor. His behaviour served as conclusive evidence of the refutation of the guarantor's offer.

With regard to the acceptance of the guarantor by the creditor, a guarantee which is offered by a bank should always be adequate. Hence it cannot be rejected as being insufficient[128]. If a plurality of guarantors guarantee the debt joint and severally, it should be taken as being an adequate guarantee if one of the guarantors fulfils the requirement of solvability[129].

b) Alternatives to the legal or judicial duty to provide a guarantor

It may be the case that a party is legally bound to provide guarantee by statutory provision or by judicial decision. If this person is unable to obtain

---

[126] Art. 1943 Italian CC: "A debtor who is bound to furnish a surety shall select a person not lacking capacity who owns sufficient property to guarantee the obligation, and who has or elects a domicile within the jurisdiction of the court of appeals where the guarantee is to be undertaken. If the guarantor becomes insolvent, another one shall be furnished, unless the surety was a person selected by the creditor".

[127] Art. 1828 Spanish CC: "A person obligated to provide a guarantor must present a person with capacity to bind himself and having sufficient assets to respond for the obligation he guarantees. The guarantor shall be understood to be subject to the jurisdiction of the court where this obligation must be performed".

[128] *Carrasco*, *Cordero* and *Marín*, 98.

[129] Pérez Alvarez, prefers a minimum requirement of two solvent joint and several co-guarantors (*Pérez Alvarez*, 142; also *Carrasco, Cordero* and *Marín*, 98).

a guarantee, then he may give a pledge or a mortgage which is sufficient to meet his obligation (art. 1855 Spanish CC). There is no parallel provision to be found within Italian law. However, the same outcome can be achieved by the analogous application of art. 2743 Italian CC.

c) *Substitution of the insolvent guarantor*

In the event of the first guarantor being insolvent[130], the creditor may demand that another solvent[131] guarantor be provided, except in the case that a precise person had been chosen by the parties for his specific qualities (art. 1943 par. 2 Italian CC and art. 1829 Spanish CC). This right of the creditor to demand another guarantor is retained until the creditor requests for payment and aims at providing protection for the creditor. Therefore, if the debt had been secured by a plurality of joint and several co-guarantors, the insolvency of one of them does not provide a sufficient basis for the creditor to demand the appointment of a new guarantor[132]. The same applies if the debt is guaranteed by a solvent sub-guarantor. However, if this sub-guarantor becomes insolvent the debtor must provide a pledge or a mortgage as a consequence of the analogous application of art. 1855 Spanish CC[133]. Hence, within consensual guarantees the risk of insolvency of the guarantor/sub-guarantor is assumed by the debtor.

d) *Jurisdiction applicable to the guarantor*

According to Italian and Spanish Civil Codes, the guarantor shall be understood to be subject to the jurisdiction of the court in which this obligation must be performed (see art. 1943 par. 1 in fine Italian CC and art. 1828 par. 2 Spanish CC)[134.] This provisions are understood to be overruled by the provisions contained in the EC Council Regulation No 44/2001 of 22 December 2000 on jurisdiction and the recognition and enforcement of judgments in civil and commercial matters (Brussels I Regulation)[135/136.]

---

130 In this context, "insolvency" must be understood as being of a factual nature; when the guarantor cannot fulfil his payments. It is not necessary to wait until the guarantor has been declared insolvent as a result of an insolvency procedure.

131 A „solvent guarantor" is understood as in art. 1828 Spanish CC: "[...] a person with capacity to bind himself and having sufficient assets to respond for the obligation he secures [...]".

132 *Pérez Alvarez*, 142.

133 *Carrasco, Cordero* and *Marín*, 99.

134 Art. 1828 and art. 1829 Spanish CC are applicable to all cases in which there is an obligation to provide a guarantor (conventional, statutory and judicial); *Guilarte*, 140 ff.; *Pérez Alvarez*, 261.

135 Official Journal L 012, 16/01/2001 P. 0001–0023.

e) Specific consequences for the judicial guarantor. Exclusion of the benefit of discussion

Those guarantees arising from a court decision are joint and several by law. This is an additional legal consequence, which is specific to judicial guarantees as established in art. 1856 Spanish CC: "a judicial guarantor has no right to demand discussion on the property of the principal debtor. A sub-guarantor, in the same case, has no right to demand discussion on the property of either the principal debtor or the guarantor".

II. Creation of the guarantee obligation

1. Conclusion of the contract of guarantee

A contract of guarantee must be founded upon the mutual assent of the parties to the agreement[137]. There must be a consensus ad idem between the parties. The purported guarantor must have made an offer which was accepted by the purported creditor. The principles relating to offer and acceptance in the case of guarantees are the same as those which apply to contracts generally[138] with certain specialties.

a) Offer and acceptance

aa) The guarantor's offer

The offer to grant guarantee is a declaration of will made by the guarantor in order to assume the guarantee. It has to be addressed to the creditor. An agreement between debtor and guarantor by which the latter assumes the liability for the debt of the principal shall not be a guarantee[139], since the creditor does not have any right against the guarantor in case of debtor's default.

---

[136] For an extensive analisys of the Brussels I Regulation see *Magnus/Mankowski*, 2007.

[137] STS 23 March 1988 [RA 1988 no. 2422]; Comentario a la STS 23 Marzo de 1988, CCCJ 16, 1988, § 429.

[138] The declaration of the will to constitute a guarantee can be subject to terms and conditions as stated in STS 25 March 1998 [RA 1998 no. 2050].

[139] It is usually considered to be a contract in favour of a third party (Cass. 4 April 1995 no. 3940, GC 1995, I, 2413). In Italy, the participation of the debtor in the guarantee contract has been accepted as being "justified participation" but the guarantee contract still exists between guarantor and creditor (Cass. 2 May 1983 no. 3018, FI, Rep. 1983, *voce* Fideiussione e Mandato di credito, no. 8).

(i) Form of the offer

(α) Express but not necessarily written form

There are no formal requirements to which the offer must adhere[140]. The Italian and the Spanish civil codes only require the explicit constitution of the guarantee (art. 1937 Italian CC[141] and art. 1827 par. 1 Spanish CC[142]). The will of the guarantor to assume the guarantee obligation does not need to be in a written format, but it must be clearly and unambiguously expressed[143]. However, the oral form is not to be recommended and in fact it is almost unknown in practice due to the difficulties of proof.

The guarantee obligation is a heavy liability for the guarantor to bear. It is therefore necessary to be sure that the guarantor understands the meaning of his obligation and that he desires to be bound to its full extent. The express assumption must therefore have regard to the will of the guarantor to be liable vis-à-vis the creditor[144]. It must also have regard to the elements which are required to determine its contents (i.e. the person being guaranteed, the obligation being guaranteed and the limits of the obligation assumed[145]).

The need to make an express declaration serves to ensure that the guarantor conducts a careful analysis of the consequences that such an obligation may have[146]. The creditor must also be confident that the guarantor

[140] The reason for this absence of formal requirements for the valid conclusion of the guarantee can be found in Roman law (see: *Jones*, 138; *Cohan*, 220).

[141] Art. 1937 Italian CC: "The will to provide a guarantee must be express" ("La volontà di prestare fideiussione deve essere espressa").

[142] Art. 1827 par. 1: "The guarantee will not be presumed: it shall be express and it cannot be extent to more than its content" ("La fianza no se presume: debe ser expresa y no puede extenderse a más de lo contenido en ella"). The wording of this provision follows art. 2015 French, Belgian and Luxemburgian CC. Art. 628 Portuguese CC also follows this principle.

[143] Cass. 26 September 1979 no. 4961, GI 1980, I, 1, 1545; *Guilarte*, 1990, 124. Even if the underlying contract must be concluded in writing, the guarantee does not require to be concluded in this manner. By contrast in § 766 German CC the declaration of will by the guarantor must be given in writing unless for commercial guarantees (see § 350 German Comm.C.). However, the word guarantee (*Bürgschaft* or *bürgen* do not need to be expressly mentioned if the will of the guarantor to guarantee is clear enough. See *Horn/Staudinger*, on § 765 no. 3.

[144] "Verpflichtungswille" in Germany: See *Horn/Staudinger*, on § 765 no. 2.

[145] *Guilarte*, 124. See: Cass. 9 May 1988 no. 3400, BBTC, 1989, II, 434. In France the guarantor's declaration of will must contain his signature and a hand written statement of the maximum guaranteed amount (art. 1326 French CC: "[...] titre qui comporte la signature de celui qui souscrit cet engagement ainsi que la mention, écrite par lui-même, de la somme ou de la quantité en toutes lettres et en chiffres".

[146] The importance of this contract is usually expressed by the words "afianza y pagarás" (guarantee and you will pay) in Spanish legal tradition. See Cass. 12 May 1942,

has really assumed the guarantee. His decision to grant credit and the conditions under which it is granted directly depend on this provision of security. Only an explicit and direct declaration of will can be sufficient to create a secure and unmistakable guarantee obligation. In the whirl of commercial activity there are plenty of situations in which a party promotes or recommends the grant of credit, without actually assuming any clear obligation in so doing[147]. A clear manifestation[148] of will thus helps to distinguish such ambiguous situations from those in which a guarantee obligation is assumed[149].

It would be highly desirable for there to be a compulsory written format for all civil guarantees. This could be modeled on the provisions which already apply to this matter within countries such as Germany (§ 766 CC) and Austria (art. 1346 par. 2 CC).

A written declaration of consent can be included in the underlying contract which gives rise to the secured obligation. Alternatively, it could be encapsulated within a separate document if the declaration stipulates the obligation which is actually being guaranteed (or the necessary elements to determine it in the case of a future or conditional obligation). If this is not observed the declaration will exist as a form of indemnity (contratto autonomo di garanzia/contrato de garantía autónomo).

(β) The meaning of the terms: 'express' and 'tacit'.

The term "expressly", which is used in both Italian and Spanish civil codes, is rather vague. To be considered express, the guarantor's declaration: a) must be clear and unambiguous[150] and b) it must express the guarantor's will to grant guarantee (animus fideiubendi)[151]. The kind of acts or

---

BBTC, 1942, II, 12; *Ravazzoni*, Le garanzie, 37; *Fragali/Scialoja/Branca*, 182; *Guilarte*, 124. See also *Jestaz*, 8.

[147] Some declarations might be comfort letters.

[148] In Germany, the use of expressions such as "guarantee" ("Bürgschaft" or "sich verbürgen") likely mean the will of the party to guarantee with a dependent guarantee. "Bei Verwendung des Ausdrucks "Bürgschaft" ist im Zweifel Bürgschaft gewollt" see *Horn/Staudinger*, on § 765 no. 3. BGH 14 December 1995, ZIP 1996, 172, 173.

[149] *Di Sabato*, 500. Italian Supreme Court did not consider that a guarantee was constituted in a case where information was given by a third party about his debtor according to which the debtor was considered "an honest person and the creditor should feel confident because he guaranteed this honesty […]" (Cass. 15 December 1975, FI 1975, no. 9).

[150] The declaration must be clear (Cass. 18 October 1994 no. 8471, FI, 1994, no. 21; Cass. 8 May 1981 no. 3027, GI, 1982, I, 1, 281; Cass. 16 Dec. 1974, no. 4314, FI, 1971, no. 7) and understandable for the creditor; without possible doubt (Trib. Milano, 6. November 1987, BBTC, 1988, II, 532).

[151] Cass. 26 June 1979 no. 4961, GI 1980, I, 1, c. 1545; Cass. 31 March 1954 no. 1011, GI 1955, I, 1, c. 383. See: *Giusti*, 89–90; *Rescigno/Bozzi*, La fideiussione, le figure affini, 211ff.

manifestations that can be understood as express or explicit in relation to the assumption of a guarantee obligation is a matter of interpretation. Gesture and other kinds of traditional communication signs have been understood as possible ways of explicit manifestation[152]. These are very much dependent on the behaviour, practice and habits of the place and community[153] in which these forms of communication have occurred. All the alternative ways to express consent must be clear enough to be considered explicit. Therefore, in order to avoid difficulties and to assist proof and security, the written form is not only generally but uniquely used in practice[154].

(γ) Compulsory written form for commercial guarantees in Spain

Art. 440 Comm.C. requires the written form for commercial guarantees[155] (art. 439–442 Spanish Comm.C.). This provision is rather surprising and its legal reasoning is not clear[156]. However, since in practice almost every guarantee (civil and commercial) is agreed in writing, scholars have not questioned this principle and case law has always required written form for the validity of commercial guarantees[157].

(ii) Proof of the constitution of the guarantee

The Italian Supreme Court has accepted that any form of proof may be admissible with regard to a guarantee[158]. This is inclusive of presumptive proof, i.e. the will of the guarantor must be express but the proof of this express manifestation might be of a presumptive nature[159]. It thus falls to

---

[152] *Aru/D'Amelio e Finzi*, 389.

[153] Cass. 14 July 1936 no. 2485, FI 1937, I, 38; *Bo*, Note sulla forma della fideisussione, 321 ff.

[154] In exceptional instances case law has also required a written form of conclusion for the guarantee: Cass. 21 May 1942 no. 1379, FI, Rep. 1942, voce *Fideiussione*, 545.

[155] Art. 439 Comm.C.: „Será reputado mercantil todo afianzamiento que tuviere por objeto asegurar el cumplimiento de un contrato mercantil, aun cuando el fiador no sea comerciante".

[156] Contrary to the Spanish regulation, § 350 German Comm.C as ammended of 13. July 2001, establishes the free form (*Formfreiheit*) for commercial guarantees in order to facilitate commercial transactions (§ 350 German Comm.C.: "Auf eine Bürgschaft, ein Schuldversprechen oder ein Schuldanerkenntnis finden, sofern die Bürgschaft auf der Seite des Bürgen, das Versprechen oder das Anerkenntnis auf der Seite des Schuldners ein Handelsgeschäft ist, die Formvorschriften des § 766 Satz 1 und 2, des § 780 und des § 781 Satz 1 und 2 des Bürgerlichen Gesetzbuchs keine Anwendung").

[157] STS 30 November 3005 [RA 2005 no. 7742].

[158] Cass. 9 September 1998 no. 8922, FI 1998 no. 21; Cass. 17 October 1992 no 11413, GI, 1994, I, 1, 1649. *Giusti*, 93.

[159] Cass. 17 October 1992 no. 11413, GI 1994, I, 1, 1649; Cass. 2 August 1984 no. 4600, GI, 1985, I, 1, 382; Cass. 16 January 1976, no. 150, FI, Rep. 1976, *voce Fideius-*

the judge to arbitrate as to the existence of the guarantee on the basis of evidence from which the intention of the guarantor can be determined. [160]

bb) The creditor's offer

Normally the offer to guarantee is made by the guarantor to the creditor. However, the creditor may also make an offer to the guarantor in order to create a contract of guarantee[161]. In this sense, if, as it is common in practice, the creditor accepts an offer sent by the guarantor but introduces insignificant changes in it, is not considered a creditor's offer or counter-offer by Spanish courts[162]. It is considered that the creditor accepted the guarantor's offer as modified by the creditor. This is only the case if the changes do not worsen the guarantor's position. If otherwise, the modifications are not clearly insignificant and the guarantee is gratuitous, it is assumed that the creditor has accepted the terms of the offer as had been made by the guarantor and the creditor's counter-offer is only a proposal of change, which needs to be accepted by the guarantor.

In any case, it is sensible to obtain an answer from the guarantor to verify the admission of the relevant terms. If the guarantee is of commercial nature, such written acceptance by the guarantor is necessary according to art. 440 Spanish Comm.C.

---

sione e mandato di credito, no. 5; Cass. 28 January 1972, no. 242, FI, Rep. 1972, *voce Fideiussione e mandato di credito*, no. 8; Cass. 10 November 1971, no. 3214, FI, Rep. 1971, *voce Fideiussione*, no. 15; Cass. 26 June 1968, no. 2154, GC 1968, I, 1796; Cass. 26 June 1968 no. 2154, GC 1968, I, 1796; Cass. 20 June 1967 no. 1455, FI 1967 no.5; Cass. 12 March 1955 no. 748, GC 1955, I, 1106; Cass. 26 June 1968 no. 2154, GC 1968, I, 1796; Cass. October 1963 no. 2664 FI, 1964, I, 600. *Biscontini/Perlingieri,* 1574. *Contra*: *Bianca*, 475; *Miccio*, 527. *Contra*: Trib. Cassino, 24 March 1965, BBTC, 1965, II, 597. In Spain this is considered possible but not desirable, see *Reyes*, 221.

[160] "La prova della fideiussione può avvenire anche mediante presunzioni, purché queste portino al convincimento di una volontà espressa di malleveria" (Cass. 14 July 1936 no.2485, FI 1937, I, c.38). See also: Cass. 11 May 1973, no. 1271, FI., Rep. 1973, *voce* Fideiussione e mandato di credito, no. 7; Cass. 9 May 1972, no. 1402, FI., Rep. 1972, *voce Contra*tto in genere, no. 150. On the testamentary proof: Cass. 7 March 1978, no. 1129, FI, Rep. 1978, *voce* Fideiussione e mandato di credito, no. 11; Cass. 9 May 1972, no. 1402, FI, Rep. 1972, *voce Contra*tto in genere, no. 150.; Cass. 6 April 1971, no. 999, FI, Rep. 1971, *voce* Fideiussione e mandato di credito, no. 12; Cass. 30 March 1971, no. 910, FI., no. 13; Cass. 21 November 1970, no. 2471, FI, no. 14; Cass. 19 May 1969, no. 1744, FI, Rep. 1969, *voce* Fideiussione e mandato di credito, no. 6.

[161] Art. 1829 Spanish CC foresees indirectly the creditor's offer when it refers to the case that the creditor has requested a specific guarantor.

[162] STS 3 November 1955 [RA 1955 no. 3564], *Carrasco, Cordero* and *Marín*, 105.

cc) Acceptance

(i) No need for acceptance of the guarantee by the debtor

The contract of guarantee only exists between the creditor and the guarantor. The debtor is not a party to the contract and therefore his acceptance is not a requirement for the valid constitution of the guarantee (art. 1936 par. 2 Italian CC and art. 1823 par. 2 Spanish CC).

The debtor is present and sometimes plays, de facto, a very important role in the creation of the guarantee. He may formally commit himself to furnish the creditor with a guarantor and so enable the granting of the credit facility. Sometimes the guarantee contract only exists as a clause within the underlying contract for the provision of credit. But in all these cases the debtor remains outside the guarantee contract. That is the reason why a guarantee can also be validly created without the debtor being aware[163] (art. 1936 par. 2 Italian CC and art. 1823 par. 2 Spanish CC[164]) and even despite his opposition thereto (art. 1823 par. 2 Spanish CC explicitly and art. 1936 par. 2 Italian CC shall be interpreted in the same way[165]).

(ii) Express acceptance of the guarantee by the creditor

(α) Is the creditor's express acceptance a constitutive requirement?

The creditor's acceptance is not expressly required by law for the valid constitution of the contract of guarantee either in Italy or in Spain[166]. Art. 1937 Italian CC clearly establishes that the only formal requisite for the constitution of a guarantee is the express will of the guarantor. The creditor's acceptance is hence not required for the creation of this contract in Italy. In Spain, art. 1827 CC does not use such clear terms. It demands the express constitution of the guarantee without clarifying whether this only relates to the guarantor's declaration of will or also to the express acceptance of the creditor. The ratio of these provisions is based on the traditional notion of guarantee as being a gratuitous contract (unilateral guarantee), by which the guarantor assumes obligations and risks without obtaining anything in return. The creditor is the beneficiary of the contract and the guarantor is the party deserving protection. Therefore, the wording of

---

[163] Following the Roman principle: "fideiusbere pro alio potest quisque, etiamsi promissor ignoret" (*Digest* 46, 1, 30).

[164] See also art. 2014 French CC.

[165] The ratio for this provision is the function of the guarantee, i.e. the reinforcement of the creditor's right. The interests of the debtor are by contrast merely factual and not considered by the law (Cass. 12 April 1984 no. 2356, FI 1985, I, 2383; Cass. 12 April 1984 no. 2456, GC 1985, I, 466).

[166] *Giuliani/Franzoni*, 940; *Guilarte*, 68.

art. 1827 CC should be interpreted as only requiring the express declaration of the guarantor for the valid constitution of a unilateral guarantee[167].

In the case of onerous guarantees, the creditor's acceptance is necessary as these are bilateral contracts that create obligations for creditor and guarantor. This acceptance might also be tacit or implicit[168]. The guarantor's will to accept is essential while notification of such will is not necessary[169].

(β) Legal effects of the creditor's acceptance of the guarantee

The creditor does not have to expressly accept the offer of a gratuitous guarantee. However if he does, this acceptance affects the moment of perfection of the guarantee. Italian and Spanish regulations present interesting differences on this point. In Spain a unilateral contract can be revoked until the moment at which the beneficiary declares his acceptance. In Italy awareness on the part of the beneficiary is sufficient to enable the perfection of the contract.

According to art. 1333 Italian CC a unilateral contract cannot be revoked once the beneficiary has received notice of the offer[170]. Moreover, the beneficiary is entitled to reject the offer within a reasonable period of time. This period is determined with regard to the nature of the contract and the common uses to which such a contract is put[171]. Therefore, the non-acceptance by the creditor of a gratuitous guarantee does not result in any negative consequences for the creditor. The perfection of the contract takes place unless the creditor acts to reject the offer within a reasonable time.

In Spain, the active acceptance by the beneficiary is decisive for the perfection of the contract. A unilateral contract may always be revoked unless the beneficiary has actually expressed his acceptance[172]. Therefore it is convenient to accept in practice either expressly or tacitly. No formalities are required for the validity of this acceptance[173]. By way of exception

[167] See *Reyes*, 222.

[168] *Santamaría*, 861; *Guilarte*, 67, 11–12; *Manresa*, 238.

[169] STS 20 January 1999 [RA 1999 no. 3]; *Carrasco*, *Cordero* and *Marín*, 105; *Santamaría*, 861. In Germany there is a need of acceptance for the valid conclusion of the contract (§ 151 CC) but such acceptance does not necessarily need to be notified. This is the case of guarantee because the creditor is beneficiary for the contract (BGH 12 October 1999, NJW 2000, 276). The implicit acceptance of the guarantee is also admitted in France (Simler, no. 933).

[170] A letter of confirmation from the creditor only serves to prove the extent of agreement which was already concluded at the moment at which the offer reached the creditor (Cass. 1 October 1993 no. 9777, GI, 1994, I, 1, 1536).

[171] Cass. 19 December 1987 no. 9468, GC, 1988, I, 971 (and BBTC 1989, II, 133).

[172] *Guilarte*, 67.

[173] *Santamaría*, 861; *Guilarte*, 67, 11–12.

acceptance by the creditor is unnecessary in some judicial and some other legal guarantees and also when the beneficiary is unknown.

2. *Object of the guarantee*

a) *In general*

The object of the guarantee is not to be fully identified with the object of the secured debt. Both are different obligations and each has its own contractually agreed elements, i.e. object, terms, conditions, legal cause (causa). However, the guarantee is an ancillary obligation, dependant on the secured debt. Due to the principle of co-extensiveness, the content of the guarantee is affected by the object of the secured debt.

As in the case of every other obligation, the guarantee needs to have a valid object (art. 1346 Italian CC and art. 1261 Spanish CC). As the law on guarantees does not establish any specific regulation on the object, the only relevant requirements are those which are established in the general law of obligations. A valid object must be possible, licit and determined or determinable. If the object of the guarantee is not possible, is illicit or it cannot be determined by any direct or indirect method, the guarantee is void. No restrictions have been introduced by Italian or Spanish law with regard to the kind of obligation that can be secured by a guarantee. According to general legal principles, it can be an obligation to provide something or to act or to refrain from acting in a particular fashion[174]. Moreover, the nature of the guarantee obligation must not be the same as that of the principal debt. An obligation to do something could be guaranteed with an amount of money or vice versa. In practice, if the guaranteed obligation is a fungible item (for example, a sum of money), the guarantor's obligation generally consists in giving the creditor a tantumdem of that which he would have received had the principal debtor completed performance. If the debtor has partially fulfilled his obligation the object of the guarantor is accordingly reduced. The guarantor is therefore only liable for the part which has not been performed by the debtor.

If the guaranteed obligation is a so called non-fungible obligation (i.e. it involves doing or not doing something), the guarantor is compelled to indemnify the creditor with an equivalent performance (fideiussio indemnitatis). This equivalent could take the form of the performance of a different obligation to do or not to do something or to pay damages to the credi-

---

[174] The obligation to do something has been considered as a possible object of guarantee only in case it is not *intuitu personae* and the guarantor is able to comply in exactly the same manner as the debtor (*Casanova Mussons*, La relación obligatoria de la fianza, Barcelona 1984).

tor[175]. When a guarantee consists of an equivalent of the secured obligation, it may be difficult to ensure that the guarantee is not of a more onerous nature than the secured obligation. Usually only monetary debts are secured by means of a guarantee for the same or similar amount as the principal debt.

In some instances the object of the guarantee will be defined by reference to the principal obligation. This is the case of the so called "undetermined guarantees"[176], which object is not fully determined in the contract of guarantee[177], as it is the case for the universal guarantees ("fideiussione omnibus"/"fianza omnibus") [178].

b) Effects of the principle of co-extensiveness on the object of the guarantee

aa) The secured obligation must be valid

A contract of guarantee can only be validly created for a valid obligation (art. 1939 Italian CC and art. 1824 Spanish CC)[179]. The underlying obligation must therefore be validly agreed, must have a valid causa or legal reason and be created on a valid object (art. 1325 Italian CC and art. 1261 Spanish CC). Such valid object must be possible, licit and determined or determinable[180] (art. 1346 Italian CC and art. 1273 Spanish CC). If the principal obligation is not valid, the guarantee cannot be considered to be valid. In this respect, Italian Supreme Court has stated that the guarantee for tort liability is valid. The object guaranteed is the damage caused by

---

[175] Cass. 9 May 1985 no. 2891 cited by *Petti*, 121; *Bianca*, 483.

[176] The term "undetermined guarantee" has been criticized within academic debate. These guarantees can be determined by relation to the principal obligation. The designation "guarantees with determinable object" has been considered to be a more accurate description (*Petti*, 119).

[177] Cass. 9 December 1997 no. 12456, GI, 1998, I, 1, 11; Cass. 1 August 1987 no. 6656 and Cass. 18 July 1997 cited by *Petti*, 119.

[178] See under Chapter 2, C., VI. The universal guarantee (fideiussione omnibus/fianza omnibus), 72.

[179] This is a direct consequence of the principle of co-extensiveness. See: Relazione al Codice Civile, no. 759 and Cass. 19 November 1959 no. 3418, FI, 1959, *voce* Fideiussione e mandato di credito, 921. Such a principle was already present in Roman Law: Digest 46, 1, 16: "fideiussor obligare non potest ei, apud quem reus promittendi obligatus non est" and Digest 46, 1, 29: "si sub impossibili condiciones stipulatus sim, fideiussor adhiberi non potest". Today such a rule is to be found in almost all legislations: § 768 and 770 German BGB, art. 2010 French CC.

[180] Guarantees on future and conditional guarantees are therefore valid if enough elements are disclosed in the contract to make possible the exact identification of the object. See under Chapter 2, C., IV. The guarantee for future obligations, 69.

the negligent act of the debtor. It is therefore a licit object and can be validly guaranteed[181].

bb) The extent of the secured obligation limits the extent of the guarantee

The extent of the object of the guarantee cannot exceed[182] or be more onerous than the guaranteed obligation. Thus the guarantee cannot be given in duriorem causam i.e. the guarantor cannot be compelled to pay more than the debtor (art. 1941 par. 1 Italian CC and art. 1826 Spanish CC). The guarantee can however be created in leviorem causam, i.e. for a part of the principal obligation or under better conditions (art. 1941 par. 2 Italian CC and art. 1826 Spanish CC)[183].

In general, once the guarantee has been created any changes regarding the content of the principal debt can only occur if they are favourable for the guarantor[184].

C. Extent of the guarantee obligation

I. In general

The extent of the guarantee can be determined by reference (per relationem) to the secured obligation[185]. Unless a specific agreement to limit the extent of the guarantee has taken place, the guarantee is presumed to cover

---

[181] Cass. 27 June 1967 no. 1590 and Cass. 8 January 1974 no. 39 cited by *Petti*, 123.

[182] It might however be more intense. This could be achieved by including a real guarantee as an extra security. See: Cass. 14 July 1971 no. 2300, FI, 1971, no. 42; Cass. 13 July 1967, no. 1738, GC, 1967, I, 1588, GI 1968, I, 1, 838 and *Moretti* 1980, 89; *Ravazzoni*, Nov.Dig.It, 281; *Guilarte*, 93.

[183] In Italy the guarantee *in leviorem causam* has been considered exceptional: So, Cass. 31 January 1968 no. 315 cited by *Macario*, La fideiussione, not published: "L'identità dell'oggetto della fideiussione e dell'oggetto dell'obbligazione del debitore principale, nella sua stessa quantità e nelle sue stesse condizioni deve considerarsi elemento normale e essenziale del vincolo che assume il fideiussore"). If any agreement has been made regarding the extent of the guarantee obligation, it shall be considered to be exactly the same as the object of the principal.

[184] *Ravazzoni*, Nov.Dig.It., 1961, 281.

[185] In Spain guarantees without an agreed limit of extent are generally denominated "indefinite guarantees". Their content is established by reference to the secured obligation. By contrast, the so-called "definite guarantees" are agreed to cover a maximum amount. This theoretical distinction is also known in other Romanic countries. In these countries, such as France, Belgium and Luxembourg the same terminology is applied. In Italy the same conceptual distinction is also applied in theory in exactly the same terms as it is done in the countries mentioned. This is the case even if there is no specific terminology for each kind of contract in Italy.

the secured obligation in its entirety. In such a case the liability of the guarantor is ex lege the secured obligation. This is thus enlarged to embrace all accessories, including the procedural costs which have arisen due to the guarantor being required to perform payment (art. 1942 Italian CC and art. 1827 par. 2 Spanish CC).

The parties may agree to create a limited guarantee. The liability of the guarantor is then limited to the amount agreed in the contract. This amount cannot be extended in any manner without a new agreement. The limited guarantee is the most common form of guarantee which is to be found within contemporary banking practice. It is especially common in the situation of guarantee for non-fungible obligations.

II. The extent of a non-limited guarantee

1. Determination of the extent of non-limited guarantees

Non-limited guarantees are valid in Italy and Spain. Their extent is limited by both civil codes to that of the secured obligation and its accessories[186]. Hence, the guarantee is subject to the same terms of amount, conditions and extension of time as the secured debt[187]. The agreement of a maximum amount for which the guarantor can be liable is not a constitutive requirement of these guarantees in Spain and in Italy it is required only for the valid creation of future guarantees (art. 1938 Italian CC).

a) The secured obligation

The secured debt does not need to be determined at the moment the guarantee is created but it has to be determinable on the basis of the guarantee contract. As a result, the guarantor has assumed a valid obligation which already exists but the extent of which can only be determined at a later moment in conjunction with the guarantee agreement itself. The guarantor is thus answerable for the secured debt once it has been determined.

b) Extensions of the secured obligation after constitution of the guarantee

Extensions of the secured obligation are not included in the guarantee unless consented to by the guarantor[188]. The guarantor is not liable for the

[186] See also 2016 par. 1 French, Belgian and Luxembourgian CC. Austrian authors interpret § 1353 Austrian CC in the sense that non-limited guarantees also cover the accessories of the secured debt (*Schwimann/Mader*, on § 1353 no. 5).

[187] The non-limited guarantee is valid until the secured debt prescribes. *Carrasco*, *Cordero* and *Marín*, 143.

[188] In Germany the extent of the guarantor's obligation is based on the extent of the secured obligation (§ 767 par. 1 sent. 1 German CC). Extensions of the secured obligation at any time also increase the guarantee obligation so long they do not arise from a

stipulations agreed between creditor and debtor to enlarge the obligation of the debtor or to make the conditions harder after the agreement of the guarantee[189]. The guarantor is thus only answerable for the debtor's obligations which are derived from the contract he has guaranteed and not for any other obligation which arises by virtue of a new and posterior agreement. This ban of the extension of a guarantee above the limits of the secured obligation is not specifically contained in Italian and Spanish civil codes as it is in other European regulations[190]. However it is considered by the Italian[191] and the Spanish[192] Courts as a consequence of the construal and application of the principle of co-extensiveness; i.e. a natural consequence of the ancillary nature of the guarantee.

The enactment of a specific provision to limit the extension of the guarantor's liability would imply a more systematic regulation of the guarantee. This is especially pertinent in those cases in which the agreements are modifications of the underlying contract, i.e. they do not result in a new contractual relationship.

c) The specific case of extension of time (prórroga)

According to art. 1851 Spanish CC, the guarantor is not bound by an extension of time which has been granted to the debtor[193]. The same conclusion is to be found in Italian case law[194] and legal theory[195], the reasoning being that an explicit or implied extension of time serves to create a new

new agreement between creditor and debtor (§ 767 par. 1. sent. 2 German CC). § 766 German CC: "Für die Verpflichtung des Bürgen ist der jeweilige Bestand der Hauptverbindlichkeit maßgebend. Dies gilt insbesondere auch, wenn die Hauptverbindlichkeit durch Verschulden oder Verzug des Hautpschuldners geändert wird. Durch ein Rechtsgeschäft, das der Hauptschuldner nach der Übernahme der Bürgschaft vornimmt, wird die Verpflichtung des Bürgen nicht erweitert". "Der Bürge haftet für die dem Gläubiger von dem Hauptschuldner zu ersetzenden Kosten der Kündigung und der Rechtsverfolgung". See *Horn/Staudinger*, on § 767 no. 36.

[189] This rule is applicable even in the case of non-limited guarantees.

[190] It is the case of Germany, France, Belgium, Luxemburg and Finland. § 767 par. 1 sent. 3 German CC sets explicitly the non-extension of the guarantee to those obligations asumed by the debtor after the agreement of the guarantee ("Durch ein Rechtsgeschäft, das der Hauptschuldner nach der Übernahme der Bürgschaft vornimmt, wird die Verpflichtung des Bürgen nicht erweitert"). Art. 2013 French, Belgian and Luxemburgian CC and § 8 par. 1 Finnish Law of Guarantees also prescribe the same rule. For Austria see *Schwimann/Mader* on § 1351 no. 14.

[191] Cass. 26 July 1956 no. 2886, FI 1957, I, 840.

[192] AP Madrid 26 January 1995 [AC 1995 no. 148].

[193] STS 20 December 2002 [RA 2003 no. 60], STS 30 December 1988 [RA 1988 no. 10075].

[194] Cass. 26 July 1956 no. 2886, FI, 1957, I, 840.

[195] *Giusti*, 151; *Moretti*, La fideiussione, 86 ff.

contract. This contract is different from that which has been guaranteed and it is, hence, not covered by the guarantee.

Art. 1851 Spanish CC is not applicable if the guarantor already knew about the possibility of the future extension of time at the moment of the conclusion of the contract. In this case it is thus unnecessary to ask for an express declaration of consent from the guarantor[196]. The Italian Supreme Court has applied the same reasoning to this matter[197].

It seems clear that in Italy and Spain[198] the extension of time is only seen as aggravation of the contractual conditions for the guarantor. In other neighbouring countries, by contrast, the extension of time is also seen as a possible benefit for the guarantor. The debtor, who is in financial difficulties at the due date, might be able to pay his obligation at a later time. The guarantor would be therefore discharged from his liability only because of the time extension. Based on this reasoning, the guarantor is not discharged in case of extension of time of the secured debt (art. 2039 French CC[199] and Austrian case law[200]).

d) Accessories

aa) In general

A guarantee which is agreed without special limitations ("indefinite guarantee") covers ex lege the content of the secured obligation and all its accessories. The Spanish CC explicitly establishes this provision in art. 1827 par. 2, with regard to the so-called indefinite guarantees. These are those guarantees in which the extent has only been determined by reference to the secured debt. Art. 1942 Italian CC establishes the same consequence for all guarantees "unless otherwise agreed", i.e. unless the accessories have not been expressly excluded (ex art. 1942 Italian CC). This provision is generally understood as being applicable to every guarantee for which there is no agreed maximum limit[201]. Therefore the accessories are not covered by the guarantee if the parties have explicitly agreed to this point or if they have established a maximum limit for the liability of the guarantor.

---

[196] STS 8 May 1984 [RA 1984 no. 2399]. The Spanish Supreme Court has accordingly declared that art. 1851 Spanish CC is not applicable to future and conditional guarantees: STS 7 January 1981 [RA 1981 no. 3399]; STS 8 May 1984 [RA 1984 no. 2399] and STS 31 October 1984 [RA 1984 no. 5153].

[197] Cass. 26 February 1960 no. 350, GI, 1960, I, 1, 613. *Contra*: *Giusti*, 152.

[198] Also in England: *Swire v. Redman* (1876) 1 QBD 536 (QB).

[199] Art. 2039 French CC is not a mandatory provision and the parties can derogate from it.

[200] OGH 6 May 1954, ÖJZ 1954, 455 no. 312.

[201] *Giusti*, 152 and 153.

If the guarantor has not limited his liability to a maximum amount, he is presumed to be willing to assume the same liability as the debtor. This liability is regarded as being of the same extent and existing on the same terms which were assumed by the debtor. This therefore also includes the accessories which may result from non-performance on the part of the debtor. By way of contrast, the parties may have expressly agreed to there being a maximum limit to the liability of the guarantor. This limitation is considered to be an absolute ceiling on the amount of the debt which cannot be enlarged in any fashion, even by virtue of its accessories.

bb) Definition of the term "accessories"

(i) In general

"Accessories" is a general term which refers to all secondary obligations arising from the non-performance by the debtor[202] or his unjustified enrichment vis-à-vis the creditor. It also refers to the obligations of restitution if the principal contract is declared invalid.

(ii) Accessories of the secured debt

The accessories of the secured obligation itself are also covered within the sphere of the accessories of the guarantee. They include the contractual interest[203] or the obligation to assign the benefits thereof as well as the penalty clauses which are agreed by the parties for the case the debtor fails to perform his obligation[204]. This extends to cover any damages which are caused by the late performance of the debtor (interesi e danni moratori/intereses y daños moratorios)[205]. The Spanish Courts have even held that

---

[202] *Giusti*, 153; *Carrasco, Cordero* and *Marín*, 140.

[203] STS 30 June 1969 [RA 1969 no. 3680]; STS 8 October 1986 [RA 1986 no. 5333]; *Guilarte*, 132; *De Maria/Franzoni*, 1489. The same is true also for Portugal (art. 634 CC; Almeida Costa, 770) and Finland (§ 4 par. 1 Law of Guarantees). In other countries guarantees only cover contractual interests if this has been explicitly or at least implicitly agreed. It is enough if the guarantor already was aware about the fact that the secured debt would bear interests (For Germany: *Horn/Staudinger* on § 765 no. 40; for England: *Andrews* and *Millet* no. 610).

[204] Cass. 30 May 1963 no. 1468 cited by *Giusti*, 154 and *Petti*, 158; STS 30 June 1969 [RA 1969 no. 3680]; STS 3 October 1985 [RA 1985 no. 4570]; STS 2 October 1990 [RA 1990 no. 7464]; *Guilarte*, 133. Penalty clauses are also considered accessories in Portugal (art. 634 CC and *Almeida Costa*, 770) and France according to French case law (Cass.com. 6 February 2001, Bull.civ. 2001 IV no. 29). In other EU countries like Germany, penalty clauses are only covered by the guarantee if it has been so agreed by the parties of the guarantee contract (BGH 15 March 1990, WM 1990, 841 and see *Horn/Staudinger* on § 765 no. 40).

[205] Cass. 23 November 1963 no. 3018, GC 1964, I, 35; *Giusti*, 155; *Petti*, 156 ff; STS 22 November 1916 cited by *Carrasco, Cordero* and *Marín*, 141; *Guilarte*, 132. In most

the guarantee covers the loss of profits (lucro cesante) which are incurred by a landlord when a lessee remains in possession of a house[206].

All these accessories derive from the secured debt and must have been agreed to before the creation of the guarantee[207]. Those accessories that have been agreed in a posterior agreement imply a novation of the contract and are therefore not covered by the guarantee.

e) Costs of legal proceedings

Art. 1942 Italian CC and art. 1827 par. 2 Spanish CC expressly refer to the costs of legal proceedings[208]. This reference is only with regard to those proceedings which occur after the guarantor has been required to perform his obligation of payment. Such requirement does not need to be of a judicial nature or to follow any special form. However, the creditor must give the guarantor an opportunity to accomplish performance. A mere notification of this requirement shall not be sufficient[209/210].

In the case of joint and several guarantees the creditor may ask for payment from the debtor or any of the co-guarantors. Any of these requests constitute a demand for performance to the guarantor[211].

2. Guarantee exceeding the secured obligation or in duriorem causam. Reduction of the exceeding extent

By virtue of the principle of co-extensiveness, the extent of the guarantee (in regard to the amount, time for payment and conditions) cannot be greater than that of the underlying obligation. A guarantee exceeding the extent of the secured debt is not totally void by reason of invalid object but its extent is reduced to encompass only the limits of the principal obliga-

---

European countries the default interests and claims for damages caused by the debtor's lack of performance are not considered accessories but they are covered by the guarantee unless otherwise agreed. In Portugal this is explicitly established in art. 634 CC; in France and Germany it has been established by case law and scholars. For France see: Cass.civ. 10 May 1988 Bull.civ. 1988, I no. 134 and Simler, no. 300 ff. For Germany see: BGH 17 May 1994, NJW 1994, 1790; *Horn/Staudinger* on § 767 no. 25.

206 SAP Asturias 13 May 1993 [AC 1993 no. 1009]; SAP Asturias 30 December 1996 [AC 1996 no. 2395] and SAP Madrid 19 April 1999 [AC 1999 no. 1666].

207 See: Cass. 13 January 1928 cited by *Giusti*, 154; *Carrasco, Cordero* and *Marín*, 140.

208 See also Germany (§ 767 par. 2 CC) and Portugal (art. 634 CC).

209 *Giusti*, 155; *Carrasco, Cordero* and *Marín*, 144.

210 The same is true for France, Belgium and Luxemburg (art. 2016 par. 1 CC) and the Netherlands (art. 7:856 par. 2 CC).

211 Cass. 30 April 1952 no. 1203, FI 1952, *voce Fideiussione*, 890; *Guilarte*, 104.

tion. The guarantee obligation is void only for the part which is in excess, as set in art. 1941 par. 3 Italian CC and art. 1826 par. 2 Spanish CC[212].

3. Convenience of establishing a maximum amount as legal constitutive requirement

a) In general

The basic limitation of the guarantor's liability is already established per relationem to the secured obligation; by virtue of the application of the principle of co-extensiveness. The parties are thus free to agree the terms and conditions that they may wish for. If they do not specify the limits of the assumed liability, the guarantor is therefore presumed to have granted the guarantee for the secured obligation (in addition of its accessories). This might be seen as a sufficient legal limitation of the guarantor's liability. However, the limitation of the guarantor's liability to a maximum amount is already very common in practice. Expert guarantors do not accept a risk which they cannot precisely define at the moment of assumption. Moreover, such limitation is known in neighbouring countries as a constitutive requirement ex lege (Switzerland, art. 493 Swiss Code of Obligations). It might therefore be arguable that it would be convenient to introduce the legal requirement to stipulate a maximum amount for every guarantee, which would contribute to the guarantor's awareness of the risk assumed and would establish a basic limitation thereof; something positive for every guarantor.

b) Special case: liability limitation for non-professional guarantors

Non-professional guarantors are usually more vulnerable than professional ones. They are commonly also financially weaker and/or more exposed to changes in their patrimonies. They deserve protection with regard to the risks that the guarantee might entail. In this sense, the awareness of the risk assumed and its limitation is desirable for this kind of guarantor. That is the reason why the legal requirement to fix a maximum amount in the case of the guarantor being non-professional has been introduced in the Netherlands (art. 7:858 par. 1 Dutch CC).

However, not every kind of guarantee entails the same level of risk for the non-professional guarantor. Limiting the liability for every kind of guarantee assumed by a non-professional appears to be an excessive protective measure. It seems more balanced to limit those types of guarantees,

---

[212] See also art. 2013 French, Belgian and Luxembourgian CC; art. 7:851 and art. 7:860 Dutch CC; § 5 par. 2 Finnish Law of Guarantees; art. 851 Greek CC; art. 631 par. 2 Portuguese CC; § 767 par. 1 sent. 1 German CC is construed in the same way (*Horn/ Staudinger* on § 767 no. 4).

which entail a higher level of risk for non-professional guarantors, such as future or universal guarantees.

c) Special case: liability limitation for future guarantees

Italian CC specifically foresees in art. 1939 that guarantees created for future debts need to be limited with a maximum amount[213].

III. The extent of a limited guarantee

The parties can limit the liability of the guarantor vis-à-vis the secured debt in terms of amount, conditions and time.

1. Limitation of the guarantee in terms of amount

The guarantor might assume the guarantee for a part of the secured debt[214]. In this case, he is liable for the accessories which correspond to that part of the debt. Moreover if the debtor has partially performed his debt it will be held to be the part which is not covered by the guarantee.

A different way of limiting the guarantor's liability is to fix a certain maximum amount above which he cannot be required to perform. The accessories of the debt are also covered by the guarantee so long they, together with the secured debt, do not surpass the maximum limit of liability established by the parties.

2. Limitation of the guarantee in terms of conditions

The guarantee can be agreed in leviorem causam i.e. it can be agreed under certain conditions which reduce the onerousity of the guarantor's liability. For instance, it is very common for a guarantee to be created under the condition that the principal debt is secured by other security interests. In other cases, the guarantee only covers those liabilities of the debtor resulting from his fraud (dolo), or it only covers after all other guarantees have failed to satisfy the creditor[215].

3. Limitation of the guarantee in terms of extension of time

The parties can also establish a time limit for the guarantee beyond which it will be extinguished. However there is a state of ambiguity with regard to the extent of the guarantee within this time limit. It may be the case ei-

---

[213] See under Chapter 2, C., IV., 3. The protection of the guarantor for future debts, 70.

[214] STS 30 January 1990 [RA 1990 no. 102] and STS 27 May 1990 [RA 1990 no. 1732].

[215] *Carrasco, Cordero* and *Marín*, 145.

ther that the debts covered by the guarantee must fall due for payment within the set time limit or that the guarantor must be requested for payment within the time limit[216]. Unless the parties have specifically addressed this issue within the contract, the court will construe the agreement on a case by case basis.

IV. The guarantee for future obligations

1. Notion of guarantee for future obligation

A guarantee can also be created for a future obligation; i.e. a debt which at the moment of constitution of the guarantee does not exist but which will be generated by an imminent undertaking or incident (art. 1938 Italian CC and art. 1825 Spanish CC[217]).

The future obligation might be an existing obligation which value is still undetermined[218]. The guarantee contract must include enough elements to be able to ascertain the future value[219]. An example is that of a guarantee for the remuneration of a freelance for the work performed before he presents the invoice. The obligation to pay exists through the contract, but its value is yet to be determined.

Another case of guarantee for future obligation is that provided for an obligation which may arise in the future between the creditor and the debtor. The principal obligation is planned but it is not fully constituted when the guarantee is agreed. This is the case when a guarantee is agreed for a loan that a bank may grant to a debtor at some future date. Banks often require that a guarantee is created before the loan is granted. Therefore, the guarantee must contain enough elements to enable determining the object of the guarantee.

2. Guarantee for future obligations and principle of co-extensiveness

It is questionable, in view of the principle of co-extensiveness, whether a guarantee can be created if the secured obligation does not already exist. The explicit recognition of the guarantees for future obligation was an innovation introduced by the Italian CC of 1942. Previous regulation in Italy did not explicitly allow for such guarantees. This explains that Italian

---

216 *Carrasco, Cordero* and *Marín*, 146.

217 The possibility to agree a guarantee for future obligation is also expressly established in § 765 German CC; art. 848 Greek CC; art. 7:851 Dutch CC; art. 628 par. 2 Portuguese CC. Guarantees for future debts are also valid in France (Simler no. 210 ff.).

218 See STS 28 February 2006 [RA 2006 no. 724].

219 STS 13 October 2005 [RA 2005 no.7340], SAP Santa Cruz de Tenerife 12 September 1994, AC 1994 no. 1517. See for Germany: BGH 30 March 1995, NJW 1995, 1886; *Horn/Staudinger*, on § 765, no. 42.

scholars[220] engaged in an extensive debate with regard to the validity of guarantees for future debts, as it was also the case in Spain to a certain extent[221].

Some authors[222] consider it essential that the underlying obligation exists previous to the valid constitution of a guarantee, as otherwise the principle of co-extensiveness would be breached. In contrast, others[223] contend that it is possible to create a guarantee on future obligations, provided the minimum number of references are made as to enable the future identification of the secured obligation (conclusive evidence of the future obligation).

The constitution of guarantees for future obligations has been admitted within case law[224]. A future guarantee can thus be created without there being a previously existing underlying obligation. The guarantor thus remains liable for the secured obligation from the moment it becomes existent.

3. *The protection of the guarantor for future debts*

a) *The maximum amount*

In Italy, guarantees for future obligations must by law establish a maximum amount (as stated in the last sentence of art. 1938 Italian CC). This provision was introduced in 1992[225] to protect the guarantor who cannot exactly know the extent of the liability he is assuming when guaranteeing a future (and therefore undetermined) obligation. The guarantee for a future obligation in Italy must therefore necessarily be created as a limited guarantee.

The limitation ex lege of the risks assumed by the guarantors is surely a positive development, with significant practical implications. This is especially true for guarantees agreed for credit lines, as the guarantor may not be able to anticipate the extent of liability that the secured obligation could eventually reach.

While the limit set in art. 1938 does provide a first layer of protection to the guarantor, it is arguable whether it should be considered enough, as the

---

[220] See references to the discussion at that time in: *Campogrande*, 300 and from a current perspective in: *Giusti*, 156 and 157.

[221] See references in *Guilarte*, 104 f.

[222] *Stolfi*, In tema di fideiussione per debiti futuri, 225; *Aru/D'Amelio e Finzi*, on art. 1936, 391.

[223] See: *Fragali/Scialoja/Branca*, 193; Cass. 17 February 1968 no. 570, GI 1969, I, 1, 748. *Guilarte*, 107.

[224] Cass. 1 June 1936 no. 1187, GI, 1936, I, 642; SAP Santa Cruz de Tenerife 12 September 1994, AC 1994 no. 1517.

[225] Art. 10 Law 17 February 1992, no. 154.

parties may agree a disproportionate limit as compared to the secured debt and the possible risk. Certainly, the fact that any limit (even a huge one) would be valid for a future obligation could jeopardize the protection effect of the provision. However, the mere fact of setting a maximum guaranteed sum serves to warn the guarantor of the possible level of risk he is assuming.

In contrast, Spanish law does not offer any protection to the guarantor even in cases of special risk like in the guarantee for future debts. The guarantor seems to be presumed to be aware of all the possible risks of granting a guarantee. Practical experience demonstrates, however, how weak, badly informed and easily manipulated guarantors can be. This is especially evident in the case of non-professional guarantors[226]. A rule, by means of which the guarantor of a future obligation limits de facto his liability to a fixed amount and is thus reminded of the risk he is taking on, would also be a positive development in Spain. In the case of non-professional guarantors, such a provision would be necessary as they are particularly vulnerable parties.

b) Guarantor's discharge (art. 1956 Italian CC)

By means of art. 1956 Italian CC, the guarantor for a future obligation is released if the creditor, without special authorisation from the guarantor, has extended credit to the third party whilst knowing that the debtor's financial conditions are such as to render the satisfaction of the claim considerably more difficult.

This mandatory rule is especially relevant in the case of the guarantee of a current account as well as in all those cases where the creditor regularly extends credit through a period of time. In the structure of a secured claim, creditors are usually the parties with more information or with the necessary structures to get such information. Through this provision, guarantors also benefit from the creditor's information with regard to the debtor and are so protected from their lack of awareness. The risk that the creditor extends credit to a debtor in financial difficulties because he thinks he will be covered by the guarantor, is limited.

This provision was introduced in art. 1956 Italian CC by art. 10 of the Italian Law 17 February 1992 no. 154 as a new protective provision regarding guarantees for future debts. A similar rule does not exist in the Spanish CC. The protection of the guarantor in this type of situations is

[226] This is the reason why art. 7:858 par. 1 Dutch CC establishes that if at the moment of constitution of the guarantee by a non-professional guarantor, the value of the secured obligation is not determined, the guarantee is only valid for the maximum amount agreed in money by the parties. The non-professional guarantor cannot derogate from this provision (art. 7:862 lit. a).

limited to proving the creditor's lack of good faith when granted subsequent credit. This is difficult, uncertain and time-consuming and therefore, the inclusion of a similar provision to art. 1956 Italian CC in Spanish law would be positive.

V. Guarantee for conditional obligations

1. In general

A guarantee may secure a conditional obligation. This possibility is specifically included in art. 1938 Italian CC and it is generally accepted as being valid in Spain[227]. The guarantee exists and is valid as soon as the agreement has been concluded. From that moment, the guarantee cannot be withdrawn[228] but the guarantor cannot be required to provide payment until the obligation has come into existence, i.e. until the condition has been fulfilled[229].

2. The nature of a guarantee for conditional obligations

Some Spanish legal authors regard the guarantee for a conditional obligation as a conditional contract[230]. Other Italian authors[231] consider that the guarantee remains a pure (non-conditional) obligation, as this contract of guarantee itself is not subject to any conditions. It can of course also be held to be a conditional contract if the guarantee obligation is subject to conditions.

VI. The universal guarantee (fideiussione omnibus/fianza omnibus)

1. The concept of universal guarantee

The term "universal guarantee" refers to the guarantee assumed for a group of obligations the content of which is still undetermined or which do not even exist but will or may fall due in the future. The content of the guarantee relates to the performance of any present and determined obligation and any future and undetermined obligation. These obligations may exist within a certain relationship or with regard to all the debts that might arise between a creditor and a debtor.

---

[227] The conditional obligation is a valid and existent obligation (see art. 1113 ff. Spanish CC) and can therefore be guaranteed. See *Guilarte*, 100.

[228] *Guilarte*, 100.

[229] *Carrasco, Cordero* and *Marín*, 149.

[230] See *Guilarte*, De la fianza, 1991, 1781; *Díez-Picazo*, Fundamentos, 424.

[231] *Fragali/Scialoja/Branca*, 195 ff.

2. *Practical applications*

a) *In general*

Many commercial relationships are of a long-term variety. In many cases there are different simultaneous contractual relationships, which serve to create a plurality of different obligations. In all these cases the creditor normally requires a guarantee for the complete operation or for the complete ensemble of relationships; i.e. a guarantee for all the claims that he may have against the debtor in present or in the future.

b) *Advantages for the parties*

In contractually agreeing a universal guarantee, the bank avoids the administrative and negotiation costs of forming a contract for every new guarantee. Moreover, the grant of continuous credits by the same bank to the same creditor could be seen as an extension of time (prórroga) or as an essential modification of the terms and conditions of the original agreed guarantee. This would introduce the risk that the guarantor would try to be discharged from some of the obligations on the basis of art. 1955 Italian CC and art. 1851 Spanish CC. The universal guarantee reduces this risk, as the parties agree a single contract of guarantee which serves to cover all obligations. These are the main reasons why banks usually prefer universal guarantee and force debtors to agree to these arrangements. In any case a universal guarantee makes the debtor's relation with the bank more flexible and easier to manage, which can be crucial for the successful running of certain businesses or in certain commercial situations. This is often the case in the context of project finance, especially if the project regards the creation of infrastructures and as such, extended over a long period of time.

c) *Clauses used in banking practice in order to create a universal guarantee*

The terms used in banking practice are usually very general. These clauses endeavour to include as many future obligations as possible or every obligation that exists between the creditor and the debtor.

The Italian Banking Association (ABI)[232] has defined the wording of atypical clause for the creation of a universal guarantee: "the guarantee covers the performance of any kind of obligation vis-à-vis the bank, which arises from banking operations of any nature, already agreed or to be

---

232 The ABI is the regulatory institution in Italian banking practice that establishes basic rules or general banking practice through the Unitary Banking Rules (Norme Bancarie Uniforme), circulars and other soft law documents.

agreed in the future"[233]. Most contracts include an exhaustive number of banking activities which are to be covered by the guarantee (obligations deriving from the current account, from a credit line, etc.[234]). The same is true in Spanish banking practice[235]. In Spain, there is no banking association with the regulatory power as the ABI in Italy, but contracts are de facto parallel to Italian ones.

The contract usually lists the activities which are specifically covered by the guarantee and contains a last general clause which includes all the future claims owed to the bank such as "in general, any operation of commercial or banking nature that the secured party might have agreed with the bank"[236] or "every sum owed by the debtor or that he might owe in the future" or "the guarantee is extensive to answer for every risk that might come out of every kind of banking operation"[237].

The establishment in Spain of a maximum liability limit is also common in Spanish practice, although not mandatory as it is the case in Italy: "Hereby I guarantee to the Bank X the payment of any debts that the company Y owes or may owe in the future, for any reason to a maximum quantity of 300.000 pesetas"[238].

Out with the sphere of banking practice, the parties may also agree to a universal guarantee for all the future obligations which are owed by the debtor to the creditor for commercial transactions: "guarantee for the transactions that the land worker X may agree with the bank Y, and accordingly we undertake hereby (...) to cover all the sums that the bank Y may request as payment for invoices, interests and charges"[239]; "guarantee also for all the supplies that the debtor may eventually purchase in the future"[240].

---

[233] See circulars of the ABI of 11 June 1964 no. 24; 24 January 1966 no. 5 and 17 June 1987 no. 20 for the adoption of uniform general conditions for universal banking guarantees.

[234] *Giusti*, 160; *Bozzi*, *voce* Fideiussione omnibus, 1993, 1.

[235] *Carrasco, Cordero* and *Marín*, 158.

[236] See STS 21 July 2003 [RA 2003 no. 5389].

[237] STS 21 July 2003 [RA 2003 no. 5389]; STS 29 March 1979 [RA 1979 no. 1235].

[238] STS 17 February 1962 [RA 1962 no. 1094].

[239] STS 3 March 1947 [RA 1947 no. 338].

[240] STS 26 October 1990 [RA 1990 no. 8051]; see also STS 31 October 1984 [RA 1084 no. 5153].

3. *Validity of the universal guarantee*

a) *In general*

Today the universal guarantee is valid and is very commonly used in commercial practice within most European countries[241]. It has been accepted within case law[242] and in academic theory[243] (as a guarantee and not as an atypical personal security right). However, the matter of its admissibility was keenly debated within Italy and many other civil law countries (with the exception of Spain).

b) *The problem of a determinable object*

The main problem with regard to the admissibility of universal guarantees was the lack of a "certain object" for the contract. This is one of the essential legal requirements for the constitution of a valid contract according to art. 1346 Italian CC and art. 1261 Spanish CC. Obviously the content of a universal guarantee remains undetermined, as the content of the underlying obligation is not determined at the moment of the contracting of the guarantee. However, this should not result in the nullity of the contract as the object of the guarantee is determinable per relationem; by reference to the underlying obligation[244]. Vice versa, the guarantee will be void, if the object of the guarantee cannot be determined; not even per relationem[245].

---

[241] Germany: *Horn/Staudinger*, on § 765 nos. 42 ff; *Erman/Seiler*, on § 765 no. 3. France: Simler no. 202. England: *Andrews* and *Millet* nos. 6.04–6.05. Finland: § 5 par. 1 Finnish Law of Guarantees.

[242] Cass. 25 August 1992 no. 9839, BBTC, 199, 237: "(the universal guarantee) pertaining the contractual scheme of the guarantee and is not an atypical contract itself" ("che va inquadrata nello schema contrattuale della fideiussione e non è un contratto atipico a se stante"). See also: Cass. 15 March 1991 no. 2790, FI, 1991, I, 2060.

[243] *De Maria/Franzoni*, 1485. See all references in this chapter.

[244] For instance, those cases in which the guarantee covers all liabilities arising from a certain legal relationship. See: Cass. 24 July 1993, no. 8291, Arch. Civ., 1993, 1270; Cass. 18 March 1991 no. 2890, GC, 1992, I, 512 and in BBTC, 1992, II, 13; Cass. 8 August 1988, no. 4871, GC, 1989, I, 2159; Cass. 5 January 1981, no. 23, FI, 1981, I, 704; Cass. 27 January 1979, no. 615, FI, 1979, I, 1, 1504, or in BBTC, 1981, II, 266; Cass. 10 November, 1971, no. 3214, FI, Rep. 1971, *voce* Fideiussione, no. 15. Also minor case law: App. Milano, 23 December 1986, BBTC, 1987, II, 591; Trib. Milano, 20 March 1986, BBTC, 1987, II, 591; Trib. Busto Arsizio, 11 October 1985, BBTC, 1986, II, 598; Trib. Milano, 16 September 1985, BBTC, 1986, II, 171; Trib. Milano, 25 July 1985, BBTC, 1986, II, 170; Trib. Milano, 18 June 1985, BBTC; App. Catania, 21 June 1983, BBTC, 1984, II, 498. In theory: Rescigno, Il problema, 1972, II, 25 f.; *Ravazzoni*, La fideiussione generale, 1980, 257; *Molle/Cicu* and *Messineo*, I contratti bancari, 1981, 245, nota 107; *Alcaro*, Fideiussione e garanzie, 1983, 612 f.; *Alcaro*, Il soggetto-banca, 1981, II, 1 f.; *Viale*, Fideiussione omnibus, 1990, 276 f.; *Barbiera*, Inefficacia parziale, 223 f.; *Terranova*, 148 f.; *Tucci*, 118.

The principal obligation to which the guarantee refers does not need to be certain at the moment of contracting the guarantee but there must be a basic and fundamental relationship between creditor and debtor that gives origin to all future obligations which are to be secured by the universal guarantee[246]. The content of the guarantee needs to be identifiable on the basis of the real link between the secured debtor and the contract of guarantee. The basis of this requirement is to ensure that it is possible to objectively determine the object. It is not designed to protect the guarantor by making him aware of the extent and possible consequences of the guarantee. Accordingly, the guarantor does not need to know or anticipate the possible content of the debt. It may be impossible to know at the moment of contracting but the contract will be valid if this content can be determined according to an objective criterion which is agreed by the parties in the contract[247]. Such objective criteria can be of a very general nature. For example the Italian courts have traditionally accepted a universal guarantee over "all debts owed by the debtor to the bank" ("quanto dovuto alla banca")[248]. In this case the objective criterion is the legal relationship between two parties ("rapporti tra la banca stessa e l'obbligato principale").

In order to avoid possible problems in relation to the validity of universal guarantees banks in Italy include a maximum amount for which it is possible for the guarantor to be liable. This was prompted by a recommendation of the ABI and in 1992 the agreement of such a maximum amount

There is also case law that holds that the universal guarantee is void because of the failure of a certain object. However this is minor case law which contradicts the Italian Supreme Court: Trib. Milano, 14 December, 1993, BBTC, 1994, II, 61; Trib. Avezzano, 14 December 1988, GC, 1989, I, 1445; App. Milano, 4 October 1988, BBTC, 1989, II, 607; App. Milano, 14 June 1988, BBTC, 1989, II, 48; Trib. Ferrara, 4 November 1987, BBTC, 1989, II, 607; Trib. Piacenza, 4 May 1985, BBTC, 1986, II, 171; Trib. Milano, 6 March 1985, BBTC, 1986, II, 170; Trib. Milano, 12 July 1984, BBTC, 1986, II, 95; Trib. Milano, 19 July 1982, BBTC, 1983, II, 219.

Some scholars have considered that the guarantee for future debts is void because the object is undeterminable. See: *Stolfi*, In tema di fideiussione generale, 1972, 529 f.; *Lanzillo*, 341 f.

[245] Cass. 15 March 1991, no. 2790, FI, 1991, I, 2060; Cass. 7 July 1989, no. 3228, GC, 1990, I, 1069.

[246] Cass. 10 November 1971 no. 3214 FI, Rep. 1971, *Fideiussione*, no. 15; Cass. 5 December 1970 no. 2575, FI, Rep. 1971, *Fideiussione*, no. 24.

[247] Trib. Milano16 January 1994, BBTC, 1996, 233: "[…] deve essere riferito soltanto alla previsione di un criterio di determinazione preventivamente convenuto tra le parti e alla sua capacità di individuare in modo rigorosamente oggettivo il rapporto obbligatorio principale". Also: Trib. Milano 20 July 1987, BBTC, 1988, 354.

[248] Cass. 6 February 1975 no. 438, FI, I, 1976, 2474.

was included as a requirement for the validity of future (and therefore also universal) guarantees[249] in art. 1958 Italian CC[250].

A similar rule is not present in the Spanish legal system. According to Spanish case law, the universal guarantee does not breach the essential requirement of "certain object" for the validity of a contract (art. 1261 Spanish CC). This is the case provided that the content of the universal guarantee can be determined[251]. In Spain, case law has been especially flexible with regard to the elements required for the validity of a universal guarantee. A court decision in 1924[252] required that there must be the previous existence of a contractual legal relationship between the debtor and the creditor to which the guarantee refers. But much of the later case law does not make any reference to specific requirements for the validity of universal guarantees[253]. Sometimes the court has made reference to the need for there to be a previous obligation. This is usually not in relation to the validity of the contract but with regard to other matters such as the need for there to be an existent due and payable debt in order to request the guarantor for performance[254], or for the lack of coverage by the guarantee of the debts which still exist after the death of the debtor[255]. Even in these cases, the need for there to be a previous relationship in order to consider the universal guarantee valid, has been regarded in very general terms. It therefore seems that a mere commercial relationship shall be sufficient to satisfy this demand[256].

---

[249] See under Chapter 2, C., IV., 3., a) The maximum amount, 70.

[250] With regard to the ratio of this provision see: *Valcavi*, Sulla nullità "ope legis" 1992, c. 791 f; *Valcalvi*, Sulla fideiussione bancaria, 1990, 558 f.

[251] STS 23 February 2000 [RA 2000 no. 1242]. According to this decision it is only necessary to determine the content in a general fashion. This is to be achieved by means of the identification of the contracting parties and an objective limitation of the maximum liability assumed by the guarantor. This last requirement is commented upon twice in the same decision but only in the form of *obiter dictum*. The limitation of liability with a maximum amount cannot be considered to be a general requirement of validity under Spanish Law. This can be said to be the case even if this is a general feature of banking practice.

[252] STS 21 November 1924 [RGLJ t. 164 no. 94] cited by *Carrasco, Cordero* and *Marín*, 158.

[253] STS 17 February 1962 [RA 1979 no. 1094]; STS 1 June 1964 [RA 1964 no. 3090]; STS 6 February 1976 [RA 1976 no. 320]; STS 29 March 1979 [RA 1979 no. 1235]; STS 31 October 1984 [RA 1984 no. 5153]; STS 20 February 1987 [RA 1987 no. 701].

[254] STS 17 February 1962 [RA 1962 no. 1094].

[255] STS 29 April 1992 [RA 1992 no. 4470 commented by Carrasco, CCJC 28 [1992] § 753.

[256] STS 29 March 1979 [RA 1979 no. 1235]. In Germany it is sufficient to refer to the obligations which result from a certain business relationship: BGH 16 January 1992, NJW, 1992, 897.

c) The principle of good faith in specifying the guarantee's object

The principle of good faith plays a very important role regarding the determination of the guaranteed object[257] and the development of the relationship between the parties. For instance, it is important to inform the guarantor of any special circumstances that may alter the balance of the previous dealing. Further, if there is a case of clear lack of proportion, the concept of unconscionable contracts may be applicable.

d) A universal guarantee included in general terms and conditions and the matter of surprising clauses

The constitution of a universal guarantee as a clause included in the general terms and conditions of a contract has explicitly been hold as valid and non-abusive by the Spanish Supreme Court[258]. In Germany by contrast, these clauses have generally been regarded in recent case law as surprising clauses[259]. The adherent/mandatory is not supposed to anticipate that such a clause will form part of this agreement. Hence in this case the clause (not the contract) is declared void[260].

Spanish Law on general terms and conditions[261] does not make any reference to the "surprising clauses" and there is no case law specifically on

[257] On the principle of good faith in relation to the validity of the universal guarantee see: Grana, 749 f.; *Di Majo/Munari*, 41; *Valignani*, 1137 f. See also: *Valcavi*, Sulla ineguatezza 1990, 1, 622 f.

[258] STS 23 February 2000 [RA 2000 no. 1242].

[259] From 1994 German case law radically limited the valid constitution of universal guarantees within the general terms and conditions of a contract (based on § 3 and § 9 AGBG (German Law on general terms and conditions). The German Supreme Court had not considered a clause where a universal guarantee was agreed as a "surprising clause" (*überraschende Klausel)* of the general terms and conditions of the guarantee contract (*Allgemeine Geschäftsbedingungen*) (see BGH 17 March 1994, WM 1994, 784 and *Horn/Staudinger*, on § 765, no. 48 ff.) but it considered that the universal guarantee clause is generally "surprising" according to § 3 AGBG in case it has not been specifically marked (BGH 18 May 1995, BGHZ 130, 19) and even if a maximum liability limit has been agreed (BGH 7 March 1996, NJW 1996, 1470; OLG Rostock 8 June 1995, WM 1995, 1533). See *Horn/Staudinger*, Vorbem zu § 765 ff. no. 44 and on § 765, no. 50 and *Drobnig/Sagel-Grande/Snijders*, 3). On the application of § 9 AGBG to the universal guarantee see BGH 18 May 1995, BGHZ 130, 19 and BGH 18 January 1996, BGHZ 132, 6.

[260] See § 308 and 309 BGB; BGH 18 May 1995, BGHZ, 130, 19; BGH 13 November 1997, BGHZ 137, 135; *Erman/Seiler*, on § 765 no. 3; *Horn/Staudinger*, vorbem zu § 765 ff. no. 45 and on § 765 no. 48 ff; *Drobnig/Sagel-Grande/Snijders*, 5. The surprising clauses as stated in § 3 AGBG are not part of the guarantee contract and those which cause the unadaquate or unreasonable lost (*unangemessen benachteiligt*) as stated in § 9 AGBG are void (§ 6 AGBG). See *Drobnig/Sagel-Grande/Snijders*, 5.

[261] Ley 7/1998, sobre condiciones generales de la contratación.

this topic as it is the case in Italy. Contracts which contain surprising clauses can however be rendered void by reason of essential mistake[262].

4. Extent of the universal guarantee

a) In general

The universal guarantee has a very extensive coverage which comprises different obligations. As previously stated, some of these guarantees are agreed in very general terms, such as guarantees for all liabilities arising from a certain commercial relationship. However, all the liabilities that are included must directly derive from the underlying contractual relationship. Non-contractual liabilities are not covered by the guarantee unless the parties have specifically agreed such coverage.

In accordance with the contra proferentem rule, those debts which are owed by the debtor to other creditors and which have been assigned to the main creditor are not covered by the guarantee. A clause, which includes these debts with regard to a non-professional guarantor, is void by virtue of the application of the principle of good faith. For the same reason, the parties cannot use novation to include within the secured obligations those debts which were already due and payable but from which the guarantor was discharged by reason of art. 1955 Italian CC/ art. 1852 Spanish CC (i.e. because the guarantor's subrogation in the rights of the debtor has been hindered by the latter)[263].

b) Universal guarantees with time limit or without time limit

aa) Guarantees with time limit

The universal guarantee can be agreed to cover a precise period of time (universal guarantee agreed with time limit). In such a case the guarantor cannot request to be discharged before that time. The same arrangement holds true if the contract is agreed for an undetermined period of time but regular enforcement intervals have been agreed. The guarantor cannot be discharged until the end of one of the specified intervals. Another similar case is that in which a universal guarantee has been agreed for an undetermined period (without time limit) but the guarantor has waived his right to ask for discharge within a certain period. This guarantee must end within a reasonable timeframe.

If a time limit has been agreed by the parties, the guarantor's liability is limited to the debts which arose within that period. Clearly, if the period is too long the guarantor is not protected by this time limit. In the Nether-

[262] See *Carrasco, Cordero* and *Marín*, 163.
[263] STS 3 March 1947 [RA 1947 no. 338], *Carrasco, Cordero* and *Marín*, 164.

lands and in Belgium, the guarantor may in any case request a discharge within a 5 years period (art. 7: 861 Dutch CC and art. 34 par. 3 Consumer Protection Act[264]), regardless of whether the guarantee was originally agreed to have a particular time limit beyond 5 years.

bb) Guarantee without time limit

If the guarantee is agreed without a specified time limit, the guarantor may request to be discharged by giving notice within a reasonable period of time or if special circumstances have arisen[265]. This right is a consequence of the analogical application of art. 1705 Spanish CC[266] but it is also normally explicitly included in most contracts[267].

5. Protection of the universal guarantor

a) Need for protection

The universal guarantee implies a high level of risk for the guarantor. The contracting terms are usually so broad that the obligation of the guarantor can become enormous. In fact this obligation is usually inestimable at the moment of contracting. A compulsory protective regulation is therefore beneficial for the universal guarantor.

b) Limitation of the guarantor's liability

In Italy the contracting parties must establish a maximum limit in relation to the guarantor's liability for guarantees provided for future debts (art. 1938 Italian CC[268]). This provision was included in the civil code by the reform introduced by the Law 17 February 1992 no. 154, art. 10 par. 1. It is part of a general European trend to set up a minimum level of protection for these particularly exposed guarantors[269]. The universal guarantor usual-

[264] Act of 12 June 1991 as amended the 1st January 2004.

[265] The same is also valid in Germany on the basis of § 242 German CC. See BGH 17 March 1993, ZIP 1994, 697, 698. *Horn/Staudinger*, on § 765, no. 47.

[266] STS 3 July 1999 [RA 1999 no. 4901].

[267] STS 29 April 1992 [RA 1992 no. 4470].

[268] A legal precedent with regard to art. 1938 Italian CC is to be found in art. 493 Swiss Code of Obligations.

[269] This tendency usually only exists in relation to non-professional guarantors. In the Netherlands and in France the liability of non-professional guarantors is limited to a maximum amount (art. 7: 858 par. 1 Dutch CC and art. 313–7 Consumption Code). By virtue of art. 34 Belgian Consumer Credit Act of 12 June 1991 as amended the 1st of January 2004, guarantees securing consumer credit must be limited to a specific amount. In Finland, universal guarantees must be limited in terms of amount and time, independently of the guarantor being professional or not (§ 5 par. 1 Finnish law of guarantees). No legal provision establishes in Germany the need to establish a maximum amount for

ly lacks information about the risk which he is assuming and the changes that might occur until the extinction of his obligation. The extension of the guarantor's obligation may ultimately be vast and have fatal consequences for the guarantor. Limiting this liability is a clear, simple and practical way to provide him with a certain level of protection.

The need to set a maximum agreed liability for universal guarantees is not legally established in Spain[270]. However there is an increasing trend to include such a limiting clause in the contracts. The Spanish Supreme Court established in one decision[271] the need to fix the maximum liability assumed by the guarantor in the contract. This maximum limit was seen as the way to identify the object of the contract. As the determination of the object is a requirement of contractual validity, the agreement of a maximum liability could be considered to be a necessary element for the valid constitution of a universal guarantee. Despite the importance of this court decision, it remains an isolated case and cannot be considered as proper "case law". Moreover, the decision is dealing with a contract which already included a maximum amount. The statement was made as obiter dictum and was not decisive for the solution of the case. The Supreme Court does not directly refer to the need to provide protection to the guarantor but only regards the need of having a certain object for the guarantee. In any case, the STS of 23 February 2000 is a first breaking point, which has been highly praised by some legal authors[272]. Irrespective of whether the court sought to create such far-reaching consequences, this decision has stimulated the discussion among legal scholars and has initiated a new approach to the treatment of the guarantor's protection. Nevertheless the decision itself is insufficient to have changed the formal requirements for validity of universal guarantees in Spanish case law. A change in Spanish regulation in the sense of granting a higher level of protection to the universal guarantor through the limitation of the guaranteed amount is desirable.

---

universal guarantees. Case law has changed from an extremely flexible view where maximum amounts where not required for the constitution of universal guarantees to more restrictive construal in recent times. See *Horn/Staudinger*, on § 765 nos. 45, 46, 47, 50.

[270] STS 21 July 2003 [RA 2003 no. 5389].

[271] STS 23 February 2000 [RA 2000 no. 1242], commented on by Infante, RDP, June, 2001, 201 f. and by Fernández, CCJC no.53, 2000, § 1451.

[272] See *Fernández*, Comment to the STS February 2000, CCJC 53 [2000] § 1451. See also *Carrasco, Cordero* and *Marín*, 162.

c) Is the agreement of a maximum amount a sufficient protection for the universal guarantor?

The agreement of a maximum amount in the contract of a universal guarantee provides a certain level of protection for the guarantor but it might be considered insufficient. The maximum amount is not determined with regard to objective parameters. It is an absolute, predetermined and freely agreed amount and can therefore be disproportionate[273]. If this is the case, it can be questioned whether the guarantor is anyhow protected.

The maximum amount helps the guarantor being aware of the levels of liability assumed, especially in relation to his own patrimony. The importance of this psychological aspect should not be undervalued in terms of protection. However it is also true that plenty of guarantors, especially those non-professionals, do not read the contract before signing. Moreover, most of these guarantors are willing to help the debtor irrespective of such contractual issues, and at the moment of signing they do not really pay attention to any clauses or conditions. The problems and difficulties arise at the moment of performance, when it is too late for the guarantor to protect his own patrimony. In the case of an extremely high maximum amount, the guarantor could adduce lack of good faith in contrahendo but this will depend on the facts and circumstances of each individual case and it will be very difficult to determine to what extent the amount was outwit a justified proportion.

A solution to this problem was given in France, where non-professional guarantors must write by hand the actual maximum amount of liability (art. 313-7 Consumption Code)[274].

d) Duty to inform the guarantor of the debtor's financial difficulties and to request authorisation in order to grant further credit

In Italy the guarantor for a future obligation is discharged if the creditor has granted credit to the third party without the special authorisation of the

[273] Italian legal authors have discussed whether the requirement of art. 1958 Italian CC shall be considered to have been fulfilled with the establishment of a maximum amount in the contract or if this amount must also be "reasonable" in respect to the general situation. See: *Rivolta*, 675; *Giusti*, 169.

[274] Art. 313–7 Code de la Consommation: "La personne physique qui s'engage par acte sous seing privé en qualité de caution pour l'une des opérations relevant des chapitres Ier ou II du présent titre doit, à peine de nullité de son engagement, faire précéder sa signature de la mention manuscrite suivante, et uniquement de celle-ci: En me portant caution de X , dans la limite de la somme de ... couvrant le paiement du principal, des intérêts et, le cas échéant, des pénalités ou intérêts de retard et pour la durée de... , je m'engage à rembourser au prêteur les sommes dues sur mes revenus et mes biens si X... n'y satisfait pas lui-même".

guarantor (art. 1956 CC[275]). This discharge occurs if the creditor was aware that the financial situation of the debtor was such as would clearly reduce the possibilities of performance. This is a mandatory provision (art. 1956 par. 2 Italian CC). Consequently, in these cases there is a duty for the creditor to provide information vis-à-vis the guarantor.

Such a rule does not exist in Spain[276]. However, a certain degree of protection can be achieved by the application of the principle of good faith. Therefore, before new credit is granted, the creditor is compelled to inform the guarantor about the significant changes that enlarge the guarantor's risk. These changes may regard the financial situation of the debtor (loss of patrimony, new unpaid debts, etc.), or his personal situation as far as it affects also the relation with the guarantor (for instance if the debtor's wife applies for a decree of divorce) and he was not aware of them.

The creditor is not supposed to incur much cost in order to attain the relevant information. But if he has notice of the information or is able to obtain it easily, and the guarantor cannot be reasonably expected to be aware of the information[277], then the creditor is compelled to inform the guarantor before granting new credit. If this action is not accomplished then the creditor is in breach of the principle of good faith.

The guarantor bears the burden of proof with regard to the creditor's lack of good faith. It is not always easy to prove that the creditor knew about the guarantor's financial situation or that he could have known about it without extreme difficulties. Therefore this form of protection is very much dependent upon the assessment of the merits of the case by the relevant court.

e) Italian protective regulation. An example for Spain?

Art. 10 of the law 17 February 1992 no. 154 introduced significant changes in Italian CC, which resulted in the development of a modern regulation on the protection of the guarantor for future obligations. This initiative is part of the general European trend to grant a higher and better structured protection to the guarantor. Most countries, have achieved this protection by means of extensive case law. This was the method favoured in Germany. In other countries, such as France and the Netherlands, statutory protection

---

[275] This provision was also included by the reform of 1992 (art. 10 Law 17 February 1992 no. 154).

[276] German case law has exceptionally also established the creditor's duty not to extend credit when, in this case not the creditor but the guarantor was in a weak financial position (OLG München NJW, 1976, 1096); *Horn/Staudinger*, on § 765 no. 47.

[277] In the opinion of Carrasco, the guarantor must have required the information in order for it to be held that the creditor was compelled to give it. *Carrasco, Cordero* and *Marín*, 163.

has supplemented case law in order to provide protection to non-professional guarantors as being particularly weak[278].

Spain has not participated within this positive protective trend. There is no specific regulation and case law has failed to provide with protection to the guarantor in general and the universal guarantor in particular. Only since the decision of 23 February 2000 there has been a moderate interest in the protection of the guarantor. This has however been indirect and limited in scope and there seems to be little enthusiasm to develop beyond this state of affairs.

It is difficult to discern the reasons for the passive attitude of the courts and also the academics with regard to this matter; the result being that the guarantor, as generally the weakest party, is not sufficiently protected. A change in the regulation of the guarantee in line with the Italian example would therefore be desirable. Also the courts should be more stringent on a case by case basis with regard to the guarantor's protection.

VII. Guarantee for an invalid obligation

1. The guarantee for a void obligation

a) In general

The validity of the guarantee depends on the validity of the secured obligation (art. 1939 Italian CC and art. 1824 Spanish CC). If the secured obligation does not exist, the guarantor shall be discharged according to the secondary nature of the guarantee. However, it might be the case that the guarantee has been agreed in such terms as to cover specifically the incidence of nullity of the principal obligation and the consequences thereof[279]. This will happen a) if the guarantor has compelled himself explicitly with regard to the case of nullity, b) he has compelled himself unconditionally and has therefore included the case of the nullity of the principal obligation[280], or c) if he knew at the moment of contracting that the secured obligation was void[281/282].

It can be concluded that the declaration of nullity of the secured obligation affects the extent of the guarantee in different ways depending on the terms in which the guarantee has been agreed and the reasons for nullity.

---

[278] See references above.

[279] This possibility is also considered valid in Germany. See BGH 12 Febraury 1987, NJW 1987, 2076. *Horn/Staudinger*, on § 765, no. 80 ff.

[280] See hereinafter Chapter 2, C., VII., b) The guarantee explicitly granted for the case of nullity of the secured obligation, 85.

[281] See hereinafter Chapter 2, C., VII., c) The guarantor's awareness of the nullity of the secured obligation, 86.

[282] See *Bozzi*, La fideiussione, 1995, 68 f.

Either the guarantee is automatically extinguished as a consequence of the nullity of the principal obligation or it is considered granted for the event of nullity of the principal obligation and is therefore valid. In that case, the guarantor will be liable for the legal consequences arising from the declaration of nullity like the duty of restitution or damages. Both cases have been admitted in Spanish case law. In a case where the secured obligation was void due to the lack of formal requirements, the guarantee was considered also extinguished as a consequence of its ancillary nature[283]. However, in a previous decision, Spanish Supreme Court had considered that the guarantee covered specifically the case of nullity of the secured obligation[284].

The guarantee agreement shall be construed as to determine whether nullity of the secured debt is covered or not. The real will of the parties to this extent shall be thereby explored ("integrative construal"[285]). Hence, if it can be determined that the parties wanted to cover the situation of nullity, the guarantee cannot be considered extinguished by the declaration of nullity of the principal debt but it will cover the negative effects arising from it.

b) The guarantee explicitly granted for the case of nullity of the secured obligation

If the guarantee expressly secures the nullity of the principal obligation, the object of the guarantee is not the underlying obligation but rather the patrimonial consequences or liabilities arising from the nullity, i.e. guarantee for the refund, damages, etc. Such guarantees are not always valid. The courts must evaluate whether it is legitimate to guarantee a situation that has been classified as void. In this sense, a guarantee may cover the nullity of the principal obligation for lack of essential formal or procedural requirements but may not cover the cases in which nullity is based on a qualitative important reason, like a mandatory provision that serves to protect the interests of a weaker group. In that case the guarantee would make possible a result that was prohibited by the law. In this respect, it is vital to analyse whether the reasons for the nullity of the principal obligation are such as to consider void the guarantee of the consequential liabilities of such nullity[286]. For instance, a guarantee can be validly constituted for the obligation to refund the payment performed by the buyer if the wife of the seller does not consent to the alienation of a common immovable asset.

[283] STS 23 November 1990 [RA 1990 no. 9044].

[284] STS 6 March 1961 [RA 1961 no. 937].

[285] *Carrasco, Cordero* and *Marín*, 152.

[286] STS 15 February 1982 [RA 1982 no. 689]; *Carrasco, Cordero* and *Marín*, 150.

The nullity of the primary liability is based on an essential formal defect and can hence be validly guaranteed.

c) The guarantor's awareness of the nullity of the secured obligation

If the guarantor secures the underlying obligation being aware that it is void, the court will endeavour to construe the real intention of the guarantor. The guarantee obligation is not necessarily extinguished by virtue of being the secondary obligation of a void secured debt. It might be the case that the guarantor desired to remain liable for the secured obligation as the primary debtor, or that he has guaranteed the consequences of the nullity (damages, etc), or that the guarantee is a penalty clause which becomes operational in the case of the nullity of the principal obligation. The courts must analyse the evidence and decide on a case by case basis.

2. Nullity of the secured obligation by reason of simulation

The secured obligation may have been simulated (relative simulation); i.e. the real will of the parties was to agree a different obligation than that declared in the contract. Since the simulation is relative and not absolute, the simulated contract shall not void but it will be converted according to the real intention of the parties. It has been controversial whether the guarantee of such void obligation remains valid if the underlying contract has been converted into a valid one. This has been considered to be possible under the condition that it can be logically and strongly presumed that the guarantor would have also guaranteed the valid new obligation, as his intention was to provide a guarantee and to assume the risk associated with it[287]. It is hence a matter of interpretation in each case. In general, if the guarantor knew the real intention of the parties then the guarantee is not void but is held to have been agreed for the "hidden" obligation[288]. In order for this conclusion to be reached there must be adequate proof of the guarantor's knowledge of the simulation. If the guarantor did not know about it, or if the simulation has been absolute (there is no hidden obligation desired by the parties), then the guarantee is void due to a lack of causa in the guarantee contract[289].

3. Nullity caused by the guarantor

The guarantor who has caused a) the nullity of the principal obligation or b) the nullity of the guarantee obligation[290] will not be entitled to allege

287 *Fragali/Scialoja/Branca*, 199; *Giusti*, 121.
288 See *Petti*, 145.
289 *Bozzi*, La fideiussione, 1995, 69.
290 STS 12 January 1989 [RA 1989 no. 100].

such nullity in order to be discharged from his obligation to perform. This is a direct consequence of the principle of good faith. In the first case, the guarantor will not be discharged of his guarantee obligation even if it is the debtor that alleges the nullity of the principal obligation. The guarantor shall be then considered principally liable[291]. Accordingly, the guarantor cannot oppose simulation of the principal obligation if he has taken part on it[292] or if he had notice of it before the creation of the guarantee[293]. Another example is the case in which the misrepresentation of the parties to the contract is previously known by the guarantor. In this case the guarantor cannot allege nullity[294].

4. *Nullity and avoidability*

If the obligation is null this means that it possesses an essential defect which invalidates its effect from the moment of its creation. Every person, including the parties to the contract, can ask for nullity to be declared. This is a right which does not prescribe. In contrast a voidable obligation is valid so long its avoidance has not been requested by one of the parties who are entitled to seek this declaration. Furthermore this declaration must be sought within a specific time limit (four years from the constitution of the contract). The guarantee of a voidable debt is valid until the secured obligation is in fact declared null. Until that moment, the guarantor cannot allege this avoidability.

5. *Validity of the waiver by the guarantor to set up the defence of nullity of the secured obligation. The case of guarantees on first demand*

In current banking practice it is common for guarantees to be agreed on first demand. These guarantees state that the guarantor must perform upon demand of the creditor. He cannot allege that the secured debt is invalid, nor can he set up the defenses which are available to the debtor. In this situation the guarantor has expressly waived rights which have been established by the law on guarantees as a consequence of the guarantee's ancillary character[295]. They are essential to its nature and they are therefore mandatory. If the guarantor renounces these rights then the contract cannot be considered to be a guarantee. Therefore the question is that of how to

---

[291] *Carrasco, Cordero* and *Marín*, 151.

[292] STS 10 July 1995 [RA 1995 no. 5561].

[293] SAP Vizcaya 10 July 1998 [AC 1998 no. 1382].

[294] STS 16 October 1989 [RA 1989 no. 6925].

[295] See for German law BGH 10 February 2000, NJW 2000, 1563 f. and references therein. This decision of the German supreme Court regards as case of guarantee on first demand (*Bürgschaft auf erstes Anfordern*) and states that guarantors of these kind keep the right to raise defences in case of abuse (*Rechtsmißbrauch*).

determine whether the guarantee is void or it can be converted into a different contract.

The autonomous or non-ancillary guarantee has been accepted within Italian and Spanish Law. Thus a guarantee which is agreed including a derogation from the rules regarding the ancillary nature is automatically converted into an indemnity (autonomous or non-ancillary guarantee)[296]. This act of derogation implies that there is an asymmetry between the parties. Hence it is only legally acceptable if the guarantor is a professional guarantor, i.e. the guarantor is not the weaker party within the contract. If such a waiver is made by a non-professional guarantor, this would thus be considered to be an unfair clause (clausola vessatoria)[297]. It would therefore be invalid by virtue of the application of consumer protection laws[298].

It can therefore be concluded that a waiver by the guarantor of his right to allege the nullity of the principal obligation in order to avoid performance, is only possible if the guarantor is a professional guarantor. An indemnity is thereby agreed. If this is not the case then the guarantee is also void.

VIII. Limitation of the extent by the agreement of certain conditions

The guarantee can be agreed under certain conditions provided they do not render the guarantor's obligation more onerous than the principal debt. Favourable conditions such as a longer term of duration; a lower rate of interest; the establishment of a different place of payment, may be agreed if they are more convenient for the guarantor with regard to the principal obligation[299].

---

[296] Italian and Spanish case law accepts the validity of clauses "on first demand" on application of the principle of free will of the contracting parties. This inclusion within a contract of guarantee, converts the contract into an atypical personal security contract (Cass. 3 September 1966 no. 2310; Cass. 31 August 1984 no. 4738; Cass. 3 February 1999 no. 920; Cass. 21 April 1999 no. 3964 cited by Petti 144; STS 12 November 2003 [RA 2003 no. 8408]; STS 31 May 2003 [RA 2003 no. 5217] with further references).

[297] According to art. 1469 *bis* par. 2 no. 2 Italian CC such a clause shall be presumed to be unfair (*vessatoria*) as it reduces the rights of the guarantor in general and it also specifically limits hid possible right to set up defences (according to no. 18).

[298] Art. 1469 *bis* Italian CC (introduced by art. 25, Italian law 6 February 1996, no. 52). Italian Law 1998 no. 281 shall also be applicable in this context. According to its content, the weaker party to a contract has the right to be treated correctly with transparency and equality within the contractual relationship. These rights cannot be renounced. Spanish Law 7/1998, of 13 April, sobre las condiciones generales de la contratación and art. 10 Law 26/1984 of 19 July, General for Consumers and Users (LGDCU). These regulations are the transposition of EU Directive 93/13.

[299] Cass. 9 December 1997 no. 12456, GI, 1998, I, 1, 11.

D. Relationship between guarantor and creditor

I. In general

The guarantee protects the creditor from an eventual lack of performance by the debtor. The completion of this security function takes place when the guarantor performs the guarantee. In this respect the kind of liability (joint and several or secondary) assumed by the guarantor is relevant. One radical difference between Spanish and Italian regulations is the type of liability assumed by the guarantor. The guarantor's liability is ex lege subsidarially in Spain (art. 1830 to 1837 Spanish CC) while it is joint and several in Italy (art. 1944 to art. 1948 Italian CC). In addition, the relationship between the creditor and the guarantor gives origin to certain rights and duties both for the creditor and the guarantor. Some of these rights and duties are established ex lege (like the creditor's duty of information), whilst others are conditions agreed by the parties in the contract.

II. Creditor's rights and duties before the debt has become due and payable

1. Creditor's right to assign the credit

According to the accessory nature of the guarantee, if the creditor assigns the underlying obligation, the guarantee is assigned together with the credit. Hence the assignee automatically acquires the original creditor's right under the guarantee[300].

[300] The assignment of the guarantee together with the underlying obligation is a consequence of the principle of co-extensiveness or the accessory nature of the guarantee, but it is specifically contained in Italian and Spanish CC. Art. 1263 Italian CC: "By effect of the assignment, the claim is transferred to the assignee with any privileges, real or personal guarantees, and other accessories. The assignor cannot, without the consent of the pledgor, give the assignee possession of the thing received in pledge; in case of disagreement the assignor retains custody of the pledge […]" ("Per effetto della cessione, il credito è trasferito al cessionario con i privilegi, con le garanzie personali e reali e con gli altri accessori. Il cedente non può trasferire al cessionario, senza il consenso del costituente, il possesso della cosa ricevuta in pegno, in caso di dissenso, il cedente rimane custode del pegno. [...]"). Art. 1528 Spanish CC: "The sale or assignment if a credit carries with it that of all accessory rights, such as guarantee, mortgage, pledge, or privilege"("La venta o cession de un crédito comprende la de todos los derechos accesorios, como la fianza, hipoteca, prenda o privilegio"). See: STS 29 June 1989 [RA 1989 no. 4797]; SAP Sevilla 18 May 1999 [AC 1999 no. 5965].

The same is valid in the Netherlands (art. 6: 142 Dutch CC). See: *Drobnig/Sagel-Grande/Snijders/Broekhuizen*, 93. For Germany see: *Horn/Staudinger*, on § 765, no. 208 f.

The creditor may assign his secured debt without the consent of the guarantor. He only needs to notify the assignment to the guarantor (and not only the debtor). If the guarantor was not informed and performs to the assignor, he will be discharged even if the debtor had been informed about the assignment.

The guarantee can only be assigned together with the secured debt. Otherwise the guarantee extinguishes, as a consequence of the principle of co-extensiveness. Accordingly, if both the creditor and the debtor excluded the possibility to assign the secured obligation, the guarantee cannot be assigned. In this case upon request for payment, the guarantor may set up against the new creditor the debtor's defence that the assignment was not allowed and avoid performance. If the guarantor agreed on the transfer, he becomes principal debtor of a new debt. In this case there is novation of the guarantee obligation.

The parties may also agree the discharge of the guarantor in case the underlying obligation is assigned.

2. *Creditor's duties before the debt has become due and payable*

a) *In general*

The creditor has certain duties vis-à-vis the guarantor even in the case of a unilateral contract of guarantee. The aim of these duties is to preserve the rights of the guarantor to be reimbursed upon performance. They are not reciprocal obligations regarding the guarantor's liability but if the creditor does not accomplish these duties, the guarantor is discharged from his duty to perform.

Moreover, the parties may agree any kind of legal conditions. For instance, if the creditor consented to remunerate the guarantor for the assumption of the guarantee, the payment of the price agreed is a condition of validity of the contract.

b) *Duty to inform about the debtor's delay in secondary guarantees*

The guarantor of a secondary guarantee[301] becomes liable upon the debtor's default. He must be informed about such default in order to perform his obligation. In contrast with other civil legislations[302], Italian and Span-

---

[301] Guarantees upon Spanish law are *ex lege* secondary. In Italy, the guarantee is secondary when the benefit of discussion has been agreed.

[302] According to art. 7: 855 par. 2 Dutch CC when the creditor requires the debtor for payment, he must also give notice to the guarantor: "De schuldeiser die de hoofdschuldenaar overeenkomstig artikel 82 van Boek 6 in gebreke stelt, is verplicht hiervan tegelijkertijd de borg mededeling te doen". If the guarantor is not professional, the provision is mandatory (art. 7: 862 lit. a).

ish regulations do not directly set up the creditor's duty to inform the guarantor about the debtor's default. However, it is a direct consequence of the principle of good faith[303], especially if the guarantor could not otherwise have known whether the debtor had performed on time or not. The mere information about the debtor's default shall be considered enough. No formalities are required.

Moreover, according to Spanish law if the creditor did not demand the guarantor to perform, the latter is discharged of the expenses of the suit (art. 1827 par. 2 Spanish CC). Such a demand does not need to be judicial but a simple requirement. The rule in art. 1827 par. 2 Spanish CC regards uniquely the expenses of the suit, which is a too weak consequence of the lack of information by the creditor. There are other expenses, like the moratory interests, which should not be covered by the guarantor who did not know about the need or possibility to perform.

c) *Duty to inform about the debtor's financial difficulties*

In Italy and Spain the creditor does not have a duty to inform the guarantor about the debtor's financial difficulties. Not even consumer guarantors in critical situations have the right to be informed until default has finally taken place.

Recent tendencies in neighbouring countries have introduced such duty at least for consumer guarantors. In France, private guarantors must be informed at least once a year about any changes in the secured obligation[304]. Also, in Belgium special regulation on consumer credit sets up the creditor's duty to inform the guarantor in case of defaults of two payments

---

In Finland the creditor must inform the guarantor of the debtor's default within one month (§ 4 par. 2 Finnish Law on Guarantee).

According to art. 505 par. 1 Swiss Code of Obligations, the creditor must notify the debtor's default six months after the obligation was due and payable. If he fails to do so, he looses his rights against the guarantor and remains liable for the damages caused (art. 505 par. 3). Art. 505: "Avis du créancier et intervention dans la faillite et le concordat du débiteur. 1. Lorsque le débiteur est en retard de six mois pour un paiement de capital ou pour l'intérêt d'un semestre ou pour un amortissement annuel, le créancier doit aviser la caution. Sur demande, il doit en tout temps la renseigner sur l'état de la dette. (…) 3. Si le créancier omet l'une de ces formalités, il perd ses droits contre la caution à concurrence du préjudice résultant pour elle de cette omission".

[303] Also in Germany but only exceptionally if lack of information would seriously damage the guarantor's interest (OLG Bamberg, 13 December 1999, WM 2000, 1582 ss).

[304] Art. 2016 par. 2 CC: "Lorsque ce cautionnement est contracté par une personne physique, celle-ci est informée par le créancier de l'évolution du montant de la créance garantie et de ces accessoires au moins annuellement à la date comvemue entre les paries ou,, à défaut, à la date anniversaire du contrat, sous peine de déchéance de tous les accessories de la dette, frais et pénalités" introduced by art. 47 par. 2 sent. 2 loi no. 98–657 du 29 juillet 1998, art. 101) and Cass. Civ. 16 March 1999, D. 1999 I.R. 99.

or a fifth of the debt by the consumer debtor and about the modifications of the contract of credit and payment facilities granted to the debtor[305]. In Finland, the duty to inform is subject to the guarantor's request[306].

This modern tendency has also been observed in the elaboration of the Rules on Personal Security of the Study Group on a European Civil Code[307], which art. 2:107 par. 1 establishes "The creditor must notify without undue delay the security provider in case of a non-performance by or inability to pay of the debtor as well as of an extension of maturity; this notification must include information about the secured amounts of the principal obligation, interest and other ancillary obligations owed by the debtor on the date of notification. No notification is required if an event of non-performance merely relates to ancillary obligations of the debtor, unless the total amount of all non-performed secured obligations has reached five percent of the outstanding amount of the secured obligation".

Such a duty of information is not too hard a charge for the creditor and means an important benefit to the guarantor, who can start taking action to avoid payment in critical situations. Italian and Spanish regulations have remained conventional on this matter but a modification would be beneficial.

d) Duty to notify the assignment

The creditor must inform the guarantor of the assignment of the principal debt (see supra under, 1. Creditor's right to assign the credit, page 91).

III. Rights of the guarantor vis-à-vis the creditor

1. The benefit of discussion

a) General notion

The benefit of discussion (beneficium excusionis) is the right of the guarantor to deny performance until the creditor has tried to find and prose-

---

[305] Art. 35 Belgian Consumer Credit Act (Loi 12 June 1991 au crédit de consummation as amended in 2003 (Loi 2003–03–24/40)) : "Le prêteur communique à la caution et, le cas échéant, à la personne qui constitue une sûreté personnelle, le retard de paiement par le consommateur de deux échéances ou d'au moins un cinquième du montant total à rembourser. Il lui communique les facilités de paiement accordées et l'informe au préalable de toute modification apportée au contrat de crédit initiale".

[306] § 14 par. 1 Finish Guarantee Law.

[307] The Rules on Personal Security have been elaborated by the working group at Max-Planck-Institute for foreign law and international private law under the direction of Prof. Dr. Dr. hc Ulrich Drobnig. Drobnig, Principles of European Law, Personal Security, 7.

cute for those goods eventually owed by the debtor[308]. Accordingly, if the guarantor is entitled to raise the benefit of discussion, his liability is secondary[309]; if not, it is joint and severally.

b) Benefit of discussion, ex lege or agreed by the parties

In Italy the guarantor is joint and severally liable together with the debtor for the performance of the debt[310]. When the underlying obligation becomes due and payable, the creditor may proceed directly against the guarantor or against the debtor indistinctly. The guarantor must perform upon request even if the debtor has not yet been requested for payment[311]. He cannot raise the benefit of discussion unless it has been specifically agreed by the parties in the contract. The possibility to agree the benefit of discussion is explicitly established in art. 1944 Italian CC, where the benefit of discussion is defined as the guarantor's right to refuse payment until a discussion (escussione) of all the goods of the principal debtor has taken place. Consequently, in Italy, the guarantor is ex lege joint and severally liable and the benefit of discussion can only be raised when it has been previously specifically agreed by the parties[312]. In that case the guarantee is converted by the parties in a secondary obligation[313].

In contrast, in Spain the guarantor's liability is ex lege secondary to that of the debtor. The guarantor enjoys the benefit of discussion; i.e. he has the right to refuse performance until a discussion has been previously made

---

308 *Lasarte*, 398.

309 "Die Einrede der Vorausklage ist Ausdruck der Subsidiarität der Bürgenverpflichtung", *Horn/Staudinger*, on § 771, no. 1.

310 See *Giusti*, 181 and *De Maria/Franzoni*, 1491. Some scholars have described the guarantee as a joint and several obligation *sui generis:* See *Rubino/Scialoja/Branca*, 134–136; *Ravazoni*, La fideiussione generale, 1980, 70; *Barasi*, 194.

311 He may claim the debtor for reimbursement afterwards: Cass. 4 March 1995 no. 2517 FI, Rep 1995, *voce* Fideisussione e mandato di credito no. 49; Cass. 28 February 1957 no. 724, FI, Rep. 1957 *voce* Fideiussione e mandato di credito, no. 28.

312 By virtue of art. 1333 Italian CC, since the guarantee is a unilateral contract in Italian Law, the benefit of discussion will be considered agreed in case the creditor has not refused on time the proposal of the guarantor to establish the benefit of discussion in the contract. The period of time might be expressly established by the guarantor in his proposal or it can be established according to the uses.

313 Cass. 15 June 1967 no. 1389, FI, I, 1976, 2540. Some Italian scholars, making an extremely theoretical analysis of the matter, have considered the benefit of discussion as a mere *beneficium ordinis*; establishing an order or rank for payment (the guarantor can only be compelled to pay upon certain debtor's default). In the opinion of these scholars, every guarantee has a subsidiary nature since as surety the guarantor is placed in a second position. Even if the guarantor must first perform, he can afterwards demand the debtor to pay him back (*Giusti*, 38; Simonetto, La fideiussione prestata da privati, 133; *Fragali*, L'inerzia del creditore, 1969, 739).

upon all the assets of the debtor (art. 1830 Spanish CC). The same is valid for most European countries[314]. However, in the business practice of all these countries such benefit is generally (almost always) excluded by the parties, opting for a joint and several liability of the guarantor[315]. This is possible since the provisions on the benefit of discussion are not mandatory. The right of the parties to agree a joint and several guarantee which means excluding the benefit of discussion[316] is even expressly contained in the guarantee regulation (art. 1822 par. 2 and 1831 par. 1 Spanish CC[317]). The former Italian CC shared this conception of guarantee as a secondary obligation. It was an inheritance from art. 2021 French CC and was changed in the CC of 1942 and adapted to the practice.

The advantages of the model based on the secondary nature of the guarantor's liability (benefit of discussion by law) have been frequently pointed out in the Spanish theory[318]. Their reasons are mainly founded in a traditional conception of the guarantee as a security given for a friend or relative, based in the personal relationship of debtor and guarantor like in old Roman times. In accordance with this model, it is logical to offer the benefactor-guarantor the benefit of discussion since he should only be liable if the debtor is unable to perform. However, the practice has changed the tenor of the law. The guarantor is de facto almost always joint and severally liable. It would make more sense according to the business practice to conceive the guarantee as joint and several and set up protective rules for the weakest guarantors (non-professional or consumer guarantor).

c) The nature of the benefit of discussion

The benefit of discussion does not create a duty for the creditor to require payment to the debtor before the guarantor[319] but it is a benefit or defence granted to the guarantor. The creditor may require the guarantor for payment, and even sue him, without having demanded the debtor for pay-

---

[314] Art. 2021 French, Belgian, Luxembourgian CC; §§ 771 ff. German CC; art. 638 Portuguese CC; art. 855 Greek CC; § 21 Finish Guarantee Law.

[315] For France: *Cabrillac* and *Mouly*, no. 322 ff. and *Simler*, no. 505 ff. Commercial guarantees are even presumed to be joint and several (Cass.com. 28 April 1966, Bull. Civ. 1966, III, no. 209); for Austria, *Schwimman/Mader* on § 1357 no. 1. For Germany, see *Horn/Staudinger*, on § 773 no. 2. The waiver to the benefit of discussion may even be agreed by a formular or general terms and conditions.

[316] STS 5 December 1991[RA 1991 no. 8917].

[317] Also in: art. 2021 French, Belgian and Luxembourgian CC; § 773 par. 1 no. 1 German CC; §1357 Austrian CC; art. 857 lit. a) Greek CC and § 3 par. 1 Finnish Guarantee Law.

[318] See extent references in *Guilarte*, 160.

[319] As it is in Austria (§ 1355 CC) and the Netherlands (art 7: 855 par. 1 Dutch CC).

ment[320]. Consequently, the discussion of the debtor's goods is not a constitutive element for a valid requirement for performance, but a benefit that the guarantor may raise in order to avoid payment unless the debtor is de facto unable to perform[321].

The guarantor can first raise the benefit when the debtor has required him for payment (art. 1944 par. 2 Italian CC and 1832 Spanish CC)[322].

The benefit grants the guarantor the right to avoid enforcement (realization of his assets) until the discussion of the debtor's assets has been done[323]. The benefit of discussion has been defined as the "rank for the procedural enforcement" (orden de ejecutabilidad procesal) that needs to be raised[324]. It is only granted by law for the personal guarantee, not for real security. The advantage of the real securities is precisely the grant of an easy and direct realization of the assets and it would be contradictory to the nature of real securities to permit the raising of a defence that hinders or delays the process to become payment.

d) The benefit of discussion and the co-guarantee

In the case of a co-guarantee, every co-guarantor is entitled to raise the benefit of discussion whenever he has been demanded for performance. If the co-guarantee is mancomunada (the co-guarantors are severally liable) each of the co-guarantors also enjoys the benefit but only for the part of the debt that he secures.

---

[320] STS 25 February 1958 [RA 1958 no. 1043]. *Contra*: STS 7 April 1975 [RA 1975 no. 1412] and STS 28 September 1977 [RA 1977 no. 3521]. These decisions of the Spanish Supreme Court considered necessary to require for payment firstly the debtor or at least both debtor and guarantor simultaneously. However such a conclusion cannot be inferred from the wording of art. 1832 Spanish CC nor could they be inferred from art. 1944 par. 2 Italian CC.

[321] The same is valid for Germany: "Es handelt sich um eine echte Einrede: der Gläubiger braucht zur Begründung der Klage gegen den Bürgen nicht zu behaupten, er habe die Vollstreckung gegen den Hauptschuldner erfolglos versucht oder sei dazu nicht verpflichtet. Der Bürge muß die Einrede vielmehr im Prozeß selvst geltend machen.", *Horn/Staudinger*, on § 771 no. 1

[322] The guarantor may give notice to the creditor of the debtor's assets before having been required for performance. At this point, he does not raise his benefit of discussion. However, if the creditor ignores this information, it could be considered bad faith and provided that the possibilities to obtain performance by the debtor become worse, the guarantor may raise the defence established in art. 1851 and art.1852 Spanish CC.

[323] *Carrasco, Cordero* and *Marín*, 217; *Pérez Álvarez*, 84.

[324] STS 14 May 1977 [RA 1977 no. 2074]. See also *Carrasco, Cordero* and *Marín*, 216.

e) The benefit of discussion for sub-guarantors

The sub-guarantor (guarantor of a guarantor) enjoys the benefit of discussion both with respect to the guarantor and to the principal debtor (art. 1836 Spanish CC)[325]. He has also the right and the duty to point out those goods of the debtor and of the first guarantor which may entirely or partly perform the principal obligation. The same is valid in Italy. Differently to the guarantor's liability, which is joint and several, the liability of the sub-guarantor in Italy is secondary regarding the debtor's and the guarantor's liability. The creditor cannot compel the sub-guarantor to pay, unless the debtor and every other guarantor are insolvent or discharged by reason of disability (art. 1948 Italian CC[326]).

f) Requirements for the application of the benefit of discussion

In case the guarantor may raise the benefit of discussion ex lege (in Spain) or by agreement of the parties (in Italy), it operates similarly in both countries.

There are three requirements for the valid application of the benefit of discussion: (i) The discussion has to be raised by the guarantor; (ii) he must point out the goods of the debtor that shall be enough to perform the payment[327] and (iii) the guarantor must anticipate the costs of the discussion (art. 1944 par. 2 and 3 Italian CC and 1832 Spanish CC). Once the guarantor has performed these requirements, the creditor must diligently sue the assets pointed out by the guarantor.

aa) The guarantor must raise the benefit of discussion

The benefit of discussion does not operate ipso iure; it is a faculty, a defence (eccezione/excepción) of the guarantor that needs to be raised against the creditor (art. 1944 Italian CC ("sia convenuto dal creditore e intenda valersi") [328] and art. 1832 Spanish CC). The creditor is always entitled to require performance from the guarantor and sue a claim against

[325] In Germany, the subguarantor may only raise the benefit of discussion against the creditor if the main guarantor may also raise it or if he waived his right to raise the benefit after the subguarantee had been agreed. See *Horn/Staudinger*, on § 771, no. 4.

[326] Art. 1948 Italian CC: "Il fideiussore del fideiussore non è obbligato verso il creditore, se non nel caso in cui il debitore principale e tutti i fideiussori di questo siano insolventi, o siano liberati perché incapaci".

[327] STS 21 February 2003 [RA 2003 no. 3109]. In this case, the guarantor raised the benefit of discussion on the basis of certain moveable assets of the debtor. However, the guarantor was not able to proof their value, their estate or the relation between those assets and the debtor. He could neither declare where they physically were and whether they could be sold. Hence the Supreme court denies the right to discussion.

[328] *Campogrande*, Trattato, 368.

him. On raising the benefit, the guarantor only stops the creditor's right to enforce his claim against him until the creditor has unsuccessfully tried to obtain payment from the debtor[329].

The guarantor can only raise the benefit of discussion for the debt he has secured. Accordingly, if the secured obligation is a co-debt and the guarantor only secures one of the co-debtors, he can only require the discussion of the assets of the debtors he guarantees[330].

bb) The guarantor must point out the goods of the debtor subject to discussion

The guarantor has the duty to point out the goods owned by the debtor that may contribute to the payment of the debt (art. 1944 Italian CC and art. 1832 Spanish CC[331]). The guarantor must contribute with the creditor to recover the money lent to the debtor and avoid an unnecessary delay of payment[332].

(i) Excessive difficulty to enforce. Explicit exclusion from the discussion of certain assets

A very long, intense or difficult discussion is not to be expected. Spanish Courts are strict in the interpretation of the guarantor's duty, so that the assets indicated must be concrete, enforceable and sufficient[333]. There is no need to consider those goods or assets pointed out by the guarantor if the circumstances of the case or the nature of the assets make it difficult to turn them into cash or would prolong the course of action[334]. It is the task of the judge to evaluate such circumstances. However in Spain the discussion is first limited by the law to those assets that "can be sold within Spanish territory and are sufficient to cover the amount of the debt" (art.

[329] *Ravazzoni*, La fideiussione, 189.

[330] *Carrasco, Cordero* and *Marín*, 217.

[331] Also art. 2023 and 2024 French, Belgian and Luxembourgian CC. German and Portuguese CC keep silent regarding the duty of the guarantor to point out the debtor's assets. However, if the debt was also secured with real security interests, the guarantor may raise those rights constituted before or simultaneously to the guarantee (§ 772 par. 2 *juncto* § 773 par. 2 German CC and art. 639 Portuguese CC). § 772 par. 2 German CC: "If the creditor has a right of pledge or lien on a moveable of the prncipal debtor, he must also seek satisfaction out of such moveable. If such a right in the thing belongs to the creditor also for another claim, this applies only if both claims are covered by the value of the thing."

[332] Aru, on art. 1955, 405; *Ravazzoni*, La fideiussione, 186; *Giusti*, 185.

[333] STS 31 January 1986 [RA 1986 no. 344]; STS 3 October 1985 [RA 1985 no. 4570]; STS 7 April 1975 [RA 1975 no. 1412] and STS 29 October 1991 [RA 1991 no. 7488].

[334] *Giusti*, 186; *Carrasco, Cordero* and *Marín*, 221.

1832 CC). A similar but even more extensive rule was also contained in art. 1909 par. 2 Italian former CC which excluded following assets from discussion: a) the property outside the jurisdiction of the court of appeal in which territory the payment must be performed ("situati fuori della giurisdizione della corte d'appello in cui si deve fare il pagamento [...]"), b) those assets which are subject to judicial procedure ("di beni litigiosi [...]") and c) the assets which have been mortgaged to secure the debt and are no longer possessed by the debtor ("o di beni già hipotecati per cautela del debito, i cuali non siano più in potere del debitore"). This provision was considered superfluous or obvious and therefore not included in the new Civil Code[335]. However, art. 1944 Italian CC is still constructed in the same or even more extensive terms: if the search for the debtor's assets would take too long, is difficult or will probably be non-fructuous, it does not need to be done by the guarantor[336]. The valuation of these facts is the task of the judge[337/338].

(ii) Need to point out sufficient assets to satisfy the creditor

In Italy it is not necessary that the guarantor points out enough of the debtor's assets to cover the whole debt. It is generally considered that the guarantor can successively give notice of the debtor's property if he was not aware of its existence without negligence or if they successively enter the debtor's patrimony[339].

The only problem in this case is the possible abuse of this right by the guarantor in order to delay the moment of performance. The judge must value in each case whether there has been an abuse or whether an extension of the procedure is justified. He must thereby also evaluate whether the guarantor's risk is so relevant that a delay of payment is justified[340].

In contrast, in Spain the guarantor needs to point out enough of the debtor's assets to satisfy the creditor (art. 1832 CC). The aim of this requirement is to avoid losing time and costs by preventing the creditor from starting new procedures. Some scholars construe the wording of this provision extensively (not literally) considering that the guarantor may raise the benefit even if he does not find enough assets owned by the debtor to cover the debt[341]. The protection of the guarantor is estimated to be more impor-

---

[335] *Distaso*, 117.
[336] Cass. 22 December 1969 no. 4032, FI, 1970, I, 421.
[337] *Ravazzoni*, Nov. Dig. It., 284.
[338] For Germany see § 773 par. 1 nos. 2, 3, 4 and § 773 par. 2.
[339] *Bo*, *voce* Fideiussione, 376.
[340] *Distaso*, 118; *Giusti*, 187.
[341] *Guilarte*, 182 ff; *Alventosa del Rio*, La fianza, 178.

tant in this point than the risk of increasing the costs of procedure[342]. Such interpretation is based on the principle of favor fideiussoris. However, in this case the legal provision is absolutely clear and does not leave any room for interpretations. The guarantor can only raise the benefit if he can identify enough assets of the debtor.

cc) The guarantor must anticipate the costs of the discussion

The discussion of the debtor's property benefits the guarantor in the first place. If it is successfully performed, he is thereby discharged of his guarantee obligation vis-à-vis the creditor. Moreover, the discussion of the debtor's assets delays the performance of payment to the creditor. It would be unfair to make him also cover the cost of such discussion which takes place only for the benefit of the guarantor.

g) Duty of the creditor to diligently discuss the debtor's assets

Once the guarantor has raised the benefit, pointed out the assets of the debtor and anticipated the costs of the discussion, the creditor must proceed diligently to make the discussion. If he does not or does not sufficiently prove his diligence on discussing, he remains liable "to the extent of the value of said property, for the insolvency of the debtor resulting from such negligence" (art. 1833 Spanish CC)[343]. Also in Italy there used to be a parallel provision in art. 1910 former CC of 1865[344]; but it was deleted in the current CC. However, the same consequence derives specifically from art. 1957 par. 1 Italian CC according to which the creditor must sue the debtor and continue diligently the actions in order to make the guarantor remain liable until six months after the obligation becomes due and payable. The general duty to perform obligations according to the principle of good faith would also be enough to expect diligent behaviour from the creditor[345]. There is no lack of diligence from the creditor when the assets are difficult to realize[346]. Such level of difficulty needs to be assessed by the judges.

If the goods of the debtor are not enough to perform the whole debt, the guarantor remains liable for the difference[347].

---

[342] Contra: *Carrasco, Cordero* and *Marín*, 221.

[343] Also in art. 2024 French, Belgian and Luxembourgian CC.

[344] Art. 1910 former Italian CC: "Qualora il fideiussore abbia fatto l'indicazione dei beni ed abbia somministrato le spese occorrenti per l'escussione, il creditore è responsabile verso il fideiussore fino alla concorrenza dei beni indicati, a cagione della non solvenza del debitore principale, sopragiunta per essersi da lui differito il procedimento giudiziale".

[345] *Giusti*, 189; *De Maria/Franzonni*, 1490.

[346] *Carrasco, Cordero* and *Marín*, 223.

[347] *Giusti*, 187; *Lacruz*, 502 f.; *Carrasco, Cordero* and *Marín*, 223.

h) Exceptions of the benefit of discussion

The Spanish CC establishes some exceptions to the secondary nature of the guarantee in art. 1831. A discussion of the debtor's assets is not required: 1° when the guarantor has expressly waived it; 2° when he has bound himself in solido with the debtor; 3° in case of bankruptcy or insolvency of the debtor and 4° when the debtor cannot be sued within the Kingdom.

Consequently, the benefit of discussion is not an essential element of the guarantee in Spain since it is excluded ex lege for certain cases and may also be excluded by agreement of the parties[348].

aa) Benefit of discussion excluded by the parties

The benefit of discussion can be excluded by agreement of the parties. If they have agreed a joint and several guarantee, the guarantor may not raise the benefit of discussion. Moreover, the guarantor may at any moment renounce his right. This waiver must be express; i.e. the intention of the guarantor must be undoubtedly, but no special form is required[349]. It may be included in the general terms and conditions of the contract.

bb) Cases of legal exclusion of the benefit of discussion

Spanish law establishes three cases in which, even if the guarantor has not renounced the benefit of discussion, it is excluded ex lege because the discussion is obviously too difficult or almost impossible. These three cases are: a) the case of debtor's bankruptcy[350] (art. 1831 par. 3 Spanish CC); b)

---

[348] In Germany § 773 CC also sets certain exceptions to the benefit of discussion: "The benefit of discussion is barred: 1. If the guarantor has waived the benefit, especially if he has assumed the guarantee in such manner that he is himself a principal debtor. 2. If the difficulty of bringin an action against the principal debtor is materially increased in consequence of a change of domicile, industrial location, or place of residence of the principal debtor, occurring after the assumption of the guarantee: 3. If bankruptcy proceedings have been instituted agains the property of the principal debtor. 4. If it may be presumed that compulsory execution on the property of the principal debtor will not lead to the sarisfaction of the creditor.

In the cases provided for by (3) and (4) the benefit of discussion is permissible where the creditor can satisfy himself out of a moveable of the principal debtor over which he has a right of pledge or lien; the provisionof 772, par. 2 sentence 2 applies." See also *Horn/Staudinger*, on § 773 no. 1 ff.

[349] *Carrasco, Cordero* and *Marín*, 223. The formal requirements are the same as those necessary for the creation of a valid guarantee. In Germany the waiver needs to given in writing as this is the compulsory form for the guarantee according to § 766 CC. See *Horn/Staudinger*, on § 773, nos. 3 and 4.

[350] See STS 31.1.1958 [RA 1958 no. 561]; STS 7 March 1992 [RA 1992 no. 2007]; STS 14 February 1997 [RA 1997 no. 1419].

when the debtor cannot be sued in Spain (art. 1831 par. 4 Spanish CC)[351] and c) for judicial guarantors and for co-guarantors (art. 1856 Spanish CC)[352].

(i) Debtor's bankruptcy

The benefit of discussion cannot be raised if the debtor is bankrupt, nor if there are clear signs of his financial crisis[353]. The meaning of "financial crisis" must be interpreted for each case.

(α) Declaration of bankruptcy

It is not reasonable to sue the debtor if it is obvious that his financial situation cannot lead to satisfactory performance of the debt. Therefore, the guarantor may not raise the benefit of discussion when the debtor has been declared bankrupt[354]. In Spain, the start of the procedure of suspensión de pagos under former bankruptcy law[355] (legal procedure previous to the declaration of bankruptcy aiming for the agreement of the creditors in order to save the company) has been considered enough reason to prevent the guarantor from raising the benefit of discussion[356]. It was factually impossible to obtain performance from a debtor in a situation of suspension de pagos since the agreements taken by the creditors on the debtor's patrimony do not leave assets to discuss on.

(ß) Factual bankruptcy

The guarantor may also raise the benefit of discussion upon the debtor's factual bankruptcy; i.e bankruptcy has not been declared but the debtor

---

[351] STS 25 February 1958 [RA 1958 no. 1043]; STS 3 March 1966 [RA 1966 no. 916].

[352] See *Guilarte*, 437 ff.; *Carrasco, Cordero* and *Marín*, 224.

[353] *Giusti*, 187; *Carrasco, Cordero* and *Marin*, 220.

[354] This is explicitly established in art. 1831 par. 3 Spanish CC. In Italy, this rule is not explicitly contained within the guarantee regulation but the same results from art. 51 *legge fallimentare italiana* and case law: Cass. 22 December 1969, 4032, FI 1970, I, 421. See *Giusti*, 187. The same is valid in France, Belgium and Luxembourg (art. 2023 CC); Germany (§ 773 par. 1 and 3 CC), Greece (art. 857 par. 3 CC), Finland (§ 21 par. 2 Guarantee Law) and also in Austria, in this case however only if the creditor has not been negligent (*nachlässig*).

[355] Spanish bankruptcy law was completely amended in the new bankruptcy law of 2003 (Law 22/2003, of 9 of July, *Concursal).*

[356] STS 7 April 1975 [RA 1975 no. 1412]; STS 6 October 1986 [RA 1986 no. 5241]; STS 24 July 1998 [RA 1998 no. 6139]. These cases regard the former bankruptcy law.

suffers an obviously critical financial position[357]. However he will not profit from the benefit of discussion[358]. In the first place, it will be difficult to find the debtor's assets to point out in order to validly raise the benefit of discussion. Moreover, the creditor cannot be compelled to start actions against the debtor which cannot be fructuous[359/360].

(ii) Impossibility to sue in Spain

The benefit of discussion can neither be raised upon the impossibility to sue the debtor within Spain[361] because in such case the discussion is too difficult and complex. The reason for this exception is the supplementary difficulty for the discussion. Therefore a more general provision as § 773 par. 1 no. 3 German CC[362], would be more satisfactory.

cc) Final remark

The reason for the exclusions of the benefit of discussion is the difficulty of execution in certain cases. However there are other cases in which execution is also very difficult or even impossible. In such cases, the benefit of discussion should also be excluded, as it is the case in neighbouring countries[363] (for instance, when the debtor's assets are all already mort-

---

[357] This case is especifically considered in Germany under § 773 par. 1 no. 4: "If it may be presumed that compulsory execution on the property of the principal debtor will not lead to the satisfaction of the creditor" ("wenn anzusehmen ist, daß die Zwangvollstreckung in das Vermögen des Hauptschuldners nicht zur Befriedigung des Gläubigers führen wird").

[358] *Carrasco, Cordero* and *Marín*, 220.

[359] See STS 30 July 1999 [RA 1999 no. 5724].

[360] The parties may limit the possibility to raise the benefit to those cases in which the reimbursement by the debtor is definitely impossible (totally or partially). Cass. 17 July 1985, no. 4218, FI, Rep 1986, *voce* Fideiussione e mandato di credito no. 33.

[361] Also in this sense: art. 640 Portuguese CC. Art. 2023 French, Belgian and Luxemburgian CC, base in the same idea but is even more restrictive: exclusion of the benefit of discussion takes place when the debtor's assets are outside the territory of the court of appeal. This limitation is not justified in modern times (Simler, no. 518).

[362] § 773 par. 1 no. 2 German CC: "if the difficulty of bringing an action against the principal debtor is materially increased in consequence of a change of domicile, industrial location, or place of residence of the principal debtor, occurring after the assumption of the guarantee" ("wenn die Rechtsverfolgung gegen den Hauptschuldner infolge einer nach der Übernahme der Bürgschaft eingetretenen Änderung des Wohnsitzes, der gewerblichen Niederlassung oder des Aufenthaltsortes des Hauptschuldners wesentlich erschwert ist").

[363] § 773 par. 1 no. 4 German CC; art. 857 Greek CC. In France: Simler no. 511, 512 and 518.

gaged[364]). A general wording including all these cases in which the debtor's performance is extremely difficult would be more practical.

2. Benefit of division. Special benefit for co-guarantors

The co-guarantors; i.e. the guarantors that guarantee together the same debt of the same debtor, may raise the benefit of division upon demand of the creditor (art. 1846 Italian CC and art. 1837 Spanish CC)[365].

3. The right to set up defences (eccezioni/excepciones)[366]

The double condition of the guarantee, as an obligation itself between guarantor and creditor on one hand and as a co-extensive obligation depending on the principal debt on the other, plays also a role regarding the defences that may be set up by the guarantor. The guarantor is liable vis-à-vis the creditor for his own guarantee obligation (different to the secured debt). Consequently, he is entitled as debtor to set up those defences deriving from his own obligation. Moreover, according to the ancillary nature of the guarantee[367], the guarantor can also set up some of the debtor's defences for his principal debt.

a) The right of the guarantor to set up the defences deriving from the contract of guarantee

According to the general law of obligations, the guarantor may set up the defences deriving from his own guarantee obligation and entirely or partly avoid the payment of his debt, or perform under more favourable circumstances. Such defences are the nullity or invalidity of the guarantee contract, the causes of extinction of the guarantee or any limit that might have been agreed by the parties for the guarantee[368].

---

[364] CA Paris, 5 February 1892: DP 1892, 2, 497 cited by Simler no. 511.

[365] See under Chapter 4, A., III., 2. Extent of liability of each one of the security rights, 231.

[366] The guarantor may raise defences not only upon demand of payment by the creditor but during the whole guarantee relationship (App. Firenze, 8 January 1965, BBTC, 1965, 622).

[367] See art. 1945 Italian CC and art. 1853 Spanish CC.

[368] Cass. 29 March 1996 no. 2909, FI, 1996, I, 1621; Cass. 20 August 1990, no. 9719, FI, 1993, I, 2171. See *Carrasco*, Fianza, accesoriedad y contrato de garantía, 229.

b) The right to set up the debtor's defences

aa) In general

The guarantor may also set up any debtor's defences which are inherent in the debt, but not those that are purely personal to the debtor (art. 1945 Italian CC[369] and art. 1853 juncto art. 1824 and art. 1845 Spanish CC). This rule is a consequence of the ancillary nature of the guarantee. The guarantor may discuss about the existence, legitimacy, validity, extent, modalities, subsistence and extinction of the principal debt[370].

The right to set up the debtor's defences is a right iure proprio[371] and not in the name of the debtor. This means that the guarantor does not depend on the debtor or his previous behaviour to use his defences, which may be set up also without agreement or even against the will of the debtor (also if the latter has expressly or tacitly renounced to set up them)[372]. Otherwise the debtor could afterwards set up his defences against the performing guarantor and refuse to pay him back the debt already paid to the creditor. Moreover, it is in the spirit of the guarantee that the creditor may not get from the guarantor what he cannot obtain from the debtor.

bb) Exception: the defense by reason of minority or disability of the debtor

The guarantor may not set up the debtor's defence of disability or minority to avoid the performance of his guarantee obligation (art. 1945 Italian CC and art. 1853 Spanish CC). Such defences are purely personal to the debtor. Hence he is the only legitimate person to set them up against the credi-

---

[369] Cass. 29 March 1996 no. 2909, FI, 1996, I, 1621; Cass. 20 August 1990, no. 9719, FI, 1993, I, 2171; Cass. 1 August 1991 no. 8475, Arch. Civ., 1992, 2, 160.

[370] *Lacruz*, 517; *Reyes*, 165; Cass. 16 November 1971, no. 3284, GC, 1972, I, 35. See also: Cass. 20 September 1971 no. 2627, FI, Rep. 1971 *voce* fideiussione e mandato di credito, no. 26; Cass. 20 June 1978 no. 3078, FI, 1979, I, 1, 1836. Regarding the guarantee of a credit account, see: Cass. 29 October 1998 no. 10808, FI, Rep. 1998, *voce* Fideiussione e mandato di credito, no. 35, 36 and 45; Cass. 11 September 1997, no. 8989, Arch. Civ., 1997, 1198; Cass. 11 March 1996, no. 1978, GC, 1997, I, 2591; App. Cagliari, 5 December 1987, GC, 1989, I, 2159.

[371] Also in Roman Law: Digest 44, 1, 19: "omnes exceptiones quae reo competunt, fideiussori quoque, etiam invito reo, competent". Cass. 22 January 1958 no. 131, FI, 1959, I, 456.

[372] Cass. 20 July 1967 no. 1861, GC, 1968, I, 324: "[…] è valido anche nei confronti del fideiussore, in relazione all'autonomo suo diritto di difesa, che si concreta nella facoltà di opporre al creditore tutte le eccezioni che spettano al debitore principale, comprese quelle che quest'ultimo non può più proporre, non potendo il comportamento omissivo di costui pregiudicare il diritto di difesa del fideiussore".

tor. The debt itself remains unaltered and consequently the guarantee obligation shall not be affected.

The wording of art. 1945 Italian CC is different to that of the Spanish equivalent provision (art. 1853 Spanish CC). While Italian CC precisely limits the exception to the debtor's defence by reason of disability, Spanish CC uses a wider expression, excluding the defences "purely personal of the debtor". The divergence is merely formal since this expression is construed as meaning exclusively the defences of minority and disability[373]. By contrast, the vices in the consent are not seen as included in the rule[374], as they are a case of general default, inherent to the debt[375]. Logically, the only case in which it is really justified that the guarantor remains liable even if the debtor is discharged is the case of a minor or disabled debtor. In these both cases, the debtor must be protected by the law in such terms that neither the creditor nor the guarantor can compel him to pay the debt. Also only in these cases it is justified that the guarantor assumes a wider risk than the debtor and suffers a worse situation. The knowledge of the guarantor about the minority or disability of the debtor does not play any role in this respect, as it does in neighbouring countries like Switzerland or Portugal (see art. 492 par. 2 Swiss Code of Obligations and § 632 Portuguese CC[376]).

The former Italian CC of 1865 (art. 1927), contained the same expression as the current Spanish CC ("debtor's purely personal defences"). The new provision meant a greater accuracy in the wording but not an important change in the meaning of the rule. Also under the former CC the defence referred to in art. 1927 was only that of disability by reason of minority, prohibition or disability of the debtor (inabilitazione) (for instance because of lack of authorisation of the husband if the debtor was a married woman). The defences of voidance or voidability by reason of vices in the

---

[373] There is no case law dealing with this matter. But the meaning of the phrase "purely personal defences" has been deeply discussed by the scholars. It is generally concluded that minority and disability are the only defences contained therein. See for all: *Guilarte*, 425 ff.

[374] By contrast in Switzerland and Portugal the vices in the content of the debtor may also be raised as exception from the guarantor under the condition that he had notice of it at the moment of granting the guarantee (see art. 492 par. 3 Swiss Code of Obligations and art. 632 Portuguese CC).

[375] *Reyes*, Fianza, 185.

[376] Art. 632 par. 2 Portuguese CC: "Sendo, porém, anulada a obrigação principal, por incapacidade ou por falta ou vício da vontade do devedor, nem por isso a fiança deixa de ser válida, se o fiador conhecia a causa da anulabilidade ao tempo em que a fiança foi prestada".

consent of the parties were considered inherent to the debt and could therefore also be set up by the guarantor[377].

cc) The guarantee of a co-debt

If the guarantee has been granted for a joint and several co-debt, the guarantor may set up against the creditor the defences of each one of the debtors of the same debt. Also if the debtor who has been asked for performance does not enjoy that defence but one of his co-debtors does, the guarantor may set it up in any case and for the whole debt.

If otherwise, the guarantee has been granted specifically for the debt of one of the debtors, the guarantor cannot set up the defences of the other co-debtors, not even if these are joint and severally liable vis-à-vis the creditor. However, according with the rules of co-debt, those co-debtors who are joint and severally liable can set up the defences of all other co-debtors. Consequently, the guarantor of any of them may also set up the defences that his own guaranteed debtor has obtained from any of his partners. These are objective defences and not the purely personal ones[378].

dd) Waiver of the right to set up defenses

(i) Validity of the waiver and consequences

It has been controversial in Italy, whether art. 1945 Italian CC is a mandatory provision or it can be waived by the parties by means of the principle of freedom of will. The relevant question is to analyse the consequences of including a waiver to set up defences by the guarantor (clausola solve et repete or senza eccezione or a prima richiesta/clausula solve et repete or a primera demanda).[379]

The clause solve et repete has been considered valid in the guarantee contract within certain limits: the guarantor would always be entitled to set up the defences regarding the guarantee obligation, as well as the nullity of the principal debt and its extinction[380]. The guarantor may also set up a defence in the case of fraud or abusive use of the guarantee[381].

The contract of guarantee including a clause solve et repete must always be construed on a case by case basis. It might be the case that the parties wanted to agree a typical guarantee. The waiver to set up the defences

---

[377] *Giusti*, 207.

[378] *Carrasco, Cordero* and *Marín*, 178.

[379] For Germany see *Horn/Staudinger*, on § 768, no. 28 ff.

[380] Cass. 29 March 1996 no. 2909, FI, 1996, I, 1621.

[381] Cass. 6 October 1989 no. 4006, BBTC, 1990, II, 1.

mentioned[382] (the clause solve et repete) is then void and does not affect the contract[383]. However, the parties might have intended to agree an atypical contract; for instance an indemnity (autonomous guarantee; contratto autonomo di garanzia)[384]. In such case, the parties may agree conditions which make the liability of the guarantor more severe than that of the debtor since it is not any more a typical contract of guarantee and art. 1941 Italian CC is not applicable any more. Accordingly, it can be considered that the waiver of the right to set up defences transforms the nature of the contract of guarantee into an atypical one, which is valid but different from a guarantee[385]. The judge must decide case by case whether the contract is a typical guarantee with a void clause or if it is an indemnity[386]. He must evaluate thereby the objective elements to reconstruct the will of the parties on making the agreement[387].

This solution is favoured in Spain, where it has been generally admitted by the scholars[388] and case law[389] that the guarantor may renounce to his right to set up defences and in such a case the nature of the contract is modified and converted into a new atypical security right[390].

---

382 See *supra* Chapter 2, C., VII., 5. Validity of the waiver by the guarantor to set up the defence of nullity of the secured obligation. The case of guarantees on first demand, 87.

383 *Petti*, 173 and *Giusti*, 208 consider art. 1945 Italian CC a mandatory provision which cannot be waived by the parties, as such waiver would become the guarantor's obligation "more onerous" than the underlying obligation (forbidden by art. 1941 Italian CC). *Contra*: *Carrasco, Cordero* and *Marín*, 180 consider that such waiver does not necessarily mean a more onerous obligation for the guarantor than that of the debtor (forbidden in art. 1826 Spanish CC).

384 STS 12. November 2003 [RA 2003 no. 8408]; STS 31. May 2003 [RA 2003 no. 5217] with further reference.

385 Cass. 7. June 1991 no. 6496, BBTC, 1992, II, 514; Cass. 16 November 1990, no. 11094, GI, 1991, I, 1, 394.

386 Cass. 7. June 1991 no. 6496, BBTC, 1992, II, 514. STS 12 November 2003 [RA 2003 no. 8408]: "... la determinación de la conceptualción judídica correspondiente a un contrato constituye un problema de interpretación del mismo en orden a su calificación, que está atribuido al juzgador de instancia...".

387 See: Cass. 22. Mai 1979 no. 2958, GC, 1979, I, 1892; Cass. Sezione Unite, 1 October 1987 no. 7341, BBTC, 1988, II, 383 commented by Costanza; Cass. 18. November 1992 no. 12341, GC, 1993, I, 1535, commented by Costanza. STS 31 May 2003 [RA 2003 no. 5217] with further reference.

388 *Guilarte*, 429 ff.; Carrasco, Fianza, accesoriedad, contrato de garantía, 210 et sequ.

389 STS 24 November 1978 [RA 1978 no. 4173]. In this case, the guarantor does not renounce specifically to raise exceptions but a more general waiver to raise any agreement taken between creditor and debtor. Accordingly, the waiver to the exceptions is also included.

390 STS 24. November 1978 [RA 1978 no. 4173]; *Carrasco, Cordero* and *Marín*, 179.

(ii) Construction of the waiver

In any case, a waiver to the rights to set up defences must be construed restrictively. Accordingly, if the clause has been formulated in a wide way, such as “for any defences”, it must be considered that the guarantor meant only those defences regarding the underlying obligation and not those defences for his own obligation (for instance, a waiver to set off, without specifying which claims, means only a waiver to set off the claims of the debtor and not his own claims against the creditor)[391].

Moreover, the right to set up the defence for extinction of the secured obligation is not considered to be included in the waiver, unless expressly established (in which case the contract cannot be considered a guarantee but an independent guarantee)[392]. Co-guarantors that waive to set up defences coming up from the underlying relationship do not waive, thereby, the defences of the other co-guarantors[393]. The construction of the waiver must also take into account the nature of the guarantor and his level of expertise with regard to the contract[394].

4. Right to make agreements with the creditor

An agreement reached between the guarantor and the creditor is valid but will not be effective against the debtor (art. 1835 par. 1 Spanish CC). The obligation of the debtor vis-à-vis the creditor does not change by agreements between the latter and the guarantor. This is a superfluous provision since it is obvious that the secured debt is not ancillary to the guarantee.

5. Right to remain unaffected by the agreements taken between creditor and debtor

Art. 1.835 par. 2 Spanish CC establishes that the agreements between creditor and debtor on the underlying obligation do not affect the liability of the guarantor, which remains in the original terms.

Actually, according to the general regulation of the guarantee, in case the agreement reduces the liability of the debtor, the guarantor’s liability

---

391 *Carrasco, Cordero* and *Marín*, 180.

392 See *supra* Chapter 2, C., VII., 5. Validity of the waiver by the guarantor to set up the defence of nullity of the secured obligation. The case of guarantees on first demand, 87.

393 *Carrasco, Cordero* and *Marín*, 180.

394 In Germany the guarantee on first demand may also be validly agreed by a private person. However this may never be agreed as a part of the general terms and conditions of the guarantee and even the contract was particularly agreed, the “on first demand” clause will not have effect if the guarantor was not aware of its effects and the bank did not properly inform him (BGH 2 April 1998, NJW 1998, 2280 f.; BGH 12 March 1992, NJW 1992, 1446 f.).

can also be diminished, since "the guarantor can obligate himself to less but not to more than the principal debtor" (art. 1826 par. 1 Spanish CC).

If the agreement between creditor and debtor increases in some way the liability of the latter, the guarantor's liability is, according to art. 1835 par. 2 Spanish CC not extinguished (like it is ex lege in other similar cases (art. 1851 and art. 1852 Spanish CC)) but remains only unaltered[395] unless he expresses his consent. The guarantor may decide himself in unclear cases whether he prefers to be affected by the agreement or not and is protected from the enlargement of his risk above the agreed terms. On the other hand, the creditor does not need to lose the guarantee because he makes an agreement with the debtor which is a novation of the original contract. It must be noted that these kinds of agreements usually aim at enlarging the chances of the creditor to be paid by the debtor.

The rule in art. 1835 Spanish CC has no precedent in Roman law nor in Spanish historical law. It is neither to be found in the regulation of neighbouring countries but is adopted from the Prussian Code[396]. It seems to offer beneficial results for both creditor and guarantor. It is applicable to any novation of the secured debt performed by the parties unless the aim of the agreement is the extinction of the debt and unless the specific agreement is explicitly ruled by the law in a different way (like the cases of art. 1849 and 1852 Spanish CC)[397]. However, the novation must regard the debt secured with the guarantee. For instance, if the agreement instead of changing the conditions of the secured debt, establishes better conditions for the following transactions, the guarantor cannot be affected. It must be construed in each case whether the agreement is a novation of the existing relationship and can therefore also affect the guarantor's liability or if it creates a new and autonomous relationship which does not regard the guarantor[398].

E. Relationship between the guarantor and the debtor

I. Introduction

The debtor is not a contracting party of the guarantee. He is usually related to the guarantor so that the latter is disposed to undertake the liability. But this is a factual relationship, which is outside the contract of guarantee. Therefore, the provisions on the guarantee do not specifically rule this re-

[395] STS 11 November 1981 [RA 1981 no. 4505]; STS 20 June 1989 [RA 1989 no. 4710].

[396] *García Goyena*, 909. *Guilarte*, 203.

[397] *Lacruz*, 532.

[398] *Carrasco, Cordero* and *Marín*, 182.

lationship. The only aspect, which is regulated by law regards the grant of remedies to the guarantor in order: a) either to be discharged in case the performance of the guarantee would imply an evident danger of non-recovery or b) in order to recover the payment he had performed as guarantor. Consequently, the legal effects of the guarantee contract between guarantor and debtor are of two kinds. On one side, the rights of the guarantor before performance of his guarantee (rilevazione/acción de cobertura or relevación). On the other, the right of the guarantor who has already performed and is therefore entitled to be refunded or indemnified by the debtor.

II. Duties of the guarantor before performance

1. Guarantor's duty to notify the creditor's request or his own intention to perform in order to prevent unjustified enrichment

There is no legal provision that sets up expressly the guarantor's duty to inform the debtor about his performance or his intention to perform. However, such duty is indirectly established since the lack of information is sanctioned by the law (art. 1952 par. 1 Italian CC and art. 1842 Spanish CC[399]). According to these provisions, the debtor who has not been informed about the payment may set up upon the guarantor's recourse all defenses that he may have set up against the creditor at the time of the guarantor's payment[400]. Hence, the guarantor who has not informed the debtor is sanctioned by the law with the risk of losing the right to reimbursement[401].

Furthermore and in any case, the guarantor's duty to inform the debtor is also a direct consequence of the principle of good faith. The debtor can only inform the guarantor about the defenses he may set up if he has notice of the payment. Therefore the guarantor must inform him of his intention to perform. Otherwise, he loses his right to be fully reimbursed, also for the payment that could have been avoided had he set up the defenses.

2. Duty of the guarantor to set up the debtor's defences

The guarantor must set up the debtor's defenses against the creditor if he had notice of them. This is not expressly contained in the civil codes as a duty but the lack of performance is sanctioned by the law as the debtor

---

[399] The same is valid according to art. 647 Portuguese CC and § 1361 Austrian CC.

[400] In other countries, like France, Belgium, Luxemburg (art. 2031 CC) and Greece (art. 859 CC), the guarantor who does not inform the debtor about payment losses automatically his claim for reimbursement.

[401] See STS 4 March 2003 [RA 2003 no. 1822]. See Chapter 2, D., III., 3. The right to set up defences (eccezioni/excepciones), 103.

may set up against the guarantor the defenses that he could have set up against the creditor (art. 1952 par. 2 Italian CC and art. 1840 Spanish CC)[402]. The debtor must prove that the guarantor knew about the defenses.

III. Rights of the guarantor before performance

1. Guarantor's right to be informed about payment performed by the debtor

There is no legal provision that sets up the specific duty of the debtor to inform the guarantor about the payment he has performed to the creditor[403]. However, the guarantor who has not been informed about the debtor's performance and pays the creditor again may claim for reimbursement and the debtor cannot deny payment. The debtor keeps his right against the creditor for unjustified enrichment. In this respect the guarantor must diligently facilitate the provision of information or he loses his right of recourse against the debtor[404].

2. Guarantor's right to request for release

a) In general

The rights available to the guarantor before he has performed are established in art. 1953 Italian CC[405] and art. 1843 Spanish CC[406]. These provisions grant the guarantor a right to request either for release or for supplementary security upon the circumstances listed. A preventative remedy is hence granted to the guarantor in order to preclude too high a risk. Therefore the rules are only applicable before the guarantor has performed[407] or if he has paid in advanced a debt which was agreed with a time limit (according to art. 1841 Spanish CC)[408].

---

[402] See under Chapter 2, E., IV., 3., d) Defences of the debtor against the claim for reimbursement, 128.

[403] Such duty is explicitly contained in art. 646 Portuguese CC. See Chapter 2, E., III. 1. Guarantor's right to be informed about payment performed by the debtor, 111.

[404] STS 4 March 2003 [RA 2003 1822].

[405] Art. 1953 reproduces the wording of art. 1919 of the former Italian CC of 1865.

[406] According to Spanish case law, art. 1843 CC is only applicable to personal guarantors and not for the grant of real securities (STS 6 October 1995 [RA 1995 no. 7022]). *Contra*: *Carrasco, Cordero* and *Marín*, 277.

[407] Cass. 13 March 2002 no. 6808 (www.dirittonotariale.it). STS 21 October 2003 [RA 2003 no. 7517]. After having performed, the remedies are others (subrogation, reimbursement). Accordingly, the payment by the guarantor extinguishes his right to be discharged.

[408] See: *Carrasco, Cordero* and *Marín*, 276.

The request for release and that to obtain supplementary security are different claims. The guarantor may renounce only to one of them or to both.

b) Guarantor's right to claim for release

Every guarantor has the right to ask for previous release. It does not make any difference whether the guarantee is remunerated or not. The guarantor who has been remunerated also has the right of reimbursement and associated rights (rights which aim to protect the reimbursement)[409].

An exception is made in Spain for the guarantor who granted in his own interest. It is considered that he is not worthy of special protection, and therefore he does not enjoy the right to be released[410].

The discharge of the guarantor according to art. 1953 Italian CC and art. 1843 Spanish CC can take place in two different ways. The guarantor may be effectively released from his liability (rilievo per liberazione/ liberación)[411]; or if full release is not possible, the debtor may provide enough security for the guarantor's eventual reimbursement (rilievo per cauzione/garantía)[412/413].

In Italy and Spain, the claims (release and security) may be set up until the debt is performed[414]. Moreover, claims are cumulative. If the guarantor tries one claim without success, he can subsidiarially try the other[415]. In any case, both options are rarely exercised in the practice. In general, the more factual option is that of granting security[416]. But even this is difficult

---

409 *Casanova*, 189 ff.; *Cian/Trabucchi*, on art. 1953, 2246 f..

410 SAP Sevilla 25 November 1999 [AC 1999 no. 2249]; *Casanova*, 184; *Carrasco, Cordero* and *Marín*, 277.

411 Cass. 13 June 1984 no. 3538, GC, 1985, I, 99.

412 Cass. 13 March 2002 no. 6808 (www.dirittonotariale.it): "Prima del pagamento, e solo prima, poiché, – in effetti – dopo il pagamento c'è solo la surrogazione e il regresso" il fideiussore nei cinque casi previsti dall'art. 1953 c.c. può, pertanto, esercitare a sua scelta contro il debitore principale o l'azione di rilievo c.d. per liberazione o l'azione di rilievo c.d. per cauzione".

413 Other European countries, also grant the possibility to choose between discharge and grant of security (§ 775 German CC, art. 648 Portuguese CC).

414 By contrast, in Germany granting security instead of guarantor's relief is only possible when the debt is not due and payable (§ 775 par. 2 German CC: "If the principal obligation is not yet due the principal debtor may give security to the guarantor instead of relieving him" ("Ist die Hauptverbindlichkeit noch nicht fällig, so kann der Hauptschuldner dem Bürgen, statt ihn wu befreien, Sicherheit leisten"). See *Horn/Staudinger*, on § 775, no. 15.

415 *Cian/Trabucchi*, on art. 1953, 2246 f.; *Carrasco, Cordero* and *Marín*, 279.

416 *Guilarte*, 299; Simler, no. 613. In Austria, the grant of security to the guarantor is the only possibility established in the law (§ 1364 sent. 1 and § 1365 *juncto* § 1373 ff. Austrian CC).

in practice since a debtor in a bad financial situation will not easily find alternative security rights.

c) Conditions for release

aa) General condition

A valid release can only take place if the debtor agreed upon the guarantee or at least had notice of it[417]. The guarantee must not have been granted against the debtor's will[418]. This condition is not explicitly established in the law[419]. However, release or grant of supplementary security increases the debtor's costs. He should not cover them if he has not consented to the guarantee. Correspondingly, the guarantor may request relief if the guarantee was granted as a result of a debtor's mandate or as a negotiorum gestio, upon the conditions established by law. In these frequent cases the debtor not only consents but even promotes the granting of guarantee. In Germany, the right to be released before performance is specifically limited to those guarantees, a) which have been assumed by reason of a debtor's mandate or b) if the guarantor has the rights of a mandatory against the debtor under the provisions relating to management without mandate (negotiorum gestio) because of the assumption of the guarantee (§ 775 par. 1 German CC[420]). By contrast, in Italy and Spain, the right to request for previous release is not limited in this sense. This means that also guarantors, who have granted guarantee without mandate, may be discharged under the circumstances established by the law. In Germany, however, an implicit mandate shall be enough (§ 670 and § 683 German CC)[421].

---

[417] *Lacruz*, La causa, 754; *Carrasco, Cordero* and *Marín*, 277. Contra: *Guilarte*, 245.

[418] *Casanova*, 182.

[419] Austrian CC contains explicitly this aspect in § 1364: "Durch den Verlauf der Zeit, binnen welcher der Schuldner hätte zahlen sollen, wird der Bürge, wenn der Gläubiger auf die Befriedigung nicht gedrungen hat, noch nicht von seiner Bürgschaft befreit; allein er ist befugt, von dem Schuldner, wenn er mit dessen Einwilligung Bürgschaft geleistet hat, zu verlangen, dass er ihm Sicherheit verschaffe. Auch der Gläubiger ist dem Bürgen insoweit verantwortlich, als dieser wegen dessen Saumseligkeit in Eintreibung der Schuld an Erholung des Ersatzes zu Schaden kommt".

[420] § 775 par. 1 German CC: „If the guarantor has assumed the guarantee by reason of a mandate by the principal debtor, or if he has the rights of a mandatory against the principal debtor under the provisions relating to management without mandate because of the assumption of the guarantee, he can demand from him release from the guarantee:" ("Hat sich der Bürge im Auftrage des Hauptschuldners verbürgt oder stehen ihm nach den Vorschriften über die Geschäftsführung ohne Auftrag wegen der Übernahme der Bürgschaft die Rechte eines Beauftragten gegen den Hauptschuldner zu, so kann er von diesem Befreiung von der Bürgschaft verlangen:"). See *Horn/Staudinger* on art. 775, no. 1 ff.

[421] *Horn/Staudinger*, on art. 775, no. 3.

bb) Specific conditions: cases for relief

(i) In general

Even if the debtor had agreed to the guarantee, the right to be release is limited by the law to specific cases. These cases are explicitly established in art. 1953 Italian CC and art. 1843 Spanish CC. Basically, the conditions for release are of two kinds; either is the debtor unable to perform his debt or the guarantor has been sued by the creditor. These two kinds of conditions are referred to in both provisions of Italian and Spanish civil codes with a parallel wording, as follows: 1) when the guarantor has been sued for payment; 2) in case of bankruptcy or insolvency; 3) when the debtor is bound to relieve him from guaranteeing within a given term and the term has expired; 4) when the term has become due because the term within which it should have been paid has expired; 5) at the end of five years in Italy (ten years in Spain), when the principal obligation has no fixed term for maturity, unless it is of such nature that it can only be extinguished in a term longer than five/ten years respectively[422].

These five cases are the only ones upon which the guarantor may require relief[423]. Analogical application is not admitted[424]. Moreover, the creditor must have notice of the intention and consent the discharge of the guarantor for the granting of a new security.

(ii) Detailed consideration of the cases for release

(α) The guarantor has been sued for payment

The guarantor may be discharged if he has been sued for his guarantee obligation. The start of judicial proceedings entails costs and risks for the guarantor[425]. Therefore, only such proceedings grant the guarantor the right to demand release. Simple demands for payment, which are not judicial, are not enough to grant the guarantor the preventative right of discharge[426]. However, it is not necessary that the creditor has obtained an enforceable judgement for satisfaction against the guarantor, like it is in Germany (§ 775 par. 1 no. 4 German CC).

---

[422] For Germany see § 775 par. 1 nos. 1, 2, 3 and 4.

[423] STS 17 October 1990 [RA 1990 no. 7976]; STS 31 October 1994 [RA 1994 no. 8007]; *Giusti*, 246; *Bo*, *voce*, *Fideiussione*, 1123.

[424] *Díez-Picazo*, Fundamentos, 438.

[425] *Giusti*, 245.

[426] *Carrasco, Cordero* and *Marín*, 280. It is clear in the wording of arts. 1953 Italian CC and 1843 Spanish CC ("convenuto in giudizio"/"judicialmente demandado").

(β) The debtor is bankrupt or insolvent

(αα) Meaning of "insolvency"

The term "insolvency" is used in this case as describing the durable and objective insufficiency of the debtor's patrimony to perform the debt (factual bankruptcy)[427]. Also the danger of insolvency has been considered enough to justify the application of art. 1843 par. 2 Spanish CC[428]. "Insolvency" is hence not used as a technical meaning for this purpose[429]. If the insolvency proceeding has been started and the debtor has been officially declared insolvent, the right to demand relief is no longer useful. The guarantor may not be discharged and no security can be granted. Therefore, the broad construction of the term "insolvency" is the only possible one[430]. As a result, the judge must decide each time, whether the debtor can be

427 *Giusti*, 245; *Carrasco, Cordero* and *Marín*, 281; *Guilarte*, 304 ff. (esp. 305).

428 *Díez-Picazo*, Fundamentos, 439.

429 As described in Italian and Spanish Bankruptcy Acts. Art. 5 par. 2 Legge Fallimentare: "Lo stato d'insolvenza si manifesta con inadempimenti od altri fatti esteriori, i quali dimostrino che il debitore non e` piu` in grado di soddisfare regolarmente le proprie obbligazioni". Art. 2 Ley 22/2003, concursal: "Presupuesto objetivo.

1. La declaración de concurso procederá en caso de insolvencia del deudor común.

2. Se encuentra en estado de insolvencia el deudor que no puede cumplir regularmente sus obligaciones exigibles.

3. Si la solicitud de declaración de concurso la presenta el deudor, deberá justificar su endeudamiento y su estado de insolvencia, que podrá ser actual o inminente.

Se encuentra en estado de insolvencia inminente el deudor que prevea que no podrá cumplir regular y puntualmente sus obligaciones.

4. Si la solicitud de declaración de concurso la presenta un acreedor, deberá fundarla en título por el cual se haya despachado ejecución o apremio sin que del embargo resultasen bienes libres bastantes para el pago, o en la existencia de alguno de los siguientes hechos:

1º El sobreseimiento general en el pago corriente de las obligaciones del deudor.

2º La existencia de embargos por ejecuciones pendientes que afecten de una manera general al patrimonio del deudor.

3º El alzamiento o la liquidación apresurada o ruinosa de sus bienes por el deudor.

4º El incumplimiento generalizado de obligaciones de alguna de las clases siguientes: las de pago de obligaciones tributarias exigibles durante los tres meses anteriores a la solicitud de concurso; las de pago de cuotas de la Seguridad Social, y demás conceptos de recaudación conjunta durante el mismo período; las de pago de salarios e indemnizaciones y demás retribuciones derivadas de las relaciones de trabajo correspondientes a las tres últimas mensualidades".

430 It concurs with Spanish historical law: The Partidas of Castilla, V, XII and XIV cited by *Díez-Picazo*, Fundamentos, 439. See Comments of García Goyena on art. 1757 Draft Spanish CC of 1851 (*García Goyena*, on art. 1757).

considered "insolvent" or not[431]. However, the guarantor has the burden of proof of the debtor's factual insolvency[432]. In modern German law the guarantor may demand release from the guarantee "if the financial condition of the principal debtor has become materially worse" (§ 775 par. 1 no. 1 German CC[433]). This wording is more accurate, practical and clearer in the context of a previous discharge of a guarantor. The use of the term insolvency is confusing. A general wording has been also chosen in § 1365 Austrian CC. The situation of the debtor must have worsened so as to fear his inability to perform; i.e. the subjective factor of a funded fear is included.

(ββ) Insolvency of the debtor

Art. 1953 no. 2 Italian CC clearly specifies that the insolvency referred to is the insolvency of the debtor. Art. 1843 Spanish CC is less accurate and does not specify whether the insolvency regards the guarantor or the debtor. The writers agree on considering that the wording of this article makes reference to the bankruptcy of the debtor[434] or any of the joint and several co-debtors[435]. This interpretation agrees with Spanish historical background[436] and with the regulation in neighbouring countries[437]. Moreover, it is difficult to understand why the insolvency of the guarantor, which does not have any legal consequences for the debtor, should allow him to anticipate his proceedings against the principal debtor[438].

---

[431] *Carrasco, Cordero* and *Marín*, 281. For Germany, *Horn/Staudinger*, on § 775 no. 8 a).

[432] *Díez-Picazo*, Fundamentos, 439; *Guilarte*, 306.

[433] § 775 par. 1 no. 1 German CC: "wenn sich die Vermögensverhältnisse des Hauptschuldners wesentlich verschlechtert haben". See *Reinicke* and *Tiedtke*, Bürgschaftsrecht, no. 438.

[434] In opinion of *Díez-Picazo*, art. 1943 par. 2 Spanish CC may also be applied in case of bankruptcy of the guarantor if the administrator of the bankruptcy considers it convenient. (*Díez-Picazo*, Fundamentos, 438).

[435] *Pérez Alvarez*, 265.

[436] Law 8°, Titles 18, Book 3°of the Fuero Real; Law 14, Title 12 of the Partida V explicitly referred to the debtor. Art. 1757 of the Draft Spanish CC of 1851 by *García Goyena*.

[437] Art. 1953 no. 2 Italian CC; art. 2032 no. 2 French CC and § 775 par. 1 sent. 1 German CC (*mutatis mutandi*).

[438] *Guilarte*, 309.

(γ) The debtor is bound to release the guarantor from his guarantee within a given term and the term has expired.

If the debtor has agreed to release the guarantor upon a term, the guarantor may require release when the term is reached[439]. He does not need to be required for payment first by the creditor. The agreement of release within a given term, may have been included in the guarantee or in a separate document afterwards. The term may be a moment in time, explicitly agreed, but it may also be a condition. The guarantor may then ask for release upon fulfilment of the condition.

(δ) The debt has become due because the term within which it should have been paid has expired.

The guarantor should not suffer the consequences of the debtor's delay in paying his debt. Therefore he may ask for release from the moment in which the debt has become due, unless the guarantee was agreed for a longer term. It is not necessary that the creditor has required the debtor or the guarantor to perform. The only condition is the expiration of the term for the principal debt[440]. The same rule is contained in § 775 par. 3 German CC[441].

(ε) At the end of five years in Italy and ten years in Spain, when the principal obligation has no fixed term.

This provision prevents the guarantor from being bound for too long time when the principal debt has been agreed without time limit[442]. The uncertainty of the guarantor is limited by the law to five years in Italy[443] and ten years in Spain[444].

This rule does not apply for those obligations which nature makes it impossible to extinguish before five/ten years[445]. It applies, by contrast, to continuing guarantees without time limit and to those conditional obligations, which may come about before or after the given terms.

---

[439] Also in art. 2032 no. 3 French, Belgian and Luxemburgian CC; art. 648 lit. d Portuguese CC and § 1364 sent. 1 Austrian CC.

[440] *Giusti*, 245, 246; *Carrasco, Cordero* and *Marín*, 281, 282.

[441] Art. 775 par. 3 German CC: "wenn der Hauptschuldner mit der Erfüllung seiner Verbindlichkeit im Verzug ist".

[442] Obligations agreed with a time limit, which overcomes five/ten years do not fall within the scope of this provision.

[443] Also in art. 646 lit. e Portuguese CC.

[444] The term of ten years is also established in art. 2032 no. 5 French, Belgian and Luxembourgian CC and used to be in art. 1919 former Italian CC.

[445] *Giusti*, 246; *Carrasco, Cordero* and *Marín*, 282.

d) Debtor's defences against the guarantor's claim for release

The debtor may set up against the guarantor's claim for release those defences arising from his relationship with the guarantor but not those based on his relationship with the creditor. For instance, he may set up as a defence the lack of claim for reimbursement of the guarantor[446].

e) Consequence of no release: damages

If the debtor fails to perform his duty to release vis-à-vis the guarantor, he remains liable for the damages caused to the guarantor[447]. It is however unusual in the practice and also fruitless since these damages are difficult to prove.

IV. Rights of the guarantor after performance

1. In general

a) Duality of claims: reimbursement and subrogation

The basic right of the guarantor against the debtor after he has performed his guarantee obligation is a right to be indemnified in respect of the amounts that he has paid by reason of the guarantee. This right is restitutionary in nature.

The guarantor's right to recover indemnification from the debtor may be founded in two claims[448]: a) reimbursement (regresso/reembolso) (art. 1950 Italian CC and art. 1838 Spanish CC) and b) subrogation to all the rights that the creditor holds against the debtor (art. 1949 Italian CC and art. 1839 Spanish CC)[449].

---

[446] *Carrasco, Cordero* and *Marín*, 278.

[447] Cass. 21 April 1965 no. 699, FI 1965, I, 2090; Guilarte, 310 ff. In France, Belgium and Luxembourg it is even included in the law (art. 2032 CC).

[448] The duality of claims is founded in French Law (art. 2028 and art. 2029 French CC). It is also contained in the modern Dutch CC (art. 7:866). Differently, German CC and Portuguese CC do not grant the claim for reimbursement in the law (only the claim for subrogation). However, a claim for reimbursement is founded on the legal relationship, which gives origin to the guarantee. Such relationship is, in most cases, a mandate or *negotiorum gestio.* See for Germany: *Seiler/Erman*, on § 774, no. 12, § 670 German CC, which grants the mandatory the claim for reimbursement of payments, necessary for the performance of the mandate. For Portugal, see *Almeida Costa*, 780).

[449] The guarantor's claim for subrogation is a right given in most European guarantee's regulations: § 774 par. 1 sent. 1 German CC; § 1358 Austrian CC; art. 2029 French, Belgian and Luxembourgian CC; § 644 Portuguese CC. By contrast it is not explicit in Dutch CC.

b) Differences between subrogation and reimbursement

The differences between the claim for subrogation and the claim for reimbursement have important practical consequences[450].

aa) The nature of the claims

The claim for reimbursement is a new claim, based on the guarantor's right to recover the money paid to the creditor. It starts at the moment the guarantor has performed his obligation. Differently, upon subrogation, the guarantor assumes the claim of the creditor, as it originally was. He "substitutes" the creditor in his rights against the debtor[451]. He is "entitled to stand in the shoes of the creditor"[452]. Therefore, the subrogated guarantor obtains the same rights[453] the creditor had against the debtor. The credit relationship remains existent but there is a change within the parties (modificazione soggetiva nel lato attivo del rapporto obligatorio[454]). Consequently, in contrast to reimbursement, the guarantor enjoys the benefit of all accessories of the credit (especially the privileges, preferences and any kind of security rights[455]) held in respect of the guaranteed debt.

bb) Extent of the claims

The extent of the claim for reimbursement is broader than that of the subrogation, since it includes the refund of judicial costs suffered as well as the interest (at least legal interest) for the sum paid by the guarantor from the moment of payment. Contrarily, upon subrogation the costs are not included, because they are not part of the creditor's rights against the debtor. The subrogated guarantor may claim for interest only as far as the creditor had this right[456]. The right of reimbursement is, hence, more advantageous if the debtor is solvable[457].

---

[450] See: *Sicchero*, 998 ff.; *Simler*, nos. 555 and 556.

[451] *Giusti*, 227.

[452] *Andrews* and *Millet* no. 11.17 cited from: Duncan Fox & Co v. North South Wales Bank (1880) 6 AppCas 1 (HL).

[453] The debtor may also raise against the guarantor all the defences, which he had against the creditor.

[454] *Giusti*, 227.

[455] The guarantor obtains all kinds of securities; those established in the civil code and by especial laws. Cass. 19 july 1967 no. 1846, FI, I, 1967, 2539: "La surrogazione legale a favore del fideiussore di cui all'art. 1203 no. 3 c.c. si estende anche ai privilegi stabiliti a favore del creditore da leggi speciali, pur se a garanzia di finanziamenti previsti per finalità di pubblico interesse".

[456] See *Giusti*, 230 and 231.

[457] *Simler*, no. 556.

cc) Prescription of the claims

The term for prescription of the claim for reimbursement starts at the day the guarantor performs his obligation. The period of prescription of the subrogated claims starts at the moment these could have been enforced; which is always prior.

c) Cumulative or alternative claims

It is indeed not clearly established in the law whether the reimbursement and the subrogation are cumulative or alternative claims. The issue has been extremely controversial. Different theories can be distinguished in this respect, but no definite conclusion has been reached.

aa) In opinion of some scholars the performing guarantor only enjoys one unique claim. For some of them the guarantor's claim is that for reimbursement, for others it is subrogation. In both cases, it is considered that the content of the claim is extended by the law. Reimbursement also contains the rights of subrogation[458] (art. 1839 Spanish CC). Subrogation is extended to the rights of reimbursement, which include the expenses and interest[459]. The reimbursement is not a new claim. It only specifies the content of the subrogation. From a technical perspective, these theories lack of consistency. Subrogation and reimbursement are different claims, with a diverse nature and extent. They should not be confused.

bb) Another theory considers that reimbursement and subrogation are two separate claims. The guarantor may choose one of them. He cannot accumulate both claims[460] but he may set up one after the other[461]. Case law has not clarified this matter, neither in Italy nor in Spain. However, some decisions seem to grant the guarantor both claims as separate and alternative[462].

---

[458] *Reyes*, Algunas consideraciones, 220; *Pérez Alvarez*, Solidaridad, 288 ff. *Mc Guiness*, refers to this combination as "quasi-subrogative rights", regarding Canadian law (The law of guarantees, 1986, 213).

[459] Cass. s.u. 15 January 1993 no. 449, GC, 1993, I, 351 ss ("il fenomeno del regresso come il momento dinamico del fenomeno della surrogazione").

[460] In Germany the guarantor may choose to claim for one or the other (OLG Köln WM, 1989, 1883, 1886) but he may also join (*verbinden*) them, so long as he is only reimbursed once: *Horn/Staudinger* on § 774 no. 5 a)).

[461] *Guilarte*, 252 ff; *Giusti*, 233.

[462] Cass. 6 June 1972 no. 1744, FI, 1973, I, 1544; Cass. 5 February 1987 no. 1120 and Cass. 14 May 1987 no. 4460; Cass. 4 February 1988 no. 1137 cited by *Giusti*, 234. STS 29 May 1984 [RA 1984 no. 2805]; STS 11 June 1984 [RA 1984 no. 3227]; STS 13 February 1988 [RA 1988 no. 1985]; STS 3 July 1998 [RA 1998 no. 5213]; STS 15 December 1997 [RA 1997 no. 8817].

cc) A third theory considers that both claims may also be raised together. The guarantor can so benefit from both claims simultaneously without being compelled to start new procedural claims after the first claim has been finished[463]. This theory appears to be the most practical one. Based on the idea of two different claims, it seems to be more efficient and save time and procedural steps. This is positive in any case and specially in countries like Italy and Spain, where Court's delay is considerably significant.

2. *Subrogation*

a) *In general*

The guarantor's subrogation into the creditor's claims as established in art. 1949 Italian CC and art. 1839 Spanish CC is a particular application to the guarantee of the general rules on subrogation (art. 1201 ff. Italian CC and art. 1209 ff. Spanish CC). According to such rules the guarantor, as performing party, subrogates into the creditor's rights (art. 1203 par. 3 Italian CC and art. 1210 par. 3 juncto art. 1212 Spanish CC). This principle is restated explicitly within the guarantee regulation.

b) *Payment to the creditor as requirement for subrogation*

The guarantor subrogates in the creditor's rights against the debtor upon performance. The term "payment" used in both Italian and Spanish CC refers to any kind of valid and effective performance; not only monetary payment. Such performance must be imputable to the guarantor, it needs to satisfy the creditor's claim[464] and discharge the debtor vis-à-vis the creditor. The payment performed before the debt was due and payable is also valid with regard to subrogation.

The lack of consent on the guarantee by the debtor does not affect the guarantor's subrogation upon performance[465]. The same is valid when the debtor was not aware of the guarantee and even if it was granted against his will. The subrogation is a legal effect established by the law for the guarantee relationship, for which the will of the debtor is irrelevant.

The guarantor cannot be subrogated if the secured debt has extinguished[466] or if it was void[467].

---

[463] *Carrasco, Cordero* and *Marín*, 258.

[464] The guarantor cannot subrogate if he performed his guarantee obligation to the debtor (Cass. 8 April 1978 no. 1648, GC, 1978, I, 1, 1854).

[465] *Giusti*, 226.

[466] Cass. 18 January 1960 no. 30, FI, 1960, I, 213.

[467] Cass. 25 November 1986, no. 6929 cited by *Giusti*, 226.

c) Content of the right of subrogation

aa) In general

The guarantor subrogates upon performance in the creditor's claims against the debtor, with the interest and the accessories, with the specific security rights that the credit may have had, its privileges and preferences and all other faculties that could be considered accessories of the credit. It is irrelevant whether the claims where constituted before or after the guarantee[468]. Accordingly, the guarantor may withdraw the underlying obligation and claim for restitution instead of payment[469]. Moreover, the debtor's rights vis-à-vis third parties to which the creditor has subrogated are also included in the guarantor's subrogation[470].

The guarantor subrogates also if debtor and creditor agreed not to assign their claims. Such agreement cannot be applied to the guarantor's detriment unless he agrees[471].

bb) Subrogation into the creditor's security rights

The guarantor subrogates into the security rights granted by the debtor in favour of the creditor (pledge, irregular pledges, reservation of title and transfer of property for security purpose, etc.). No special formalities are required. The guarantor does not need to inform or notify. Debtor and creditor do not need to explicitly accept. The guarantor must only perform those general requirements for the enforcement of the respective rights according to their nature. If the creditor was secured with a pledge, he must transfer to the guarantor the possession of the secured asset (unless they agree that the creditor remains possessor for the guarantor)[472]. Mortgages can only be subrogated if the general requirements for assignment of mortgage are fulfilled (art. 2843 Italian CC and art. 149 Spanish Ley Hipotecaria).

---

[468] By contrast, in art. 507 par. 2 Swiss Code of Obligations, securities constituted after the guarantee are not subject to subrogation ("Von den für die verbürgte Forderung haftenden Pfandrechten und andern Sicherheiten gehen aber, soweit nichts anderes vereinbart worden ist, nur diejenigen auf ihn über, die bei Eingehung der Bürgschaft vorhanden waren oder die vom Hauptschuldner nachträglich eigens für diese Forderung bestellt worden sind. Geht infolge bloss teilweiser Bezahlung der Schuld nur ein Teil eines Pfandrechtes auf den Bürgen über, so hat der dem Gläubiger verbleibende Teil vor demjenigen des Bürgen den Vorrang").

[469] *Bo*, voce Fideiussione, 1119 with further references; *Giusti*, 229; *Carrasco, Cordero* and *Marín*, 261.

[470] Cass. 26 June 1968 no. 2154, GC 1968, I, 1796; *Carrasco, Cordero* and *Marín*, 261, 262.

[471] *Carrasco, Cordero* and *Marín*, 261.

[472] *Carrasco, Cordero* and *Marín*, 261.

cc) Items excluded from subrogation

Subrogation serves to indemnify the performing guarantor. It is hence limited in its extent by the effective payment performed by the guarantor. In that order, the guarantor may not fully subrogate in those rights which would grant him a better position or a more valuable asset than the performed payment. He may not get more in return than what he has actually performed (art. 1839 par. 2 Spanish CC)[473]. Consequently, if the guarantor's subrogation results for instance in the recovery of a more valuable asset than the credit paid, that asset must be sold and the guarantor only obtains an equivalent of his payment[474].

It has been controversial whether the subrogated guarantor may exercise all the creditor's contractual rights vis-à-vis the debtor (nullity, voidance, withdrawal, etc.) or only those which are deemed to recover the payment. Most scholars correctly limit subrogation to those rights which could effectively serve to indemnify the guarantor for the performed payment[475].

Moreover, subrogation is limited to the scope of the guaranteed obligation[476].

Lastly, the guarantor cannot subrogate in the rights of the creditor vis-à-vis third parties, which are not accessories of the performed claim.

d) Partial subrogation upon partial performance

The guarantor also subrogates in the rights of the creditor upon partial payment[477]. According to the general rules on subrogation, in the case of partial payment the subrogated party and the creditor are co-creditors of the debtor in proportion to what is due to them, unless there is an agree-

---

473 *Guilarte*, 276.

474 *Carrasco, Cordero* and *Marín*, 262.

475 The performing guarantor for a flat's rental fee does not subrogate in the creditor's rights against the landlord. He can neither use the flat nor has he any further rights to be paid for the future rents (SAP Barcelona, 14 November 1995, RJC, 1996, 398). The same example had already been considered by Italian scholars: *Giusti*, 229: "Il fideiussore solvens ha acquistato, attraverso la surrogazione, il diritto di credito con i suoi accessori, […] in funzione del recupero di quanto ha fatto conseguire al creditore; ma non avrebbe assunto la qualità di parte nel rapporto contrattuale tra debitore e precedente creditore, perché tale assunzione non sarebbe conforme alla tipica funzione recuperatoria dell'istituto"; *Carrasco, Cordero* and *Marín*, 262. *Contra*: *Campogrande*, Trattato, 475.

476 The creditor's claims against the debtor coming from the parties' personal circumstances, such as claims for salaries, are not transferable to the guarantor. STS 27 June 1989 [RA 1989 no. 4787] commented by *Cabanillas Sánchez*, CCJC 20 [1989] § 536; *Miccio*, 545.

477 *Ravazzoni*, Le garanzie, 111; *Carrasco, Cordero* and *Marín*, 264. The guarantor's claim for subrogation as established in the law is not limited to full performance. Therefore a partial payment is also valid (see Simler, no. 592).

ment to the contrary (art. 1205 Italian CC[478] and art. 1213 Spanish CC[479])[480]. These provisions are applicable in general to subrogation and also specifically to the subrogation of the performing guarantor. The creditor, who has received only a part of the debt from the guarantor, keeps his right to claim for the rest as a preferential creditor[481]. This is explicitly ruled in art. 1213 Spanish CC, which is a concretisation of the adage "nemo contra se subrogasse videtur"[482]. The creditor must have accepted the partial payment.

If the credit was secured with a personal security right, the performing guarantor subrogates in the corresponding part of it. Real security rights cannot be divided. They can be fully exercised by the creditor and by the guarantor. In practice, the guarantor usually waives his right to subrogate in the creditor's real security rights, upon partial payment, in order to avoid practical difficulties.

The performing guarantor may claim against the debtor for the partial payment, even before the creditor has required performance of his part. In such a case, the creditor may defend his preference starting the so called "claim of better right" (tercería de mejor derecho)[483].

e) Effectiveness of the subrogation

The subrogation is effective vis-à-vis the debtor and vis-à-vis any other guarantor. No formalities are required. They do not need to be informed or to agree on the subrogation.

---

[478] Art. 1205 Italian CC: "In case of partial payment, the subrogated third person and the creditor are co-creditors of the debtor in proportion to what is due them, unless there is an agreement to the contrary". ("Surrogazione parziale. Se il pagamento è parziale, il terzo surrogato e il creditor concorrono nei confronti del debitore in proporzione di quanto è loro dovuto, salvo patto contrario").

[479] Art. 1213 Spanish CC: „The creditor to whom a partial payment has been made may exercise his right to collect the rest with preference to the person subrogated in his place by virtue of the partial payment of the same credit". ("El acreedor, a quien se hubiere hecho un pago parcial, puede ejercitar su derecho por el resto con preferenciaal que se hubiere subrogado en su lugar a virtud del pago parcial del mismo crédito").

[480] In Germany the guarantor's partial subrogation upon partial payment is specifically established in the rules on the guarantee (§ 774 par. 1 sent. 1 German CC: "As far as the guarantor satisfies the creditor, the claim of the creditor against the principal debtor is transferred to him" („Soweit der Bürge den Gläubiger befriedigt, geht die Forderung des Gläubigers gegen den Hauptschuldner auf ihn über").

[481] In Germany, the creditor's preference to collect his part of the claim is indirectly established in the rules on the guarantee; § 774 par. 1 sent. 2: "The transfer may not be enforced to the detriment of the creditor" („Der Übergang kann nicht zum Nachteil des Gläubigers geltend gemacht werden").

[482] See Simler, no. 592.

[483] *Carrasco, Cordero* and *Marín*, 264.

f) Protection by the law of the right of subrogation

If the guarantor cannot subrogate in the rights of the creditor by an act performed by the latter, the guarantee is extinguished (art. 1955 Italian CC and art. 1852 Spanish CC). The guarantor's right of subrogation is so protected by the law.

g) Waiver by the guarantor to his right of subrogation

The guarantor may waive his right to subrogate[484]. Such waiver is common in the practice, but usually limited to the case of partial subrogation by reason of partial payment. An agreement by which the guarantor renounces to subrogate while the creditor still has enforceable claims against the debtor must be considered abusive if the guarantor is a non-professional (consumer).

3. The claim for reimbursement

a) Source of the claim: the relationship between debtor and guarantor

The guarantor's claim for reimbursement is firstly justified by a common sense of equity. It would be simply unfair to make the guarantor totally liable for the debt. Beyond this instinctive reason, there is a legal rationale for the claim based on the relationship between the debtor and the guarantor. This factual relationship gives also a legal reason for the guarantee. In some cases the debtor mandates or pleads the guarantor to grant. The claim for reimbursement is then based on the mandate[485]. The mandatory has a right to be indemnified after performance (art. 1720 Italian CC and art. 1729 Spanish CC). Sometimes the guarantor himself simply wishes to benefit the debtor. In this case, the claim for reimbursement is based on the negotiorum gestio[486] (art. 1705 Italian CC and art. 1717 Spanish CC).

Other Spanish scholars consider that the guarantee does not need to be identified either with the mandate or with the negotiorum gestio. The connexion between the guarantee relationship and these contracts (mandate/negotiorum gestio) is factual and not specifically established in the law. The guarantee is considered as a contractual relationship sui generis[487].

---

[484] For Germany see *Horn/Staudinger*, on § 774, no. 24.

[485] Art. 1703 ff. Italian CC and art. 1710 ff. Spanish CC.

[486] *Carrasco*, *Cordero* and *Marín*, 254. This concept is common in other European contries: France: Simler, 507, no. 558; Germany: *Erman/Seiler* on §774 no. 12 and Portugal: Almeida Costa, 780. Differently as in Italy, Spain or France, the claim for reimbursement is not contained in the German and Portuguese guarantee regulation.

[487] *Cassanovas*, La relación obligatoria de la fianza, 145 ff.

b) Payment to the creditor as requirement for reimbursement

Only the performing guarantor has the right to reimbursement[488]. Payment is considered any kind of performance by the guarantor to the creditor for the satisfaction of the secured debt. The guarantor is entitled to claim for reimbursement automatically upon performance.

c) The content of the claim for reimbursement

The content of the claim for reimbursement is explicitly established in art. 1950 par. 2 and 3 Italian CC and art. 1838 Spanish CC. These rules shall apply irrespectively of whether the debtor had notice or not about the constitution of the guarantee (art. 1838 in fine Spanish CC).

aa) The total amount of the debt

The claim for reimbursement seeks to indemnify the guarantor for his effective payment. The performing guarantor is entitled to be fully indemnified to the extent of the loss which he has suffered and no more. Hence the guarantor is entitled to recover the sum which he paid to discharge the debtor's liability to the creditor, together with expenses and legal interest[489] on that sum running from the date on which the debtor has been notified of the payment[490] (art. 1950 par. 2 and 3 Italian CC and art. 1838 Spanish CC). If higher interest was agreed for the debt, the guarantor has the right to recover this interest[491]. The same is valid for higher moratory interest[492]. The guarantor's right to interest on the amounts he has paid to the creditor compensate him for being kept from his money until he recovers it from the debtor. Therefore this right is unaffected by the fact that the underlying debt was paid free of interest[493].

If the guarantor partially performs, the debtor must only reimburse this partial payment. It is irrelevant whether the guarantor simply did not pay a part or if he had been partially released by the creditor (for instance as a result of donation)[494].

If the debt was fully paid by assignment of assets, the guarantor may claim for the principal sum, whether the value of the asset is higher or lower.

---

[488] *Giusti*, 234.

[489] The interest for the debt are considered part of it (STS 22 November 1967 [RA 1967 no. 4708]; STS 29 December 1987 [RA 1987 no. 9710]).

[490] STS 22 November 1967 [RA 1967 no. 4708].

[491] Art. 1950 par. 2 sent. 2 Italian CC. For Spain: *Carrasco, Cordero* and *Marín*, 259.

[492] See SAP Madrid 17 March 1990, RGD, 1991, 736.

[493] See *Andrews* and *Millet*, 338 no. 10.18.

[494] The same in England: *Andrews* and *Millet*, 337 no. 10.18.

bb) Costs after notifying the debtor of the demand for payment against him

The guarantor may claim for reimbursement of the expenses incurred after informing the debtor about the demand for performance (art. 1950 par. 2 Italian CC and art. 1838 no. 3 Spanish CC).

The guarantor is entitled to recover the costs only if the debtor had notice of the demand. No formalities are needed in this respect. The simple acknowledgement of the debtor entitles the guarantor to demand the costs[495]. The guarantor has a general duty (onere/carga) to inform but is not liable (obligo/obligación) vis-à-vis the debtor for the lack of information, the only consequence of which is the loss of the right to recover the costs.

In any case, the guarantor must generally behave in good faith and diligently. Thus, if he gave the debtor notice of the creditor's demand, but he does not set up the defences that he should have known upon average diligence, the debtor may set up them against the guarantor when he claims for reimbursement[496].

The limitation of the claim to the costs incurred after notification is inadequate. The guarantor should be entitled to recover all the expenses which must be reasonably incurred as a consequence of the judicial or non-judicial requirement for payment; whether incurred before or after notification. The limit would be established on application of the principle of good faith. The costs of a claim raised by the guarantor recklessly, against the will of the debtor, cannot be recovered by the guarantor 497, while costs for any reasonable claim should be recovered whenever it has been raised.

It is unclear whether the guarantor is entitled to recover from the debtor the costs incurred in resisting a claim of the creditor against him. This must be decided for each case on appliance of the principle of good faith.

cc) Damages, when appropriate

The right to claim for reimbursement of the damages suffered by the guarantor is explicitly contained in art. 1838 no. 4 Spanish CC and generally admitted in Italy. The express mention of damages was excluded from the current Italian CC498, as it was considered superfluous.

This Spanish provision lacks of clarity in its wording. In first place, according to its terms (damages will be reimbursed "when appropriate"). The

---

[495] The guarantor does not need to inform the debtor himself. It is enough if he already knew. STS 24 November 1992 [RA 1992 no. 9370]. *Giusti*, 237, 238.

[496] *Giusti*, 238; *Carrasco, Cordero* and *Marín*, 259.

[497] *Carrasco*, *Cordero* and *Marín*, 259.

[498] Art. 1915 former Italian CC explicitly included the damages.

meaning of this expression is not clear. It can refer to the need that there are actual damages that can be proved or it also might refer to the imputation of these damages to the debtor according with the general rules of tort law.

On the other hand it is also difficult to think of possible damages apart from those mentioned in number 3 of this provision[499]. Except from the expenses mentioned above, any other damage should have been considered by the guarantor as a normal consequence of his guaranteeing activity.

d) Defences of the debtor against the claim for reimbursement

aa) Debtor's defenses against the creditor may be set up against the guarantor

(i) In general

If the guarantor pays without notifying the debtor, the latter can set up against him all the defences that he could have raised against the creditor at the time payment was made (art. 1952 par. 2 and art. 1840 Spanish CC).

Moreover, if the guarantor paid the creditor although he could have raised the debtor's defences against the creditor, the debtor keeps his right to set up the defences against the guarantor. The rule establishes a sanction for the guarantor for his lack of diligence regarding the rights of the debtor. He assumes the risk that the debtor sets up the defences against him[500], but he does not lose his claim for reimbursement[501], like in France.[502].

The behaviour of the guarantor should not worsen the debtor's position.

(ii) Requirements

(α) Guarantor's duty to inform the debtor about his intention to perform

The guarantor needs to know the defences available to the debtor. If he did not have notice of them by any other way, the debtor must inform him. This is only possible if the guarantor notifies his intention to pay and gives the debtor time enough to answer. This way the debtor has the opportunity

---

[499] See Chapter 2, E., IV., 3., c), bb) Costs after notifying the debtor of the demand for payment against him, 127.

[500] STS 14 November 1981 [RA 1981 no. 4510].

[501] The same is valid in § 1361 Austrian CC and art. 647 Portuguese CC.

[502] Art. 2031 par. 2 French, Belgian, Luxembourgian CC: "Lorsque la caution aura payé sans être poursuivie et sans avoir averti le débiteur principal, elle n' aura point de recours contre lui dans le cas où, au moment du paiement, ce débiteur aurait eu des moyens pour faire déclarer la dette éteinte; sauf son action en répétition contre le créancier".

to inform the guarantor about the defences he may set up against the creditor.

The debtor can only set up against the guarantor the defences that he could have raised against the creditor if the guarantor had not informed him about his intention to perform[503]. Such information must be given before payment has been made either voluntarily or upon request[504]. Moreover, the guarantor must leave a reasonable time between notice of his intention to perform and the effective payment. The debtor should not be damaged by an extremely sudden payment of the guarantor. If the guarantor had not informed the debtor about the request for performance but he had notice of it, the debtor loses his right to set up the defences against the guarantor[505].

The guarantor's duty to inform the debtor is founded upon the principle of good faith. Moreover, if the guarantee relationship is considered as a mandate, the guarantor must preserve the interests of the mandatory and give him the opportunity to inform the guarantor of his defences[506].

(β) Defences at the moment of guarantor's performance

The debtor may set up against the guarantor all defences that he could have raised at the moment of payment by the guarantor. The defences which arose after that moment cannot be set up by the debtor.

(iii) Exceptions

(α) Lack of defences

If the debtor either had no defences or he does not set up them against the performing guarantor, the latter must be reimbursed for the total amount performed.

---

[503] The same in France, Belgium, Luxembourg, art. 2031 par. 2 CC. *Contra*ry according to art. 7: 868 Dutch CC the guarantor may raise against the debtor the defences he had against the creditor, also if he had not informed about his intention to perform.

[504] In French, Belgian and Luxembourgian CC it is a specific requirement that the guarantor's payment has been performed without being sued ("sans être poursuivie"). See also Simler, no. 606. In Italy and Spain the provisions are applicable also if payment has been performed upon request.

[505] STS 14 November 1981 [RA 1981 no. 4510]; STS 24 November 1992 [RA 1992 no. 9370].

[506] So is the reasoning applied in German Law because there is no specific provision on this point in German CC (See *Horn/Staudinger* on § 765 no. 106 f.).

(β) Defences already set up

The debtor cannot set up against the guarantor those defences already raised by the guarantor against the creditor.

bb) Debtor's defences against the guarantor for anticipated payments

If the guarantor performed before maturity of the underlying obligation, the debtor may deny reimbursement until expiration of term (art. 1841 Spanish CC) because too spontaneous a reaction of the guarantor regarding the payment should damage the debtor reducing his terms of payment. The guarantor does not lose his right to be reimbursed but it will be postponed to the moment of maturity of the underlying obligation. Interest and costs originated by the early payment will not be reimbursed.

Defences may not be raised if the term of payment for the underlying obligation has been reduced by the creditor. If it has been extended but the guarantor was not informed, the defence may not be raised either[507].

cc) Defence for a double payment

(i) The guarantor performs without notifying the debtor

The guarantor who pays without notifying the debtor loses his right to be reimbursed if the debtor, who did not know about the payment, also performs (art. 1952 par. 1 Italian CC and art. 1842 Spanish CC[508]). The guarantor has a right of recourse against the creditor for undue payment. Although an express reference would not have been necessary, this provision is specifically included in art. 1952 par. 3 Italian CC and art. 1842 in fine Spanish CC[509]. The claim for reimbursement set up by the guarantor before the creditor required the debtor for payment is enough notification.

(ii) The debtor performs without notifying the guarantor

If the debtor did not inform the guarantor of his performance and the latter paid the creditor again, the debtor may not set up the defence that the debt

---

507 *Díez-Picazo*, Fundamentos, 443 f. In opinion of Guilarte the debtor may not raise defence in case of extension of time even if he had informed the guarantor (*Guilarte*, 286 f.).

508 Also in art. 2031 par. 1 French, Belgian, Luxembourgian CC; art. 645 par. 1 Portuguese CC and art. 7: 867 Dutch CC.

509 See also art. 645 par. 2 Portuguese CC: "O fiador que, nos termos do número anterior, perder o seu direito contra o devedor pode repetir do credor a prestação feita, como se fosse indevida". *Carrasco, Cordero* and *Marín*, 273. Art. 646 Portuguese CC: "Aviso do cumprimento ao fiador: O devedor que cumprir a obrigação deve avisar o fiador, sob pena de responder pelo prejuízo que causar se culposamente o não fizer".

had been performed and the guarantor's payment was undue. In this case, the guarantor may claim for reimbursement to the debtor and keeps his claim against the creditor for undue payment. If the debtor reimburses the guarantor, he has a claim against the creditor for unjustified enrichment. This has been even expressly established in Portuguese CC, art. 646.

F. Extinction of the guarantee contract

I. Causes of extinction of the guarantee

There are three different types of causes of extinction of the guarantee: a) the causes of extinction that are established in the Civil Codes for common obligations when they concur within the guarantee[510] (direct causes of extinction[511]); b) the same causes of extinction, when they affect the underlying obligation (indirect causes of extinction[512]), and c) certain specific causes of extinction of the contract of guarantee that are established in the provisions within the law of guarantees.

As the two first groups (the direct and the indirect causes of extinction) derive from the nature of the guarantee; i.e. an obligation which is ancillary to the principal debt, the regulation of the guarantee does not need to refer to them again. This is the reason why Italian regulation on the guarantee avoids any reference to the direct and the indirect causes of extinction[513] and refers only to the specific causes of extinction of the guarantee. These special causes are: a) the release of the guarantor when the creditor distresses his rights of subrogation. The guarantee is extinguished when the subrogation of the guarantor into the rights, mortgages, and privileges of the creditor has become impossible because of actions taken by the creditor (art. 1955 Italian CC); b) the release of the guarantee for future obligation. The guarantee for a future obligation (see art. 1938 Italian CC) is released if the creditor, without a special authorisation from the guaran-

---

[510] The general causes of extinction of the obligation are ruled in art. 1176 ff and art. 1230 ff Italian CC and art. 1156 ff. Spanish CC.

[511] In Germany "selbständige Beendigungsgründe": See *Horn/Staudinger*, on § 765, no. 225.

[512] For Germany: see *Seiler/Erman*, on § 765 no. 8 and *Horn/Staudinger*, on § 765 no. 225 ff. and on § 767 no. 10 and on § 768 no. 16.

[513] The former Italian CC contained a specific reference to the direct causes of extinction in art. 1925 former Italian CC: "L'obbligazione che nasce dalla fideiussione, si estingue per le stesse cause per cui si estinguono le altre obbligazioni". This provision followed art. 2034 French CC: "L'obligation qui résulte du cautionnement, s'éteint par les mêmes causes que les autres obligations". However, a specific reference to the general causes of extinction within the regulation of the guarantee was later considered to be irrelevant and deleted from the current Italian CC.

tor, has granted credit to the third party whilst being fully aware that the debtor's financial conditions have become such as to make satisfaction of the claim considerably more difficult (art. 1956 par. 1 Italian CC) and c) after six months of the maturity of the primary obligation. The liability of the guarantor is extinguished after six months from when the principal obligation became mature. This is the case unless the creditor has sued the debtor and has diligently pursued the action (art. 1957 par. 1 Italian CC). This term will be reduced to two months if the guarantor has expressly limited his own obligation to the moment of the payment of the principal debt (art. 1957 par. 2 and 3 Italian CC). It is interesting to observe that the legal reasoning for all of the cases of extinction of the guarantee in the Italian CC is based on a particular behaviour on the part of the creditor, which perturbs the situation of the parties with regard to the obligation. This behaviour takes the form of: a) not being diligent in requiring the payment of the debt, b) avoiding the efficient subrogation of the guarantor in the rights or guarantees of the secured debt, and c) ignoring an evident danger of insolvency but still granting more credit to the debtor, whilst not performing the benefit of discussion or not applying the right of set-off[514].

In contrast to Italian law, art. 1847 Spanish CC explicitly refers to the direct and indirect causes of extinction of the guarantee[515]. Arts. 1848 to 1852 Spanish CC set those specific causes of extinction of the guarantee, which also regard the behaviour of the creditor towards the guarantor: a) if the creditor grants an extension of time in relation to the secured debt without the consent of the guarantor, the guarantee is thereby extinguished (art. 1851 Spanish CC); b) when the creditor prevents the guarantor from being subrogated into his rights, mortgages and privileges, the guarantor is discharged with regard to his guarantee obligation (art. 1852 Spanish CC) and c) when the creditor voluntarily accepts an immovable, or any other object, in payment of the debt, even if he thereinafter loses them because of eviction, the guarantor is also discharged (art. 1849 Spanish CC).

The Spanish provisions on the extinction of the guarantee appears to be obsolete and rather confused. First, being the guarantee an obligation itself, reference to the direct and the indirect causes of extinction seems indeed unnecessary and redundant. Further, art. 1853 Spanish CC should systematically not have been included in the chapter on extinction. It refers to the right of the guarantor to raise against the creditor all the exceptions that are inherent in the debt, but not those that are purely personal to the debtor. While extinction of the guarantee may under circumstances follow

---

[514] *Giusti*, 253.

[515] Art. 1847 Spanish CC: „The obligation of the guarantor shall expire at the same time as that of the debtor, and for the same causes as other obligations".

upon the application of this provision, it does not seem to make sense to introduce this wording while regulating extinction.

Spanish regulation on the extinction of the guarantee could be shortened and be given a greater degree of precision. In this regard, the Italian regulation would provide with a good example.

II. The extinction of the underlying obligation as the reason for the extinction of the guarantee: the indirect causes of extinction.

1. Extinction of the guarantee upon performance of the underlying obligation

a) Payment to the creditor

aa) Payment by the debtor

The natural way for a guarantee to be extinguished is by the debtor performing the underlying obligation[516]. The guarantor will be released upon the debtor's discharge (as a consequence of the principle of co-extensiveness).

bb) Payment by a third party

The guarantee extinguishes upon the discharge of the debtor, not upon the satisfaction of the creditor. The payment performed by a third party might satisfy the creditor but not necessarily discharge the guarantor. If the performing party is subrogated into the rights of the creditor, the guarantee is not extinguished. According to art. 1204 Italian CC and art. 1212 Spanish CC, by means of subrogation, the credit is transferred along to the party subrogated, with the rights annexed thereto, whether they run against the debtor or third parties (guarantors or holders of mortgages).

If the performing party is not subrogated into the rights of the creditor but only enjoys a right of reimbursement, the guarantee is extinguished by the payment or performance. The right to subrogate is compatible with the right of reimbursement. There will only be a mere right of reimbursement when it has been proved that the subrogation did not take place[517].

Consequently, if a third person performs the payment, this will only serve to extinguish the guarantee if the party performed in name of the debtor and with the intention of extinguishing the debt[518]. However, if the

---

[516] Arts. 1176–1200 Italian CC and arts. 1160–1169 Spanish CC, which deal with the valid performance of general obligations are applicable.

[517] *Nanni/Franzoni*, 784 ff; *Díez-Picazo*, Fundamentos, 215.

[518] For instance, if a debt secured with a guarantee is performed with the money obtained from a new loan, granted by a different creditor; the original guarantee does not

third party who affected performance is subrogated into the rights of the creditor against the debtor then the guarantee will not be extinguished until the debtor is fully discharged[519] (art. 1204 Italian CC and art. 1212 Spanish CC)[520].

cc) Typical cases of performance by third parties

(i) A joint and several co-debt

In case of a joint and several co-debt the guarantee will only be extinguished by performance on the part of the debtor in whose favour the guarantee was granted.

The guarantee is not extinguished if the payment is totally performed by one of the co-debtors in favour of whom the guarantee was not granted because the performing party still has a right of subrogation against all other debtors and thus retains his right against the guarantor of any of his debtors (see art. 1299 Italian CC and art. 1145 Spanish CC)[521].

(ii) The third party performs for the account of the guarantor

A different situation is that of the third party performing for the account of the guarantor. In such case, the third party enjoys a claim for reimbursement (art. 1158 Spanish CC). In practice it is not easy to know whether the payment was performed for the account of the guarantor or for the account of the debtor. The concrete facts and circumstances of the case must be considered. Generally the payment of a secured debt must be regarded as being performed for the account of the debtor and of the guarantor. The performing party is therefore presumed to be willing to retain the corresponding claims against both other parties[522].

(iii) Payment performed in good faith to the person in possession of the title

The debtor is discharged if the payment is fulfilled in good faith to the person in possession of the title (art. 1189 Italian CC and art. 1164 Spanish

---

secure the second credit; i.e. it extinguishes upon performance of the debt it is guaranteeing. See: *Carrasco, Cordero* and *Marín*, 228.

[519] About the subrogation and its effects see: *Díez-Picazo*, Fundamentos, 214 and 215.

[520] The subrogation is presumed in the cases that are established in arts. 1201–1203 Italian CC and art. 1210 Spanish CC.

[521] *Giusti*, 255. Art. 1299 Italian CC and art. 1145 Spanish CC refer to right of "reimbursement". However, this term has been generally construed as a right of subrogation. See. *De Maria/Franzoni*, 902).

[522] *Carrasco, Cordero* and *Marín*, 229.

CC). As a result, the guarantor will be also discharged even if the creditor's interest is not fully satisfied.

If as a result of the debtor's bankruptcy, the debt is extinguished by enforcement of the debtor's patrimony (ejecución forzosa) (allocation of his assets to perform the debt), both debtor and guarantor are thereby discharged. The effects of the enforcement are the same as those which occur as a result of payment; the principal and the guarantee obligations are extinguished.

dd) Void or undue payment

If the payment is void, the guarantor is not discharged (art. 1160, art. 1162 and art. 1165 Spanish CC). This is the case unless the payment is later validated (art. 1160 Spanish CC) or has become useful for the creditor (art. 1163 Spanish CC).

If the debtor has performed an undue payment, he may claim for the return of that payment. The guarantor cannot set up such a claim and remains liable for the guarantee obligation that is not extinguished.

ee) Partial payments

Partial payment extinguishes the part of the guarantee that corresponds to that payment. Moreover if the debtor makes payment by assigning some of his assets, he will only be discharged with regard to the liquid value of the assigned assets (art. 1175 Spanish CC). This will be the case unless something different has been agreed by the parties. The guarantor will also be discharged with regard to the same amount and will still be liable for the rest of the unpaid debt.

ff) Imputation of the payment performed by the debtor

(i) In general

In the absence of any express agreement, the mere existence of a guarantor does not affect the rights of the creditor and the debtor to impute payments. According to the general law of obligations, the debtor who has different debts in relation to the same creditor, may chose which one of the subsisting debts shall be considered to have been performed upon payment i.e. to which one of the debts the payment shall be imputed (art. 1193 par. 1 Italian CC and art. 1172 Spanish CC).

If the debtor does not impute the payment to any of his debts, this will be done in application of the law as established in art. 1193 par. 2 Italian CC and art. 1174 Spanish CC.

The Italian CC establishes a very concrete and detailed order of imputation: a) in the first place the payment must be imputed to the debt that is already due and payable; b) if there are different debts which are already due and payable, the least secured debt will be the debt which is considered to have been performed; c) if there is a plurality of due and payable debts that are all equally secured, then the more onerous debt must be considered to have been performed by the payment; d) among different debts which are equally onerous, the most ancient debt will be considered to have been performed.

According to art. 1193 par. 2 Italian CC, if a debtor has a plurality of debts which relate to the same creditor, the payment that is performed by the debtor must be imputed first to the less or non-guaranteed debts.

The solution to the same case is different according to Spanish law. Spanish CC lacks of the accuracy of Italian CC in this respect. As stated in art. 1174 Spanish CC, when the payment cannot be imputed pursuant to the rules in the civil code, the debt that is most onerous to the debtor from those that are matured shall be deemed to be the one paid. In case all the mature debts are equally onerous, the payment is imputed a pro rata among all. If there is a plurality of debts that are secured with guarantees then the payment must be imputed to the most ancient obligation, which is considered to be the most onerous obligation by Spanish Supreme Court[523].

No reference is made in the Spanish CC to the situation in which a plurality of debts is secured with a guarantee. In such cases the application of art. 1174 Spanish CC results in the imputation of the payment first to the debts that are secured with a guarantee because they are more onerous for the debtor than those that are not secured[524]. It must be stressed that the criteria of onerousity relates to the debtor and not the guarantor. Accordingly, if the guaranteed debt is not the most onerous one that exists in relation to the debtor, the payment will not be imputed to that one. For instance, if the debtor has two debts with the same creditor, one secured with a guarantee and another one secured with a mortgage, a payment that is performed by the debtor without express reference to whom it should be imputated, must be considered to have been made for the fulfilment of the mortgaged debt. This is because the mortgaged debt is more onerous for the debtor than that which is secured with a personal guarantee. The guarantor does not have any right to assume that the payment has been made to fulfil the debt that is guaranteed by him[525].

---

[523] STS 16 May 1989 [RA 1989 no. 3770].
[524] *Bercovitz*, 209.
[525] *Carrasco, Cordero* and *Marín*, 229.

(ii) Imputation in the case of a debt partially secured with a guarantee

If a debt has been partially guaranteed and the debtor also performs only partially, it is questionable as to which part of the debt will be considered extinguished: a) the part secured with the guarantee or b) the part of the debt which has not been guaranteed.

The Italian and the Spanish regulations are radically different in this regard. The application of art. 1193 Italian CC results in the imputation of the payment to the part of the debt which has not been guaranteed. By contrast, according to the wording of art. 1174 Spanish CC, the payment that is performed by the debtor without an express declaration about its appropriation, should be imputed to the part of the debt that has been guaranteed. The guarantee is therefore extinguished, either in part or completely. The part of the debt that is secured with a guarantee is more deemed to be onerous for the debtor than the part that is not guaranteed[526].

(iii) Imputation of a partial payment in the case of a guarantee for a limited amount

The issue of the imputation of a partial payment is different if there is a unique debt vis-à-vis the creditor and only a part of this debt has been secured with a guarantee (guarantee for a limited amount). Since there is only one debt, any payment will be imputed to that debt. But to which part of the debt: the part that is secured with the guarantee or the part not secured? In the first case the guarantee would be extinguished, in the second case, the guarantee will still be valid for the rest of the debt.

Art. 1193 Italian CC and art. 1172 Spanish CC are not applicable to this situation as there is only one relevant debt. The creditor is entitled to accept or refuse payment and accordingly he can also adjudicate as to the ascription of the payment. If he does not express his will in regard to this matter, payments must be assigned to the non-guaranteed part of the debt, in view of creditor's interests and the security function of the guarantee[527].

It is normal contractual practice to include a clause in the guarantee contract by means of which the guarantor is only fully discharged upon the complete performance of the underlying obligation.

(iv) Imputation in the case of a debt secured with different guarantees

If there is a single debt between the debtor and the creditor and different parts of the debt have been secured with different guarantees that are inde-

526 *Guilarte*, 359 f.

527 *Carrasco, Cordero* and *Marín*, 230.

pendent from each other[528] (i.e. not a co-guarantee), then the rules on the imputation of payments are not applicable. The debtor cannot make a free election with regard to the part of the debt to which the payment shall be imputed. Unless the guarantors have made an agreement on this point, the payment will be imputed pro rata among all the guarantors (art. 1193 par. 2 in fine and art. 1174 par. 2 Spanish CC)[529].

b) Alternative legal ways for performance (surrogati del pagamento/ subrogados del pago)

Payment is the normal way to perform an obligation. However the general law of obligations also establishes alternative ways to fulfill performance: tender and deposit (deposito/consignación); set off (compensazione/ compensación) and payment by assignment of assets (prestazione in luogo dell'adempimento /dación en pago).

aa) Tender and deposit (deposito/consignación)

The tender and deposit (consignation) of the amount that is owed has the same effects as the fulfillment of the obligation by normal payment. Consequently, the debt is extinguished and thereby also the guarantee (art. 1210 to 1213 Italian CC and art. 1176 to 1181 Spanish CC).

Moreover, according to art. 1181 Spanish CC, guarantors and co-obligors are discharged if „subsequent to tender and deposit of the thing owed, the creditor authorises the debtor to withdraw it". The same shall be valid in Italy where a specific provision is missing.

bb) Set-off (compensazione/compensación)

The existing claims between the debtor and the creditor may be set-off by the debtor or directly by the guarantor[530]. In that case the guarantee extinguishes together with the secured debt.

The right of the guarantor to set-off de iure proprio[531] the claims of the secured debtor vis-à-vis the creditor is specifically established in art. 1247

[528] See Chapter 4, A., II., 1., b) Plurality of personal guarantees independent from each other, 228.

[529] *Carrasco, Cordero* and *Marín*, 230.

[530] The origins of this rule are already in Roman Law; Digest, 16, 2, 4 and Digest, 16, 2, 5. The same was included in the traditional Law of Castilla; in the Partida V, Title 14, Law 24: "[…] non tan solamente los debdores principales pueden descontar un debdo por otro, mas aun sus fiadores lo pueden fazer tamiben de la debda que deviessen a aquel a quien fiaron, como de la que deviesen a el mismo [...]".

The Roman rule was also included in the Code Napoleon, art. 1294. The Draft Spanish CC of 1851 by García Goyena contained also a parallel rule. Spanish CC changes the structure of the provision but maintains the content in art. 1197.

Italian CC and art. 1197 Spanish CC. In the case of Spain, this is a legal exception to the general rule in art. 1196 par. 1 CC, according to which, a set-off can only take place when both obligors are principally liable.

This rule often applied when the secured claim is already enforceable but neither the debtor nor the creditor effectively set off and extinguish the debt. This case is not to be seen as extension of time but rather as just an extension of the guarantor's uncertainty. The rule aims at protecting the guarantor against such uncertainty by allowing him to set-off the debtor's claims in order to be sure that he is discharged of his guarantee obligation.

cc) Assignments of assets (prestazione in luogo dell'adempimento/ dación en pago)

The assignment of assets is a valid way of performing any obligation. The extinction of the secured debt by the assignment of assets as established in the law of obligations, automatically results in the extinction of the guarantee (principle of co-extensiveness). Furthermore, art. 1849 Spanish CC specifies the application of assignment of assets for the guarantee. The guarantor is definitely discharged when the creditor voluntarily accepts an immovable or a movable object in payment of the debt. This remains a valid discharge even if the creditor thereafter loses this object by virtue of eviction.

The content of art. 1849 Spanish CC followed the wording of art. 2038 French CC. The same wording was also adopted in art. 1829 former Italian CC. It was excluded from the guarantee regulation in the current Italian CC of 1942 and included in the general provision on the assignment of assets[532] (art. 1197 par. 3 Italian CC: "In any case security furnished by a third person is not revived"[533]. The results are though the same as in Spain.

2. Extinction of the guarantee by release of the debtor (condonazione/ condonación)

a) In general

If the creditor releases the debtor from his debt by means of a valid and binding legal agreement, the principal obligation extinguishes and the gua-

---

[531] *Zuddas*, 6.

[532] This criterion was also followed in Portugal where the effects of the assignment of assets in the guarantee are included in art. 839 Portuguese CC and not in the guarantee regulation.

[533] Art. 1197 par. 3 Italian CC: "In ogni caso non rivivono le garanzie prestate dai terzi".

rantor is thereby also automatically discharged of his obligation[534]. This is explicitly provided for in the Italian and the Spanish civil codes. Art. 1238 juncto art. 1239 par. 1 Italian CC and art. 1190 Spanish CC establish that the "remission of the principal debt extinguishes the accessory obligations; but the remission of the accessory obligations does not affect the principal debt". These provisions are however superfluous since the same results occur by application of the general law of obligations and the ancillary nature of the guarantee.

b) Acceptance to be released

The guarantor's discharge is dependent on the factual extinction of the secured debt. This only takes place upon the creditor's declaration to release the debtor and the debtor's acceptance to be released. Therefore, if the debtor does not accept the offer to be released[535], the guarantor will not be discharged and the guarantee will not be extinguished[536].

The guarantor cannot be compelled to perform the guarantee until the debtor accepts or refuses the creditor's offer of release. This is the case even if the guarantee is actually not yet extinguished[537].

c) Partial release

If the creditor only releases the debtor from a part of the debt, the guarantee will be also reduced in the same quantity as the reduction that is performed on the debt. In the case of a co-guarantee, the liability of each co-guarantor will be proportionally reduced.

d) Pactum de non petendo

If the creditor renounces his right to sue the debtor but explicitly retains his right against the guarantor, then there is not a release of the debt but a pactum de non petendo in personam[538]. In this situation the debt has not been extinguished and the creditor therefore maintains his right against the guarantor. Accordingly, upon the performance of the guarantee the guaran-

[534] See *Luminoso*, 10; *Tilocca*, 412; *Allara*, 304 f.; *Giusti*, 257; *Guilarte*, 362; *Carrasco*, *Cordero* and *Marín*, 243.

[535] About the renounce to be release: *Di Prisco/Rescigno*, 297 ff (spec. 230).

[536] *Giusti*, 256. *Contra*: *Rescigno*, Studi sull'accollo, 1958, 118.

[537] *Perlinguieri/Scialoja/Branca*, 247 ff.

[538] Cass. 11 July 1942, no. 1962, FI, Rep., 1942, *voce Fideiussione*, 545; Cass.12 July 1958, BBTC, 1958, II, 333.

tor is subrogated into the rights of the creditor against the debtor and retains his right to sue the debtor for reimbursement[539].

3. Extinction of the guarantee by novation of the secured debt (novazione/novación)

When the secured obligation is extinguished by novation the guarantee is also extinguished. This natural consequence of the principle of co-extensiveness is implicitly established in art. 1207 Spanish CC: "when the principal obligation is extinguished by the effect of novation, accessory obligations can remain in effect only insofar as they benefit third parties who did not consent to the novation". In the Italian CC there are two similar provisions which relate to the contracts of pledge and mortgage (art. 1232 and art. 1233 Italian CC), but not to the guarantee. However, Italian writers agree that the guarantee is rendered extinct upon the novation of the secured debt unless the parties have reached a contrary agreement with regard to the effects of novation[540].

If the secured debt has been novated by a change of the parties; subjective novation (novaciones subjetivas), the guarantee is thereby also extinguished. This is considered to be the case unless the guarantor has consented to the novation (art. 1235 juncto 1275 Italian CC). If such consent is granted, it must be of an explicit nature[541].

4. Extinction of the guarantee by confusion between the creditor and the debtor

The convergence of the two parties of a contractual relationship into the same person is called confusion.

The secured debt is extinguished upon confusion of debtor and creditor; i.e. when the same person becomes the creditor and the debtor of the same debt (art. 1253 Italian CC and art. 1192 Spanish CC). The guarantee is thereby also extinguished[542]. This is a direct consequence of the principle of co-extensiveness and it is also specifically established in art. 1253 in fine Italian CC543 and art. 1193 sent. 1 Spanish CC544.

[539] *Rescigno/Bozzi*, 266; *Carrasco, Cordero* and *Marín*, 243; *Guilarte*, 362. See for Germany and mutatis mutandis *Horn/Staudinger*, on § 774 no. 49.

[540] *Giusti*, 255; *Salvestroni*, 96; *Buscisano*, 8.

[541] *Rescigno*, *voce* Debito, Nss.dig.it., 1960, 193.

[542] STS 4 May 2007 [RA 2007 no. 4327].

[543] Art. 1253 *in fine* Italian CC: "When the qualities of debtor and creditor are united in the same person the obligation is extinguished and third persons who have given a guarantee for the debtor are discharged".

[544] Art. 1193 sent. 1 Spanish CC: "The confusion falling on the person of the debtor or of the principal creditor benefits the guarantors".

In the case of a joint and several co-debt, the confusion of the creditor with one of the joint and several co-debtors results in the extinction of the whole debt (art. 1143 Spanish CC). The guarantors may set up all the debtor's defences against the creditor. Accordingly, all guarantors are discharged upon confusion of any of the co-debtors with the creditor. This is the case even if the guaranteed debtor was not the one affected in first place by the confusion.

5. Extinction of the guarantee by prescription

a) In general

The guarantee may be extinguished upon the prescription of the secured debt (i.e. prescription of the right to demand the performance of the debt). Moreover, a debt that has already prescribed cannot be guaranteed[545].

According to art. 1937 Spanish CC, the guarantor may set up the defence of prescription of the secured debt, even if the debtor has waived his right to set up this defence.

The dies a quo for the start of the period of prescription is that of the maturity of the secured obligation. It is considered to be irrelevant as to whether or not the respective obligations of creditor and guarantor were originally agreed upon different terms.

b) Interruption of prescription of the secured debt

The prescription of the secured debt is interrupted by a judicial demand for performance. Such a demand, which must be of a judicial nature, also interrupts the prescription of the guarantee[546]. This is explicitly regulated in art. 1975 Spanish CC[547]. According to this provision: a) if the prescription of the secured debt is interrupted "by judicial demand of the debt", the prescription of the guarantee is also automatically interrupted and b) if the prescription of the secured debt has been interrupted by "extra-judicial claims of the creditor or private acknowledgements of the debtor", the terms of the prescription of the guarantee are not interrupted thereby. The

[545] It has been discussed by Italian scholars (not in case law) whether a guarantee granted for a debt, which has already prescribed, should be considered valid. Some of them give a positive answer based on the difference between the moment of prescription and the moment the prescription is raised as defence by the debtor. Other scholars consider invalid the guarantee granted for a prescribed obligation, even if the defence has not been raised. See references in *Petti*, 225.

[546] *Petti*, 225.

[547] Art. 1975 Spanish CC: "The interruption of prescription against the principal debtor by judicial demand of the debt is also effective against the guarantor; however, the interruption arising from extra-judicial claims of the creditor or private acknowledgements of the debtor shall not prejudice the guarantor".

secured debt will thus remain as valid and enforceable for a longer period than the guarantee.

III. The extinction of the guarantee obligation: the direct causes of extinction

1. Payment by the guarantor

a) In general

As with any other obligation, the guarantee is extinguished upon the event of a valid and effective payment or performance by the guarantor. Such payment only serves to extinguish the guarantee. It does not affect the underlying obligation, first because the secured debt is not the ancillary obligation and also because if the debt would extinguish, the guarantor could not be subrogated into the creditor's right[548]. Hence, the secured debtor is not discharged by the payment of the guarantee obligation. He continues to be liable vis-à-vis the guarantor for the part of the debt he has performed and vis-à-vis the creditor for the rest.

b) Imputation of the payment

If there are debts that exist between the guarantor and the creditor other than that of the guarantee obligation then the eventual payment performed by the guarantor must be imputed to one of these debts. In this respect, the general provisions on the imputation of payment shall be applicable (art. 1193 par. 2 Italian CC and art. 1172-1174 Spanish CC). According to these provisions, unless the parties specifically determine the debt that has been actually performed, the payment shall be imputed to the most onerous debt between them. Presumably the guarantor will consider as most onerous debts those for which he is primarily liable and not only guarantor.

2 Alternative legal ways for the guarantor to perform (subrogados del pago/surrogati)

As in the case of any other legal obligation, the guarantee is extinguished by performance through any of the legal ways that are established in the law as valid alternatives to payment.

---

548 *Fragali/Scialoja/Branca*, 453. *Contra*: *Bo*, *voce* Fideiussione, 1130.

a) Tender and deposit (deposito/consignación) and assignment of assets (prestazione in luogo dell' adempimento/dación en pago)

If the creditor refuses to accept the payment, the guarantee may be extinguished by tender and deposit of the sum that is owed by the guarantor[549], in accordance with the general rules on tender and deposit (arts. 1210–1213 Italian CC and arts. 1176–1181 Spanish CC).

The guarantee obligation may also be performed by assignment of assets as ruled in art. 1197 Italian CC and art. 1175 Spanish CC.

b) Set-off (compenssazione/compensación)

aa) Set-off by the guarantor of his own claims

Where the payment of the guarantee obligation is effected by means of a set-off against the creditor's corresponding liability, the guarantor will be discharged. This does not present any problems within Italian law (arts. 1241–1252 Italian CC). However, in Spain such a discharge is conditional upon the fulfilment of the requirements that are established in art. 1196 Spanish CC. First the obligors need to be mutually, principally liable. The guarantor is not a principal but an ancillary debtor. However, the set-off is considered to be valid for the guarantee obligation for the following reasons: a) as the guarantor may set-off the debtor's claims against the creditor (art. 1197 Spanish CC), he should also be entitled to set-off his own claims against the same person i.e. the creditor; b) at the moment of payment of the guarantee, the guarantor acts as a principal debtor in relation to the creditor[550] and c) art. 1847 Spanish CC states that all causes of extinction that are established by the law for the common obligations are applicable to the guarantee, including the right to set-off.

Moreover, the Italian regulation on set-off, which is analogous to the Spanish one does not request that the parties of a set-off be principally liable. Art. 1196 Spanish CC should not be interpreted so literally as to consider this requirement as conditio sine qua non for the applicability of the guarantor's right to set-off in Spain and so exclude the set-off from the direct causes of extinction of the guarantee contract[551].

It can thus be concluded that the set-off may be applied to the guarantee, provided that the reciprocal debts between the guarantor and the creditor are due and enforceable.

---

[549] *Guilarte*, 352.
[550] *Guilarte*, 353.
[551] *Pérez Alvarez*, 217; *Guilarte*, 353 ff.

bb) Moment in which a set-off may be raised

The guarantor may affect a set-off when he has been required to perform payment[552].

Moreover, the guarantor is discharged if the creditor performs his claim vis-à-vis the debtor when he could have affected a set-off. He will also be discharged if the debtor and the creditor have agreed that the creditor will perform the claim that could have been set-off. In this case, the agreement must have taken place when the claims can effectively be set-off[553].

c) Release of the guarantor (condonazione/condonación)

aa) In general

The creditor, as direct beneficiary of the guarantee, always retains the power to unilaterally release the guarantor of his obligation[554]. The accord of the debtor is not necessary but in some cases the creditor and the debtor agree on the release granted in favour of the guarantor[555]. In any case, the guarantor does not participate in the decision but he merely needs to be informed[556].

The discharge of the guarantor by virtue of such a release does not affect the underlying obligation (art. 1238 Italian CC and art. 1190 Spanish CC). The principal debtor is still liable for the whole debt, also in the case the guarantor is only released for a part of the debt.

bb) Effects of the release in case of co-guarantee

The effects of the release of one co-guarantor vis-à-vis the other co-guarantors are specifically governed by art. 1239 par. 2 Italian CC[557] and art. 1850 Spanish CC[558]. According to these provisions the release of one

---

[552] *Fragali/Scialoja/Branca*, 456; *Guilarte*, 353; *Carrasco, Cordero and Marín*, 233.

[553] *Jimenez Mancha*, 576.

[554] *Guilarte*, 406 ff.

[555] App. Brescia 29 November 1962, BBTC, 1963, II, 62; *Moreti*, La fideiussione, 178 ff.; *Giusti*, 260.

[556] *Moretti/Nicita/Visalli*, 178.

[557] Art. 1239 par. 2 Italian CC: "The release granted to one of the sureties, does not discharge the rest but for the part of the discharged surety. (...)". ("La remissione accordata a uno dei fideiussori non libera gli altri che per la parte del fideiussore liberato. (...)").

[558] Art. 1850 Spanish CC: "The discharge of one of several guarantors by the creditor without the consent of the rest benefits all to the extent of the part of the guarantor discharged". ("La liberación hecha por el acreedor a uno de los fiadores sin el consentimiento de los otros, aprovecha a todos hasta donde alcance la parte del fiador a quien se ha otorgado").

guarantor benefits all the co-guarantors on a pro rata basis unless they have previously consented[559] to a variation[560].

These provisions only apply provided: a) it is a case of co-guarantee (as different to a plurality of independent guarantees). The guarantors must have agreed to act together to guarantee the same debt in relation to the same debtor. If the guarantees have been agreed as independent from each other, the release of one of the guarantors will not affect the position of the others[561]; and b) the co-guarantors have not consented. The co-guarantors only benefit from the release of one of them if they have not agreed. If all guarantors consent to the release of one of their number, then they all remain liable for the total debt (art. 1239 par. 2 in fine Italian CC[562] and art. 1859 Spanish CC[563]). The right of regress (regreso/regresso) among co-guarantors as set in art. 1954 Italian CC[564], is deemed to have been renounced if one of the co-sureties has consented to the release[565]. If some of the co-guarantors give their consent to the release, this provision will be applicable to them. Consequently, those guarantors who did not consent to the release of one co-guarantor are released from their obligation while those who consented are not benefited by the release.

No special form is required for the release. Thus an oral agreement would be binding but is not recommended due to the difficulties of proof.

---

559 Also according to Portuguese case law: RL Coimbra 28 February 1989, CJ XIV, I, 69. According to § 774 par. 2 *juncto* § 426 par. 1 German CC, the release of one co-guarantor follows the proportional release of his co-guarantors. See *Horn/Staudinger*, on § 774, no. 49.

560 In relation to this point the Spanish and the Italian regulation differ from the Austrian and the French regulation. According to art. 1285 and 1287 *juncto* 1288 French CC, the co-guarantors are either fully or partly discharged upon the release of one co-guarantor. Surprisingly, § 1363 sent. 3 Austrian CC sets up that any guarantor is affected by the release of any of his co-guarantors. Accordingly, the release of one co-guarantor is *de facto* a *pactum de non petendo* by the creditor. The released guarantor remains liable vis-à-vis his co-guarantors for reimbursement in case they perform.

561 *Guilarte*, 388.

562 Art. 1239 par. 2 *in fine* Italian CC: "If the other guarantors have consent the discharge, they remain obliged for the whole". („Tuttavia se gli altri fideiussori hanno consentito la liberazione, essi rimangono obbligati per l'intero").

563 Art. 1.850 Spanish CC: "The discharge of one of several guarantors by the creditor without the consent of the rest, (…)". ("La liberación hecha por el acreedor a uno de los fiadores sin el consentimiento de los otros (...)").

564 Art. 1954 Italian CC: "If more than one person has acted as guarantor for the same debtor and for the same debt, a guarantor who has paid has recourse against the co-guarantors for their respective shares". („Se più persone hanno prestato fideiussione per un medesimo debitore e per un medesimo debito, il fideiussore che ha pagato ha regresso contro gli altri fideiussori per la loro rispettiva porzione.(...)").

565 *Pellegrini/D'Amelio/Finzi*, 142 and *Perlingieri*, Manuale, 249.

(i) Controversy regarding art. 1850 Spanish CC

The deficient and unclear wording of art. 1850 Spanish CC has given rise to controversy. According to this provision, "the discharge of one of several guarantors by the creditor without the consent of the rest benefits all to the extent of the part of the guarantor discharged". This wording has been construed in two different ways. On one hand, it has been considered that when one co-guarantor is discharged, each one of the other co-guarantors is proportionally discharged in relation to the debt which has been released. All the co-guarantors thus share the benefits of the release.

However, it has also been considered that the benefit to which art. 1850 Spanish CC refers is that the discharge of one co-guarantor does not increase the liability of the other co-guarantors[566]. The release would thus result in the partial extinction of the guarantee. The proportional risk of insolvency with regard to each of the co-guarantors that is assumed by each one of the groups would decrease due to the reduction of the amount of the total guarantee.

If a creditor releases one of the co-guarantors, he probably wants to fully discharge him of his obligation. It is not the case that he only wants to affect a partial discharge, which would proportionally affect the other obligors. The creditor should have the freedom to release any of his co-guarantors to any extent that he deems to be desirable. The second construction of art. 1850 Spanish CC is therefore more appropriate in the light of the foregoing considerations. Moreover, this construction agrees with the tenor of Italian regulation on this matter. The wording of art. 1239 par. 2 Italian CC is more lucid on this point and does not give rise to the different constructions that are borne of the Spanish regulation. In contrast to Spanish law, the Italian regulation of this matter has been included among the general provisions on the law of obligations. It was removed from the guarantee regulation, in which it was accommodated under the former civil code. This is consistent with the systematic regulation on the extinction of the guarantee under the civil code of 1942, which is mainly regulated by the provisions on the extinction of general obligations.

3. Novation

The guarantee may be transformed into a new obligation (novation) and thereby extinguished. An example of this can be seen when the guarantor transforms a guarantee into a different security right (e.g. a real estate security interest). In this case the guarantee is extinguished and a new obli-

[566] *Perez Alvarez*, 230; *Guilarte*, Comentario, Ministerio de Justicia, 1993, 1847.

gation is created. However the co-guarantors are not thereby discharged[567] unless they are joint and severally liable[568].

4. Confusion

Confusion as a direct cause of the extinction of the guarantee may occur between the guarantor and the debtor or between the guarantor and the creditor.

a) Confusion between the guarantor and the debtor

In Italy a guarantee remains valid and is not extinguished upon the confusion between guarantor and debtor if it is the case that the creditor may have an interest in the continued existence of the guarantee (art. 1255 Italian CC[569]). By contrast, the possibility of confusion between the guarantor and the debtor is not included in the Spanish regulation of confusion. Art. 1192 and art. 1193 Spanish CC treat the case of confusion between the party who owes the performance of an obligation (posición deudora) and the party to whom that performance is owed (posición acreedora). But both the debtor and the guarantor are liable for the same obligation; both are "debiting parties". The case of the confusion of two debiting patrimonies is not specifically regulated within the Spanish CC. However the guarantee shall be considered extinguished upon the confusion of the guarantor and the debtor. Different reasons justify this statement: i) the extinction of the guarantee is a logical effect of the advent of confusion. If this is not the case then the same person would be rendered as being liable for the same debt by reason of two different obligations; ii) moreover, according to the general principles of the law of the guarantee, nobody can guarantee his own debt with a personal guarantee. This is exactly the scenario that would arise if there was a case of confusion between the guarantor and the debtor; iii) lastly, the extinction of the guarantee by the advent of confusion between debtor and guarantor has also been held to be implicitly contained in art. 1848 Spanish CC[570] (which is paralleled by art. 1926[571] of the former Italian CC of 1865 and art. 2034 French CC). These provisions refer to the

---

[567] *Guilarte*, 335.

[568] *Pérez Alvarez*, 199 and 209.

[569] Art. 1255 Italian CC: "If the qualities of guarantor and principal debtor are united in the same person, the guarantee remains in force if the creditor has an interest in its continuations". ("Se nella medesima persona si riuniscono le qualità di fideiussore e di debitore principale, la fideiussione resta in vita, purché il creditore vi abbia interese").

[570] *Guilarte*, 369.

[571] Art. 1926 former Italian CC: „La confusione che si effettua nella persona del debitore principale e del suo fideiussore, quando divengono eredi l'uno dell'altro, non estingue l'azione del creditore contro colui che ha fatto sicurità pel fideiussore".

case of confusion between debtor and guarantor, and establish that the sub-guarantee is thereby not extinguished. If the sub-guarantee is not extinguished, and no reference is made to the guarantee, it can be concluded that the latter has been extinguished as well[572].

However, there are important practical reasons that serve to justify the continued existence of the guarantee. Most of these reasons were considered by Italian scholars under the former CC and provided the reason for the introduction of art. 1255 in the present Italian CC.

Firstly, confusion renders the same person as being the guarantor and the debtor in relation to the same debt. However he might be liable by virtue of two different titles (the debt on the one hand and the guarantee on the other). Such duplication of title is only justified if there are practical reasons that make it convenient[573]. The creditor may have a substantial interest in retaining the title of the guarantee despite the confusion between the guarantor and the debtor[574]. This situation might arise if the guarantor has granted additional securities (real security interest). If the guarantee is extinguished upon the occurrence of confusion then all additional guarantees will be extinguished with it and the creditor will lose a supplementary right[575]. Another typical situation in which the duplication of title is convenient and beneficial for the creditor, is that which is present when the guaranteed debt is invalidated by reason of the lack of capacity of the debtor. The guarantee for such debt remains valid according to art. 1945 and art. 1939 Italian CC and art. 1824 par. 2 Spanish CC. The guarantor is not entitled to set up the defences that are available to the debtor. In this instance the creditor could chose to avail himself of the existing guarantee and avoid the eventual utilisation of defence ex parte debitoris[576].

In consequence of the consideration of these practical issues, the Italian legislator of the current civil code, introduced art. 1255 Italian CC[577/578].

---

[572] This would be in accordance with Roman law: Digest 46.3 93.2 and 46.3.95.2 and 3.

[573] *Fragali/Scialoja/Branca*, 457 ff ; *Delgado*, Elementos de derecho civil, 530; *Guilarte*, 370; *González Porrai*, 394 ff; *Abril Campoy*, 301; *Cicu*, 182 ff.: "Nulla vieta che la medesima persona sia obbligata per due diversi titoli ad una medesima prestazione, se una ragione giuridica essista per dare rilevanza a tale duplicità di titolo, e quindi se vi sia concreta utilità alla persistenza di essi".

[574] See *Sesta*, 2 f.

[575] This case was explicitly content in art. 1926 former Italian CC: "La confusione che si effettua nella persona del debitore principale e del suo fideiussore, quando divengono eredi l'uno dell'altro, non estingue l'azione del creditore contro colui che ha fatto sicurtà pel fideiussore". See *Ravazzoni*, La fideiussione, 45; *Rescigno/Bozzi*, 266.

[576] See *Sesta*, 2 ff.; *Giusti*, 259; *Campogrande*, 579; *Perlingieri/Sialoja/Branca*, 438; *Guilarte*, 371; *Carrasco, Cordero and Marín*, 237; *Pérez Alvarez*, 221.

[577] Art. 1255 Italian CC: "If the same person becomes surety and principal debtor of the same debt, the guarantee keeps alive, while the creditor may have an interest in it"

The rationale of this provision is to prevent the creditor from being the recipient of damages that are caused by reason of the confusion of the debtor with the guarantor. The creditor should have the same opportunity of obtaining performance before and after the confusion of those parties has taken place[579]. The practical importance of the regulation of this matter is manifest. The absence of such regulation in the Spanish CC is clearly disadvantageous. The introduction in the Spanish CC of a provision to facilitate the subsistence of the guarantee upon the confusion of the guarantor and the debtor should be encouraged.

b) Confusion between debtor and one of the joint and several co-guarantors

The confusion between the debtor and one of the joint and several co-guarantors does not affect the guarantee[580].

c) Confusion between the creditor and the guarantor

The guarantee is extinguished upon the event of confusion between creditor and guarantor. This conclusion can be directly deduced from the wording of art. 1253 Italian CC[581] and art. 1192 par. 1 Spanish CC[582]. These are general provisions that establish the extinction of any obligation upon the occurrence of confusion between debtor and creditor. The guarantor is also a debtor and one cannot be creditor for one's self, not even if the obligation is of an ancillary nature. The security function of the guarantee vanishes upon this confusion. Accordingly, the debtor may not set up any defenses against the creditor that the debtor may have raised against the guarantor after payment has been affected by the latter. The creditor will

---

("Se nella medesima persona si riuniscono le qualità di fideiussore e di debitore principale, la fideiussione resta in vita, purché il creditore vi abbia interesse").

[578] Also art. 509 par. 2 Swiss Code of Obligations. French and German CC do not have a specific provision on this matter but the legal solution given in the legal practice of these countries is coincident; the guarantee does not extinguish: *Simmler*, 593 and *Horn/Staudinger*, on §765, no. 224.

[579] *Perlingieri/Scialoja/Branca*, 438.

[580] *Carrasco, Cordero and Marín*, 237 f.

[581] Art.1253 Italian CC: "When the qualities of debtor and creditor are united in the same person teh obligatin is extinguisehd and third persons who have given a guarantee for the debtor are discahrged" ("Quando le qualità di creditore e di debitore si riuniscono nella stessa persona, l'obbligazione si estingue, e i terzi che hanno prestato garanzia per il debitore sono liberati".)

[582] Art. 1192 par. 1 Spanish CC: "The obligation shall be extinguished when the status of creditor and debtor are merged in the same person". ("Quedará extinguida la obligación desde que se reúnan en una misma persona los conceptos de acreedor y de deudor").

ask the debtor to accomplish performance in his capacity as a creditor and not as a guarantor who has affected performance and then asks for reimbursement[583]. However, if the guarantor has accomplished performance before the confusion has taken place, the guarantor/creditor has the right to seek reimbursement against the debtor[584].

d) Confusion between the creditor and one of the guarantors in the case of a plurality of independent guarantees

A debt may be secured by a plurality of guarantees, with each guarantee bing separately constituted in relation to the whole debt (the so called plurality of guarantees that exist independently from each other). In this situation the extinction of one guarantee by confusion between creditor and guarantor does not affect the other guarantees.

e) Confusion between the creditor and one of the co-guarantors

In the case of a co-guarantee there must be a distinction made as to whether or not the co-guarantors are joint and severally liable or severally liable i.e. mancomunidad.

aa) Co-guarantors that are separately liable (mancomunidad)

In a co-guarantee mancomunada (several liability), each co-guarantor is liable for his corresponding part of the debt and the creditor can only require that each guarantor affects performance with regard to his particular portion of the debt. In this situation a confusion between the creditor and one of the co-guarantors does not affect the other co-guarantors. The other co-guarantors remain liable for their corresponding part of the debt vis-à-vis the creditor (that is now the co-guarantor that has entered into confusion with the creditor) (art. 1194 Spanish CC)[585].

bb) Co-guarantors that are joint and severally liable (solidarietà/ solidaridad)

If the confusion occurs in relation to one of the joint and several co-guarantors (co-fianza solidaria), it is debatable whether the guarantee remains valid for the other co-guarantors, or if it is extinguished and all the co-guarantors are thereby discharged.

---

[583] See *Abril Campoy*, 282 ff.
[584] *Carrasco, Cordero* and *Marín*, 236.
[585] *Guilarte*, 366.

Some scholars[586] consider that the co-guarantee is extinguished by confusion between the creditor and one of the co-guarantors. This view is based on the Spanish regulation of the co-debt, which these writers apply to the co-guarantee. In contrast to other European regulations[587], Spanish law holds that the confusion between the creditor and one of the joint and several co-debtors serves to extinguish the whole debt (eficacia colectiva y no parcial/Gesammtwirkung der Konfussion) (art. 1143 Spanish CC). The application of this provision together with art. 1145 and art. 1146 Spanish CC allows concluding that the confusion between the creditor and one of the joint and several co-guarantors extinguishes the guarantee.

However, although certainly a number of similarities can be found between the co-guarantee and the co-debt, there are also differences. The guarantee is an ancillary obligation and not the principal one. It can thus be said that if a guarantee served to secure a principal debt, then there is no reason to hold that if one of the guarantors becomes a creditor then the guarantee is extinguished[588]. The obligation of the guarantor affected by the confusion is of course extinguished, but the debt will continue to exist after the confusion. The principal obligation remains valid and existent. All other co-guarantors have agreed to the guaranteeing of the debt and there is no reason for this protection not to continue.

An aspect which has not received any academic treatment is that of whether the remaining co-guarantors are held to be liable for the total amount of the guarantee or only for their corresponding part of the total amount. The confusion of creditor and guarantor is an accidental event for which none of the parties is responsible. It may benefit the guarantor concerned but it should not serve to damage all the other co-guarantors. Therefore, it is to be concluded that the guarantee remains valid but only in relation to the part which exists with regard to the co-guarantors that are not affected by the confusion. The same result is achieved by the analogous application of art. 1239 par. 2 Italian CC and art. 1850 Spanish CC. According to these provisions the discharge can be granted by the creditor to one of the co-guarantors. Such a discharge serves to benefit all the other

---

[586] *Caffarena Laporta*, 255; *Pérez Alvarez*, 220; *Abril Campoy*, 288; *Carrasco, Cordero* and *Marín*, 238. Contra: *Guilarte*, 366.

[587] § 425 par. 2 German CC as ammended by the reform of the law of obligation 26.11.2001 ("Einzelwirkung der Konfusion"): "(1) Andere als die in den §§ 422 bis 424 bezeichneten Tatsachen wirken, soweit sich nicht aus dem Schuldverhältnis ein anderes ergibt, nur für und gegen den Gesamtschuldner, in dessen Person sie eintreten. (2) Dies gilt insbesondere von der Kündigung, dem Verzug, dem Verschulden, von der Unmöglichkeit der Leistung in der Person eines Gesamtschuldners, von der Verjährung, deren Neubeginn, Hemmung und Ablaufhemmung, von der Vereinigung der Forderung mit der Schuld und von dem rechtskräftigen Urteil". See *Seiler/Erman*, on § 425, nos 1 ff.

[588] *Guilarte*, 366, 367.

co-guarantors by discharging them of liability in respect of the part that corresponds to the guarantor discharged.

If the co-guarantors were liable for different percentages of the total debt, each one remains liable for his corresponding portion.

cc) Confusion between co-guarantors

The confusion between two co-guarantors does not affect the guarantee. The guarantee remains valid. The co-guarantor that is affected by the confusion is liable for the two parts of the guarantee (or the sum of the percentages of liability assumed by both) vis-à-vis all other co-guarantors.

dd) Exception to the confusion

According to art. 1192 par. 2 Spanish CC[589], the confusion based on inheritance does not have any effect if the inheritor has accepted the inheritance "a beneficio de inventario"; i.e. the inheritor wishes to keep his patrimony separate from the patrimony he obtains by inheritance.

5. Prescription

As with any other obligation, the guarantee may be extinguished on the basis of prescription. The prescription of the guarantee does not necessarily concur with that of the debt. The terms of the prescription of the guarantee are not interrupted if the prescription of the debt has been interrupted by "non-judicial claims of the creditor or private acknowledgements of the debtor" (art. 1975 Spanish CC[590]). The principal debt will remain valid and enforceable for a longer period than the guarantee. This also holds true in the Italian context[591]. This rule aims to protect the guarantor from the possible effects of simulated non-judicial agreements between the debtor and the creditor, which would act to interrupt the prescription of the debt and, as a consequence, would also extend the guarantor's liability[592].

---

[589] Art. 1192 Spanish CC: "The obligation shall be extinguished when the status of creditor and debtor are merged in the same person. An exception is made in the case where confusion takes place by virtue of inheritance, where the inheritance is accepted under benefit of inventory". ("Quedará extinguida la obligación desde que se reúnan en una misma persona los conceptos de acreedor y de deudor. Se exceptúa el caso en que esta confusión tenga lugar en virtud de título de herencia, si ésta hubiese sido aceptada a beneficio de inventario").

[590] Art. 1975 Spanish CC: "The interruption of prescription against the principal debtor by judicial demand of the debt is also effective against the guarantor; however, the interrumption arising from extrajudicial claims of the creditor or private acknowledgments of the debtor shall not prefudice the guarantor".

[591] See *Petti*, 225.

[592] *Manresa*, 952 ff.

Some scholars have argued that it should also be possible to interrupt the prescription of the guarantee by means of the non-judicial claims of the creditor against the debtor, provided that the guarantor has been informed of such claims[593] but this approach plays against the rational of the rule and against the basic principle of the guarantor's protection. The guarantor may always extend the guarantee if he so wishes after extinction.

It has also been questioned whether the prescription of the guarantee should be interrupted by the non-judicial claims of the creditor against the guarantor or if it is necessary to initiate a judicial claim in order to affect such an interruption. The prescription of any obligation cannot be interrupted by claims which are not judicial (art. 1975 Spanish CC). Hence, only judicial claims may interrupt the prescription of the guarantee[594]. A number of scholars[595] lay more emphasis on the ratio of the rule, and consider it only applicable to principal debts. The prescription of the guarantee may therefore be interrupted by any kind of claim (i.e. extra-judicial or non-judicial claims).

IV. Special causes of extinction for the guarantee

1. Release of the guarantor by reason of the impossibility to subrogate caused by the creditor

a) In general

The guarantee is extinguished when the subrogation of the guarantor into the rights, pledges, mortgages and privileges of the creditor has become impossible due to the creditor's actions[596]. This is one of the causes of extinction that are specific to the guarantee and are therefore explicitly stated within the guarantee rules (art. 1955 Italian CC and art. 1852 Spanish CC[597]). These provisions contain the legal sanction for the case the creditor has adversely affected the right of subrogation that it is granted by the law to the guarantor in case of performance[598/599].

---

[593] *Díez-Picazo*, La prescripción, 1964, 150.

[594] *Guilarte*, 355 ff; *Santamaría,* Comentarios al código civil, II, 1958, 1030.

[595] *Pérez Alvarez*, 273, no. 434; *Carrasco, Cordero* and *Marín*, 245.

[596] See: *Fínez Ratón*, La extinción, 9 ff.

[597] Both provisions derive directly from art. 2037 French CC: „La caution est déchargée, lorsque la subrogation aux droits, hypothèques et privilèges du créancier, ne peut plus, par le fait de ce créancier, s'opérer en faveur de la caution. Toute clause contraire est réputée non écrite". Other neighbouring countries have similar provisions: art. 653 Portuguese CC; §776 German CC. About the differences between the civil laws see: *Bozzi*, La fideiussione, 267; *Simler*, no. 593 ff; *Mouly*, 490 ff; *Horn*, Bürgschaft, on §776.

[598] Art. 1945 Italian CC and art. 1839 Spanish CC. *Ravazzoni*, Le garanzie, 89.

[599] In Italy and Spain the sanction for the behaviour of the creditor is the automatic discharge of the guarantor. This is so in most neighbouring countries (for instance:

The performing guarantor should enjoy the same legal protection as the creditor against the debtor[600]. If the guarantor looses part of his rights by virtue of actions taken by the creditor, the guarantor shall be discharged because the conditions under which the guarantee was granted have been changed to his detriment.

b) Requirements for release: a harmful act of behaviour on the part of the creditor

aa) In general

The discharge of the guarantor in the case we are treating is based on a particular behaviour on the part of the creditor that serves to damage the rights of the guarantor. In Spain the behaviour of the creditor does not need to be a culpable or an illicit act. It may be a mistake (error excusable) or a legitimate act or omission that results in the guarantor losing his right to be subrogated into the rights of the creditor (like the postponing of a mortgage)[601]. In Italy there is a certain level of controversy with respect to the qualification of the creditor's behaviour. According to some Italian case law it must be of a culpable character-fault (culposo) or be that of an illicit act[602] and render impossible for the guarantor to be subrogated into the rights of the creditor. However, academic opinion holds that it is not

---

France: Belgium and Luxemburg, art. 2037 CC; Germany: §776 CC; Greece: art. 863 CC; Portugal: art. 653 CC; England: Andrews and Millet, no. 9. 40 ff). However, other countries also sanction the lost of the right of subrogation of the guarantor by reason of the creditor's acts or omissions, but with a claim for damages instead of with discharge (Austria: § 1364 par. 2 CC; The Netherlands: art. 7:850 par. 3 *juncto* art. 6: 12 and art. 6:154 CC).

[600] Cass. 26 April 1937, no. 1318, Riv. Dir. Priv. 1937, II, 141 as to art. 1928 former Italian CC of 1865; *Giusti*, 261.

[601] *Carrasco, Cordero* and *Marín*, 199. See: STS 7 October 1933 [RA 1993 no. 322] and STS 9 October 1962 [RA 1962 no. 3631]. Other examples of discharge of the guarantor by an act of the creditor which damages his rights to recover: the creditor consents the cancellation of a mortgage (SAP Asturias, 8 November 2000 [AC 2000 no. 301]; the creditor consents the cancellation of the attachment (STS 30 December 1988 [RA 1988 no. 10075]; SAP Las Palmas 26 September 1998 [AC 1998 no. 1864]); the creditor looses or gives back an asset given as pledge or over which a reservation of title has been agreed (STS 9 July 1908, RGLJ, t. 111, no.125 cited by *Carrasco, Cordero* and *Marín*, 196); the creditor does not make use of the reservation of title (STS 1 March 1983 [RA 1983 no. 1412]; the creditor looses his rights in the bankruptcy (STS 1 July 1988 [RA 1988 no. 5551]; SAP La Coruña 22 May 1996, [AC 1996 no.1939].

[602] "Il fatto del creditore deve consistere in un fatto quanto meno colposo o comunque illecito" (Cass. 11 April 1997, no. 3161, GC, 1997, I, 2441); Cass. 7 January 1982 no. 63, FI, Mass. 1982, 17) *Calderale*, 76.

necessary for such behaviour to be qualified as a fault[603] and the mere connection between the cause and the effect is enough to justify the guarantor's discharge. Hence, in both Italy and Spain there must be a causal link (nesso causale/nexo causal) between the behaviour of the creditor (cause) and the loss of the right to be subrogated that is suffered by the guarantor (effect)[604].

bb) The act of the creditor: active and passive

Both the Italian and the Spanish civil codes use the word "act" in order to refer to the behaviour of the creditor that limits the guarantor's right to subrogation. Such term must be understood as describing both the acts and omissions that can be imputed to the creditor[605].

An omission has occurred when there has been a failure to fulfil a duty to perform a certain act of behaviour in order to maintain the validity of the right of subrogation of the guarantor[606]. These "duties" of the creditor are not legal obligations but general duties derived from the application of the principle of good faith[607]. For instance, the creditor should effect a timely registration of the mortgage in order to maintain its validity. However, the creditor also has the right to try to protect his own interests (reduce his costs). Thus the creditor does not need to request the debtor to provide payment only in order to protect the guarantor[608]. He may refuse partial payment and is not obliged to acquire supplementary securities in order to create a benefit for the guarantor[609]. The creditor is not even obliged to accept securities for the debt after the guarantee has been already

---

[603] *Villani*, 309 ff; spec. 311 cited by *Giusti*, 262; *Fragalli*, Fideiussione – Mandato di credito, on art. 1955–57, 472.

[604] Cass. 28 July 1965, no. 1812, GC, 1966, I, 1180; Cass. 25 February 1969, no. 619, FI., Rep. 1969, voce Fideiussione e mandato di credito, no. 22; Cass. 28 July 1965, no. 1812, GC, 1966, I, 1180; Cass. 28 September 1971, no. 2659, FI, Rep. 1971, *voce Fideiussione e mandato di credito*, no. 28; Trib. Milano, 18 January 1988, BBTC, 1989, II, 183; Cass. 20 April 1982, no. 2461, GI, 1983, I, 1, 1316.

[605] In Germany, by contrast, it is generally considered that neither omissions nor the negligence of the creditor are sanctioned in §776 German CC. Only willful acts shall be considered sanctioned. See: BGH 15 July 1999, NJW 1999, 3195, 3197; Münchener Kommentar/Habersack, on § 776, no. 8; *Contra*: *Horn/Staudinger*, on § 776, no. 12.

[606] Cass. 16 March 1995, no. 3080, FI, Rep. 1995, *voce Fideiussione e mandato di credito*, no. 43; Cass. 27 March 1990, no. 2472, BBTC, 1991, II, 350. See: STS 7 October 1933 [RA 1933 no. 322] and STS 9 October 1962 [RA 1962 no. 3631].

[607] *Carrasco, Cordero* and *Marín*, 199.

[608] Cass. 28 July 1965, no. 1812, GC, 1966, I, 1180.

[609] Cass. 22 December, 1939, FI, 1940, I, 559 (regarding art. 1928 former Italian CC of 1865 parallel to art. 1955 Italian CC); *Fragali/Scialoja/Branca*, 469.

granted[610]. Hence he does not need to register a mortgage that is granted after the guarantee has been constituted[611]. Furthermore, the guarantor is not discharged if the creditor omitted to require a legal measure to secure an attachment[612], or if he omitted to inform the guarantor of the execution of a mortgage[613].

cc) Damaging effect: loss of the right to subrogate

The guarantor will only be discharged provided the creditor has caused a loss of the guarantor's right to be subrogated into the pledges, mortgages, privileges and rights of the creditor that already existed at the moment the guarantee was granted[614/615].

The impossibility to subrogate must have caused an effective damage to the guarantor[616]. Accordingly, if the debt was secured with a supplementary security and the creditor substitutes such a security with a different one, the guarantor is not released unless it is proved that his potential to recover payment has been diminished[617]. He will neither be released if a deposit of money that was constituted to secure the debt has been substituted by a mortgage[618], nor when a procedural advantage is lost (acción procesal privilegiada cambiaria o ejecutiva) but the right may still be enforced by means of a different procedure[619].

---

[610] It is generally considered in case law that the creditor only affects negatively the guarantor in the sense of art. 1955 Italian CC if his behaviour affects the security interest existing previously to the guarantee and not to those constituted afterwards; Trib. Napoli, 22 November 1975, FI, Rep. 1975, voce Fideiussione e mandato di credito, no. 24.

[611] Trib. Napoli, 22 November 1975, FI, Rep. 1975, voce Fideiussione e mandato di credito, no. 24; Cass. 24 December 1992, no. 13661, Vita not., 1993, 769; Cass. 10 February 1977 no. 595; Cass. 2 May 1980 no. 2899 cited by *Giusti*, 265.

[612] STS 7 October 1933 [RA 1933 no. 322].

[613] STS 20 October 1993 [RA 1993 no. 7753].

[614] See: *Calderale*, 75.

[615] By contrast, in Germany those rights that are agreed after the grant of the guarantee are also comprised in the subrogation package (§776 German CC).

[616] The guarantor cannot be discharged if he did not suffer any damage: STS 22 November 1916, RGLJ, t. 138, no. 119. In the decision SAP Asturias 8 November 2000 [AC 2000 no. 301], the guarantor was considered damaged because a van over which a chattel mortgage had been granted, was sold privately and not by judicial procedure. This decision must be critised since the procedure of the sale did not affect the value of sale for the van. (Also in this sense: *Carrasco, Cordero* and *Marín*, 203).

[617] Damage is not caused in the sense of the provision if the recovery of the performed payment has become more difficult but only if it is effectively lost: Cass. 11 April 1997, no. 3161, GC, 1997, I, 2441; Cass. 20 Augost 1992, no. 9719, FI, 1993, I, 2171.

[618] *Fragali/Scialoja/Branca*, 471.

[619] STS 22 November 1916 RGLJ, t. 138, no. 84 cited by *Carrasco, Cordero* and *Marín*, 196.

The damage that is caused to the guarantor by the actions of the creditor has been defined by Italian judges as “legal damage”. It is therefore not deemed to be mere “economic” damage. Thus the damage is caused by the loss of the right itself and not by the increased difficulty to obtain the payment due to the debtor’s decreased patrimony[620]. Hence, the guarantor is not discharged by virtue of art. 1955 Italian CC (or 1852 Spanish CC) if the creditor is secured by means of a joint and several guarantee and he has not already requested payment from the debtor or the co-guarantors[621]. Furthermore, the guarantor will not be discharged if the solvency of the debtor has only decreased because the debtor entered into new business arrangements with the creditor[622], or if the different creditors of the debtor have informally agreed how they will share the debtor’s assets[623].

If the potential for the guarantor to be subrogated into the rights of the creditor upon performance is only diminished to a partial extent, the guarantor will only be discharged with respect to that particular part. The guarantor must suffer de facto that partial damage. This is the case if an act of the creditor caused one of the supplementary securities to be lost. The guarantor will only be discharged in relation to the part of the guarantee that was covered by this security, and only if the debtor is insolvent or will not be able to pay the guarantor back in the event of performance.

c) Behaviour of the guarantor

Spanish case law[624] states that the guarantor cannot rely on the defence of art. 1852 Spanish CC (art. 1955 Italian CC) if he could have avoided the loss of the rights. He has the duty to avoid or minimise the damages by doing what would be considered reasonable in this respect. For example if the guarantor could have avoided the loss of the rights by doing what the creditor has failed to do[625] or by other normal means[626].

---

[620] “che il creditore abbia, con il suo comportamento causato al garante un pregiudizio giuridico e non soltanto economico, vale a dire la perdita del diritto di surrogazione ex art. 1949 o di regresso ex art. 1950, ovvero che il creditore abbia omesso l’esplicazione di un’attività che la legge o il contratto impongano al fine specifico di rendere giuridicamente possibile la surrogazione” (Cass. 8 June 1976, no. 2090, FI, 1977, I, c. 154); Cass. 20 August 1992, no. 9719 FI 1993, I, c. 2173; Cass. 2 February 1998, no. 1024, FI., Rep. 1998, voce Titoli di credito, no. 38; Cass. 14 August 1997, no. 7603, Fallimento, 1998, 381; Cass. 5 March 1999 no. 1870 cited by *Petti*, 201. See *Trabucchi/ Cian*, on 1955, 2248 f.

[621] Cass. 29 February 1960 no. 380, GI 1961, I, 1, 218.

[622] STS 14 February 1978 [RA 1978 no. 296].

[623] STS 31 March 1927, RGLJ, t. 174 núm. 109.

[624] STS 1 March 1983 [RA 1983 no. 1412]; STS 20 June 1989 [RA 1989 no. 4710].

[625] STS 22 November 1916, RGLJ, t.138, no. 84.

[626] STS 1 March 1983 [RA 1983 no. 1412].

This Spanish case law has so modified the principle of favour fideiussoris without any real justification. The guarantor's position is already significantly disadvantageous. He should not be expected to be alert and proactive with regard to the protection of his right to be discharged in this case. Art. 1852 Spanish CC should be literally applied[627]. The guarantor must be discharged simply upon the loss of the right to recover payment if this loss is caused by the behaviour of the creditor and if such behaviour is contrary to the principle of good faith.

d) Waiver by the guarantor of his right to be discharged

There is no provision in either Italy or Spain that serves to prohibit the waiver by the guarantor of the rights that are set in art. 1955 Italian CC and 1852 Spanish CC[628]. Therefore the guarantor may renounce the protection that is provided by law[629]. Such a waiver may be tacit if the guarantor does not raise the defence at the moment he is requested to perform[630] but it may be invalid if it serves to justify an action on the part of the creditor that is contrary to the mandatory principle of good faith[631].

Such a waiver does not extend to include third parties such as the sub-guarantor. Hence the sub-guarantor may set up the defence even if the guarantor has renounced his right[632].

A further limit on the right of renunciation has been included in the Dutch CC in order to protect consumer guarantors. According to art. 7:862 lit. b CC, consumer (non-professional) guarantors may not renounce this right (art. 6:154 Dutch CC). Non-professional guarantors very often sign contracts without having a full understanding of their meaning and implications. A waiver of this protective right is damaging to the non-professional who should be legally protected from injurious clauses inserted by the stronger party to the contract. This Dutch provision is therefore positive and is in conformity with the recent European policy trend to enlarge consumer protection.

---

[627] *Guilarte*, 407 ff; *Carrasco, Cordero* and *Marín*, 204; *Alonso Sánchez*, 158 f.

[628] By contrast, in France any derogation of art. 2037 must be considered as not taken by the parties (art. 2037 par. 2 as introduced by art. 49 loi no. 84–148 du 1 mars 1984.

[629] Cass. 18 October 1960 no. 2811, GI, 1962, I, 1, 260 considered valid a clause of renounce to the right of discharge according to art. 1955 Italian CC. *Calderale*, 77. Also in Germany: BGH 24 September 1980, NJW, 1981, 748. *See*: *Horn/Staudinger*, on §776, no.20 and 21.

[630] Cass. 18 October 1960, no. 2811, BBTC, 1961, II, 186.

[631] In Germany: BGH, 17 December 1980, NJW 1981, 756.

[632] *Fínez Ratón*, La extinción, 54.

2. *Extinction of the guarantee for future debts*

a) In general

According to art. 1956 Italian CC, the guarantee for future obligations is extinguished if the creditor, without special authorization from the guarantor, has extended credit to the third party whilst knowing that the debtor's financial conditions have become such as to make satisfaction of the claim considerably more difficult.

This provision protects the guarantor, who has entered into a guarantee for future obligations. He granted the guarantee on the basis of the circumstances of the parties at the moment of the agreement. From that moment until the extension of the guarantee, the financial situation of the debtor may deteriorate in a way that the guarantor would not have granted a security under such conditions. However, the creditor may extend the provision of credit to an even greater degree, irrespective of the new circumstances, and the guarantee will cover that extension. In order to prevent the guarantor from being treated unfairly art. 1956 Italian CC provides for the extinction of the guarantee if the creditor was aware of the deterioration that has occurred in relation to the debtor but has elected to grant further credit without an express authorisation from the guarantor[633].

The rule contained within art. 1956 Italian CC sets a limit to the discretion of the creditor with regard to his right to unilaterally extend the liability of the guarantor. It is applicable if such an extension may serve to damage the guarantor[634].

This protective provision is grounded on the creditor's duty to behave in accordance with the principle of good faith[635]. As a consequence, a bank will be breaching this principle also if it extends credit to the debtor exclusively on the basis of an existing general guarantee covering the client's liabilities[636]. The bank does not valued the credit in the objective manner

---

[633] Trib. Milano 20 April 1995, BBTC, 1996, 332: La norma "è giustificata dall'esigenza di tutelare il fideiussore di obbligazioni future contro un obiettiva modificazione a posteriori del peso degli impegni assunti".

[634] Cass. 9 December 1997 no. 12456, GI, 1998, I, 1, 11: "la normative assolve la finalità di consentire al fideiussore di sottrarsi, negando l'autorizzazione, all'adempimento di un'obbligazione divenuta, senza sua colpa più gravosa".

[635] Cass. 1 July 1998 no. 6414, FI, Rep. 1998, voce Fideiussione e mandato di credito, no. 32: "…un comportamento contrario a la buona fede, sanzionato con l'inefficacia della garanzia fideiussoria"; Cass. 13 June 1967 no. 1320, GI, 1968, I, 1, 332; *Calderale*, 83; *Stolfi*, In tema di fideiussione generale, Riv. Dir. Civ., 1972, I, 529 ff.; Ravazzoni, La fideiussione generale, 275 ff.

[636] Cass. 23 September 1966 no. 2386, FI 1966, I, 1660.

which would have been the case if the guarantee had not been secured. The consequence of this lack of good faith is the guarantor's discharge[637].

b) Requirements for the application of art. 1956 Italian CC

The application of art. 1956 Italian CC depends on a particular variety of circumstances: i) the creditor extends credit to the debtor and this credit is secured by the guarantor; ii) the financial situation of the debtor has become such as to render it difficult for the debt to be performed and iii) the creditor must be aware of the deterioration in the financial situation of the debtor at the moment credit is extended.

i) The creditor extends credit.

The creditor must decide to grant the credit. The debts derived from moratory interests are not considered to form an extension of credit in the sense of art. 1956 Italian CC[638].

ii) The financial situation of the debtor has become such as to make it difficult for the debt to be performed.

The courts must evaluate on a case-by-case basis whether or not the changes in the patrimony of the debtor are enough to consider art. 1956 Italian CC to be applicable[639]. It is difficult to determine the precise circumstances that allow to consider the debtor is under "financial difficulties". This is a general notion that cannot be identified with the insolvency of the debtor and depends very much on the precise circumstances of each case. For instance, if the guarantor underestimated the risk involved in the guarantee, the creditor is not required to assume this risk a posteriori[640]. If the diminished financial prosperity of the debtor was only provisional and had improved by the time the creditor extended the credit, art. 1957 Italian CC would neither be applied[641].

---

637 Cass. 1 July 1998 no. 6414, FI, Rep. 1998, voce Fideiussione e mandato di credito, no. 32.

638 Trib. Brescia, 8 November 1967, Corti Brescia, Venezia, Trieste, 1968, 594.

639 *Aru/D'Amelio/Finzi*, 337; *Falaschi*, 187.

640 Cass. 9 April 1990 no. 2965, GC, 1990, I, 2359, and GI, 1991, I, 1, 322; Cass. 30 June 1959, no. 2035, GC, 1959, I, 1178; *D'Amelio e Finzi/Aru*, 425.

641 Cass. 2 December 1992 no. 12862, FI, Rep. 1992, voce Fideiussione e mandato di credito, no. 51.

iii) The creditor is aware of the financial deterioration of the debtor's position.

Art. 1956 Italian CC is only applicable if the creditor was really acquainted with the new situation ("conoscenza")[642] by employing a normal degree of diligence[643] i.e. the creditor does not need to have acted with dolus. This condition is considered indispensable in Italian case law[644].

The guarantor will not be discharged if the creditor was not aware of the changes that had occurred in the financial situation of the debtor or if the debtor was already in a difficult financial situation before the guarantee was granted but nobody gained notice of this until after the grant had been effected.

It has been established by Italian case law that two basic criteria must be applied in order to determine whether or not the creditor was apprised of the reduced financial circumstances of the debtor at the moment of the extension of the credit. First, there must be a comparison of the debtor's solvency at the moment at which the guarantor granted security and the moment at which the credit was extended. Second, the solvability of the debtor at the moment of granting must be valued by giving consideration to all factors which may have a bearing on this matter[645].

After the evaluation of these various aspects it must be clear that there has been an objective deterioration of the debtor's solvability and that this was apprehended by the creditor. Suppositions, suspicions or deductions are not enough to satisfy this requirement[646]. If these two factors are not evident, then art. 1956 Italian CC cannot be applied[647]. Moreover, the guarantor bears the burden of proving that the rule was violated by the creditor[648].

c) Authorisation by the guarantor to the creditor to grant credit despite the financial difficulties of the debtor

If the creditor wants to grant further credit to a debtor who is undergoing financial difficulties, the creditor may ask the guarantor for a "special au-

---

642 *Ravazzoni*, Le garanzie dell'obbligazione, 144.

643 Cass. 2 December 1992 no. 12862, FI, Rep. 1992, *voce* Fideiussione e mandato di credito, no. 51.

644 Cass. 2 December 1992 no. 12862, FI, Rep. 1992, *voce* Fideiussione e mandato di credito, no. 51.

645 Trib. Napoli, 21 January 1974, BBTC, 1976, II, 363.

646 *Ravazzoni*, Le garanzie dell'obbligazione, 144.

647 Trib. Milano, 20 April, 1995, BBTC, 1996, 332: "risulti un obiettivo deterioramento delle condizioni di solvibilità del debitore".

648 Cass. 28 July 1997 no. 7050, FI, Rep. 1997, *voce* Fideiussione e mandato di credito, no. 47.

thorisation". The guarantor's authorisation must be a precise declaration of the extent of the new credit in relation to the actual diminished patrimonial situation of the debtor. It must be clear that the guarantor is freely agreeing to provide security under the difficult financial circumstances which are faced by the debtor. Therefore it cannot be a general authorisation to facilitate any grant of future credit but rather an explicit and specific declaration of extent[649]. The exact amount of new credit and the new economic circumstances which pertain to the situation must be mentioned. Thus it must be made clear that the guarantor is willing to assume this supplementary risk. The authorisation must therefore be given ex informata ratione. It will not be valid if it is based on an answer to a request from the creditor in which the exact circumstances of the case are not explicitly stipulated[650].

If after an authorisation has been made for the granting of new credit, the debtor's financial situation becomes even worse or the creditor wants to grant further new credit, a new authorisation must be given. Otherwise the guarantor will be discharged in relation to this further credit.

d) Waive by the guarantor of the right granted in art. 1956 Italian CC

The guarantor may not waive his right to be discharged (art. 1956 par. 2 Italian CC[651]). This rule was introduced in 1992[652] to convert art. 1956 into a mandatory provision. Until that moment, the guarantor could renounce this right. The general terms and conditions of the contract for the guarantee for future debts (especially for the general guarantee (omnibus)) included a clause discharging the bank of the duty of requiring the guarantor for special authorisation to enable the further extension of credit[653]. This clause was admitted within the context of Italian case law[654] provided the creditor behaves in accordance with the principles of correctness and good faith (according to art. 1175 and art. 1375 Italian CC)[655]. The creditor

[649] *Falaschi*, 187; *Giusti*, 274.

[650] *Agostino*, 334.

[651] Art. 1956 par. 2 Italian CC: "It is not valid for the guarantor to effect a prior renunciation of his right to be discharged".

[652] The rule was introduced by art. 10 of the law 17 February 1992 no. 154.

[653] Such clause was also included in the formular of the Italian Banking Association (ABI) for general guarantees (*fideiussione omnibus*) (art. 5 dello schema-tipo dell'ABI relativo alle fideiussioni omnibus).

[654] See *Petti*, 204–206 for a long explanation of the reasoning of Italian case law to justify the validity of a derogation of the provision.

[655] See Cass. 28 July 1999, no. 8176, FI, Rep. 1999, *voce Fideiussione e mandato di credito,* no. 32; Cass. 14 Augost 1997, no. 7603, FI, Rep. 1997, *voce Fideiussione e mandato di credito*, no. 32; Cass. 29 August 1995, no. 9099, BBTC, 1996, II, 596; Cass. 3 March 1994, no. 2115, FI, Rep. 1994, *voce Fideiussione e mandato di credito*, no. 29;

could thus not abuse the clause of renunciation. If the clause had been included in the contract, the creditor did not need the special authorisation of the guarantor in order to grant credit, yet the creditor did have to inform the guarantor of the new circumstances. If the clause of renunciation was abused the guarantor could set up the defence of bad faith (exceptio doli generalis). This is the way in which Italian case law tried to reconcile the needs of commercial practice with the need for honest transactional relations[656]. However, scholars generally considered such clauses unfair vis-à-vis the guarantor and they advocated that they should be banned[657]. This criterion followed the new European trend to grant consumers a higher level of protection. Par. 2 of art. 1956 Italian CC was enacted as a consequence of the adoption of the new European conception of public economic order in Italy[658].

e) The principle of good faith in the guarantee for future obligations under Spanish Law

The Spanish CC does not contain any special rule in line with art. 1956 Italian CC. This absence is mirrored in the German and the French legal systems and within all other regulations of the guarantee within the EU. However similar results are derived from the application of the principle of good faith in these other European contexts (art. 7 Spanish CC; § 242 German CC[659]).

In Spain the creditor does not have a general duty to provide information to the guarantor about the financial situation of the debtor[660]. However, according to the principle of good faith, the creditor has a duty to provide information to the guarantor in specific instances. Firstly, if the guarantor requires information about the debtor which may be easily obtained by the creditor without incurring any further cost and which cannot be easily obtained by the guarantor himself. Secondly, in the case of a general guarantee (omnibus) if the creditor is deciding whether or not to grant further credit and the creditor presumes that the guarantor would not have provided a guarantee under the new circumstances. It should be recognised that these new circumstances can be of a personal (i.e. if he knows that the

---

Cass. 20 July 1989, nos. 3385 and 3386, FI, 1989, I, 3102. See a critical analysis of the case law: *Mariconda*, 3102 ff.; *Cantillo/Munari*, 62 ff.

[656] *Benfatti/Munari*, 115. See also, *Costanza*, 221 ff.

[657] *Simonetto*, La fideiussione prestata da privati, 101 ff.

[658] See *Petti*, 205 ff.

[659] In Germany, if the debtor's financial situation has gravely worsened, it is considered a serious reason as to discharge the guarantor for future debts (BGH 21 January 1993, NJW – RR 1993, 944, 945).

[660] STS 20 October 1993 [RA 1993 no. 7753].

relationship between the parties has changed; like in the case of divorce) or financial nature[661].

In Germany there is no general duty to provide information about the financial situation of the debtor. Information must only be presented in exceptional circumstances on the basis of the principle of bona fides (§ 242) and provided that the guarantor suffers an extreme injury[662]. Moreover, § 610 is applied by analogy and allows for the discharge of the guarantor if the creditor granted further credit without regard to the fact that he was aware of the new financial difficulties of the debtor[663].

In France the creditor is liable for the damage that is suffered by the guarantor if the credit was granted fraudulently. The guarantee is extinguished by a set-off against the damages[664]. Moreover, France has included a provision in favour of the consumer guarantor who grants a guarantee without stipulating a time limit. These guarantors have the right to be annually informed about the financial situation of the debtor (art. 2016 French CC; art. 47 par. 2 sent. 2 Madelin Act).

3. Extinction of the guarantee by reason of time. Discharge of the guarantor after maturity of the underlying obligation (scadenza dell'obbligazione garantita ed inerzia del creditore)

a) In general

The creditor is free to require the debtor for performance at any time from the maturity of the debt until it has prescribed. The guarantor does not have any influence on this decision although he is directly affected by it. Between the time of the maturity of the debt and the time of the demand for performance, the potential for the debtor to effect payment may have considerably increased or be reduced. As a result it is difficult to determine whether or not a passive attitude of the creditor with regard to the demand for payment is positive or negative for the guarantor. In any case the mere uncertainty regarding the performance may be considered negative enough for the guarantor, especially if it is extended over an excessively long period. On this basis, art. 1957[665] was introduced in the Italian CC of 1942.

---

[661] *Carrasco*, *Cordero* and *Marín*, 108 and 163.

[662] OLG Köln 7 February 1995, WM 1996, 1965; OLG Bamberg 13 December 1999, WM 2000, 1582.

[663] BGH 6 December 1984, WM, 1985, 155.

[664] Cass.comm. 24 May 1976, Bull. Civ. 1976, IV, no. 171. *Mouly*, Les causes, 471.

[665] Art. 1957 Italian CC: "The liability of a guarantor remains in effect even after the primari obligation has matured, provided that the creditor, within six months, has instituted an action against the debtor and has diligently pursued it. This provision applies even if the guarantor has expressly limited his guarantee to the same period as that of the primary obligation. In such case, however, the action against the debtor shall be insti-

This rule sets a new cause of extinction in order to prevent there from being an excessively long period of uncertainty for the guarantor in relation to his liability due to the creditor holding a passive attitude with regard to the demand for payment of the debt[666]. The inactivity of the creditor with regard to the recovery of the claim during a period of six months after maturity of the debt, is sanctioned with the extinction of the guarantee. If the guarantor had limited his liability to the same period as that of the secured debt, the guarantee extinguishes if the creditor did not take action against the debtor within two months.[667]

In contrast, Spain has no provision to establish time limits for the validity of the guarantee. The parties may agree to a time limit in the contract but there are no legal limits to the length of time for validity. This lack of specific regulation must receive some criticism. The guarantor remains liable until the creditor requires that the debtor should effect performance. During that period the guarantor suffers a degree of uncertainty with regard to his duty to perform, which is unnecessarily harmful. Moreover, the creditor is not rendered as being in a less secure position if the validity of the guarantee is legally limited by a reasonable time constraint.

b) The extinction of a guarantee agreed without time limit

aa) In general

In Italy a guarantee that is agreed without a time limit is extinguished within six months after the underlying obligation has matured. This is the legal position unless the creditor has instituted an action against the debtor and has diligently pursued it (art. 1957 par. 1 Italian CC[668]).

Italy is the only country within the EU that has placed a general legal limitation on the extension of a guarantee that is agreed without a time limit. Some countries have established legal limits for global guarantees or for guarantees for future debts without time limit, but there is not a general

---

tuted within two months. The action instituted against the debtor also interrupts prescription with respect to the guarantor". ("Il fideiussore rimane obbligato anche dopo la scadenza dell'obbligazione principale, purché il creditore entro sei mesi abbia proposto le sue istanze contro il debitore e le abbia con diligenza continuate. La disposizione si applica anche al caso in cui il fideiussore ha espressamente limitato la sua fideiussione allo stesso termine dell'obbligazione principale. In questo caso però l'istanza contro il debitore deve essere proposta entro due mesi. L'istanza proposta contro il debitore interrompe la prescrizione anche nei confronti del fideiussore").

[666] *Bozzi/Rescigno*, La fideiussione, le figure affini, 209.

[667] Art. 866 Greek CC also establishes a combined system of time limits and diligence of the creditor in the requirement for performance. The creditor has to take legal action and pursue it diligently within one month after the expiration of the fixed time.

[668] See also: art 652 Portuguese CC and art. 511 par. 1 Swiss code of obligations.

rule that covers guarantees for existing obligations that do not include a time limit[669]. Other countries have provided general limitations to the extension of guarantees that are agreed without time limit. However this has been achieved by means of case law rather than by statutory provision[670].

In Portugal the secondary guarantor will be discharged after the expiry of two months from the moment at which he required the creditor to ask the debtor to effect performance. Notice from the guarantor is effective (one month after notification) if the creditor has not sued the debtor within this time. Art. 652 Portuguese CC states that upon the maturity of the underlying obligation the secondary guarantor has the right to demand the creditor to sue the debtor within two months after the expiry of the one month that follows from the moment at which the guarantor provided effective notice to the creditor.

In Spain and in Germany[671] there is no legislation that establishes any limit to a guarantee agreed without a time limit[672]. The guarantee therefore remains valid for the period that the underlying obligation remains valid, provided that the legal right to require the performance of the secured debt has not prescribed.

bb) Global guarantees and guarantees for future debts without time limit

In Italy, the guarantor of global guarantees and guarantees that are granted for future obligations without a time limit may extinguish the guarantee by giving notice to the creditor[673/674].The guarantee covers those obligations

---

[669] Countries like Finland and the Netherlands have included provisions limiting the extension of global guarantees and guarantees for future debts respectively without time limit. France has included a provision protecting the consumer guarantor, by which the professional creditor is obliged to inform annually the consumer guarantor about his right of revocation of the guarantee (art. 47 par. 2 sent. 2 Madelin Act 11 February 1994).

[670] The case law of countries like Austria or France has recognised the right of the guarantor to terminate the guarantee without time limit by giving notice to the creditor (Austria: OGH 8 November 1970, JBl, 1971, 257; France: Cass. Comm 3 December 1979, JCP G 1980 IV, 67). One decision of the Austrian Supreme Court required a reasonable length of the guarantee (OGH 22 June 1993, ÖBA 1994, 239). This is also the tenor in art. 2.10 RPS: "Limiting Guarantee Without Time Limit. (1) Where a guarantee has no time limit, its duration may be limited to cover existing obligations only by any party giving notice of reasonable length to the other party. (2) The guarantor's maximum liability is limited to the amount of the secured claim and its accessories as defined in art. 2.5 par. 2 and 3 as of the date at which the limitation becomes effective".

[671] *Seiler/Erman*, on § 765, no. 8.

[672] In Spain only one recent decision of a minor court established the possibility to terminate a guarantee without limit on appliance of the principle of good faith (SAP Córdoba 12 June 2000 [RA 2000 no. 2070].

[673] Trib. Milano 15 September 1993, BBTC, 1994, II, 548, *De Maria/Franzoni*, 1486; *Giusti*, 165.

that exist until the moment of termination[675]. The date of termination is that which is chosen by the guarantor in accordance with the requirements of notice[676/677].

By way of contrast, in Spain it is not possible to unilaterally terminate the guarantee. This is the case even for continuing guarantees and even if the secured obligation may be indefinitely extended in time. The guarantee that is granted for a future obligation is not legally limited in terms of time. The guarantor remains indefinitely liable until the obligation has been agreed and has matured. Therefore the guarantor is not protected from an eventual excessive long duration of his liability.

In Germany, the lack of regulation with regard to the termination of the guarantee without a time limit has been moderated by case law[678]. Those guarantees for future obligations that lack a reasonable time limit are hold extinguished. This is an exceptional measure only justified if a reasonable time[679] has elapsed since the agreement was made, or there is another grave reason[680]. These exceptions are based upon the principle of bona fides, established in § 242 German CC and also upon the criterion that it must be possible to terminate long term relations in order to facilitate future freedom of contract[681]. The same reasoning could be applied in Spain in order to limit guarantees for future debts or global guarantees without time limit which would contribute to the protection of the guarantors.

---

[674] Dutch CC establishes the same legal rule in its art. 7: 681 par. 1 lit. a and the recent Finnish law on dependent guarantees too (§ 6 par. 1).

[675] *De Maria/Franzoni*, 1484.

[676] Trib. Milano 15 September 1993, BBTC 1994 II, 548; *De Maria/Franzoni*, 1486.

[677] The same is explicitly established in art. 7:861 par. 2 Dutch CC. In Germany, the obligations covered by the guarantee are also those arisen until the termination is effective, i.e. after the guarantor has given notice (Habersack, Münchener Kommentar,on § 765 no. 57. *Contra*: Derleder, NJW, 1986, 97, 102).

[678] BGH 21 January 1993, NJW – RR 1993, 944 ff.; Habersack, Münchener Kommentaar, on § 765 no. 55; *Seiler/Erman*, on § 765, no. 8.

[679] A period of three years has been considered enough in German case law and literature (BGH 4 July 1985, NJW, 1985, 3007, 3008; Bülow no. 807). The notice for termination given by the guarantor is generally effective after a reasonable period which depends on the circumstances of the case (BGH 4 July 1985, NJW 1985, 3007, 3008) but generally three months (Habersack, Münchener Kommentaar, on § 765 no. 55; OLG Celle 5 October 1988, NJW – RR 1989, 548, 548). Only in the case of termination by severe reason the period of notification may be shorter (four to six weeks according to OLG Celle 5 October 1988, NJW – RR 1989, 548, 548) or even immediate (BGH 4 July 1985, NJW 1985, 3007, 3008) under special circumstances.

[680] BGH 4 July 1985, NJW 1985, 3007, 3008; *Seiler/Erman*, on 765, no. 8.

[681] *Reinicke* and *Tiedtke*, Bürgschaftsrecht, no. 130; OLG Düsseldorf 24 November 1998, ZMR, 2000, 89.

c) Extinction of the guarantee limited to the moment of maturity of the underlying obligation

In Italy, if the guarantor has expressly limited the guarantee to the same period as the underlying obligation, the guarantee will be extinguished upon the same conditions but within two months of the moment of extinction of the underlying obligation (art. 1957 par. 2 Italian CC)[682/683].

In Spain there is no regulation to establish that the guarantee will remain valid during a certain (short) period of time after the maturity of the underlying obligation. The Spanish creditor must prove that he required the guarantor to perform at the moment at which the debtor was obliged to do so (constiutido en mora/mora debitoris). The creditor must be alert and extremely diligent in making his request for performance. This could be deemed excessively onerous for the creditor just to avoid losing his right vis-à-vis the guarantor.

As a solution, the guarantee could be held to remain valid until the date in which the secured debt prescribes[684]. However, in most cases there is a clearly established time limit in relation to the guarantee. Moreover, it may actually be damaging for the guarantor to remain liable for a longer period than that which he would have been liable for if the guarantee had been limited to the term that was originally agreed. Therefore, in order to be fair to both, the creditor and the guarantor, it would be necessary to follow the example of neighbouring countries and establish a period of time after maturity of the underlying obligation during which the guarantee remains valid and within which the creditor must make his request for performance.

d) Extinction of the guarantee agreed with a specific time limit

In Italy and in Spain if the guarantee is agreed to have a specific time limit[685] the guarantor will be automatically discharged upon the expiration of such time limit. This is the case unless the creditor has taken action against the debtor or the guarantor; i.e. the creditor has requested performance before the expiration of the time period. Such demand does not need to be

682 Cass. 20 August 1992 no. 9719, FI, 1993, I, 2171 and GI, 1993, I, 1, 1256; Cass. 28 March 1990 no. 2545, BBTC, 1990, II, 683; Cass. 8 February 1989 no. 786, GI, 1990, I, 1, 460.

683 §777 German CC, art. 510 par. 3 Swiss Code of Obligations.

684 *Carrasco, Cordero* and *Marín*, 227.

685 The time limit for the guarantee must be after the time of maturity of the underlying obligation. The period between maturity of the debt and maturity of the guarantee must also be reasonable, so that the creditor had enough time to require the debtor for performance. Moreover, the time limit does not need to be a certain date. It may also be established by reference to a certain event that may come (see: BGH 6 May 1997, NJW 1997, 2233).

of a procedural nature. The guarantor must be informed of the actions that are being taken against the debtor[686]. This creditor's duty to inform the guarantor has, though, not received the statutory establishment that has been granted in other countries like Germany[687] or Greece[688].

In Germany, a joint and several guarantee that is agreed for a fixed term is extinguished upon the expiration of that term. This is the case unless the creditor informs[689] the guarantor of his intention to demand that performance should be effected immediately after the specific point in time was reached (§ 777 par. 1 sent. 2)[690]. If the guarantee is secondary, the creditor must proceed against the debtor immediately after the expiration of the fixed term, pursue the legal proceedings without significant delay and inform the guarantor immediately of his intention to require performance (§ 777 par. 1 sent. 1 German CC)[691].

The criteria that are followed in Italy and Spain are more favourable to the guarantor. The creditor must start the action before expiration of the time limit established by the parties. No difference is observed to exist between joint and several and secondary guarantees.

---

[686] *Giusti*, 149 and 253; *Carrasco, Cordero* and *Marín*, 226.

[687] § 777 par. 1 German CC: „If a guarantor has assumed the guarantee for an existing obligation for a fixed time, unless the creditor proceeds without delay to the collection of the claim pursuant to § 772, continues the procedure without serious delay, and, after the termination of the procedure, notifies the guarantor without delay that he has recourse against him. If the guarantor does not have the claim for prior execution against the principal debtor he is discharged after the expiration of the fixed time, unless the creditor gives him notice without delay". ("Hat sich der Bürge für eine bestehende Verbindlichkeit auf bestimmte Zeit verbürgt, so wird er nach dem Ablaufe der bestimmten Zeit frei, wenn nicht der Gläubiger die Einziehung der Forderung unverzüglich nach Maßgabe des § 772 betreibt, das Verfahren ohne wesentliche Verzögerung Fortsetzt und unverzüglich nach der Beendigung des Verfahrens dem Bürgen anzeigt, dass er ihn in Anspruch nehme. Steht dem Bürgen die Einrede der Vorausklage nicht zu, so wird er nach dem Ablaufe der bestimmten Zeit frei, wenn nicht der Gläubiger ihm unverzüglich diese Anzeige macht").

[688] Art. 866 Greek CC: „Wer sich nur für eine bestimmte Zeit verbürgt hat, wird von der Bürgschaft befreit, wenn nicht der Gläubiger innerhalb eines Monats nach dem Ablauf dieser Zeit seine Forderung gerichtlich geltend macht und das Verfahren darüber nicht unverzüglich fortsetzt" (German Translation: *Gogos*, Das Zivilgesetzbuch von Griechenland, Berlin/Tübingen, 1951).

[689] The information does not need to comply with formalities (*Habersack*, Münchener Kommentaar sub § 777 no. 5).

[690] Also in Greece, the creditor has a period of one month after the fixed term, but in this case he has to take legal action and pursue it without delay and not only inform about his intention (art. 866 Greek CC).

[691] In opinion of some scholars, the guarantee limited on time may also terminate for serious reasons as has been declared by case law for the guarantees without time limit (*Habersack*, Münchener Kommentaar, on § 765, no. 56.

The guarantee for future obligations that is limited by time may cover the debts that are created before the time limit set in the contract. However, such a guarantee may only cover those debts that are enforceable before that particular date. The contract should be clear in its stipulation upon this point. If the contract is unclear, the clause that establishes the time limit must be construed to determine the position on this issue. According to Italian and the majority of Spanish case law, the guarantor is only liable for the obligations that are created before the time limit agreed in the guarantee contract. This is the case even if the debt matures after the time limit has elapsed[692]. However, it has occasionally been considered that the time limit set in the contract is meant to be the final point at which the guarantee may be enforced[693].

It is the responsibility of the creditor to demand the guarantor for performance before the expiry of the agreed term. This demand does not need to be of a judicial nature[694].

e) The terms established in art. 1957 Italian CC

The dies a quo of the terms (generally six months, but occasionally two months for guarantees that have been expressly limited to endure for the same period as that of the principal obligation) starts at the moment at which the secured obligation matures[695]. That moment of maturity is established by the parties in the contract.

If no specific term has been established, the obligation matures according to the regime set in art. 1183 Italian CC[696]. In the case of a current account, the term starts from the moment at which the account was closed[697].

---

[692] Cass. 8 August 1988, no. 4871 cited by Petti, 215; STS 27 January 1961 [RA 1961 no. 293]; STS 24 November 1982 [RA 1982 no. 6929]; STS 26 June 1986 [RA 1986 no. 3796]; STS 28 December 1992 [RA 1992 no. 10658]; SAP Madrid 2 June 1997, RGD 1998, 1189.

[693] In a case, the debt already existed at the time of agreement of the clause limiting the time (STS 31 October 1985 [RA 1985 no. 5135]).

[694] STS 28 September 1993 [RA 1993 no. 6748].

[695] Cass. 14 February 1975, no. 566, FI , Rep. 1975, *voce* Fideiussione e mandato di credito, no. 28; Cass. 7 November 1986, no. 6547 BBTC, 1988, II, 184; *Bozzi/Rescigno*, La fideiussione, le figure affini, 271.

[696] Art. 1183 Italian CC: "If the time for performance is not specified, the creditor can demand it immediately. However, when by usage or the nature, manner or place of performance, a time is necessary, it is fixed by the court, in the absence of agreement between the parties.

If the time of performance is left to the discretion of the debtor, it is also for the court to establish it according to the circumstances; if it is left to the discretion of the creditor, it can be fixed by the court at the request of the debtor who wishes to free himself of the obligation".

[697] App. Napoli 11 October 1962, BBTC, 1963, II, 55.

In the case of continuing obligations, it starts from the moment of the maturity of each of the debts. The guarantee that is granted for continuing obligations, serves to secure all of the liabilities that must be performed within the scope of the contract. These liabilities form a single entity as they are all derived from the same contract. However, they can all be fully identified and distinguished from each other by virtue of their own elements. The guarantor may be sued in relation to each of the liabilities; i.e. if there is a failure to perform with regard to any of these liabilities. Accordingly, the guarantor must be sued within the terms that are established in art. 1957 Italian CC for each liability or the guarantee will be extinguished in relation to that specific liability[698].

f) Requirements to avoid the extinction of the guarantee within the given term

aa) In general

Art. 1957 Italian CC protects the guarantor from the adverse consequences that may result from a lack of activity on the part of the creditor with regard to the requirement for performance. Consequently, the guarantee is not extinguished on the basis of the provision if the creditor has taken appropriate action ("istanze") against the debtor and has diligently pursued it. In such a case the creditor has done everything that he could do in order to obtain payment and he should not be made to assume any risk above that originally established in the contract.

bb) An action against the debtor

The term "take action" ("istanze") is a general term and its meaning has been the source of some controversy in Italy. Case law and certain prestigious scholars have construed the term in a very restrictive fashion with regard to judicial actions[699]. The judicial action may be of any kind. An example would be that of the retention of the goods of the debtor by the creditor ("sequestro conservativo di beni del debitore principale anterior-

---

[698] Cass. 26 Febraury 1985 no. 1655, FI 1985, I, c. 2672; Cass. 14 October 970 no. 2028, BBTC, 1971, II, 207; Cass. 17 February 1968 no. 570, GI, 1969, I, 1, c. 748.

[699] The notion of "istanze" has been described as "tutti i vari mezzi di tutela giurisdizionale esperibili al fine di conseguire il pagamento, indipendentemente dal loro esito e dalla loro concreta idoneità a sortire il risultato sperato; resta, invece escluso che, in quello stesso termine possa rientrare un semplice atto stragiudiziale, o una denuncia o una querela da presentare in sede penale o un ricorso per accertamento tecnico preventivo" (Cass. 14 january 1997 no. 289, FI Rep. 1997, voce Fideiussione e mandato di credito no. 54); Cass. 11 January 1983 no. 183, FI, Rep. 1983, voce Fideiussione e mandato di credito, no. 27; *Fragali*, L'azione del debitore, 508; *Calderale*, 79.

mente al giudizio di merito")[700]. A simple requirement for payment or an invitation to pay is not sufficient to prevent the discharge of the guarantor within the given terms of the contract[701]. However, the parties may choose to derogate from the need to commence a judicial action. They may explicitly agree that a simple (non-procedural) request for performance is enough to prevent the extinction as established in art. 1957 Italian CC[702].

A minority of scholars disagree with this interpretation of the term "istanze". They consider that this term is not restricted to procedural measures but that it includes any kind of action that is performed in order to require that the debtor effects performance. This opinion is based mainly on the rationale of art. 1957 Italian CC. The aim of this provision is to prevent the creditor from exhibiting a lack of interest and activity in relation to making a request for payment. A non-judicial action would be enough in this respect[703].

In Spain the request for performance by the creditor does not need to be of a judicial or procedural nature. Accordingly, if the creditor and the debtor are negotiating payment, the guarantee will remain valid until such negotiations are complete.

In the case of joint and several guarantees the creditor may initiate the judicial action against the guarantor or against the debtor in order to prevent the extinction of the guarantee[704].

cc) Diligent pursuit by the creditor prevents the extinction

The creditor must take actions and also diligently pursue these actions. This is a necessary corollary of the rationale of this provision[705]. The guarantor is only in receipt of proper protection if the creditor does everything

---

[700] Cass. 19 December 1985 no. 6498, FI 1986, I, 685; Cass. 4 September 1991 no. 9364, GC, 1992, I, 3134.

[701] Cass. 5 September 1966 no. 2315; Cass. 10 July 1968 no. 2393; Cass. 26 April 1972 no. 1305 and Cass. 22 July 1976 no. 2828 cited by *Giusti*, 288 and 289; Cass. 11 January 1983, no. 183, FI Rep. 1983, *voce* Fideiussione e mandato di credito, no. 27; Cass. 14 July 1994 no. 6604, BBTC 1995, II, 422; Calderale, 78; *Fragali*, L'azione del debitore, 508.

[702] Cass. 3 April 1996 no. 3085, GI 1997, I, 1, 944. Italian Supreme Court has declared that the parties may agree in the guarantee contract that instead a judicial procedure, an arbitral one started within the terms established in art. 1957 Italian CC may be enough to avoid the extinction of the guarantee: Cass. 23 September 1996 no. 8405, FI Rep 1996, voce Contratto in genere, nos. 265–266.

[703] *Biscontini*, Solidarietà 167; *Girino*, 544 ff.

[704] Cass. 13 September 1977 no. 3952, FI, 1978, I, 678. See also: Cass. 11 January 1983 cited by Calderale. *Contra*: Cass. 3 June 1977 no. 2263, FI 1978, I, 679 and *Biscontini*, Soliedarietà fideiussoria, 164 ff.

[705] Cass. 22 May 1979 no. 2958; GC, 1979, I, 1982: "non far ricadere sul fideiussore la mancanza di diligenza del garantito".

he can in order to obtain payment from the debtor at the most immediate opportunity. He needs to engage in appropriate diligence but he does not need to be successful in it[706].

g) Art. 1957 Italian CC: a non mandatory rule

aa) Validity of the waiver of art. 1957 Italian CC

Art. 1957 Italian CC is not a mandatory rule[707]. The guarantor may renounce his right to be discharged upon the terms and conditions that are established in art. 1957 Italian CC[708]. The renounce may be of an express or a tacit nature[709]. It might be agreed as a valid clause included in the general terms and conditions[710]. Italian case law has expressly stated that the contents of art. 1957 Italian CC do not affect any principle of public order (such as good faith)[711]. Also most scholars agree that this provision is non-mandatory and it can therefore be expressly or implicitly derogated from by the parties[712]. However, a small body of case law[713] and a minority of scholars[714] consider that a derogation from art. 1957 Italian CC is not-valid. The main reason adduced is that the content of the provision is an application of the principle of good faith. As this principle is mandatory, no derogation is possible.

This provision simply serves to grant an indirect protection to the guarantor against a potential act on the part of the creditor that is contrary to

---

706 Cass. 3 April 1996 no. 3085, GI, 1997, I, 1, 944.

707 Cass. 31 August 1984 no. 4738, FI 1985, I, 506. See also: Cass. 20 April 1982, no. 2461, Diritto fallimentare, 1982, II, 980; cited by *Calderale*, 79; Trib. Milano 22 December 1988, FI, Rep. 1989, *voce* Fideiussione e mandato di credito, 1054; App. Milano 5 February 1988, BBTC, 1989, II, 160; Trib. Milano 25 February 1988, BBTC, 1988, II, 464.

708 Cass. 22 April 1986 no. 2828, FI, Rep 1987, *voce*, Fideiussione e mandato di credito, no. 24.

709 Cass. 2 May 1980 no. 2901, GI, 1980, I, 1, 1416. Cass. 12 November 1988 no. 6142, BBTC 1989, II, 412 and Cass. 8 February 1989 no. 786, GI, 1989, I, 1, 1517 declare not abussive the clause in which the guarantor renounces to the rights granted in art. 1957 Italian CC. Cass. 20 August 1992, FI 1993, I, 2171; Cass. 6 April 1992 no. 4208 and Cass. 22 June 1993 no. 6897 cited by *Giusti*, 290.

710 Cass. 22 April 1986 no. 2828, FI, Rep. 1987, *voce* Fideiussione e mandato di credito, no. 24.

711 Cass. 9 December 1997 no. 12456, GI, 1998, I, 1, 11; Cass. 20 August 1992 no. 9719, FI, 1993, I, 2171 and others. *Contra*: Trib. Milano 1986, BBTC, 1987, II, 980; Trib. Pordenone, 11 May 1993, BBTC, 1994, II, 565.

712 See *Dolmetta*, 412 ff.

713 Trib. Milano 11 June 1986, BBTC, 1987, II, 216 commented by Benfatti; Trib. Pordenone 11 May 1993, BBTC, 1994, II, 565.

714 *Valcavi*, Sulla inderogabilità dell'art. 1957 cc, GI, 1990, I, 1, 460.

the principle of good faith[715]. The law establishes a certain distribution of the risk but it seems to be legitimate for the parties to distribute the risk in a different way from that which is established by the law. The non-mandatory nature of art. 1957 Italian CC is also suggested by the fact that the changes established by art. 10 of the Law no. 154 in 1992 in the guarantee regulation modified art. 1956 Italian CC and established its mandatory character but avoided mentioning art. 1957. This would have been a good opportunity to specify the mandatory nature of this provision if that had been considered to be desirable. As it was not introduced, it can be inferred that a waiver is allowed[716].

bb) Form of the waiver: express or tacit

The waiver of art. 1957 Italian CC may be of an express character. The standard contracts published by the ABI (Italian Banks Association) for the general guarantee (fideiussione omnibus) include a clause of explicit renunciation by the guarantor[717]. However, the waiver may also be implicit. For instance, a clause by which the parties agree that the guarantee will remain valid until the moment when the debtor is discharged functions as an implicit renunciation to art. 1957 Italian CC[718].

4. Extension of time (prórroga)

a) Extension of time in the Spanish regulation

aa) In general

If an extension of time is granted by the creditor to the debtor with regard to the principal debt but this extension is granted without the consent of the guarantor then the guarantee will be extinguished (art. 1851 Spanish CC). The reasoning for this provision is that the extension of the duration of the secured debt will have an adverse effect upon the position of the guarantor, who is forced to assume the risk of non-performance on the part of the debtor for a longer period of time[719]. Moreover, the financial condi-

---

[715] *Nappi*, 564 ff.

[716] Trib. Crema 2 January 1993, FI, 1993, I, 2175.

[717] "La banca non è tenuta ad escutere il debitore o il fideiussore [...] entro i termini previsti dall' art. 1957, che si intende derogato".

[718] Cass. 19 July 1996 no. 6520, FI, Rep. 1996, *voce Fideiussione e mandato di credito*, no. 49; Cass. 24 March 1994 no. 2827, BBTC, 1995, II, 558; Cass. 20 August 1992 no. 9719, FI 1993, I, 2173; Cass. 19 June 1987 no. 5373, BBTC 1989, II, 32.

[719] Also in England: Swire v. Redman (1876) 1 QBD 563 (QB). The reasoning however is that an extension of time to the debtor prevents the guarantor from his right to pay off and demand the debtor for reimbursement.

tions of the debtor may deteriorate during that extra time. The prevention of such uncertainty, thus, justifies the extinction of the guarantee[720].

However, the application of art. 1851 Spanish CC can also be negative as it prevents the creditor from being tolerant in respect of temporary difficulties that the debtor may be experiencing. The generous attitude of the creditor towards the debtor by postponing the moment of payment results in the forfeiture of the guarantee. The creditor may be thus "sanctioned" for something that is of no benefit to his own position, and although sometimes it is precisely this tolerance with regard to the timing of performance that allows the debtor to improve his financial situation, effect payment and thereby discharge the guarantor. It is then the case that an extension of time may also be beneficial for the guarantor. This is the reason why in some neighbouring countries the guarantor is not discharged upon an extension of the time to the principal debtor[721]. In Germany § 767 par. 1 sent. 3 CC states that if agreements are reached between the creditor and the debtor after the assumption of the guarantee and these agreements serve to significantly negatively effect the position of the guarantor, then such agreements are not binding in relation to the guarantor[722].

The clear literal terms of art. 1851 Spanish CC have been construed[723] in an extremely restrictive way. In fact, this provision specifically refers to the extension of the dies solutionis or the term for performance[724]. However, the expression "extension of time" is interpreted as referring to an extension of the principal obligation. Thus, it is seen as relating to a novation of the principal contract and not as an extension of the dies solutionis i.e. the moment of the performance of the original obligation. Such construction is based on the legal history of this provision. Art. 1851 Spanish CC was introduced in the Draft Civil Code by García Goyena. According to this project, the modification of terms causes the novation of the contract. This would be the only reason to consider the extension of the terminus solutionis as a cause of extinction. However, modification of terms does not result in the novation of the obligation in the current Spanish CC. Therefore this phenomenon should not cause the extinction of the guaran-

---

720 *Manresa*, Comentarios, 367; *Gullón*, Curso, 1968, 442.

721 Art. 2039 French and Belgian CC for secondary guarantees. Art. 2039 CC: "La simple prorogation de terme, accordée par le créancier au débiteur principal, ne décharge point la caution, qui peut, en ce cas, poursuivre le débiteur pour le forcer au payement ". See Simler, no. 469. For Austria: OGH 6 May 1954, ÖJZ 1954, 455 no. 312.

722 *Seiler/Erman*, § 767, no. 9.

723 *Carrasco*, *Cordero* and *Marín*, 188; *Díez Picazo*, Fundamentos, 457.

724 Díez-Picazo considers that the extension of time should only have an extinctive effect regarding the guarantee if it means a novation of the obligation. On the contrary, in case of extension of the *terminus solutionis*, an extinction of the guarantee would be a too significant privilege for the guarantor (*Díez-Picazo*, Fundamentos, 457).

tee. Moreover, the guarantor is protected from the moment at which the principal debt has become due and payable. From that point in time the guarantor is entitled to require that he should be discharged or that adequate security should be obtained if the secured debt has not been performed (art. 1943 par. 4 Spanish CC). Art. 1851 Spanish CC would thus appear to be superfluous. If any change results in a novation of the principal obligation the guarantee is automatically extinguished as a consequence of the principle of co-extensiveness. Moreover, according to art. 1843 par. 4 Spanish CC if the terminus solutionis has been extended without the consent of the guarantor, the latter may require to be either discharged or secured.

bb) Explicit extension of time and tolerance for the non-performance by the debtor

Art. 1851 Spanish CC is technically deficient as it only refers to the extension of time which has been explicitly granted by the creditor. It omits mentioning the very common situation of there being a tolerance on the part of the creditor for the lack of performance by the debtor; i.e. the debtor is simply not required to effect payment[725].

An explicit extension of time may be construed as being a novation and it may therefore cause the guarantee to become extinct. However, if no explicit extension has been granted but the creditor does not require the debtor to perform or the creditor is tolerant with the lack of performance then there is not a novation of the secured debt. Extensive case law[726] in Spain has declared that in such cases there is no legal "extension of time" (prórroga) and therefore the guarantee is not extinguished. This criterion serves to reduce the practical relevance of art. 1851 Spanish CC. In most cases the creditor does not explicitly grant the extension of time and avoids so the application of this provision. Furthermore, if the creditor wants to avoid losing the guarantee by applying art. 1851 Spanish CC, this can be accomplished by privately requesting the debtor to effect performance (by a simple private phone call). He may even promise the debtor that he will not be required to perform until a certain or currently undetermined point in the future. If the creditor unofficially requests performance he retains the guarantee, while he will lose it if he makes a formal request for performance. This appears to be both illogical and unfair.

---

[725] *Guilarte*, Comentario, Ministerio de Justicia, 1993, 1850.

[726] STS 24 June 1940 [RA 1940 no. 674]; STS 3 November 1955 [RA 1955 no. 3564]; STS 7 April 1975 [RA 1975 no. 1412]; STS 6 November 1981 [RA 1981 no. 4465]; STS 8 October 1986 [RA 1986 no. 5333]; STS 10 April 1987 [RA 1987 no. 2545]; STS 29 October 1991 [RA 1991 no. 7488]; STS 30 December 1997 [RA 1997 no. 9667]; STS 16 December 1997 [RA 1997 no. 8778].

cc) Practical application

Art. 1851 Spanish CC is applied to all guarantees, including those which are joint and several. In the case of a general guarantee (omnibus) the extension of the time limit of one of the guaranteed obligations does not result in the extinction of the entire guarantee[727]. Even if such extension causes the novation of that debt, the new obligation (with a different term of performance) would also be secured by the general guarantee[728].

A different case is that of a guarantee that is limited by time but the time limit is actually posterior to the time limit of the secured debt. The guarantee is not extinguished upon the extension of the time limit of the principal debt, provided that the extension is not beyond that of the time limit of the guarantee[729]. The guarantor has already assumed the risk that will exist until that moment. His situation does not become worse by reason of the extension.

The extension of time for continuing obligations (such as a debt for a rent) does not cause the extinction of the guarantee for those debts which were due and payable before the original term was reached. However, the guarantee is extinguished with regard to the new debts that are assumed after that moment[730].

Finally, joint and several co-guarantees are regulated by art. 1148 Spanish CC and therefore excluded from the application of art. 1851 Spanish CC.

dd) Extension of time established by law (proroga/prórroga)

According to Spanish case law[731] the guarantee is not extinguished if the extension of time is legally compulsory or is made compulsory by a judicial or administrative decision. If the creditor is not responsible for the extension of time he should not be punished with the extinction of the guarantee. The reasoning is based on the idea that an extension of time is a negative development for the position of guarantor[732].

---

[727] See STS 31 October 1984 [RA 1984 no. 5153].

[728] STS 30 December 1997 [RA 1997 no. 9667] commented by *Alonso Sánchez*, CCJC 47 § 1272.

[729] *Carrasco, Cordero* and *Marín*, 190; *contra*: *Fínez Ratón*, La prórroga forzosa, 94.

[730] *Fínez Ratón*, La prórroga forzosa, 94.

[731] STS 5 February 1955 [RA 1955 no. 731]; STS 27 February 1981 [RA 1981 no. 633].

[732] Carrasco considers these case law non congruent with the regulation on extension of time but correct; *Carrasco, Cordero* and *Marín*, 190.

ee) The consent of the guarantor to the extension of time for the secured debt

The guarantee is not extinguished if the guarantor has agreed to the extension of time[733]. The real will of the guarantor to consent on the extension needs to be clear. Thus, if such consent is expressed in the guarantee contract[734] or it has been communicated simultaneously with the extension of time, then there will be no problem. Sometimes the guarantor renounces the right that is granted in art. 1851 Spanish CC in the original guarantee contract. Such waiver is valid even if it was included in the general terms and conditions of the contract[735] and also if the guarantor is a consumer[736]. The right will be considered renounced if "according to the terms agreed in the contract of guarantee, this remains valid so long the secured debt has not extinguished, including all extensions and renewals granted by the creditor to the debtor"[737]. In some cases it is explicitly stated in the contract that the guarantee will cover the secured debt in the event of an extension of time. This is a common provision with regard to continuing obligations (such as lease contracts).

If the situation is unclear, the contract must be interpreted. If the possibility of extension was included in the principal contract and the guarantor was aware, the extension of time in relation to the principal debt shall be considered to be validly consented by the guarantor[738].

In one minor case it was held that the guarantor had consented because the contract for the underlying obligation included a clause which stated that a tacit extension of time could be indefinitely granted by the creditor[739].

There is no doubt of the consent if the guarantor has required the extension of time to be granted[740]. The fact that the guarantor has an interest in the underlying obligation does not allow concluding that he might be will-

---

733 STS 7 April 1975 [RA 1975 no. 1412]; STS 23 May 1977 [RA 1977 no. 2135]; STS 30 December 1988 [RA 1988 no. 10075]; STS 10 September 1997 [RA 1997 no. 6401].

734 STS 31 January 1980 [RA 1980 no. 174] ; STS 3 October 1985 [RA 1985 no. 4570]; STS 10 September 1997 [RA 1997 no. 6401]; STS 3 October 1985 [RA 1985 no. 4570] commented by *Delgado Echeverría*, CCJC 9 [1985] § 236.

735 SAP Zaragoza 10 March 1999 [AC 1999 no. 501].

736 *Carrasco, Cordero* and *Marín*, 194.

737 SAP Zaragoza 10 March 1999 [AC 1999 no. 501].

738 STS 27 February 1981 [RA 1981 no. 633]; STS 8 May 1984 [RA 1984 no. 2399]; Commentary on the STS 8 May 1984 by *Delgado Echeverría*, CCJC, 5 § 135.

739 SAP Madrid 13 October 1998 [AC 1998 no. 2097].

740 STS 7 April 1975 [RA 1975 no. 1412].

ing to consent to the extension of time. In most of these cases the Spanish Supreme Court[741] has considered the guarantee to have been extinguished.

ff) Good faith and consent

Even if the guarantor has renounced to his right to be discharged in accordance with art. 1851 Spanish CC, the extension of time must be granted in good faith. Therefore, if it was granted in order to damage the guarantor's right to receive reimbursement, or if the risk of the guarantor has been greatly increased in comparison to the possible benefits gained by the extension, the guarantor retains the rights in art. 1851 Spanish CC[742].

b) Extension of time in other regulations

The Spanish regulation on the effects on the guarantee of the extension of time for the secured debt is an exception among the European regulations. In the most relevant neighbouring countries such extension of the term of payment of the principal debt, freely granted by the creditor does not serve to cause the extinction of the guarantee. The French CC makes explicit reference to the extension of time. However, art. 2039 French Civil Code[743] states that the guarantee is not extinguished by the extension of time for the secured debt.

Other civil codes (such as the German, the Italian or the Portuguese) do not explicitly regulate the voluntary extension of time for the secured debt but the guarantor is protected by a time limit within which the guarantee remains enforceable beyond the moment of the enforceability of the secured debt. This regime is effective if the creditor has acted to sue the debtor (§ 777 German CC; art. 1957 par. 1 Italian CC and art. 652 Portuguese CC). Hence these civil codes limit the liability of the guarantor with regard to the possible tolerance of the creditor in relation to the non-performing debtor. The guarantor is thus protected by the law from the problem of uncertainty. The Italian and the Portuguese civil codes followed the German model by changing their traditional regulations on the extension of the secured debt. They established a new system of protection for the guarantor based on the absence of activity on the part of the creditor in relation to an enforceable debt.

---

[741] STS 23 May 1977 [RA 1977no. 2135]; STS 8 May 1984 [RA 1984 no. 2399], commented by *Delgado Echeverría*, CCJC, 5 § 135; STS 30 December 1997 [RA 1997 no. 9667], commented by *Alonso Sánchez*, CCJC 47 § 1272.

[742] See *Carrasco, Cordero* and *Marín*, 194.

[743] Art. 2039 French CC: „La simple prorogation de terme, accordée par le créancier au débiteur principal, ne décharge point la caution, qui peut, en ce cas, poursuivre le débiteur pour le forcer au payement".

The concrete solutions to this topic that are offered in each of the legal systems present some notable differences. In the German CC the guarantor will be discharged at the moment of the enforceability of the secured debt unless the creditor immediately acts against the debtor. The different situations which may take place are explicitly governed in § 777 German CC[744]. The Italian CC (art. 1957) opted for a mixed formula of periods and diligence on the part of the creditor[745]. According to art. 652 Portuguese CC "if the principal obligation has a term, the guarantor which enjoys the benefit of levy may demand, upon the enforceability of the obligation, that the creditor proceeds against the debtor within two months, from the moment of enforceability, upon sanction of expiration of the guarantee."

The Spanish solution of art. 1851 Spanish CC is in line with the French formula in the specific consideration of the extension of the principal obligation. However, the Spanish solution is different in its extinctive character with regard to the guarantee. In contrast to the German, Italian and Portuguese solutions, the only protection that is provided to the Spanish gua-

[744] § 777 BGB: „Hat sich der Bürge für eine bestehende Verbindlichkeit auf bestimmte Zeit verbürgt, so wird er nach dem Ablaufe der bestimmten Zeit frei, wenn nicht der Gläubiger die Einziehung der Forderung unverzüglich nach Maßgabe des § 772 betreibt, das Verfahren ohne wesentliche Verzögerung Fortsetzt und unverzüglich nach der Beendigung des Verfahrens dem Bürgen anzeigt, dass er ihn in Anspruch nehme. Stehet dem Bürgen die Einrede der Vorausklage nicht zu, so wird er nach dem Ablaufe der bestimmten Zeit frei, wenn nicht der Gläubiger ihm unverzüglich diese Anzeige macht.

Erfolgt die Anzeige rechtzeitig, so beschränkt sich die Haftung des Bürgen im Falle des Absatzes 1 Satz 1 auf den Umfang, den die Hauptverbindlichkeit zur Zeit der Beendigung des Verfahrens hat, im Falle des Absatzes 1 Satz 2 auf den Umfang, den die Hauptverbindlichkeit bei dem Ablaufe der bestimmten Zeit hat."

[745] According to art. 1957 Italian CC there will be a full discharge of the guarantor within a general limit of six months provided that it was the case that the creditor had not started and diligently continued any action against the principal debtor to enforce his debt. If the guarantor has expressly limited his guarantee obligation to the same period of time as that of the principal obligation the acts by the creditor against the debtor will have to take place within a period of two months. Art. 1957 Italian CC: "The liability of a guarantor remains in effect even after the primary obligation has matured, provided that the creditor, within six monts, has instituted an action against the debtor and has diligently pursued it. This provision applies even if the guarantor has expressly limited his guarantee to the same period as that of the primary obligation. In such case, however, the action against the debtor shall be instituted within two months. The action instituted against the debtor also interrupts prescription" ("Il fideuissore rimane obbligato anche dopo la scadenza dell'obbligazione principale, purché il creditore entro sei mesi abbia proposto le sue istanze contro il debitore e le abbia con diligenza continuate. La disposizione si applica anche al caso in cui il fideiussore ha espressamente limitato la sua fideiussione allo stesso termine dell'obbligazione principale. In questo caso però l'istanza contro il debitore deve essere proposta entro due mesi. L'istanza proposta contro il debitore interrompe la prescrizione anche nei confronti del fideiussore".).

rantor occurs if the creditor positively grants an extension to the principal debtor.

G. Spanish foral laws and the guarantee contract

I. The plurality of co-existent civil law regimes in the Spanish territory

Some Spanish regions (Vizcaya and Alava, Cataluña, the Balearics, Galicia, Aragón and Navarra) developed throughout centuries certain civil law provisions (so called foral law) that have remained applicable in those specific territories beside the Spanish general civil law (derecho civil común)[746]. These foral laws were codified during the 20th century into legal texts called Compilaciones that are applicable today within the respective regions[747]. According to the Spanish Constitution (art. 149 par. 1 no. 8[748]) the respective regional legislators can amend and even develop the regulation contained in the respective Compilaciones. This means that new foral legislation on the contract of guarantee will only be possible in those regions in which this contract is already regulated by foral law and this is only the case in the Compilación Navarra.

Besides the Compilaciones, the derecho civil común also applies in the foral regions. It is subsidiarily applicable in the fields subject to regulation in the respective foral law (aplicación subsidiaria del derecho común) and primarily as regard to all other fields of civil Law and to the more general provisions contained in Spanish CC[749].

---

[746] See *Villiers*, 109.

[747] The Spanish CC sets the requirements for their application (art. 13 to art. 15 Spanish CC) as well as the rules applicable in the cases of conflict of these laws (art.16 Spanish CC).

[748] Art. 149 par. 1 no. 8 Spanish Constitution: "the State holds exclusive competence over the following civil legislation, without prejudice to the preservation, modification, and development by the autonomous communities of civil "fueros", or special rights, where they may exist; in any case, the rules relative to the application and effectiveness of legal norms, civil-legal relations having to do with the form of matrimony, regulation of registers and public instruments, the bases for contractual obligations, norms for resolving the conflicts of laws, and the determination of the sources of the law, in this last case, with respect to the norms of the "fueros" and special law".

[749] Art. 13 Spanish CC: "The provisions of this preliminary title, insofar as they determine the effect of laws and the general rules for their application, and those of Title IV of Book I, except for the latter's rules concerning the matrimonial property regime, shall be of general and direct application in all Spain. In all other matters, and with full respect to special or territorial laws of the provinces and territories where they are in force, the Civil Code shall govern, as suppletive law in default of the law that may be applicable in each of them in accordance with their special rules".

This plurality of co-existent applicable civil regulations must be taken into account for the study of any field of civil law. In the case of the guarantee, only the region of Navarra has today a valid legislation. In the past also the foral laws of Aragón, Cataluña and the Balearics contained regulations on the guarantee but developments in recent times led to their complete disappearance. However, the guarantee relationship might also be affected by the foral regulation of other fields of law. That is the case of the provisions on matrimonial property, which affect the liability of the parties of a guarantee contract and are included in several Compilations.

II. The contract of guarantee in the foral laws

1. The regulation on the guarantee in the region of Navarra

The only foral law which provides a detailed regulation of the guarantee is the Compilación of Navarra (or Fuero Nuevo de Navarra)[750] in the Leyes[751] 525 to 531. However these Laws present a similar regulation to that contained in Spanish CC. Ley 525 regulates the promise to grant guarantee by means of which the promissor is compelled to perform the obligation of the debtor upon his default. The benefit of discussion, the right of reimbursement and the beneficium divisionis are also defined in this Ley as they are in the Civil Code.

The Ley 527 establishes some particular rules on the capacity of the guarantors. Parties whose lack of economic means is notorious by virtue of their religious condition (votos religiosos) cannot be guarantors. Moreover, lawyers who are involved in a guarantee relationship cannot take part in the procedures which are related to it.

If the debtor cannot be found (paradero desconocido) and the guarantor is asked to fulfil the obligation then the guarantor benefits from a period of 30 days before he has to effect payment (Ley 529). He can also require the judge to officially enter a notification (notificación preventiva) in the Register in order to prevent the debtor from selling or agreeing to the constitution of securities over his goods before the guarantor can ask him for payment (Ley 530).

According to Ley 531, the liability of the debtor shall be transferred to the heirs. Nevertheless if they consider it too onerous, they can ask the judge to adjust the obligation[752]. It should also be noted that in contrast to

---

[750] This compilación is called *Fuero Nuevo de Navarra* and was adopted by the Ley 1/1973 of 1 March 1973.

[751] The term Leyes (Ley) is used in this *Fuero Nuevo de Navarra* as a sinonim for articles or provisions.

[752] See the Ley 493.

the Civil Code, the compilation of Navarra regulates the mandate in order to provide credit in Ley 526[753].

2. Aragón

The contract of guarantee was regulated under the traditional foral law of Aragón[754]. There used to be four different types of guarantee (cablevadoras): cruz, derecho, salvedad and indemnidad and the liability of the guarantor was joint and several[755].

When the foral law of Aragón was codified in the new Compilación of 1967 any express reference was made to the guarantee. Since then Aragón adopted the guarantee regulation of the Spanish CC and lost thereby the right to further develop its own legislation on the guarantee.

3. Cataluña

The contract of guarantee has never been fully regulated in the foral law of Cataluña. However, art. 321 and art. 322 of the Compilación of 1960 regarded the guarantee relationship. Both provisions served to create a limitation on the women's right to assume liability which is derived from a contract of guarantee. Art. 321 set that "a woman shall not be liable by virtue of a guarantee or debt's intercession for another person and she is entitled to require repayment for anything she might have paid or performed as undue payment". According to art. 322: "the guarantee granted by a wife in favour of her husband is void, unless the credit would have been inverted to her benefit".

The adoption of the Spanish Constitution in 1978 rendered this provisions void as they were contrary to art. 14[756] (principle of equality of all Spaniards before the Law) and art. 32 par. 1[757] (principle of equality between spouses).

The Courts of Barcelona declared art. 321 and 322 of the Compilación of Cataluña unconstitutional[758] and the Law of 20 March 1984 of the Parliament of Cataluña amended the Compilación and incorporated thereby the regulation on the guarantee of the Civil Code.

---

[753] See *infra* Chapter 3, A. The mandate to provide credit for a third party, 186.

[754] See *Mellado/Nieto/Bonet*, 186.

[755] *Mellado/Nieto/Bonet*, 186.

[756] Art. 14 Spanish Constitution: "Spaniards are equal before the law, without any discrimination for reasons of birth, race, sex, religion, opinion, or any other personal or social condition or circumstance".

[757] Art. 32 par. 2 Spanish Constitution: "Man and woman have the right to contract matrimony with full legal equality".

[758] SAP Barcelona, 11 October 1982 and 15 October 1982 cited by *Mellado/Nieto/Bonet*, 187.

4. The Balearics

The Balear Compilation of 1961[759] included in art. 4 in fine a provision regarding the guarantee that stated: "the married woman can grant a guarantee in favour of her husband, remaining severally liable with him". This text was derogated by the new compilation of 1990[760], Spanish Civil Code remaining applicable.

759 Real Decreto Legislativo de 6 de septiembre de 1990.

760 Texto Refundido de la Compilación de Derecho Civil de las Islas Baleares, Decreto Legislativo 79/1990.

Chapter 3

Other typical personal security rights under Italian and Spanish law

A. The mandate to provide credit for a third party

I. The basic concept of mandate to provide credit

The mandate to provide credit for a third party (m.p.c.) (mandato di credito/mandato de crédito) is a contract between two persons, the mandator (mandante) and the mandatory (mandatario). The mandator orders the mandatory to grant credit in his own name and for his own account to a third party, whereupon the mandator then holds himself liable as surety for future debts arising from the granting of such credit.

The purpose or causa of the contract is to facilitate the grant of credit. This aim is achieved by a complex structure, which consists, on the one hand, of the mandatory's obligation to grant credit, while on the other hand, the concomitant guarantee obligation of the mandator. This structure can be considered: a) as a special kind of guarantee for a conditional obligation (the condition being the grant of credit) or simply as a guarantee, preceded by a singular order[1]; b) as a simple bilateral contract following the structure of the mandate[2] or c) as a mixed contract, which initially adopts the structure of a contract of mandate and then subsequently, from the time credit is granted, is converted into a contract of guarantee[3].

II. Historical background: Roman Law

The contract of mandate used for the purpose of guaranteeing a credit obligation was considered in Roman law to be a form of liability for the debts of a third person ("mandatum qualificatum" or "mandatum pecuniae credendae")[4]. No specific definition of the m.p.c. was given. However a de-

---

[1] *Rothemberg*, 223 ff.

[2] It is so understood by the majority of German authors. See *Horn/Staudinger*, on §778, no. 1.

[3] See *Almeida*, 789.

[4] For a number of references about the m.p.c. in Roman Law, see: *León*, 1077–1083; *Arcos*, 22–32. See also, Espinosa, Mandato de crédito. „*El Mandatum pecunia credendae*" en el Derecho Romano, Barcelona, 1994; Constadaky, Le mandat du crédit,

scription of the contract and the features differentiating it from other similar institutions was provided[5]. The m.p.c. was firstly considered to be a form of intercessio by which the mandator intervened between creditor and debtor in order to stand surety for the debtor's obligation. Upon default of the debtor, the creditor had the freedom to choose between suing the mandator or the debtor. If it is the mandator (mandante) who performs, he would then enjoy the creditor's rights against the debtor, as derived from the contract of mandate ("actio mandati" or "actio negotiorum gestorum"). Moreover, he would also enjoy the benefits of discussion and division, as found in guarantee.

Yet although the structure and elements of this relationship have significant similarities with the contract of guarantee, it was not considered a guarantee in post-classical Roman Law, but rather a combination of two different contracts. The first created a credit relationship between the debtor and the creditor; the second, a mandate and guarantee relationship between the creditor and the mandator. Hence the mandatory had a claim against his debtor derived from the credit relationship and also a secondary claim (upon default of the debtor) against the mandator (actio mandati contraria[6]).

The nature of the mandatory's liability in terms of the m.p.c. differs from the liability of a guarantor in terms of a guarantee. First, while the mandator is liable to compensate the creditor for the damages caused by the debtor's default, the guarantor is not liable for the indemnification of the creditor but for the normal fulfilment of the debt in place of the debtor. Moreover, the mandator within a m.p.c. can revoke his mandate, provided that the credit has not been granted. This again contrasts with the guarantee in which the guarantor is not free to revoke his guarantee obligation.

But the m.p.c. was neither considered to be a form of mandate in the Roman post-classical period. This was because while in a typical mandate the mandator is the dominus negotii, in the m.p.c. the dominus negotii is the mandatory. In a mandate, the mandator was the party who had an interest in the debtor's performance. The mandatory could grant credit in his own name but this was done for the benefit of the mandator and the performance was always due to the latter (negotium alienum). By contrast in

---

Paris, 1932; Segré, Mandato, Mandato di Crédito e fideiussione, Temi Emiliana, 1925, 102.

[5] Digest I, 17, 48–1°: "Quum mando tibi, ut credendo pecuniam negotium mihi geras, mihique id nomen praestes meum in eo periculum, meum emolentum sit, puto mandatum posse consistere". See *León*, 1982, 1078.

[6] Digest I, 46, 41-1°.

the m.p.c. the mandatory grants the credit in his own name; only the risks belong to the mandator[7].

During Justinianian's period the m.p.c. was assimilated into the contract of guarantee, due to the common purpose of both contracts. The mandator (mandator) was considered to be a guarantor (fideiussor)[8]. Nevertheless, there was still a number of differences between the two contract types in Justinianic law[9].

III. Evolution of the mandate to provide credit in Europe. Current situation

The m.p.c. is included in the civil regulations of various European countries. In Germany a provision on the m.p.c. (§778) was included in the rules on the contract of guarantee in the Civil Code. Also in Switzerland, the m.p.c was regulated by art. 418 to art. 421 of the former Swiss Code of Obligations of 1881 and these rules were reproduced by art. 408 to art. 411 of the Swiss Code of Obligations of 1912. Surprisingly, certain countries which had first not included any regulation on the m.p.c. in their civil legislation opted to introduce it in later reforms of their Civil Codes. This was the case in Italy, where the m.p.c. was first introduced in the Italian CC of 1942 (art. 1958 and 1959), although it was not included in the former Civil Code. Similarly in Portugal, the m.p.c. was not included in the Civil Code of 1867, and was only introduced into the Civil Code of 1967 (art. 629)[10]. Also the Greek CC, enacted in 1946 regulates the m.p.c. in art. 870. However, none of these countries have demonstrated a significant academic interest in the m.p.c. Furthermore it is not commonly used in practice and accordingly there is no relevant case law.

By way of contrast, the Spanish CC does not regulate the m.p.c., although the concept of the m.p.c. was present in Roman law and in the Castillian traditional Law (Las Partidas[11]) as a specific form of security contract[12]. The lack of regulation justifies the almost inexistent academic interest until recent times[13]. Moreover only two decisions of the Spanish Su-

---

[7] This reasoning is refutable, as even though the contractor is the person granting the credit, the business does not necessarily have to be done in his interest. The risks are being assumed by the principal.

[8] Digest 41, 8, 28.

[9] Digest III, 41, 35–10° and I, 46, 41–1°.

[10] *Vaz Serra*, 287 ff.

[11] Ley 20 ff., Título XII, Partida V.

[12] For an extensive explanation about the reasoning and the process of this change from the Spanish traditional Law of the Partidas, see Arcos, 42.

[13] Apart from some brief remarks in general texts, a very few articles have been written on this topic: Rubio Torrano, El mandato de crédito (a propósito de la ley 526 de la Compilación navarra), Revista jurídica de Navarra, no. 4, julio-diciembre, 1987, 101 f;

preme Court had ever dealt with m.p.c.[14], the relevance of which was very limited due to the very tangential treatment of the matter, and the fact that the cases were not concerned with typical examples of m.p.c.

The m.p.c. is regulated in the Law 526 Fuero Nuevo de Navarra within the rules on guarantee[15]. It is only applicable in the Spanish region of Navarra (Comunidad Autónoma de Navarra).

IV. Legal provisions applicable to the m.p.c.

1. Legal provisions on the m.p.c.

In Italy and the Spanish Territory of Navarra there are specific provisions which provide a general frame of regulation for the m.p.c.. Art. 1958 Italian CC[16] and Ley 526 Fuero Nuevo de Navarra[17] describe the m.p.c. and art. 1959 Italian CC concludes the regulation by considering the case of the supervening insolvency of the mandator or the third person[18]. These brief provisions do not exhaust the regulation required for such a complex contract as the m.p.c.. It, hence, needs to be supplemented with the application

---

Robles Alvarez de Sotomayor, El mandato de crédito, RCDI, 1948, 531 f.; *León*, El mandato de crédito, RDP, 1982, 1075 f.. The first monography on the m.p.c.: "El Madato de Crédito" was written by Arcos in Pamplona in 1996, as a PhD on the regulation of the m.p.c. in the Foral Compilation of Navarra. Torres has recently developed the study of this institution in the book "El mandato de crédito como garantía personal", 1998.

[14] STS 8 October 1927 and STS 22 December 1941 [RA 1941 no. 1400] commented by Polo in RDP, 1942, 414 f.

[15] The introduction of this provision in the Compilation of Navarra was a deviation from the historical law of Navarra, and also from general Spanish civil law. See: *Arcos*, 53.

[16] Art. 1958 Italian CC: "If a person directs another to extend credit to a third person in the name and for the account of the person thus directed, and the latter binds himself to act accordingly, the person so directing is answerable as a guarantor for a future debt. The person who has accepted the mandate cannot renounce it, but the mandator can revoke it, subject to his duty to compensate the other party for damages".

[17] Ley 526 *Fuero Nuevo de Navarra*: "The person, who directs another to borrow a sum or extend credit to a third person, binds himself as guarantor for the obligation accepted by the latter. The person who has accepted the mandate can be released if the financial conditions of the principal have become such as to render the satisfaction of the claim more difficult".

[18] Art. 1959 Italian CC: "If, after aceptance of the mandate, the financial conditions of the principal or of the third person have become such as to render the satisfaction of the claim considerably more difficult, the person who has accepted the mandate cannot be compelled to carry it out".

by analogy of the respective regulation on the guarantee and on the mandate[19].

As there is no specific regulation on the m.p.c. in the Spanish CC, if a m.p.c. is agreed upon in Spain, the rules on the contract of mandate and on the guarantee must also be applied[20]. However this application is not by way of analogy in Spain.

2. *The rules on the mandate applicable to the m.p.c*

The rules on the mandate that do not present difficulties of application with regard to the m.p.c. are following:

a) art. 1710 par. 1 Italian CC and art. 1718 Spanish CC respectively on the diligence required by the mandatory;
b) art. 1710 par. 2 Italian CC on the duty of the mandatory to inform of any supervening circumstances which might cause revocation or modification of the mandate;
c) art. 1711 par. 2 Italian CC and art. 1714, art. 1715 and art. 1719 Spanish CC, on the duty to follow the instructions of the mandator and on the potential to depart from these instructions if circumstances unknown to the mandator which cannot be timeously communicated to him, reasonably create an assumption that the mandator would have given his approval;
d) art. 1712 par. 1 on the duty of the mandatory to give notice of performance;
e) art. 1713 Italian CC and 1720 Spanish CC as well as art. 263 Spanish Comm.C., on the duty to render account;
f) art. 1722 Italian CC and 1732 Spanish CC on the causes of extinction and e) art. 1727 Italian CC and 1733 Spanish CC on renunciation by the mandatory.

3. *Regulation on the contract of guarantee*

Once the mandatory has granted the credit, the mandator is automatically answerable as guarantor for the credit. At this moment and with regard to this guarantee relationship, the rules on the guarantee are applicable.

---

[19] Since the m.p.c. can neither be fully identified with the contract of guarantee nor with the contract of mandate, the provisions of these contracts can only be applied by analogy.

[20] For a concrete reference see: *Fernandez/Nieto/Bonet*, 837, 838.

V. Parties to the contract

The contracting parties in a m.p.c. are the mandator, ordering the grant of credit and being thereby liable as guarantor; and the mandatory, who grants the credit to the third party. The latter, also known as the beneficiary, remains outside the contractual relationship. This is because he does not obtain any right by virtue of the mandate, but only a possibility to obtain credit.

1. The mandatory

On performing a m.p.c., the mandatory enjoys a double position: in the first place, he is the creditor for the credit granted to the third party, and secondly he is the creditor for the guarantee.

2. The mandator

By giving order to the mandatory, the mandator shall be fully capable and offer an appearance of economic solvency. This appearance will provide the creditor with the necessary certainty to perform the business. This certainty shall be a general perception and never a provision of funds, as in such an instance the contract would be a loan granted by an intermediary. The aim of this relationship at the first stage is not to provide the monetary funds themselves, but only to offer a guarantee in order to create the conditions in which the creditor will be prepared to provide such monetary funds[21].

In the second phase, the mandator effectively guarantees the credit which has been already granted from the mandatory to the third party. The function of the mandator in this second phase, may be seen in a double perspective: a) in relation to the mandatory, the economic risk of the latter is limited by the guarantee of the mandator and b) regarding the third party, the mandator allows the provision of the relevant funds.

---

[21] Art. 1943 par. 1 Italian CC and art. 1828 Spanish CC (as well as Leyes 527 and 528 *Fuero Nuevo de Navarra*) require a special financial capacity of the guarantor. The guarantor must therefore be the owner of sufficient goods to fulfil his obligation. However these provisions are not applicable to the contract of m.p.c. as they only apply in those cases in which the debtor (third party) is obliged to provide a guarantor. In any case, the solvency of the guarantor will be a decisive reason for the creditor to decide whether to grant credit. This is the reason why some scholars have considered art. 1829 Spanish CC (respectively art. 1943 par. 2 Italian CC) to be applicable to this point. According to this article, if it has been agreed that a specific person will serves as a guarantor due to his personal characteristics, his financial situation will not affect the contract of guarantee (See *Fernández/Nieto/Bonet*, 834).

VI. Conclusion of the contract

The contract of m.p.c. is concluded by agreement of the parties. The general rules on conclusion of the contract are thus applicable.

1. Mandate

The mandate must be clearly formulated and must include references to the beneficiary and the object of the contract[22]. A recommendation, simple authorization or requirement to grant credit by the mandator is not enough[23]. There must be a voluntary intention to enter into the contract, which can in the case of the mandator be implied from his interest in the relevant business transaction (the grant of credit)[24]. However this is only a sign and is not enough to conclude that the will of the mandator is to be liable as a guarantor[25]. Once a contract of mandate has been freely agreed it results in the mandator assuming liability as guarantor for the credit he has asked the mandatory to grant. An express assumption of the guarantee liability shall not be necessary, because it is an automatic legal consequence[26]. However, in the few cases which have dealt with the m.p.c., an assumption of guarantee liability has usually been expressly accepted[27].

The m.p.c., particularly in its written form does not require any set format in order to be validly concluded[28]. However, since the madator will be liable as a guarantor, the provisions on the form of the guarantee must be considered[29]. Neither in Italy nor in Spain is a written form required to validly conclude a contract of guarantee. However the will to assume the guarantee obligation must be explicit and cannot be presumed. Accordingly it is highly prudent for there to be an explicit assumption by the mandator of the guarantee which is derived from the mandate.

In Spain commercial guarantees must be concluded in writing according to art. 440 Spanish Comm.C. This provision is not applicable to the m.p.c., since its conclusion is governed by the general regulation on the mandate (art. 1710 Spanish CC according to which, no special form is required). A non-valid commercial guarantee in Spain caused by a failure to observe

---

[22] *Sesta/Cendon*, 1769.

[23] *Horn/Staudinger*, on § 778, no. 2; *Contra*: Guilarte, 44 ff., who consideres that the circumstances of the cases shall be valued.

[24] BGH 28 March 1956, WM 1956, 1212; *Stoll*, 760, 762.

[25] *Horn/Staudinger*, on 778, no. 2–4.

[26] In Spain, as this issue is not legally regulated, the guaranteeing function must thus be expressly assumed by the principal.

[27] See *Horn/Staudinger*, on § 778, no. 4.

[28] *Giusti*, 295; art. 1710 Spanish CC; *Horn/Staudinger* on § 778 no. 6.

[29] On the formal requirements for the constitution of the guarantee see under Chapter 2, B., II. Creation of the guarantee obligation, 52.

formal requirements could potentially be converted into a mandate in order to provide a guarantee. This could be a way to avoid the application of a provision which is of doubtful merit. However, it could be considered a case of fraud of law (fraude de ley) and according to art. 6 par. 4 Spanish CC[30] it would therefore be rendered invalid.

In any case a mandate is usually made in writing, a simple letter being enough for its valid constitution[31].

2. Acceptance

The mandatory must accept the concrete mandate of the mandator (with the terms and conditions included in the offer). By virtue of this acceptance, he is compelled to enter into the credit relationship with the third party. The amount and conditions of the credit are pre-established by the parties and the mandatory is automatically guaranteed for the risk of this credit. The acceptance may also be tacit and deemed to exist by implication from circumstance. The mere fact of granting of the credit might be held to be conclusive evidence of the acceptance[32]. The granting of the credit must take place immediately after the order/offer of the mandator and be upon the conditions given by him. In Italy, according to art. 1327 CC, the mandatory must also inform the mandator of the grant of credit[33]. If this requirement is not observed then the contract is not validly concluded, and the mandator is not liable as guarantor[34].

There is a considerable degree of controversy in Italy regarding the applicability of art. 1333 CC to the m.p.c.. According to this provision, a direct proposition to conclude a contract from which only obligations for one party arise is not revocable from the moment it reaches the receiver. The latter can refuse the proposition within a reasonable time; otherwise, the contract is concluded. The Italian Supreme Court has occasionally taken all the rules applicable to the guarantee, including art. 1333 CC[35] and applied them by analogy to the contract of m.p.c. Some authors agree with this application although they are not in concurrence with regard to the guaranteeing nature of the m.p.c.[36]. However the application by analogy is

[30] Art. 6 par. 4 Spanish CC: „Acts realized under the protection of the text of a norm that seeks a result prohibited by the legal order or that is contrary thereto, shall be considered in fraud of the law and shall not prevent the appropriate application of the law sought to be evaded".

[31] *Fernández/Nieto/Bonet*, 836.

[32] Trib. Milano 30 May 1983, BBTC, 1984, II, 333 ff.

[33] Rapone, note to the Supreme Court decision: Cass. 9 April 1990, no. 2965, GI, 1991, I, 1.

[34] *Sesta/Cendon*, 1769.

[35] Cass. 1964 no. 2548 and Cass. 1974 no. 1433 cited by *Sesta/Cendon*, 1769.

[36] *Bozzi/Rescigno*, 274.

not easy to justify as the mandate creates bilateral obligations for both parties and not solely for the mandator. This has been posited to be the case by the majority of scholars[37] and by the Supreme Court itself in other decisions[38].

An express acceptance of the order and the conditions of the credit relationship is to be recommended in order to avoid misunderstanding.

VII. The object of the contract

The object of this contract is the grant of credit by the mandatory himself with funds from his patrimony to a third party. The grant of credit must be considered in a broad sense, especially within current business practice (to open a credit line, extension of a loan already granted, credit on goods, acceptance of bills of exchange, assignment of concrete things, etc)[39].

According to the general rules, the object must be possible, licit and determinable (art. 1346 Italian CC and art. 1271 Spanish CC). It does not have to be determined before the debt becomes due; it must only be determinable (like in the case of a credit line whose final object depends on the use the debtor makes of it). This possibility is considered under art. 1348 Italian CC and art. 1273 in fine Spanish CC; as well as in art. 1938 Italian CC and art. 825 Spanish CC on guarantee for future debts.

VIII. Relationships between the parties to the contract

1. In general

The structure of the m.p.c provides the basis for a complex configuration of relationships between the three parties who are de facto involved within it.

The development of the m.p.c. can be seen as occurring in three different moments; each moment giving rise to a different legal relationship.
At the first stage, the mandator orders the mandatory to grant credit to a third party and the mandatory accepts doing it. The legal scheme is that of a contract of mandate.

---

[37] *Giusti*, 306; *Ravazzoni*, Le garanzie, 164; *Galgano*, 447. See also references in *Sesta/Cendon*, 1769.

[38] Cass. 9 April 1990 no. 2965, GI, 1991, I, 1, 321 and Cass. 17 Mai 1974 no. 1433, FI 1974, I, 3380.

[39] *Horn/Staudinger*, on § 778, no. 3; *Giusti*, 296.

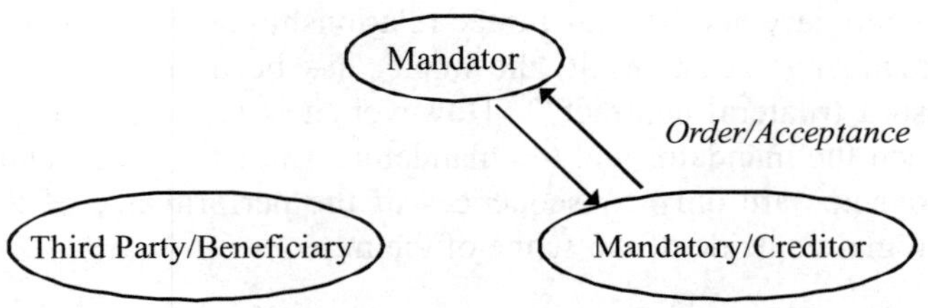

At the second stage, the mandatory performs the mandate by granting credit to the third party. In doing so he creates a credit relationship with this beneficiary. This credit is ex lege automatically guaranteed by the mandator. The structure of this relationship is that of a credit secured with a personal guarantee.

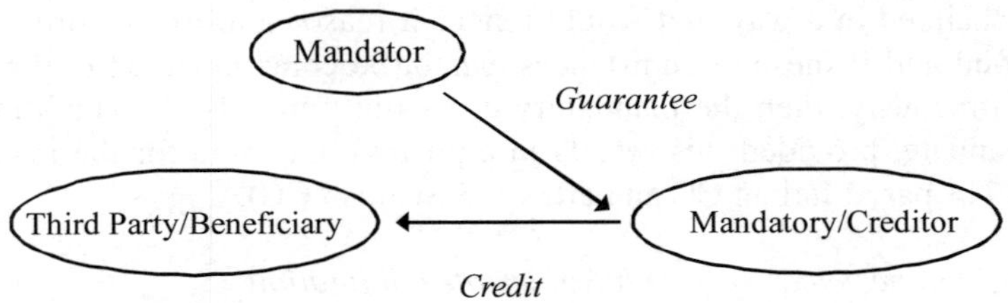

The third stage only occurs upon the default of the beneficiary in repaying his debt. In such a case, the mandatory is entitled to require performance by the mandator of his guarantee obligation and the latter on so doing receives subrogation of the rights against the beneficiary. The relationship among the parties at this stage is the typical of a guarantee contract.

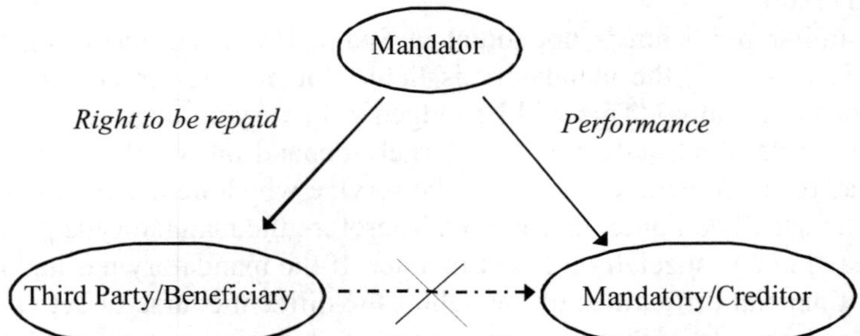

The m.p.c. is concluded in the first stage. The performance of the mandate then gives origin to two different relationships completely independent from the contract of m.p.c.: a) a credit relationship between the mandatory and the beneficiary and b) a guarantee relationship between the mandatory and the mandator. As a result, the m.p.c. has been considered as being "lato sensu a trilateral contract"[40]. However, it is stricto sensu a bilateral one between the mandator and the mandatory since the credit and guarantee relationships are only consequences of the performance of the m.p.c. and thus remain outside of the scope of the m.p.c.

2. *Rights of the mandator vis-à-vis the mandatory*

a) *Right to the performance of the mandatory on the agreed terms*

The first right of the mandator is to obtain the effective performance of his order by the mandatory. According to art. 1958 and art. 1710 par. 1 Italian CC and 1718 and 1719 Spanish CC, the mandatory is compelled by his acceptance to perform the mandate diligently and according to the terms and conditions agreed. However, if certain circumstances of the mandate have changed in a way that would render it reasonable for the order to be modified and if these circumstances cannot be communicated to the mandator timeously, then the mandatory can validly modify the conditions of the mandate, provided this results in a positive outcome for the mandator (art. 1711 par. 2 Italian CC and art. 1715 Spanish CC).

b) *Right to be released from his guarantee obligation*

Art. 1956 par. 2 juncto art. 1958 Italian CC on guarantees for future debts is applicable to the m.p.c.. This application comes into operation if the mandatory grants credit without authorisation from the mandator and if the mandatory is aware that the financial conditions of the debtor have become such as to render the satisfaction of the claim considerably more difficult. Thus the mandator is henceforth released from being guarantor for the extended credit.

A similar provision is not found in Spain. However, according to art. 1726 Spanish CC, the mandatory is liable not only for fraud (dolus) but also for fault (culpa). This will be judged with varying degrees of severity by the courts. Such judgment will largely depend on whether the mandatory has received compensation for the service which he has provided. The m.p.c. is usually an onerous contract. Therefore the mandatory is presumed to behave in an especially diligent manner. If the mandatory has had notice of the financial difficulties of the debtor the diligent course of action is for the mandatory to inform the mandator of this circumstance before the credit is granted. Furthermore the mandatory should not grant credit until

---

[40] *Simonetto*, Il Mandato di Credito, 150.

the mandator has authorised the grant in the light of the new circumstances. Such a departure from the instructions received by the mandator contradicts the mandatory's basic obligation to perform the mandate in the agreed terms but it is allowed if it results in a positive effect for the mandator (art. 1715 Spanish CC and also in art. 1711 par. 2 Italian CC). If the effect is not positive and the mandatory has granted the credit even though he was aware that the debtor might have repayment difficulties, then he is liable for the damage suffered by the mandator.

c) Right to be informed: "render of account"

The mandator also has a right to be informed by the mandatory of the results of his performance (art. 1713 Italian CC and art. 1720 Spanish CC and art. 263 Spanish Comm.C).

d) Right to be subrogated in the rights of the mandatory

If the mandate has been performed and the mandator has made payment as guarantor, he is then subrogated into the mandatory's rights against the third party (art. 1949 Italian CC and art. 1839 Spanish CC).

e) Right of the mandator to revoke the mandate

The mandator enjoys a right to revoke the mandate in Italy, Navarra and the rest of Spain. As the exercise of this right extinguishes the contract it shall be treated as a way of extinction hereinafter[41].

3. Rights of the mandatory vis-à-vis the mandator

a) Right to performance of the mandator upon default of the beneficiary

This is a right granted ex lege by art. 1958 Italian CC and by the contract of mandate in Spain (art. 1727 Spanish CC and in art. 253 and art. 254 Comm. C., by which the mandator remains liable for the obligations which have been agreed within the limits of the mandate). On performing the mandate, the mandatory automatically obtains a guarantee from the mandator; hence upon default of the third party, the mandatory has the right to be paid by the mandator, in accordance with the rules on the guarantee.

b) Right to perceive the remuneration stipulated

The parties can agree a specific remuneration for the performance of the mandate (see art. 1709 Italian CC and art. 1711 Spanish CC), different to

---

[41] See under Chapter 3, A., IX., 1. Revocation by the mandator, 199.

the interests for the credit. In this case, the mandatory has the right to receive it from the mandator on the agreed terms.

c) Right to recover costs which are separate from the provision of funds

Art. 1719 Italian CC and art. 1728 Spanish CC enshrines the right of the mandatory to receive from the mandator the means necessary to perform the mandate and to fulfil the obligations which the mandatory has undertaken in his own name. These provisions are not applicable to the m.p.c. as the funds for the credit must belong to the mandatory himself. Otherwise, If it would be the mandator who was actually granting the credit, the economic sense and the legal reason (causa) of this contract would be lost.

d) Right to be indemnified for the damages suffered due to the performance of the mandate

Those costs and damages which are incurred by the mandatory in performing the mandate (as distinct from the insolvency of the third party) and which are not caused by his own negligence, shall be covered by the mandator (art. 1720 Italian CC and art. 1729 Spanish CC and 278 Spanish Comm.C.).

e) Right to be discharged of the duty to grant credit

This right is expressly provided for the m.p.c. in art. 1959 par. 1 Italian CC and Ley 526 sent. 2 Fuero Nuevo de Navarra. According to this provision, the mandatory can be discharged of ("cannot be compelled to") performing his obligation if the financial situation of the mandator or the third party has become worse and the performance of the debt would therefore be more difficult.

The paying capacity of the beneficiary and the mandator-guarantor are the economic reason for the granting of credit. Therefore it is reasonable to give the mandatory the opportunity to avoid the contract if the relevant circumstances change.

As the mandatory has the right to renounce the mandate, it has been contended that he also has the right to be discharged[42]. The difference is mainly that the right to be discharged needs a fair reason (such as the supervening insolvency of the mandator or of the third party). Accordingly, the mandatory is not liable for possible damages which are due to the discharge, which contrasts with the case of renunciation.

---

[42] *Arcos*, 254 ff.

f) Right to waive the contract

The mandatory's right to renounce the contract has been recognised as valid in Italy and Spain. As it causes the extinction of the contract it shall be treated hereinafter[43].

IX. Extinction of the m.p.c.

Since the regulation of the m.p.c. does not contain any provision regarding its extinction, the general rules on mandate shall be taken to be applicable to this matter in Italy, Navarra and the rest of Spain (art. 1722 ff. Italian CC juncto art. 78 Legge falimmentare, applicable by analogy[44]; Ley 559 Fuero Nuevo de Navarra and art. 1732 Spanish CC). Accordingly, the m.p.c. shall be extinguished by revocation, waiver, death, incapacity or by reason of the insolvency of the mandator or the mandatory.

1. Revocation by the mandator

The mandator has the right to extinguish unilaterally the contract of m.p.c. if his confidence in the mandatory has deteriorated in any way. The right of the mandator to revoke his m.p.c. is expressly established in art. 1958 Italian CC. The nature of the contract justifies this provision, since the mandator is the person assuming the risk of the contract. Furthermore this contract is based on a relationship of trust between the parties. However, the wording of art. 1958 Italian CC contradicts the general rule on revocation of a mandate given in the interest of the mandatory or the third party (art. 1723 par. 2 CC). This suggests that the m.p.c. is constituted as a mandate given for the interest of the mandator himself[45] and therefore art. 1723 to art. 1726 CC shall not be applied to this contract.

Revocation must take place before the credit has been effectively granted (on application of the general contractual rules, art. 1373 CC)[46]. If only a part of the mandate has already been fulfilled, there may possibly be a revocation of the rest.

In Navarra and the rest of Spain the right of revocation is established within the rules on the mandate (Ley 559 of the Fuero Nuevo de Navarra and art. 1733 to art. 1735 Spanish CC as well as 279 Spanish Comm.C), applicable hereto[47]. It can be express or tacit if the behaviour of the man-

---

[43] See *infra* Chapter 3, A., IX., 2. Waiver by the mandatory, 200.
[44] *Giusti*, 312.
[45] See *Giusti*, 309.
[46] *Giusti*, 309; *Fernández/Nieto/Bonet*, 843. Contra: *Sesta/Cendon*, 1769.
[47] *Robles*, 541 ff.

dator is absolutely incompatible with the subsistence of the mandate (for example, when the mandator gives the same order to a new mandatory)[48].

The possibility to revoke the mandate is one of the features distinguishing the m.p.c. from the guarantee for future debts. If the mandator revokes his mandate, he will have to indemnify the mandatory for the damages caused (general damage and lost of profit) (art. 1958 par. 2 in fine Italian CC).

The right of revocation is not mandatory. However, the parties to the mandate may contractually stipulate that the m.p.c. will be irrevocable. Spanish case law has established implied irrevocability of the mandate not being based on a personal trustworthy relationship but existing as a consequence of another contract[49].

2. *Waiver by the mandatory*

In Italy, the regulation on the m.p.c. does not explicitly establish the right of the mandatory to waive this contract. However this has generally been held to be a valid legal right by academic theorists in Italy, Navarra and the rest of Spain[50].

Some Italian authors justify the approval of this cause of extinction through art. 1256 par. 2 Italian CC (extinction of the obligation if its performance has become impossible for a cause not imputable to the debtor). The waiver would only take place if the patrimonial difficulties are not limited to short-term financial difficulties, the appraisal of this situation depending on the circumstances of the case. At a first stage, the contract might be suspended; i.e. it is not extinguished but only left without effect until the situation becomes clear[51]. However in the case of the mandate, the obligation of granting credit does not become impossible only because

---

[48] Art. 1735 Spanish CC; *Farré*, 1752.

[49] STS 27 October 1989 [RA 1989 no. 6964] and STS 11 May 1993 [RA 1993 no. 3538]: „La irrevocabilidad del mandato deviene no sólo cuando exista pacto expreso que así lo establezca siempre que tal pacto sea conforme a su finalidad y no esté en contradicción con la moral en cuanto es una manifestación de la renuncia de derechos, sino también cuando el mandato no es simple expresión de confianza o del simple interés del mandato, sino que responde a exigencias de cumplimiento de otro contrato en el que están interesados, no sólo el mandante o representado, sino también el mandatario y terceras personas; es decir cuando el mandato es en definitiva mero instrumento formal en relación jurídica bilateral y plurilateral que le sirve de causa o razón de ser y cuya ejecución o cumplimiento exige y aconseja la irrevocabiidad para evitar la frustración del fin perseguido por dicho contrato subyacente por la voluntad de uno solo de los interesados“. Contra: *Farré*, 1752.

[50] *Simonetto*, Il Mandato di Credito, 164; *Giusti*, 310; *Arcos*, 254; *Fernández/Nieto/Bonet*, 843.

[51] *Ravazzoni*, Le garanzie, 168.

the mandator or/and the beneficiary suffer patrimonial difficulties. Accordingly, art. 1256 CC does not offer a genuinely acceptable legal way to allow the mandatory to waive the contract.

The respective regulations on mandate, applicable hereto, do contain a right for the mandatory to renounce the mandate (art. 1727 Italian CC and art. 1736 Spanish CC and also the Ley 559 par. 2 and 3 of the Fuero Nuevo de Navarra). According to these provisions, the mandatory shall compensate the mandator for damages caused by the waiver unless it is due to a fair cause. In the case of a m.p.c., if the patrimony of the beneficiary or the mandator has been so strongly reduced that it no longer suffices for paying or guaranteeing the credit, then there will be reason enough to waive the mandate without any need to indemnify.

3. Death

If either the mandator or the mandatory dies or is not able to perform the mandate, the contract is extinguished. This results from the rules covering the extinction of the mandate (Ley 559 Fuero Nuevo de Navarra[52], art. 1722 juncto art. 1728 Italian CC and art. 1732 Spanish CC). The actual effects of the death of one of the parties depend on the moment at which it occurs.

a) Death before the performance of the mandate

If any of the parties die before the mandatory has granted credit, the m.p.c. shall be automatically extinguished. The heirs of the decedent do not have any rights vis-à-vis the surviving party except for the costs of the activity already accomplished and any damages caused before the extinction had taken place. As the credit has not been granted, these costs and damages will be almost irrelevant. Moreover, the damages derived from the extinction of the m.p.c. itself are not included, as art. 1720 Italian CC and 1729 Spanish CC as well as the Ley 559 Fuero Nuevo de Navarra all serve to limit the answerability for the damages to those which are actually sustained in the execution of the mandate. Therefore the mandatory is not entitled to ask the heirs for lost profits caused by the non-performance of the mandate.

b) Death after the performance of the mandate

If the credit has already been granted, the general rules on succession apply and the heirs succeed the decedent in all rights and obligations.

---

[52] The mandate post-mortem, specifically regulated by the Ley 559 par. 1 *in fine*, remains excluded.

If the mandator dies, the mandatory loses the guarantee for the credit granted, which was one of the main reasons to accept the mandate. The heirs shall be answerable vis-à-vis the mandatory for the damages or losses that the diligent performance of the mandate might cause. Also if the mandatory decides to break the credit relationship with the third party by reason of the mandator's death, the heirs will also be liable for the losses[53].

If the mandatory dies, the obligation to perform cannot be transmitted to his heirs. The latter cannot be compelled to accept the mandate and the mandator cannot accept them as mandatories, since the m.p.c. is a contract which is very much based on personal reliance. The contract of m.p.c. is therefore usually extinguished and the costs and damages to which it has given origin shall be paid off. Yet the rights already acquired by the mandatory for the partial or total performance of the mandate shall be transmitted to his heirs. So the credit that had been granted by the decedent mandatory must be repaid to his heirs.

4. *Supervening incapacity*

Art. 1722 juncto 1728 Italian CC and art. 1732 Spanish CC[54] consider the incapacity of the mandator or the mandatory as a justified cause of extinction of the contract. Art. 1732 Spanish CC also includes the declaration of prodigality as a cause of extinction. The legal reasoning is the same as in the general supervening incapacity; the person is not trustworthy enough to perform the mandate as agreed.

5. *Insolvency*

Art. 1722 Italian CC juncto art. 78 Legge Falimmentare, as well as art. 1732 Spanish CC include the insolvency of mandator or mandatory as a cause of extinction of the mandate. These rules do not specify if the insolvency must be legally declared or if a de facto insolvency shall be enough to extinguish the mandate. According to the legal reasoning of this provision i.e. mutual personal confidence, a factual insolvency will generally be considered to be enough[55] to sanction extinction.

6. *Exception in case of enterprises*

According to art. 1722 par. 3 in fine Italian CC "a mandate concerning the completion of transactions connected with the operation of an enterprise is

[53] *Arcos*, 248 ff.
[54] As ammended by the Ley Orgánica 1/1996, de 15 de enero.
[55] *Gordillo*, 1582.

not extinguished if such operation continues, subject to the right of the parties or of their heirs to withdraw from the mandate".

X. Function of the m.p.c.

There are plenty of commercial situations in which a person is interested in the ability of another to obtain credit. He might intend to become a partner in a profitable business or to win customers by enabling them to obtain the essential funds through a credit. The m.p.c. to a third party offers an adequate legal instrument for these instances. The businessman requiring a credit institution to grant credit to one of his future partners/customers is thereby also assuming the guarantee for it. A similar case takes place when a holding requires a bank to provide credit to one of the companies under its control. Another example is an architect who administrates the finances of a construction in progress and requires the supplier to deliver materials on credit. Thus he also assumes thereby the guarantee for the payment of the goods[56].

A m.p.c. offers a useful and functional legal solution in normal commercial practice. The development of business traffic and the world of finance has not made this instrument obsolete. Yet it is almost unused in practice as a legal way to obtain credit. This is partly due to the broad use of the guarantee for future obligation or letters of comfort, especially in cases where the m.p.c. could also quite properly be used.

It seems that the scope of application of the m.p.c. may be restricted in practice to minor financing contracts. An example of this could be the situation in which parents order a bank to open an account for their minor son, whilst declaring that the latter will operate within a maximum amount[57].

XI. Similar security rights to the m.p.c.

1. The m.p.c. and the letter of comfort

The letter of comfort[58] operates to facilitate the granting of a personal security. The issuer of the letter promotes and enables the grant of credit to the third party (the subsidiary) by issuing a letter of comfort which provides the creditor with a certain level of security. The creditor's protection upon default of the debtor depends on the terms in which such letter is drafted. Generally, letters of comfort are divided in so called "strong" and "weak" letters of comfort. The wording used in the letter is key to identify

---

[56] OLG Frankfurt, NJW 1967, 2361.

[57] *Giusti*, 298 f.

[58] See *Sánchez Guilarte*, 871 ff.

the level of protection provided. In the practice, interpretation of these letters has given origine to conflicts solved by a large case law in both countries[59]. The issuer is personally interested in the grant of credit[60]. The letter of comfort shares a common aim with the m.p.c. but there are important differences between both contracts.

The issuer of a letter of comfort promotes the grant of credit because he makes the creditor feel confident in relation to the recovery of the credit. However he does not order the grant of the credit. This contrasts with the function of the mandator of a m.p.c.. The decision to grant is exclusive to the creditor. It is also the case that it falls to the creditor and the beneficiary to establish the terms and conditions of the contract. Accordingly, the letter of comfort usually precedes the grant of credit while in a m.p.c. the guarantee is a consequence of the performance of the mandate.

The kind and level of security provided by a comfort letter depends on its wording which is usually subject to careful construction. In a m.p.c. the security constituted is always a typical contract of guarantee and the parties cannot agree otherwise. Once the mandatory has granted the credit on performance of the mandate, the mandator is answerable as guarantor. The strongest letters of comfort also provide a security very similar to the contract of guarantee but this is subject to the will of the issuer and the construction of the wording of each letter.

The content of the letter of comfort is in many cases not strictly defined. In some cases, it shall cover a sum of different debts or even the complete balance due. On the contrary, the object of the m.p.c. is strictly defined in the contract. The mandatory must grant the credit for the sum ordered and the mandator guarantees this object.

Therefore, although the final aim of both personal security rights is similar, their respective structure and effects differ. This allows drawing a distinction between them and using each of them in different situations within commercial activity.

2. *The m.p.c. and the documentary credit*

Documentary credits are payment and financing instruments for international transactions[61]. The aim is to guarantee the payment of a trading price

---

[59] See for Italy, Aletti and for Spain Medina, Chapter I.5.

[60] These are usually parent companies which are contributing to the operation of a subsidiary company (Supreme Court decision STS 16 Dec. 1985 [RA 1985 no. 6442]. Recently there are also cases of comfort letters between private persons. An example of this is the situation of solvent parents of a poor tenant issuing a letter of comfort to the landlord in order to provide satisfactory security. The interest in these cases is usually personal.

[61] In practice they are governed by the ICC Uniform Rules on Documentary Credits.

between two different places. The bank (issuer bank), following the instruction of his client, shall perform a payment, as well as accept or sell a bill of exchange that the beneficiary may draw, or permit the payment, to acceptance or sale of such bills of exchange by another bank, upon the delivery of the documents if the agreed terms and conditions have also been performed.

Many similarities are to be found between the documentary credit and the m.p.c.. There is an instructing party, ordering the issuing bank to perform payment to a third party upon delivery of the agreed documents. There is a credit relationship between the issuing bank and the instructing party. Nevertheless, there are a number of differentiating elements. In first place, both contracts have a different content. The documentary credit is usually based on a commercial relationship, focused on the transaction of property while the m.p.c. is based on a future financial debt.

The interests of each of the parties involved in these contracts are also different. In a m.p.c. the mandator aims to enable the grant of credit to a third party and therefore guarantees the credit provided by the mandatory. In a documentary credit, the payment to the third is a consequence of a commercial transaction. The aim of the instructing party is to guarantee its commercial partner the performance of his commercial debt, previously existent as a consequence of their commercial relationship. But the person accepting the credit is the instructing party and not the third i.e. the mandator of a documentary credit is liable as a credit receiver (debtor), while the mandator of a the m.p.c. only guarantees and will therefore be liable in the exceptional case of non performance by the third party ("ope exceptionis").

The liability of the bank in a documentary credit regards the credit relationship while in a m.p.c. it is based on the acceptance of the mandate.

Moreover, in the situation of documentary credit, a second bank may enter the relationship, by adding its own guarantee to the beneficiary.

3. The m.p.c. and the letters of payment (Cartas orden de crédito)

The so called "cartas órden de crédito" are instruments of payment provided for in art. 567 f. Spanish Comm. C. They are issued by a trader to another trader or to accomplish a commercial operation. They must be issued in favour of a determined person and for a fixed and specific amount or within a maximum limit previously settled. The receiver of the letter pays the person in favour of which it has been issued and the issuer remains answerable for the amount agreed in the letter and has a right of repayment against the debtor. This can be utilised if the issuer is called on to perform. The structure and function of the letters of payment may appear to exist in parallel to the m.p.c. However, the letter of payment is not an order or mandate to the receiver to provide credit. The efficacy of this instrument depends on the will of both the beneficiary, who asks for the amount established in the letter and the receiver who must decide whether or not he wishes to pay. These factors are discretionary for both parties.

The beneficiary might not ask for the amount. His right to do so is limited by time to the term agreed in the letter or to the legal one established in art. 572 Spanish Comm. C (six months within Europe and twelve within the rest of the world). If he does not ask the receiver of the letter for payment within the time limit, the letter of payment is rendered void.

The receiver of the letter is not obliged to perform the payment. If he does perform, the issuer remains answerable for that payment. But it must be emphasised that the receiver has an unfettered discretion as to whether or not he will perform. This is the main difference with the contract of m.p.c.

The structure of both instruments is very similar. There are three parties, one grants credit to a third and the promoter of that credit remains liable for it. However, the letter of payment is not a mandate, since the receiver is never compelled to grant credit. Moreover, the letter of payment is exclusively applied within commercial transactions.

XII. Legal nature of the m.p.c.

A functional approach to the contract of m.p.c., shows a complex structure combining elements of two different typical contracts (mandate and guarantee). This surprising configuration gives origin to a considerable uncertainty on the nature of the m.p.c.. This remains as being the primary matter of controversy among scholars on this topic since Roman Times.

In view of the elements of the contract and their significance, the m.p.c. has been identified with the contract of guarantee and with the contract of mandate. It has also been treated as an atypical contract with a particular legal nature combining elements of both contracts.

1. The m.p.c. as a contract of guarantee

The m.p.c. has been identified with the contract of guarantee[62] on the basis of the guarantee for future debts. A certain identification of both contracts is generally accepted[63], as the second phase of the m.p.c. is actually the constitution of a guarantee. Furthermore, the possibility of constituting guarantees for future debts seems to facilitate the identification of both contracts.

---

[62] *Campogrande*, 132 ff.. See also long references in *Graziani*, 322; *Giusti*, 301 and *Leon*, 1086.

[63] *León*, 1086.

However, certain features of the m.p.c. serve to distinguish it from the classic contract of guarantee. In the m.p.c. the guarantee obligation is the source and the consequence of the mandator obligation (connessione causale[64]/interconexión causal[65]). In a typical credit relationship it would be unusual for the constitution of the mandator obligation to be so directly connected with the constitution of the guarantee[66].

In the m.p.c. the credit is granted because it is already guaranteed. Simultaneously, the guarantee obligation is automatically created when the credit is granted. Accordingly, while the archetypal guarantee can be constituted before or after the establishment of the mandatory's obligation, in the m.p.c. the guarantee has to be constituted before.

Moreover, by contrast to the guarantee, the mandatory of a m.p.c. has the obligation to grant the credit. This allows the revocation of the mandate as long as the mandatory has not yet granted the credit. This is not possible in the case of a classic guarantee, even if the guarantee has been given for a future debt.

2. *The m.p.c. as a contract of mandate*

It has also been contended that the m.p.c. is a special form of mandate[67]. In countries such as Italy which have enacted a specific legal regulation covering the m.p.c. formal reasons are cited in support of this theory.

In the first place, the nomen iuris of this contract contains the term mandate („mandato di credito"/„Kreditauftrag"). This can thus be related to the classic contract of mandate which is regulated within the civil codes. Moreover, the regulation of the m.p.c contains other terms which are typical of the contract of mandate ("incarico"/"beauftragt"). Terminology of this nature is also present within the regulation of certain special kinds of mandate (like in art. 1756 or art. 1742 Italian CC).

If this argument is followed then the liability of the mandator can be seen to be derived from the contract of mandate. The content of art. 1958 Italian CC would be taken as a particular application of art. 1720 par. 2 Italian CC. Therefore, the mandator would remain liable for damage suffered by the mandatory by reason of the mandate. In the particular instance of the m.p.c. this liability is only pre-established on the basis of the guar-

---

[64] *Graziani*, 315 ff.

[65] *León*, 1086.

[66] "La teoria della fideisussione incontra un ostacolo insormontabile nell'essistenza della obligazione del c.d. mandatario a concedere il mutuo, obbligazione che assolutamente è assente nella fideiussione dove a carico del creditore non sorge nessuna obbligazione", *Graziani*, 322.

[67] "*Sottospecie di mandato*", *Ravazzoni*, Le garanzie, 165. See *Fragali/Scialoja/Branca*, 532; *Simonetto*, 154 ff. See also long references in *León*, 1089.

antee[68]. However the liability of the mandator as guarantor does not possess the typical indemnifying character of the mandate. This discrepancy in the nature of the mandator's liability seems significant enough to reconfigure the entire nature of the contract. Accordingly, the m.p.c. cannot be considered to be a special form of mandate, although many constitutive elements are shared between both contracts.

In Spain the m.p.c is not governed by statutory provisions. Therefore, if the parties agree to make the mandator liable as a guarantor upon default of the third party, the mandator must indemnify the damages caused to the mandatory on the occurrence of the default as stated in the rules of mandate.

The mandatory bears the burden of proving the loss which has been created. Furthermore he will only obtain damages from the mandator if he justifies the damages i.e. the liability of the mandator is issued ope exceptionis (on application of the exceptio dolis generalis) and not ipso iure. The security of the mandatory would thus be based upon the rules of the mandate. This would thereby create a particular scheme for the obtaining of compensation for damage caused by any default. This gives the security an indemnifying character which is atypical of the contract of guarantee.

If this concept of m.p.c. is followed and the guaranteeing liability of the mandator is agreed, then the indemnifying nature of this contract is changed into being of a guaranteeing nature. Moreover, in the contract of the m.p.c. the mandator is not the dominus negotii, even though he is the party who is assuming its risk. This state of affairs serves to distance the m.p.c. from the contract of mandate. However this last objection can be easily refuted as the mandator of a m.p.c. has greater status than that of being a simple guarantor. He is the verus dominus; the de facto legal and economic centre of the whole structure which has been created on his own initiative, risk and interest. The mandatory is only the intermediary which serves to facilitate the possibility of the business taking place, while the mandator is the direct cause of the credit granting by the mandatory (who granted because of the promise to cover the debtor's insolvency). The risks are taken into account when the estimated profits are being calculated. Moreover the mandator determines who will be the beneficiary. This action is done in the expectation of the obtaining of commercial returns from this relationship, which is another manifestation of the dominus character of the mandator.

The agreement between the mandatory and the third person which enables the credit to be granted changes the role occupied by the mandator. Within this trilateral relation the mandator is thus converted into a guarantor. This agreement may therefore have an impact on the mandator's pat-

[68] See *Giusti*, 300.

rimony. Thus it could be argued that this erodes the dominus position of the mandator, but that was the exact aim of the mandator in electing to issue the mandate.

3. *Autonomous legal nature of the m.p.c.*

Within the m.p.c. elements of the contract of guarantee and the contract of mandate are intermingled in order to compose a financial instrument[69]. Such interconnection is so strong that the nature of the m.p.c. cannot be fully identified with the nature of either of the two contracts under analysis. It must rather be construed as possessing an independent or autonomous character. This autonomous character however does not prevent it receiving the application of the rules on mandate in the appropriate circumstances. This application will thus be appropriate if it is compatible with the special characteristics of this contract and the regulations which cover the guaranteeing function of the mandator in the second phase of the contract. This theory appears to be the most convincing one with respect to the legal nature of the m.p.c..

XIII. Convenience to regulate the m.p.c. in Spanish legislation

The question of whether it is necessary to include the m.p.c. in Spanish legislation is of a rather theoretical variety. Spanish commercial practice does not seem to suffer any disadvantage due to the absence of a specific regulation of the m.p.c. Parties are free to agree a contract of mandate with the same characteristics and effects as the m.p.c. Yet they neglect to do so within the commercial sphere. Even in legal systems which have a specific regulation for the m.p.c., its use is almost non-existent.

From a theoretical point of view, the m.p.c. is moderately problematic. The contract of mandate in Spain was regulated in accordance with the French model, on the basis of representation. The mandatory represents the mandator in the performance of the contract. However, as it is the case that within a m.p.c. the mandatory grants the credit in his own name and account, the representing role of the mandatory is lost. Accordingly, the m.p.c. cannot be fully considered to be a form of mandate in Spain. Accordingly, it would be also difficult to admit the applicability of the regulation of the mandate to the m.p.c.. This was probably the main reason for the omission of a specific regulation of the m.p.c. within the Spanish Civil Code, despite the fact that important precedents such as Roman law and the old law of Castilla contained a regulation of the m.p.c.

---

[69] See *Fernández/Nieto/Bonet*, 832 and *Giusti*, 303.

However, these theoretical barriers could be overcome if the m.p.c. were to be regulated in Spain. Important legal authors[70] have considered possible the existence of a non-representative mandate (mandato no representativo) under Spanish Law as the wording of art. 1709 and art. 1717 Spanish CC is suggestive of a broader conception of the mandate. This would make it possible to regulate the m.p.c. in Spanish CC, but the practical experience of the neighbouring countries makes it doubtful as to whether there is any real need for it.

B. Guarantee for a bill of exchange (l'avallo/el aval cambiario)

I. The basic concept of guarantee for a bill of exchange

The guarantee given for a bill of exchange (avallo/aval[71]) is a personal security right specifically aimed at securing the payment of a bill of exchange (or a cheque or promissory note). It is a declaration, by means of which the surety undertakes to be answerable for the total or partial payment of the exchange obligation.

The function of the guarantee for a bill of exchange is identical to that of the contract of guarantee, namely to secure the creditor and thereby facilitate the grant of credit[72]. The guarantee obligation undertaken by the surety is a separate obligation, and the surety assumes a joint and several liability regarding the primary obligation. The declaration is made on the bill itself and must specify the limits of the liability assumed by the surety. Unless otherwise specified, the surety's liability will be considered granted for the totality of the mandatory's obligation.

II. Terminological uncertainty in Spain

The term aval is not only used to describe the abovementioned guarantee for a bill of exchange but is also rather confusingly used as a synonym for guarantee (fianza). Originally it referred specifically to contracts of guarantee granted by qualified guarantors, like banks or public institutions, but its meaning was later extended to include every kind of guarantee and be-

---

[70] *Díez Picazo*, La representación en el Derecho Privado, Madrid, 1979. See long references in *Arcos*, 83–161.

[71] See *Vicent/Nieto/Bonet*, 383; *Añoveros*, 1992; *Blanco*, Aval, 677 f.; *Sánchez-Calero Guilarte*, El aval, 331 ff; *Sánchez Calero*, Instituciones, 80 f.

[72] *Bozzi/Rescigno*, 288; *Thietz-Bartram*, 36; *Vicent/Nieto/Bonet*, 383; *Rojo/Menendez*, 549; *Sánchez Calero Guilarte*, El aval, 331 ff.; *Guilarte*, 48. See *supra* Chapter 1, C. The practical functions of security rights: Law, economics and social implications, 14.

came so an alternative to the word fianza[73]. The term is regularly used in this latter sense in daily practice, case law[74], legal studies[75] and even legislation[76]. It is hence the task of the courts to determine in each case which kind of contract is contained in a document before the forum. The lack of precision in the use of this legal term should be avoided, particularly within legislation.

III. Legal nature and regulation

The guarantee for a bill of exchange is conceived of as an independent obligation which remains valid even if the primary obligation becomes invalid[77]. This independent nature was always clear under Italian law[78] but not in Spain, where an intensive doctrinal debate took place until the enactment of the Ley Cambiaria y del Cheque (LCC) in 1985. The wording of art. 475 to art. 478 Spanish Comm. C. were ambiguous[79]. Some writers, following the Italian construction, considered the guarantee for a bill of exchange to be an autonomous security right[80], while authors who supported the French theories considered it a kind of contract of guarantee; accessory[81]. After years of debate and uncertainty[82], the matter was clari-

---

[73] Blanco refers to a semantic study of the term *aval*; *Blanco/Sánchez-Calero* and *Sánchez-Calero Guilarte*, 171; Infante, Un equívoco del TS, IV.

[74] As a way of example see: STS 15 June 2008 [RA 2008 no. 4377] and STS 7 Jan. 1981, BMIJ no. 1240, 37.

[75] *Suso*, 519 f.

[76] Art. 284 Ley de Sociedades Anónimas (LSA); regarding Mutual guarantee societies: art. 1 RD of 26 of July 1978. For long references see: *Blanco/Sánchez-Calero* and *Sánchez-Calero Guilarte*, 172.

[77] Art. 37 Legge Cambiaria (LC) and art. 37 par. 1 Ley 19/1985, cambiaria y del cheque (LCC). *García Cortés/Nieto/Bonet*, 508; *Sánchez Calero*, Instituciones de derecho mercantil, 88.

[78] *Bozzi/Rescigno*, 288; Trabucchi, 624 and 724; *De Marco/Sparano*, 185.

[79] For long historical references: *García Cortés/Nieto/Bonet*, 509. *Guilarte*, 48.

[80] They based their opinion on the term "independently" in art. 486 Comm. C.: "The payment of a bill of exchange, can be guaranteed with an obligation written independently of the one assumed by the acceptor and the endorser, known as guarantee for a bill of exchange." ("El pago de una letra de cambio podrá afianzarse con una obligación escrita independientemente de la que contraen el aceptante y el endosante, conocida con el nombre de aval").

[81] They base their opinion on the guarantee function of the guarantee for a bill of exchange. The term "independently" in art. 486 LCC regards the parties and not the obligations. Moreover the extent of the guarantee for a bill of exchange is flexible according to art. 487 Spanish Comm. C., but is always restricted to the limits of the underlying obligation.

[82] For long references see *Guilarte*, 49.

fied by the LCC[83]. The imprecise wording of the Spanish Comm.C. (art. 486 ff.) is clarified in art. 37 par. 1 LCC[84], where the autonomous character of the guarantee for a bill of exchange is expressed in the same words as in Italian art. 37 L.C.

Italy ratified the Geneva Uniform Law on Bills of Exchange and Promissory Notes of 1930 and adopted the text as national law[85] in the LC. Spain never ratified the Geneva Conventions but adopted the text of the Uniform Law[86] in the LCC[87]. The guarantee for the bill of exchange is governed by art. 35 to art. 37 of both statutes. Furthermore, in both countries the law on guarantees has been declared to be subsidiarily applicable to the bill guarantee by analogy[88]. Due to the different nature of a guarantee and a guarantee for a bill of exchange[89], they may both be simultaneously granted by the same surety[90].

It is interesting to note that Spain has not signed the UNCITRAL Convention on International Bills of Exchange and International Promissory Notes, which was adopted the 9th of December, 1988. The Convention was an attempt to reconcile the approaches of different legislative systems in this regard[91]. However, this Convention has not yet entered into force and will probably never do so.

---

[83] The explaining motives of the law expressely refer to the autonomous nature in the motive III: "[…] the need to clarify this matter, opting for its definition as autonomous obligation…".

[84] Extremely surprising is the Supreme Court decision of 28 March 2003 (STS 28 March 2003 [RA 2003 no. 3039] werer it is clearly estated that the gurantee for a bill of exchange is an ancillary contract, which extinguishes upon the extinction of the secured debt. This decisions referes to a large case law, all previous to 1985, year in which the LCC clarified the matter *ex lege*. This case law must be strongly critized and not taken into account with regard to the configuration of the guarantee for a bill of exchange.

[85] *Jahn*, Wechselrecht, 1.

[86] *Jahn*, Bills of Exchange, 6.

[87] See Explanation Motive III of the Spanish LCC.

[88] Cass. 11 November 1953 no. 3026; Cass. 8 June 1976 no. 2090; Cass. 11 September 1997, no. 8990; Cass. 7 May 1998 no. 4618, cited by Petti, 267. For a deep study: *Bozzi/Rescigno*, 288 f.; *Rojo/Menéndez*, 500 f.

[89] *Guilarte*, 48.

[90] Cass. 8 August 1967, no. 2114, GI, 1968, I, 1, 314; Cass. 25 July 1978, no. 3710, BBTC, 1979, II, 141.

[91] *García Cortés/Nieto/Bonet*, 510.

C. The contract of guarantee insurance

I. The basic concept of guarantee insurance

The guarantee insurance is now a very common way of providing security[92] through an insurance contract taken out by a debtor in favour of his creditor. It covers the creditor for any loss or damage which he may suffer in the event of the debtor failing to perform his legal or contractual obligations.

In Italy and Spain these contracts are not strictly regulated and a great deal is left to be agreed by the parties. As the parties involved are usually companies and professionals, there is normally no need for the application of special consumer protection rules[93]. Flexibility and adaptability to their needs is generally sought out by the parties and so there are a number of different kinds of insurance policies which fulfil this function in practice.

II. Relations between the parties to the contract

The guarantee insurance creates a three party relationship between the insurer, the party taking out the insurance (the debtor) and the beneficiary of the contract (the creditor).

1. Relationship between the debtor and the creditor

The debtor and the creditor enjoy a contractual relationship, which gives rise to an obligation to perform, or not to perform or to pay. In order to guarantee the fulfilment of such obligation, the creditor (beneficiary) requires a guarantee of performance (cauzione/caución). This relationship is the underlying obligation, which is basis for the insurance contract.

The guarantee insurance is most commonly used in the export trade as well as in connection with contracts agreed with the State, for which guarantees are required by law.

2. Relationship between the debtor and the insurer

The insurance policy is agreed between the debtor and the insurer, either by mandate of law or by agreement between the parties. In terms of such policy, the insurance company is obliged to pay a sum of money to the creditor upon the happening of the stipulated contingency, i.e. the failure of the debtor to perform its obligation/s to the creditor. If the insurer is

[92] Baldini (http://www. Tidona.com/versionestampa/stampa_aprile01_2.htm). See STS 26 January 1995 [RA 1995 no.172], STS 19 May 1990 [RA 1990 no. 3741].

[93] If, however, a consumer enters a guarantee insurance, the general rules on consumer protection will be applied thereto.

required to make such payment it retains a right of recourse against the debtor[94]. The debtor pays the premium of the insurance policy, which is calculated according to general insurance practices[95].

3. Relationship between the insurer and the creditor

The creditor obtains an individual certificate of guarantee insurance[96]. This provides that the insurance company insures the performance of the debtor's obligation/s to the creditor and that the insurer will pay a sum of money to the creditor as an indemnity or penalty if the debtor does not perform.

III. Economic function of the guarantee insurance

By means of the guarantee insurance, the creditor is assured of the performance of the debtor's obligation and the automatic payment of damages in case of non-performance. The goal of security is achieved without further burdening the debtor's balance sheet with an additional guarantee, which would also require an increase of the immobilised capital reserves or a supplementary guarantee. Moreover, guarantee insurance is tax-deductible and more cost-effective. Insurance companies usually have extensive national and international networks, allowing for higher flexibility and lower costs in providing guarantees.

IV. Types of guarantee insurance contracts

The kind of protection provided by the guarantee insurance is required by the law in certain cases. In other situations it is contractually agreed by companies who need to secure performance in order to guarantee the safe conduct of their business[97]. Accordingly, different types of guarantee insurance contracts can be distinguished[98].

---

[94] *Mazza/Franzoni*, 1430; *Tamburrino*, 525.

[95] *Simone, Dizionario Simone*, „Polizza fideiussoria“ (http:www.simone.it/cgi?local/Dizionari/newdiz.cgi?*voce*,5,4155).

[96] In Spanish insurance practice these certificates are also called "aval" but are simply one of the documents formalising the insurance. The use of the term "aval" in this context has created confusion with regard to the legal nature of the contract.

[97] See STS 21 April 1989 [RA 1989 no. 3248] commented by Embid, La Ley 1990, II, 198; STS 19 May 1990 [RA 1990 no. 3741]; STS 30 July 1991 [RA 1991 no. 5431] and STS 5 June 1992 [RA 1992 no. 5002] commented by Embid, CCJC, 1992, § 776.

[98] Extensive references about the modalities of the guarantee contract in European business practice: *Cavatorta*, 11 ff. cited by *Tirado/Motos/Albadalejo*, 428.

1. Guarantee insurance required by law

Guarantee insurance contracts are prescribed by law in certain instances for the protection of interests that are considered valuable for the benefit of the community[99]. The most obvious illustration of this in commercial practice is the requirement of a guarantee insurance contract when the public administration acts as a contracting party in commercial activities.

a) Insurance contract in favour of the public administration

The party that contracts with the public administration must often provide a guarantee for the obligation assumed[100]. There are a number of different situations in which a guarantee is required by law in this respect[101]. All private companies bidding for public work must provide a guarantee to the public administration ensuring that they will accept the tender should it be awarded. When a company is awarded a public tender it must then provide another guarantee to ensure the due performance of its obligations in terms of its contract with the public administration. All guarantees provided by other companies will be cancelled then.

b) Insurance contract to guarantee sums of money invested in the construction of a private residence[102]

In Spain, the law protects those individuals who have made advanced payments in respect of the building of their private residence. This is because such an action is considered to be an essential social good[103].

Usually, the most convenient means of payment for those people who are not able to afford a built flat is to pay part of the purchase price before it is completed. They thereby assume the risk that the construction of the

---

[99] See *Tamburrino*, 524.

[100] See art. 49 Directive 2004/18/EC of the European Parliament and of the Council of 31 March 2004 on the coordination of procedures for the award of public works contracts, public supply contracts and public service contracts, *Official Journal L 134, 30/04/2004, 0114 – 0240.*

Italy: see art 30 Legge 109/94, quadro in materia di lavori publici, as amended and its further developments through the DPR 554/1999 (art. 100 to art. 108). The Decreto legge 123/2004 sets the official forms for the guarantee and insurance contracts in the context of public contracts.

Spain: art.83 to art. 92 Ley 30/2007, de 30 de octubre, de Contratos del Sector Público (Ley 30/2007). On guarantee insurance see art. 84.1c of the Ley 30/2007.

[101] For legal and theoretical references, see *Tamburrino*, 524; *Sánchez-Calero/Tirado/Motos/Albadalejo*, 431; *Francisco* (http://www.5campus.org/leccion/ segucau).

[102] For long references: *Carrasco, Cordero* and *Gonzalez*, 375 ff.

[103] See STS 7 June 1983 [RA 1983 no. 3450]; STS 8 March 2001 [RA 2001 no. 2731]; STS 26 Feb. 2000 [RA 2000 no. 1020]; See references in *Tirado/Motos/Albadalejo*, 429.

building may not be completed. As the buyer is usually the weaker of the contracting parties he is often obliged to accept unfavourable conditions or to provide money upfront without being able to calculate the real risk involved. The consequences of non-performance of such construction contracts can thus be severe for the persons involved, their families and the community as a whole. Moreover, the high level of fraud within the field of private residential construction in practice has given rise to justified social concern.

In order to protect the buyers, Ley 57/1968 de 27 julio[104] compels any individual or legal person involved in the construction of a building to guarantee the return of any money received in advance. Such a guarantee is achieved by concluding an appropriate guarantee insurance contract with a registered and officially authorised insurance company. This type of guarantee contract is governed by the Order of 29th November 1968 (BOE 5 December 1968).

The constructor must therefore take out a guarantee policy in respect of all the buyers purchasing units in a specific building. He must assume payment of the premiums of the policy without passing the costs thereof onto the buyers. Furthermore, when the buyers make upfront payments for their respective dwelling places, they receive a so-called insurance certificate which protects them in the event of the constructor's non-performance[105]. The purpose of this guarantee insurance is to ensure that the sums paid are really invested in the construction of their dwelling places, or that their money will be returned if construction fails to be completed[106]. It does not insure the building risks themselves[107].

The right to be indemnified only arises once the following two conditions have been fulfilled: a) the construction of the building is not completed (or there is no administrative certification of the completion of construction) and b) proof is given of a demand from the buyer to the constructor to return the advanced sums of money[108]. A third additional requirement has been added by the courts[109]: the advanced sums of money must have been paid into a special current account created for this purpose (art. 2 of the Law 57/1968).

---

[104] This law has been ratified by the derogatory disposition (par. 2 lit h) of the Law 33/1984 of 2 August, de Ordenación del Seguro Privado.

[105] *Tirado/Motos/Albadalejo*, 429 ff; *Muñoz de Dios*, 1067.

[106] See Motives of the Ley 57/1968 and STS 8 March 2001 [RA 2001 no. 2731].

[107] STS 18 February 1993 [RA 1993 no. 1243] and STS 14 April 1993 [RA 1993 no. 2879].

[108] See SAP Cáceres 1 February 2000 [AC 2000 no. 776].

[109] SAT Madrid 31 October 1986, RGD 1987, 3396 ff.; SAP Alicante 7 Feb. 1997 [AC 1997 no. 375].

c) Guarantee insurance against property damage caused by construction deficiencies or defects

Art. 17 of Law 38/1999 of 5 November 1999 of the Building Act (Ley de Ordenación de la Edificación, LOE), establishes the constructor's liability for damage to property caused by construction faults or defects. This liability must be secured in accordance with art. 19 LOE which refers to guarantee insurance as a valid way to provide this security[110]. In other countries other types of security are more commonly used for this purpose; for instance guarantees on first demand (Bürgschaft auf erstes Anfordern) in the German practice[111].

2. Guarantee insurance by agreement of the parties

Guarantee insurance contracts are also often concluded by agreement between private parties. In most cases they are used to guarantee the performance of a contractual obligation[112]. However they can also be used to guarantee moratory interest of a payment or the quality of a construction[113].

V. Legal nature of the guarantee insurance

The legal nature of the contract of guarantee insurance has been the subject of much controversy[114]. The combination of elements of a guarantee obligation together with elements of an insurance contract creates some doubt about the legal nature of the guarantee insurance and the legal provisions applicable thereto[115]. Moreover, the confusion on this subject is aggravated by terminological uncertainty in Italy and Spain. Terms like guarantee, aval, guarantee insurance, suretyship insurance, insurance by means of guarantee[116] are common in insurance practice[117]. A significant effort to

---

[110] For longer references, see *Carrasco, Cordero* and *Gonzalez*, 265 ff.

[111] See BGH 2 April 1992, NJW 1992 no. 1881.

[112] *Francisco* (http://www.5campus.org/leccion/segucau).

[113] *Zuliani*, 30 ff., 384 ff.; *Sánchez-Calero/Tirado/Albadalejo*, 432.

[114] The study of this matter began in Italy and was then followed by Spanish authors on the basis of the Italian theories. See references in: *Embid/Alonso Ureba/Martinez-Simancas*, 1851 ff. and *Camacho de los Ríos/Nieto/Bonet*, 769. See STS 12 March 2003 [RA 2003 no. 2573] with extensive references; see also STS 26 February 2000 [RA 2000 no. 1020]; STS 13 December 2000 [RA 200 no.10438]; STS 20 December 1999 [RA 1999 no.8983]; STS 30 December 1998 [RA 1998 no.9983].

[115] *Ravazzoni*, Nuove riflessioni, 553 ff; *Camacho de los Ríos/Nieto/Bonet*, 769.

[116] In Italy: "assicurazione fideiussoria", "polizza fideiussoria", "polizza fideiussoria cauzione", "polizza fideiussoria per il cuazionamento". Despite this variety of terms, „assicurazione fideiussoria" (equivalent to guarantee insurance) is the consolidated form commonly used in contemporary practice. In Spain: "seguro de caución",

interpret the exact terms of the contract is required in order to determine its nature as insurance or guarantee contract.

1. The insurance elements in the contract of guarantee insurance

The basic elements of a contract of guarantee insurance are typical of an insurance contract. On this basis, guarantee insurance would appear to fall within the scope of the insurance.

a) Insurance company

In Spain, the major difference between a guarantee and guarantee insurance is the involvement of an insurance company[118]. This is different from Italy[119] in which both insurance companies and financial institutions are allowed to provide guarantee insurance[120]. The insurance company in such cases is usually a specialist in guarantee and/or credit insurance contracts.

b) Indemnifying character

By means of the insurance policy, the creditor is ensured that if the debtor does not perform this action then the insurance company will pay an agreed sum of money as an indemnity or penalty. The insurer therefore covers the risk of patrimonial damage to the creditor that may be caused by the debtor's default. As this indemnifying character is a typical characteristic of insurance for damages[121], the guarantee insurance has been classified as a pure contract of insurance for damages[122]. As with insurance for damages, the risk assumed by the insurer in the guarantee insurance is the contingency that the creditor may suffer patrimonial damages as a result of the debtor's default (the "covered incident" in insurance terminology). However, most contracts of guarantee insurance set a fixed limit of indemnity in the contract and in insurance practice the creditor is not required to prove his damages, but needs only showing a failure to perform by the

---

"afianzamiento", "en concepto de fianza", "aval", "seguro de fianza" etc. The term "seguro de caución" has been consolidated by the Law but all others are still to be found in practice.

[117] See *Ravazzoni*, Nuove riflessioni. 548.

[118] In the opinion of Camacho this is the *only* difference between both contracts. *Camacho de los Ríos/Nieto/Bonet*, 799.

[119] Norme 106 and 107 Testo Unico Bancario (http://www.itlex.it/ITA/ARCHIVIO/Norita/FINANZA/TUEC385/FFTUEC385.htm).

[120] *Baldini*, 1 (http://www.tidona.com/versionestampa/stampa_aprile01_2).

[121] *Mazza/Franzoni*, 1430.

[122] *Ippolito*, 94; Concordato cauzione, credito, Mercato, cauzione e credito in Italia (http://www.concordato.it/ccmerca.htm). Find long references in *Camacho de los Ríos/Nieto/Bonet*, 771 and *Tirado*, 814.

debtor. This position could be judged as being incompatible with the principle of indemnity for damages. However it can also be considered as an anticipatory, bilateral estimate of the damages. Upon this viewpoint, the external composition is undoubtedly that of an insurance contract, even if, in practice the real insured risk is only the debtor's default[123] instead of the actual damages. The differences with a contract of guarantee are extremely diffuse on this point.

The Spanish Supreme Court[124] stated that in cases where the insurer must perform, he will do so as a result of his own (indemnifying) obligation, whilst a normal guarantor performs the liability of another person. This is however, an easily refuted line of reasoning, since the guarantor is also considered to perform his own guarantee obligation. The Supreme Court itself modified its opinion in a later decision[125].

In any case, all other typical formal elements of the insurance contract are also identifiable in the guarantee insurance contract. These include: cover of a risk; an event giving rise to the coverage; participation of an insurance company, etc.

The application of the insurance regulation is justified by the presence of these typical elements in the guarantee insurance.

2. *The guarantee elements in the contract of guarantee insurance*

Despite the insurance elements present in this contract, a large number of legal writers in Italy[126] and Spain[127] have concluded that the guarantee insurance must be considered to be a guarantee. Their opinion is based on the guaranteeing nature of this contract and its economic purpose. Despite its classification by the law as a contract of insurance for damages, the real aim of the parties is not stricto sensu to insure the damages caused by the debtor's lack of performance but rather to perform his obligation, providing the creditor with immediate coverage in the case of default[128]. This

---

[123] See *Carrasco, Cordero* and *Marín*, 441.

[124] STS 20 February 1989 [RA 1989 no. 1212]; STS 19 May 1990 [RA 1990 no. 3741]; STS 12 March 2003 [RA 2003 no. 2572].

[125] STS 25 February 1994 [RA 1994 no. 1196]. See *Camacho de los Ríos*, Comentario and *Camacho de los Ríos/Nieto/Bonet*, 771.

[126] *Bonvicini*, 630, *Donati*, 75; *Fragalli*, Fideiussione e assicurazioni, BBTC, 1956, I, 135; *Gambino*, 57; *Geri*, 127; *Hermannsdorfer*, 211; *Mungari*, 654 ff; *Ravazzoni*, Fideiussione in luogo de cauzione, 266; *Tamburrino*, 522; *Camacho de los Rios/Nieto/Bonet*, 775.

[127] *Camacho de los Ríos/Nieto/Bonet*, 811; *Embid/Alonso Ureba/Martinez Simancas*, 1863; *Embid*, 6 ff; *Vicent*, Compendio, 569; *Font*, Comentario a la STS de 16 de febrero de 1983, 243; *Carrasco*, Comentario a la STS de 19 de mayo de 1990, 611 ff; *Carrasco, Cordero* and *Marín*, 443.

[128] *Embid/Alonso Ureba/Martinez Simancas*, 1863.

guaranteeing function is not necessarily incompatible with the indemnifying character of the insurer's obligation, as the amount of indemnity is previously agreed by the parties and is equivalent to the debt[129].

a) Guarantee insurance on first demand

In practice, contracts of guarantee insurance usually include "on first demand" clauses. Accordingly, the insurer is compelled to immediately pay in case of default by the debtor, even if it was due to irresistible or superior force (fuerza mayor o caso fortuito). In such cases, the contractual nature of guarantee insurance is that of a guarantee on first demand.

b) Guarantee insurance as a dependent guarantee

Other policies make the obligation of the insurance company dependent on the principal debt. This creates a relationship which is thus similar to the contract of guarantee. The main characteristic of such policies is therefore their accessory nature[130]. In these cases, all provisions on the guarantee, which derive from the principle of co-extensiveness are also applicable to the contract of guarantee insurance[131]. So, the extent of the guarantee obligation is limited in relation to the principal debt. The guarantor's liability may be less, but cannot be more, than the debtor's liability, both in respect of the amount owed as well as with regard to the onerousness of any conditions imposed on the debtor (art. 1941 Italian CC and art. 1826 par. 1 Spanish CC). The extent of the guarantee insurance is the damage caused as a result of the debtor's default. This includes the debt and its accessories[132]. In practice, the insurance obligation is usually limited to the debt itself or a lower sum.

A controversial situation arises in the event of the debtor's default being caused by a fortuitous event or force majeur. Such events extinguish the principal obligation and any accessory obligations such as guarantees. However, they do not extinguish the indemnifying obligation of the contract of guarantee insurance. Accordingly, the insurer must make the payment, even though the debtor is not obliged to. This appears to be irreconcilable with the accessory nature of the contract of guarantee insurance, as it means the insurer's obligation is greater than that of the debtor[133]. A more intricate analysis of this issue is not appropriate at this point. The

---

[129] *Font*, Comentario a la Sentencia del Tribunal Supremo de 16 de febrero de 1983, 243.

[130] *Baldini* (http://www.tidona.com/versionestampa/stampa_aprile01_2.htm).

[131] STS 20 February 1989 [RA 1989 no. 1212].

[132] *Vicent*, Compendio, 569.

[133] For a deeper study, see: *Camacho de los Rios/Nieto/Bonet*, 782 ff.

practical relevance of this matter is minimal as the parties usually exclude fortuitous events and force majeur from the actual contract of insurance.

Lastly, art. 1945 Italian and art. 1853 Spanish CC are also applicable to the contract of guarantee insurance. The guarantor may set up against the creditor all the debtor's defences, which are inherent in the debt except the purely personal to the debtor.

3. Conclusions and law applicable to the guarantee insurance

In respect of its formal or structural elements, the contract of guarantee is undoubtedly an insurance contract. In the context of the Spanish legal system this position is actually specified in the Insurance Act, the LCS[134], which is clearly insufficient[135]. Yet the obvious guaranteeing function of the contract suggests that it is a contract of guarantee. Accordingly the guarantee regulation should also apply concurrently with the provisions of insurance law[136]. In practice, the question of which provisions are applicable will usually depend on the specific wording of the policy in question[137].

---

[134] Art. 68 Ley 50/1980 del Contrato de Seguro (LCS) is the only rule applicable to guarantee insurance: "By a guarantee insurance the insurer obliges himself, in case of non-performance by the taker of the insurance of his legal or contractual obligations, to indemnify, with title of indemnity, the ensured person for the patrimonial damage suffered, within the limits of the Law or the contract. Every payment performed by the insurer must be repaid by the taker of the insurance".

[135] *Embid/Alonso Ureba/Martinez Simancas*, 1852 ff.

[136] *Embid/Alonso Ureba/Martinez Simancas*, 1863. With regard to the provisions on the guarantee of the Italian and Spanish Civil Codes applicable to the guarantee insurance see *Tamburrino*, 533; *Carrasco, Cordero and Marín*, 443–444. STS 20 February 1989 [RA 1989 no. 1212]; STS 19 May 1990 [RA 1990 no. 3741]; STS 12 March 2003 [RA 2003 no. 2572].

[137] *Tamburrino*, 524; *Carrasco, Cordero* and *Marín*, 441–445.

D. The contract of credit insurance (assicurazione di credito/seguro de crédito)

I. The basic notion and legal nature of the credit insurance

Credit insurance is an insurance contract taken out by the creditor to protect himself against damages suffered due to the debtor's insolvency[138].

The extent of the insured risk is the final loss suffered by the creditor upon definite insolvency of the debtor (i.e. when the debtor has insufficient assets to perform all of his debts)[139].

II. Historical evolution and economic function in contemporary commercial activity

1. Historical background

The contract of credit insurance was already known in the 18th century in Europe, but it was not significantly used in practice until more than a century later. This form of insurance practice then underwent considerable development in the period preceding the economic crisis of 1929. Lloyd's of London played a particularly important role in this phenomenon, circa 1870. After World War II the increase of commerce, credit and the development of new techniques on risk management, contributed to the worldwide expansion of the concept of credit insurance[140].

2. Economic function

a) Commercial use of credit insurance

Credit insurance is now particularly common in the field of operational risk for commercial activities. Companies selling on credit are continuously exposed to default due to the insolvency of their business partners. These defaults create additional expenditure which results in a deceleration of company development and restricted potential for expansion. Continuous failure by debtors to make payment is especially dangerous for small and medium-sized companies[141].

---

[138] Univelex, dir. Di Brina, La copertura assicurativa, Assicurazione del credito (http://univelex.unive.it/diritto-commerciale/menu/mf400000.htm); *Vicent/Nieto/Bonet*, 387.

[139] See *Tirado*, 447.

[140] For historical references and bibliography: Univelex, dir. Di Brina, Nascita e sviluppo delle assicurazioni del credito, Assicurazione del credito (http://univelex.unive.it/ diritto-commerciale/menu/mf400000.htm).

[141] About the special difficulties of small and medium-sized companies and the advantages of credit insurance see: ALASECE (http://alasece.com/bolentin3.htm).

The commercial risk is increased by the fact that in most cases the creditor lacks information about his clients and their ability to perform. This is especially evident in the case of international transactions. It is difficult and costly for creditors to obtain information about foreign countries. This is particularly problematic with regard to information which concerns legislation and the procedural aspects of insolvency. Such information is nevertheless of great importance for companies wishing to expand their activities into new markets.

In most cases, the size of the company does not make it possible or efficient to maintain a whole department for the purpose of client control as such a department does not generate direct revenues for the company. It is therefore more convenient to concentrate on its primary activities and leave the control of clients to professional specialists such as insurance companies which concentrate upon credit insurance.

The companies which specialise in credit insurance have developed highly detailed information systems concerning the credit history and solvability of potential clients. In many cases, they only use this system in order to make a decision about insuring certain debts. The mere fact that insurance is granted indicates to the insured creditor the solvability of each client. Moreover, in credit insurance practice, the creditor is usually granted access to the information relating to his clients. Furthermore, the costs of the insurance contract are tax deductible, and the benefits of such contracts outweigh the cost thereof[142]. The negative consequences of a high level of bad debts are so limited.

As with any other mechanism, insuring the creditor against eventual defaults, credit insurance also encourages the grant of credit.

b) Recent use of credit insurance in banking practice: Mortgage Insurance

Mortgage Insurance (MI) is a type of credit insurance designed to protect lenders for the risk of a secured loan (mortgage). It is a case of concurrency of security rights[143]. It has been used in the international markets since decades as an effective mitigant for credit risk exposures.

Typically, lenders require borrowers to make a reasonable down-payment or deposit towards the purchase price of the house -typically 15 %; the remaining 85 % of the purchase price is financed as a mortgaged credit. This structure results in a mortgage Loan To Value (LTV) ratio of 85 %. Depending on the first down-payment that the borrower can afford,

---

[142] *Francisco* (http://www.5campus.org/leccion/segucre).

[143] See Chapter 4, Plurality of security rights.

the LTV ratio will be higher or lower (should the borrower put 5 %, the mortgage LTV would be (95 %).

Clearly, the likelihood of defaulting on the mortgage payments increases with high LTV loans. Other factors like high housing prices, economic variables or market conditions also affect severely the lender's risk for mortgage lending (flow or portfolio).

When borrowers put down less than 20 % to purchase mortgages, lenders may use mortgage insurance to protect themselves against the increased risk.

From the lenders perspective, the purchase of MI effectively reduces the loss, were a loan to default. Effectively, where the loan granted by the lender to his borrower is ultimately foreclosed by the lender with a resulting loss, MI would assess the claim and pay it immediately.

This means that MI removes risk, supporting the solvency and stability of lenders in periods of high mortgage default through risk transfer. The Loan To Value (LTV) ratio of a mortgage is the single most important indicator of potential loss for a lender and is used extensively by rating agencies to assess the credit-worthiness and security of lending institutions and the quality of mortgage-baked securities. The use of MI also enables the lender to participate more fully in the higher LTV end of the market, thereby securing new borrowers whilst mitigating much of the increased risk. It allows a greater focus on risk selection through the employment of risk-selection techniques introduced by the insurers, and enhances the quality of mortgage baked securities and mortgage bonds.

Indeed there is a significant level of credit risk transfer in the use of this credit insurance policy. MI reduces the Loss Given Default by acting as a "first loss cover", where the proceeds of sale on foreclosure are insufficient to cover the outstanding debt of the borrower. The flexible nature of the product means that lenders can set the level of cover to ensure that they suffer no losses in the event of default by the borrower. Depending on the level of cover chosen, losses can either be completely eliminated, or substantially reduced.

MI can also play a role in a lender's risk management strategy. Basel II and the Capital Requirements Directive (CRD)[144] place greater emphasis on risk management, both in general terms, and more specifically under Pillar 2. A lender's risk management processes can be improved through the use of more sophisticated underwriting, risk management and loss mitigation techniques as a result of third party oversight in the mortgage lending process. Furthermore, third party provision of mortgage scoring

---

[144] See Chapter 5, Personal security rights as Credit Risk Mitigators in the Basle II Accord and in the Capital Requirements Directive, 248.

mechanisms,[145] in addition to the origination data and performance data requirements create a further layer of reporting requirements, which will not only help to improve a lender's internal risk management, but will also improve transparency.

III. Legal nature of the credit insurance

It may be questioned whether credit insurance falls within the scope of personal security rights[146]. As it is a form of insurance contract and the insurance elements are clearly predominant, credit insurance is not usually studied as a personal security right. However, from a functional perspective, the "surety" (insurance company) covers the creditor against the risk of loss as a consequence of the debtor's default. It does not guarantee the payment of the debtor upon default, but rather undertakes a principal obligation to indemnify the creditor's losses upon the uncertain event of default of the debtor. The guaranteeing function derives from its indemnifying character. The insurer's obligation is therefore principal, conditional and also always onerous, as it is exercised by professional insurance companies.

IV. Legislation applicable to credit insurance contracts

Credit insurance in Italy and Spain has become increasingly regulated in the last thirty years by insurance legislation. In Italy credit insurance was governed by art. 440 former Comm. C. of 1882, but it is not specifically mentioned in art. 1904 f. Italian CC of 1942[147] as one of the different types of insurance for damages (assicurazione danni). However, the general regulation on insurance contracts is applicable as well as the special regulation referring to this contract[148].

---

[145] Mortgage scoring is more sophisticated than credit scoring, which only takes into account the borrowers credit score. Mortgage scoring considers not only this variable, but also takes into account the mortgage product, duration of the mortgage, repayment type, property type etc.

[146] The issue of the legal nature of credit insurance has been controversial in neighbouring countries (see references in Mouly, 304) but has not been treated in Italy and Spain.

[147] Current Italian CC unified former Civil and Commercial Codes.

[148] The different types of credit insurance are also indicated in the Decreto Legislativo no. 175 of 17th of March 1995. Circolare Ministeriale dell'industria e commercio no. 433 of 16th of November 1979 and its predecessor, Circolare Ministeriale in materia di assicurazione del credito no. 145 of 7th of December 1960. See Univelex, dir. Di Brina, Natura specifica del contratto di assicurazione del credito, Assicurazione del credito (http://univelex.unive.it/diritto-commerciale/menu/mf400000.htm).

In Spain the first regulation of credit insurance was provided by the Ordenanzas de Seguro Marítimo de Bilbao of 1737, which par. XLIII allowed insurance of "the risks of payments or borrowed sums". However, subsequent legislation, first the Comm. C. of 1829 and later the Comm. C. of 1885 (in force today), avoided any reference to credit insurance. Paradoxically, credit insurance began then to be used in practice in terms of art. 438[149] Comm. C. of 1885. Since 1980, the contract of credit insurance is specifically regulated by art. 69 to art. 72 Ley 50/1980 del Contrato de Seguro (LCS). The different types of credit insurance are contained in the 1st disposición adicional of the Ley 30/1995, de Ordenación y Supervisión de los Seguros Privados.

[149] Rules on Insurance Contract, derogated in 1980 by Ley 50/1980 del Contrato de Seguro (LCS). For more extensive historical references see: *Tirado/Motos/Albadalejo*, 451 f.

Chapter 4

Plurality of security rights

A. Relationship among sureties in case of concurrency

I. In general

It is very common in present business practice to secure an obligation with more than one security right. Creditors are usually professionals trying to run their business as safely as possible. As in many cases they cannot be sure about the payment capability of their debtors, they seek to obtain security from more than one person for the case the debtor defaults. These security rights may be personal, real or a mixture of both. They might have been assumed together for the same debt (as in the case of co-guarantee) or independently from each other. Hence, there are different possible combinations of security rights. These combinations give rise to different external relationships between the sureties and the creditor, and different internal relationships between the sureties themselves.

II. Constellations of plurality of security rights

1. Plurality of personal security rights

a) The co-guarantee (confideissione/co-fianza)

The first case to be mentioned is that of the so called "co-guarantee". According to academic theory, in Italy and Spain a co-guarantee allows a plurality of guarantors to assume a guarantee in favour of the same creditor, for the same debt of the same debtor. All of these guarantors are rendered as being in the same position within the contract and have the same kind and level of liability regarding the secured debt. They must assume the guarantee together. This requirement of collective assumption relates to the subjective link of the guarantors and is independent from the external features of the assumption. This means that all co-guarantors must have a common target or interest in the guarantee, even if they do not assume their respective liabilities simultaneously or in the same document[1].

---

[1] *Ravazzoni*, Le garanzie 1993, 74; Cass. 12 July 1962 no.1862, GC, 1962, I, 2099.

b) Plurality of personal guarantees independent from each other

The co-guarantee has been distinguished from the case of the "plurality of personal guarantees independent from each other"[2]. In this case there is a plurality of guarantors that ensure the obligation of one debtor. Therefore, each guarantor is party to a different guarantee that exists independently from the others. There is a common debtor and a common debt, which is secured by virtue of different guarantors that do not have any relationship to each other. It is a case of the coexistence of different personal guarantees that are independent and autonomous from each other. Each of the guarantees secures the whole debt[3]. The subjective element or interest in granting security is different for each guarantor. They do not assume the obligation collectively and they may even ignore the existence of other guarantees or they may simply wish to constitute each guarantee independently from the others[4]. There are as many obligations as there are guarantors[5].

c) Legal regulation of both cases

The Italian and Spanish Civil Codes regulate the situation of the co-guarantee, but do not provide an explicit definition not do they distinguish between co-guarantee and plurality of guarantors independent from each other.

The Spanish Civil Code lacks terminological accuracy. Some provisions (art. 1837, art. 1844, art. 1850, art. 1852) use the very general expression "plurality of guarantors" (which actually refers to both, the co-guarantee and the plurality of guarantees that are independent from each other) although the title of the whole section[6] refers to the co-guarantee and the term "co-guarantors" ("co-fideiusores") is used again in art. 1845.

Case law and legal writers[7] have construed arts. 1837 together with art. 1844 ff. as to develop a definition of co-guarantee. This is the case regu-

---

[2] The Spanish writers have largely ignored the study of this matter and Supreme Court decisions are recent occurrences. In Spain see: *Guilarte*, 231–232 and *Carrasco*, *Cordero* and *Marín*, 290 ff. The situation is different in Italy, where both case law and scholars have developed a clear view of both constellations and the differences between them. See: *Fragali*, Confideiussione, 1963, I, 196 ff.

[3] *Ramón*, La distinción entre cofianza (http://www.uv.es/~ripj/5cof.htm).

[4] *Giusti*, 211; Cass. 12 July 1962 no. 1862, GC, 1962, I, 2099.

[5] *Ramón*, La distinción entre cofianza, (http://www.uv.es/~ripj/5cof.htm); esp. punto 2 "Distinción con la pluralidad de fianzas independientes".

[6] Chapter II, Title XIV, Book IV, section three Spanish CC (arts. 1844 ff.) is entitled "About the effects of the co-guarantee among co-guarantors".

[7] STS 4 May 1993 [RA 1993 no. 3403]; RGD no. 585, june 1993, 5861 f.; La Ley, 1993–3, 336; Ramón, La distinción (http://www.uv.es/~ripj/5cof.htm).

lated in the Spanish CC and which is thus distinct from other kinds of plurality of personal guarantors. The same position is to be found in Italy8 with regard to arts. 1946, art. 1947 and art. 1954 Italian CC.

In order to determine if a case of plurality of guarantors is a co-guarantee, it must be decided whether the interests of the guarantors were autonomous or independent from each other or if they wished to guarantee together[9]. This can only be observed on a case by case basis. However, there will be a presumption of common interest (co-guarantee) if the position cannot be deduced from the circumstances[10]. In any case, the plurality of guarantees is not specifically regulated in either of these Civil Codes. The rules on co-guarantee cannot be applied[11] (not even by analogy)[12] due to the different nature of both situations[13]. However, the general regulation on the guarantee shall be applied.

2. *Plurality of personal and real securities*

Another possibility is that of the concurrency of personal and real security rights. This situation is not regulated in Italian or in Spanish Civil Codes. Each security obligation is regarded as independent from the others and the circumstances that may affect one of them is not taken to affect the others.

III. Relationship of the different sureties vis-à-vis the creditor

There are no special provisions regarding the relationship between the co-guarantors and the creditor. The civil code applies in general and especially the rules on the guarantee mutatis mutandis.

1. *Order of payment*

The laws of Italy and Spain are both silent with regard to the rank or order of payment in case of plurality of securities. If the liability of the surety is joint and several (solidaria) in relation to the main debt, the surety might

---

[8] Cass. 18 March 1999 no. 2459 l. 2253, FI, no. 7–8, July–August, 1999; Cass. 18 July 1997 no. 6635 in *Giusti*, 211; Cass. 11 July 1967 no. 1712, FI, 1968, I, 212; *Rescigno/Bozzi*, La fideiussione, le figure affini e l'anticresi, 256; *Fragali*, Confideiussione, 196 f.; *Petti*, 191.

[9] Cass. 12 July 1962 no. 1862, GC, 1962, I, 2099; *Carrasco, Cordero* and *Marín*, 290.

[10] *Giusti*, 211.

[11] STS 18 September 1997 [RA 1997 no. 6705], La Ley, no. 4405, miércoles 29.10.1997, 7 ff.

[12] *Ramón*, La distinción entre (http://www.uv.es/~ripj/5cof.htm); punto 2 „Distinción con la pluralidad de fianzas independientes".

[13] *Díez-Picazo*, Fundamentos, 445 ff.; *Gullón*, Sobre el atículo 1844 del Código, 1030; *Contra*: *Lacruz*, Elementos, 1986, 541 ff.

be compelled to perform before default of the debtor. This order of events cannot occur if the security is a secondary obligation.
The possible combinations of the plurality of security rights are the following:

a) if all securities are joint and several with regard to the principal debt, the creditor may request performance from any of the sureties from the moment the debt is due and payable[14];
b) if some of them are joint and several while others are secondary in relation to the principal debt, the creditor can enforce payment from the principal debtor or the sureties that are joint and severally liable while secondary sureties enjoy the benefit of discussion; and
c) obviously if all securities are secondary to the principal debt, all of them will enjoy the benefit of discussion.

Therefore, if there is a plurality of securities, the creditor is free to demand fulfilment from any of his sureties, provided these securities are enforceable and it is a matter of hazard as to which one of them will be requested to perform. The person who provides payment first will assume the risk of the insolvency of the parties from whom he may be reimbursed[15].
It has been intensively discussed in Germany whether the guarantor should enjoy a priviledged position with regard to the other sureties. The reasons adduced by the scholars in favour of this position regard mainly the especial risk assumed by the personal guarantor as he remains liable with his present and future patrimony for the secured debt[16]. A proof of this is certainly the growing tendency in the German Supreme Court to consider that the guarantor's position should be strengthened[17]. However, in this case the Supreme Court has decided that the guarantor should not enjoy a privileged position as to the other sureties that secure the same debt[18].

---

[14] See SAP Barcelona 13 June 2008 WL no. 329/2008: A plurality of joint and several co-guarantors, guarantee a plurality of guarantors, severally liable. The co-guarantors are jointly liable only for the part of the debt which was not fulfilled by one of the guarantors.

[15] Alternatives are perhaps preferable as to avoid the effect of hazard regarding the performing surety. Personal securities could be privileged with regard to real ones, or the order of payment could be determined upon the moment of the conclusion of the guaranteeing contract. The treatment of this matter is related to the study of the internal relationships between the different sureties. This is because it seems to be important to determine who will finally suffer the patrimonial detriment upon the demand for payment, and not only who will be the performing party in first place. See *infra* Chapter 4, A., IV. Internal relationship among the different sureties, 236.

[16] *Horn/Staudinger*, on § 774, no. 68; *Reinicke* and *Tiedkte*, 2000, 422 ff.

[17] See *Tiedtke*, Rechtsprechung, 1015 ff.

[18] BGH 26 une 1989, BGHZ 108, 179 and BGH 24 September 1992, W 1992, 3228. See comment in *Reinicke* and *Tiedtke*, 2000, 422 ff.

2. Extent of liability of each one of the security rights

a) In the co-guarantee

aa) Regulation

In Italy the liability of the co-guarantors is conceived of as being joint and several (art. 1946 Italian CC[19]). The benefit of division may also be agreed to by the parties, in which case each co-guarantor is only liable for his part of the debt and the creditor cannot compel any of them to perform with regard to the total obligation (art. 1947 sent. 1 Italian CC[20]). Only if any of the co-guarantors is insolvent at the time at which the original benefit is agreed, the co-guarantors are proportionally liable in relation to the share of the other guarantor (art. 1947 sent. 2)[21].

The Spanish regulation on the co-guarantee is extremely contradictory as compared to the Italian. In Spain the liability of the co-guarantors can be a) joint and several (solidaria) or b) several (mancomunada simple)[22].

According to art. 1837 sent. 1 Spanish CC[23], the co-guarantors are severally liable (mancomunidad). Every guarantor is liable only for his share of the whole debt[24]. Thus each guarantor exists independently from each of their co-guarantors, whose insolvency will thus only affect the position of the creditor. Guarantors are not able to set up defences that pertain to the other co-guarantors, nor do they enjoy a right of recourse between each other.

---

[19] Art. 1946 Italian CC: "If a plurality of persons has provided guarantee to the same debtor and for the same debt, each one of them is compelled for the entire debt, unless the benefit of division has been agreed."

[20] Art. 1947 Italian CC: "If the benefit of division has been agreed, each one of the co-debtors being required for the payment of the entire debt can compel the creditor to reduce the content of the claim to the part that he owns."

[21] *Petti*, 178.

[22] If an obligation is *mancomunada* the debt is vis-à-vis the creditor, divided among the debtors (per capita unless otherwise agreed) and each one of them is only liable for his own part of the debt. The creditor must rise a claim against each one of them and they do not have a right of recourse against the others in case of payment. This is the general regime for co-debt in Spanish law, unless the *solidarity* (joint and several regime) is expressly agreed. See art. 1137 Spanish Civil Code: "The concurrence of two or more obligees or two or more obligors in a single obligation does not imply that each of the former has a right to demand or that each of the latter is bound to perform, the obligation in its entirety. This shall only take place when the obligation provides for it expressly, the obligation being contracted as solidary."

[23] Art. 1837 sent. 1: "When there are several sureties of only one debtor and for one debt only, the obligation of responding herefor shall be divided among all. The creditor can only demand from each surety his corresponding share, unless solidarity has been expressly stipulated."

[24] See art. 1137 Spanish CC on several liability of co-debtors.

The position of several liability among co-guarantors is not the normal rule within modern continental regulations[25]. It is surprising that the Spanish CC, extremely similar to the French, creates an exception in this area, distancing itself from its own near-historical background[26]. Nevertheless, a system of several liability for co-guarantors is a perfectly feasible alternative.

Therefore, apart from historical reasons, it would be quite acceptable for art. 1837 Spanish CC to finish at the stage of its first sentence. However, the second part of this provision[27] unexpectedly refers to the benefit of division, which can only occur within joint and several obligations. It therefore seems to be a point of debate as to whether the co-guarantee is a joint and several or a several obligation in the Spanish context.

The wording of art. 1837 has received academic analysis which has yielded a variety of different conclusions. One of the suggested solutions[28] is that the co-guarantee should be held to be a several obligation. This view is put forward as the wording of art. 1837 sent. 1 is clear and is parallel to the general regulation in art. 1137 and art. 1138 Spanish CC, which establishes the several liability for the co-debtors (mancomunidad = division). However, this theory does not explain the inconsistency between sent. 1 and 2 of art. 1837.

For this reason another group of scholars[29], place a great deal of importance on the historical background of this provision[30]. They consider that the first sentence is a "last moment adherence" in a coherent whole that should be maintained unaltered (art. 1844 to art. 1846 and art. 1850 Spanish CC are all based on the benefit of division and therefore apparently on the joint and several liability between co-guarantors).

---

[25] Art. 1946 Italian CC, § 774 German CC; *Horn/Staudinger*, on § 774, no. 43; art. 2025 French CC. For a comparative study, see: Guilarte, Notas sobre la cofianza, 891 ff. This conception of the liability in the co-guarantee has its origins in Roman Justinianian Law, where co-guarantors were liable *in solidum*, but the *benefitium divisionis* could be agreed among them. In this last case, each co-guarantor were allowed to compel the creditor to require payment of the respective parts of the debt to each one of the co-guarantors.

[26] The Draft Spanish CC of 1851 of García Goyena, followed in its art. 1750 the French solution as well as Spanish historical Law of the Partidas (joint and several liability with the possibility to agree the benefit of division).

[27] "The benefit of division agains co-sureties ceases in the same cases and for the same causes as that of discussion against the principal debtor."

[28] *Lacruz*, Elementos, 1986, 537; Guilarte, Notas sobre la cofianza, 891–920. Recently also *Carrasco, Cordero* and *Marín*, 284.

[29] *Castán*, 707; *Cristóbal*, 51 ff. For other references see: *Guilarte*, 227.

[30] The first paragraph was only lately introduced and it is a direct translation of the Belgian Project of Laurent. The second, however, derives from the important Project on a Spanish Civil Code of 1851, where the liability of guarantors was joint and several.

The Spanish Supreme Court[31] has agreed with the first opinion and has thus declared that the co-guarantors are severally liable unless otherwise agreed. According to this viewpoint, it is to be concluded that: a) the benefit of division is not a special kind of benefit but a normal effect of the several (mancomunada) nature of the co-guarantee[32] and b) unless otherwise agreed by the parties, each of the co-guarantors are severally liable (mancomunadamente responsables) and each one can therefore only be required to pay his or her particular part of the total debt. The wording of this last sentence of art. 1837 (benefit of division) refers to those cases in which an exception to the several liability shall be permitted. These exceptional cases are the same as those for which the benefit of division ceases for the principal debtor as set in art. 1831 Spanish CC: a) when the guarantor has expressly renounced his right to the benefit of division; b) in case of bankruptcy[33] of any of the co-guarantors and c) when the guarantee of any of the co-guarantors cannot be enforced in the Spanish Kingdom.

In these cases, the other co-guarantors are severally liable for the part of the debt which belongs to the co-guarantor who has fallen under one of the abovementioned situations. Therefore, the share of the latter will be divided among all other co-guarantors and added to their respective partial liabilities. This is conceived of as being a benefit for the creditor, who must therefore take action to implement his right timeously. For example, if a bankruptcy proceeding has already been commenced against one of the co-guarantors and the creditor requires partial payment from each of the other co-guarantors, he loses the possibility to set up art. 1837 sent. 2 after a certain point in time[34].

bb) In the business practice

(i) Express agreement of the parties

The technical problems that are created by the deficient regulation of the co-guarantee in the Spanish CC, are minimised in commercial practice. Almost every guarantee and co-guarantee contract in Spain is agreed within the rules of solidarity; i.e. as joint and several guarantees. In this case the application of the regulation on co-guarantee is not problematic as it is

[31] STS 3 June 1968 [RA 1968 no. 3064]; STS 4 May 1993 [RA 1993 no. 3403].

[32] Spanish CC keeps silent about the establishment of a concrete moment to allege the division of the debt. See STS 4 May [RA 1993 no. 3403]. *Contra*: *Carrasco, Cordero* and *Marín*, 285.

[33] A restrictive interpretation of art. 1837 sent. 2 prevails (*Guilarte*, 246). Accordingly financial difficulties are not be considered enough but a bankruptcy proceeding (*quiebra* or *concurso de acreedores*) must have been open in order to apply this exception.

[34] *Guilarte*, 247.

mostly the same as the general rules on joint and several obligations that are established in art. 1137 ff. Spanish CC.

The most common scenario is for there to be the agreement of joint and several liability of all parties, including the principal debtor and the co-guarantors. These contracts include a clause of waiver to "all benefits"[35]. Sometimes, the guarantors are joint and severally liable with regard to the inner relationship, but secondarily with respect to the principal. A mixture of several, and joint and several co-guarantees for the same debt is also possible.

(ii) Construction of unclear contractual terms

The co-guarantors are free to make agreements regarding their internal relationship within the guarantee. If an agreement is not clearly formulated the real will of the parties must be construed with regard to the facts and circumstances of each individual case. However, the same terminological formulas with identical imprecise terms are recurrently used in practice. Therefore it is useful to suggest a construction that will be generally applicable to the same recurrent cases[36]. Firstly, the assumption of a guarantee together by a plurality of persons should be considered to be a co-guarantee. If the co-guarantors have agreed that there should be a joint and several liability between them, this does not make them joint and severally liable in relation to the principal debt[37]. Furthermore, a co-guarantor may constitute a guarantee for the risk of not-being repaid by the debtor if the guarantee is performed. The person who guarantees this right of one co-guarantor against the debtor is not thereby the sub-guarantor of the creditor[38].

In some instances of joint and several co-guarantee it is the case that one co-guarantor promises to indemnify another co-guarantor if he is called on to perform. If the promisee has performed, he is able to recover the total amount from the promisor. If it is the promisor the one who is performing, then the promisor does not enjoy a right of recourse against the other co-guarantor. Moreover, the promisor is not to be considered to be a sub-guarantor for the promisee's liability vis-à-vis the creditor.

Furthermore, in neighbouring countries it is common for there to be an agreement to provide a guarantee for a maximum percentage of the debt. If this is agreed by a plurality of guarantors (for example A ensures a 100 % of the debt, while B and C guarantee only a 30 % each) it is difficult to

---

35 "...con renuncia a los beneficios de excusión, orden y división"
36 See *Carrasco, Cordero* and *Marín*, 289.
37 STS 3 June 1968 [RA 1968 no. 3064].
38 See SAP Barcelona 28 May 1997 [AC 1997 no. 1164].

know what level of liability must be performed by each of the guarantors[39]. However this situation does not seem to be common in practice. There is no case law regarding this matter and there is no theoretical discussion of this possibility. The only reference to this issue has stated that such a contract is to be construed as a joint and several co-guarantee[40].

The partners of a firm may act together to guarantee a debt of their firm. In this situation it is taken to be the case that each one of them is liable not per capita but proportionally, according to their respective shares of the firm.

b) In the case of plurality of security rights (personal and real)

In the case of a plurality of security rights that are assumed independently from each other, every surety is liable for the totality of his obligation against the creditor. This is the case provided that the security is already enforceable and the principal obligation has not been extinguished.

3. Defences

a) In the co-guarantee

The regulation of the guarantee on this matter is applicable to each one of the co-guarantors.

Every co-guarantor can set up all his personal defences. This includes those arising from the principal debt and also the defences of the other co-guarantors if the liability has been agreed to be joint and several.

If the creditor discharges one of the co-guarantors, the other co-guarantors may set up a defence[41] in order to reduce their own liability with regard to the part of the guarantee which has been discharged[42].

This situation must be distinguished from the instance in which creditor and guarantor have set-off mutual claims. A release of the latter with regard to having to perform payment does not mean that there has been a discharge. The party who has been released has not received a benefit. Therefore, the other co-guarantors should not receive any advantage on this basis.

---

[39] For Gemany see *Glöckner*, 821.

[40] *Carrasco, Cordero* and *Marín*, 288.

[41] The personal defence of the discharged guarantor.

[42] This is regulated in art. 1850 Spanish CC, although a specific provision would not be necessary.

b) In the case of plurality of security rights

If there is a plurality of security rights the sureties can only set up personal defences and defences arising from the principal debt. A discharge of one of the guarantors does not affect the rest.

IV. Internal relationship among the different sureties

The performing surety enjoys a right to receive a contribution from the other sureties of the same debt depending on the type of relationship between them. This will be different if it is a case of

a) co-guarantee,
b) a plurality of personal security rights, independent form each other or
c) a plurality of personal and real security rights.

1. Internal relationship among co-guarantors

a) Right of recourse

In a joint and several co-guarantee, a co-guarantor who fulfils performance for the entire guarantee, enjoys a right of reimbursement and a right of subrogation in the rights of the creditor against the debtor and the co-guarantors (art. 1203 par. 3 Italian CC and 1210 par. 3 Spanish CC)[43]. As against the other co-guarantors, the performing party will have a right to be reimbursed for the total amount of the debt, except for his original part.

The internal right of recourse between co-guarantors is regulated in art. 1954 Italian CC[44] and based upon the rule of proportionality. The performing co-guarantor enjoys ope legis a right to be refunded by all other co-guarantors for their respective shares of the debt. If no agreement has been reached and no other criteria of division can be applied, the respective shares are presumed to be equal with regard to the total debt (division per capita). This result is attained by the application of the rules on co-debt (art. 1298 CC)[45].

[43] *Franzoni*, 785 and art. 1210 par. 3 sent. 2 Spanish CC: "Subrogation shall be presumed to exist (...) 3) When payment is made by a person having interest in the performance of the obligation, saving the effects of confusion with respect to the part belonging to him". See STS 20 July 2007 [RA 2007 no.5301]; SAP Zaragoza 25 June 2007 [AC 2007 no. 299859].

[44] "If a plurality of persons has provided a guarantee for the same debtor and the same debt, the surety that has performed has a right of refund against the other sureties for their respective part. If one of them is insolvent, art. 1299 must be considered".

[45] *De María/Franzoni*, 1496.

If the parties have agreed to the benefit of division[46], each co-guarantor will only be liable for his part of the obligation, unless any of the co-guarantors is insolvent when the benefit is plead. In this case the other co-guarantors are proportionally liable for the share of the insolvent party (art. 1947 sent. 2 CC). Moreover, if one of the co-guarantors performs the whole debt, while he was not compelled to do so, he will have a right of recourse against the other co-guarantors on the basis of the principle of unjustified enrichment.

The system of recourse between co-guarantors is consistent with the joint and several liability of the co-guarantee in Italy. In contrast, the Spanish regulation of this matter is confusing. If one has recognised the several nature of the co-guarantors' liability under Spanish Law, then art. 1844 Spanish CC is rather bewildering. In its first paragraph, this provision[47] establishes a basic right of recourse among co-guarantors on the basis of proportionality (per capita unless otherwise agreed according to art. 1145 CC on co-debt). In an ordinary co-guarantee (several) the co-guarantors are only liable for their corresponding part of the debt. Therefore, each co-guarantor can only be compelled to perform his share of the debt. The applicability of art. 1844 Spanish CC to this situation is hence questioned by leading scholars[48]. Some writers have considered this provision to be applicable to those co-guarantors that have agreed a joint and several liability[49]. However, the right of recourse in this case is already governed by art. 1145 Spanish CC[50].Therefore, the regulation of this situation under art. 1844 would be superfluous[51]. Thus, the only right of recourse that is provided by art. 1844 is for a co-guarantor who, despite his possession of several liability, also performs the obligations of the other

[46] See Chapter 2, D., III., 2. Benefit of division. Special benefit for co-guarantors, 103.

[47] Art. 1844 par. 1 Spanish CC: "When there are two or more sureties of only one debtor and for the same debt, the one that pays the debt may demand from each of the others the part for which he is proportionally liable. When one of them is insolvent, his part shall be borne by all in the same proportion. In order for the provisions of this article to apply, payment must have been made as a result of a suit or after the principal debtor became insolvent or bankrupt."

[48] *Gullón*, Sobre el artículo 1844, 1030 ff.; *Lacruz*, Elementos, 1986, 543.

[49] *Sierra* and *Gullón*, Comentario 2000, 189.

[50] Spanish Case Law has declared a preference to apply art. 1145 Spanish CC in case the co-guarantors are joint and severally liable with the debtor if the payment has not been malicious (STS 18 September 1997 [RA 1997 no. 6705] and STS 29 November 1997 [RA 1997 no. 8436]; STS 4 May 1993 [RA 1993 no. 3403] and STS 2 December 1988 [RA 1988 no. 9287]).

[51] Accordingly some scholars exclude the joint and several co-guarantee from the scope of art. 1844 Spanish CC. See *Carrasco, Cordero* and *Marín*, 294; *Pérez Alvarez*, 220.

co-guarantors. Strictly considered, this payment would be partly the performance of his own debt and partly the performance of the liability owed by other persons. As the case of performance for another person is already regulated in art. 1158 Spanish CC, there would not be any need to enact a special provision to cover the case of co-guarantee. According to the general regulation, a co-guarantor that fulfils the performance of the other co-guarantors has a right to be refunded by virtue of being a third party who is performing the debt of another person.

Despite the bad use of legislative language, art. 1844 is not unnecessary as it contains the restrictions that exist in relation to the right of refund. These are included in the third sentence of the provision, according to which, the action of refund will be granted only if: a) payment has been made as a result of a suit or b) after the principal debtor became insolvent or bankrupt. This provision would make sense if it was the case that in Spain the liability of the co-guarantors was joint and several. However, this is simply not the case.

It seems peculiar that by virtue of his status as a co-guarantor, an individual who has completed performance of an obligation that he did not owe (namely the obligations of the other co-guarantors), possesses a right of refund that is inferior to the one that is granted by the general regulation of the Spanish Civil Code. It is submitted that his position should not be distinguished from that of any person who performs the debt of another person[52]. Therefore, art. 1844 in fine Spanish CC should at least be construed in a non restrictive way. This criterion has been followed by the Spanish Supreme Court, which thus has avoided the strict application of its wording (also in cases of joint and several co-guarantees[53]). In the words of the Supreme Court, "the aim of art. 1844 is to avoid a possible damage to the co-guarantors by reason of a reckless, premature or malicious payment"[54/55]. Therefore, by application of the principles of good faith and equity, a right of refund shall always be present when all the co-guarantors have benefited from the payment[56], a judicial suit not being "absolutely necessary".

---

[52] For critical views see: *Albadalejo*, Compendio, 1997, 294; *Díez-Picazo*, Fundamentos, 452. *Contra*: *Carrasco*, *Cordero* and *Marín*, 294.

[53] STS 9 July 1958 [RA 1958 no. 2718]; STS 20 January 1984 [RA 1984 no. 355] and STS 4 May 1993 [RA 1993 no. 3403].

[54] STS 19 November 1982 and STS 7 July 1988 cited by *Sierra* and *Gullón*, 190.

[55] However, in case of arbitrary payment of the whole debt by one of the con-guarantors, the others can always set up their defences against the performing one.

[56] According to STS 24 May 1994 [RA 1994 no. 3741] the performing guarantor must not have been sued for payment in order to ask the co-guarantors for reimbursement if all of them have benefited from the payment. This benefit might simply be the avoidance of an increase of the debt because of procedural costs (STS 7 July 1988 [RA 1988 no.

Furthermore, with regard to the second restriction of art. 1844 par. 3, a factual insolvency or bankruptcy of the debtor is enough to render the guarantor entitled to request reimbursement[57].

b) The case of insolvency of one of the co-guarantors

According to art. 1954 par. 2 juncto art. 1299 Italian CC, if one of the co-guarantors is bankrupt, his part of the debt will be assumed by the other co-guarantors. They will thus assume their share proportionally in relation to the performing guarantor. The latter must prove that at the moment of reimbursement, the relevant co-guarantor was insolvent[58]. The same rule is to be found in art. 1844 par. 2 Spanish CC.

A logical application of this provision only takes place within co-guarantees that have been agreed as being joint and several, or if the "benefit of division" has been lost (cases listed in art. 1831 par. 1). Otherwise, i.e. in the normal case of several liability, the guarantors are not legally compelled to reimburse the performing party. If full performance is freely given, then he thereby assumes the risk of insolvency.

c) The right of the co-guarantors to set up defences against other co-guarantors

If one co-guarantor has performed on behalf of his fellow co-guarantors (joint and several ex lege in Italy or if the benefit of division has been lost according to the law in Spain[59]), the co-guarantors can set up any defences against the performing guarantor (solvens) that they could have raised vis-à-vis the creditor. Moreover, every co-guarantor can set up his own personal defences against the solvens.

2. Internal relationship between a plurality of sureties that are independent from each other

a) Plurality of guarantees, independent from each other

As previously observed, the rules on co-guarantee are not applicable to the case in which a plurality of personal securities are independent from each

---

9287]; STS 7 June 1991 [RA 1991 no. 4428] and STS 16 July 1999 [RA 1999 no. 6770]); but also the cases of special interest of the co-guarantors in the principal debt (STS 2 December 1988 [RA 1988 no. 9287] commented by *Guilarte*, CCJC, 1988, 18 § 483; STS 24 May 1994 [RA 1994 no. 3741], commented by *Tur*, CCJC, 1994, 36 § 970 and STS 29 November 1997 [RA 1997 no. 8437]).

[57] STS 18 September 1997 cited by *Sierra* and *Gullón*, 190.

[58] See *Petti*, 193.

[59] See *supra* Chapter 2, D., 2. Benefit of division. Special benefit for co-guarantors, 103.

other[60]. Hence, there is no right of recourse between the different sureties. However, the general rules on guarantees are applicable. In this respect, according to arts. 1949 Italian CC and art. 1839 Spanish CC[61], the performing guarantor is subrogated in all of the rights of the creditor, including the security rights for the debt [62]. Therefore, it is also a matter of hazard as to which one of the guarantors shall be requested to perform in first place and which one will finally perform.

b) Plurality of personal and real securities independent from each other

The same results are present in the situation of there being a plurality of personal and proprietary sureties[63]. By virtue of art. 1203 par. 3 Italian CC and art. 1210 par. 3[64] Spanish CC, the surety (personal and/or real) that performs the obligation is subrogated into all the rights of the creditor. The rights that are annexed to the credit are also the object of subrogation[65]. Therefore, the surety who fulfils the payment is subrogated into all the rights of the creditor. This subrogation therefore includes any other security that ensures the principal debt.

As the creditor is free to act against any of the sureties that are guaranteeing the same principal debt it is a matter of hazard as to which surety will be required to provide payment. The one who has been chosen has to furnish payment, but he thus obtains the possibility to sue the other sureties. However, this right is of little use if the other sureties are insolvent. It is thus an unpredictable matter as to which of the sureties will finally suffer the patrimonial damage. This appears to be particularly unfair as the ultimate loss is thus dependent on the will of the creditor, which may be whimsical or based on mere personal preferences.

---

[60] STS 4 May 1993 [RA 1997 no. 3741]; *Díez-Picazo*, Fundamentos, 445 ff; *Petti*, 192.

[61] "By virtue of payment the surety is subrogated in all the rights that the creditor had against the debtor. (...)"

[62] Cass. 7 April 1998 no. 3575 cited by *Petti*, 192.

[63] *García Medina*, La doctrina jurisprudencial del art. 1852 del Código Civil (LEG 1889, 27), y la extinción de la fianza, Boletín Aranzadi Civil-Mercantil num. 47/2002, 2003.

[64] Subrogation shall be presumed to exist: (...) 3° When payment is made by a person having an interest in the performance of the obligation, saving the effects of confusion with respect to the part belonging to him".

[65] Cass. 27 December 1963, no. 3221, FI, Rep. 1963, voce *Fideiussione e mandato di credito*, 24; *Tafuro/Franzonni*, 785 and art. 1212 Spanish CC: "A subrogation transfers to the party surrogated the credit along with the rights annexed thereto, whether they run against the debtor or third parties, whether guarantor or holders of the mortgages" ("La subrogación transfiere al subrogado el crédito con los derechos a él anexos, ya contra el deudor, ya contra los terceros, sean fiadores o poseedores de las hipotecas").

c) *Possible solutions to the unfairness of the lack of right of recourse among sureties*

aa) *In general*

As we have observed, the absence of regulation on the plurality of independent sureties has given origin to inequitable situations regarding the internal right of recourse among the sureties. Scholars in Italy and Spain have chosen to ignore the study of this matter[66]. However, the case law in Italy and in other countries such as Germany, has applied general legal principles in order to provide a satisfactory and fair solution to these situations.

bb) *Solution based on the principle of bona fides*

(i) *Application in neighbouring countries*

The logic of fairness suggests that if several persons are prepared to risk their own patrimony or certain assets in order to secure the obligation of another person, all of them should be deemed to be co-debtors for a part of the liability that arises upon the non-performance of the principal debtor[67]. The courts and scholars of certain neighbouring countries with no specific regulation of this issue have already accepted such a solution on the basis of general legal principles such as equity or bona fides[68].

The Italian Supreme Court has reached the same solution to this issue. This court held[69] that the performing guarantor is subrogated into all the

---

[66] The only reference to this case has been first recently made in *Carrasco*, *Cordero* and *Marín*, 290–291.

[67] *Reinicke* and *Tiedtke*, 183 und 187 f.

[68] In Germany on the basis of § 242 BGB (*bona fides*), BGH 29 June 1989, BGHZ 108, 179, 183, 186. In Common Law a right of contribution between co-sureties has been recognised to all co-sureties on the basis of the principle of equity. So, "The right of a surety to contribution is not limited to those who have jointly or jointly and severally bound themselves by the same instrument or even by different instruments expressly connected with each other... The rights of a surety and the effect of the conduct of the creditor upon them rest, broadly speaking, upon two principles which are quite distinct from each other: One is merely a principle of the law of contract. (...) But sureties have other rights not based upon contract at all, but resulting from the equitable right to contribution in all cases where there are sureties for the same debt, even though bound by different instruments, for different amounts an in different terms. In all such cases the extent of each surety's rights must depend not only upon the rerms of the instrument by which the other sureties are bound, and the extent of this relief may be measured by the extent to which the conduct of the creditor has affected the surety's right to contribution" (Molson Bank v. Konvinsky [1924] 4 D.L.R. 330 at 335–36 (Ont. C.A.); *Mc Guiness*, 226.

[69] Cass. 7 April 1998 no. 3575 in *Petti*, 192; See also *Franzoni*, 1497.

rights of the creditor (art. 1203 Italian CC). This guarantor therefore has a right to receive reimbursement from each of the other guarantors. This reimbursement is to be proportional to the percentage that each guarantor provided with regard to the total provision of security. Therefore the performing guarantor should receive a sum that is equivalent to the entire sum of the guarantee, with the exception of an amount that represents the proportion of the total security that was provided by himself[70]. Altogether it can be observed that the Italian Supreme Court has overcome dogmatic problems in order to provide a sensible solution.

(ii) Application of the "Bona Fides" solution in Spain. Difficulties

A similar solution to that used in Germany or Italy could also be applied under Spanish Law. However, there is some difficulty in this matter with regard to the concept of co-debt. According to the wording of art. 1137 Spanish CC, co-debtors are severally liable, unless a different agreement has been reached on this point. If a plurality of sureties that are independent from each other are considered to be co-debtors, they are thus held to be severally liable with regard to the external relationship. The creditor would therefore only be entitled to request that each one of them fulfils his respective obligation. This would therefore mean that each co-debtor would only have to provide a payment in relation to the debt that was proportional to his or her individual share of the total security.

This solution is obviously different to that which is desired by the parties. This can be seen to be the case as their aim was to secure the total debt with different securities that were additional to each other. Moreover, sureties must not receive any notice of the existence of other sureties. This is to prevent them from being unaware of the amount for which they are liable. If they were unaware they might not be able to set up a defence that might arise if an excessive amount should be requested. The result of this construction would be that in order to solve an unfair situation that was present within the internal relationship, a separate unfair or undesired situation is created within the external relationship.

Spanish case law has modified the application of art. 1137 Spanish CC in order to restrain the exigency of the express constitution of a joint and several co-debt by application of the principle of good faith (art. 7 Spanish CC). According to a number of decisions the joint and several character of

[70] If no special agreements have taken place, all securities have the same rank. The sureties are considered co-debtors and according to the rules on co-debt they will be liable *pro rata (*per capita unless otherwise agreed), (art. 1298 Italian CC). The same has been applied by the German Supreme Court in BGH 24 September 1992, NJW 1992 no. 3228 in *Reinicke* and *Tiedtke*, 183 (§426„*nach Köpfen*").

a co-debt may be deduced from the intention of the parties or from the nature of the agreements[71].

In case there is a plurality of sureties, they might act separately from -or even not have notice of the existence of- each other. However, all of the securing obligations seek to achieve a common legal result; i.e. to satisfy the same creditor for the same debt. Hence, they are joined by this common aim. Therefore, according to the case law on co-debt[72] the sureties might be considered to be joint and several co-debtors. This may even be the case if the parties have ignored the request in art. 1137 Spanish CC and have not expressly agreed to such a position.

A second theoretical difficulty arises from the fact that if there is a plurality of sureties then there are as many obligations as there are securities. These obligations are independent from each other and also from the principal debt. Certain legal writers hold that a joint and several co-debt creates a unique obligation that is owed by different persons. This theory has been contradicted by other academics who consider that a joint and several co-debt always creates a plurality of obligations: "the external unity derives in a real plurality"[73]. Moreover Spanish case law on co-debt has also held that even if the different obligations of the individual debtors are independent to a certain extent, they are unified by their common purpose of fulfilling the interest of the creditor[74].

It can therefore be concluded that in Spain a plurality of sureties of the same rank, that secure the same debt for a common debtor can be considered to be joint and several co-debtors. Hence, arts. 1140–1148 Spanish CC should be applied to such instances.

(iii) Consequences of the application to this solution

Consequently the provision of compensation for the benefit of a performing co-debtor shall be applicable for the benefit of a performing surety. In general the compensation of the performing co-debtor can be based on two different claims: reimbursement and subrogation.

In Germany, Italy and Spain the performing debtor has claim for reimbursement against his co-debtors with regard to their respective parts of the

---

[71] STS 15 March 1982 [RA 1982 no. 3403]; STS 6 March 1999 [RA 1999 no. 2247] and STS 7 April 1983, STS 14 April; STS 20 October 1986, STS 12 May 1987, STS 26 July and STS 11 October 1989, STS 28 May and STS 17 December 1990, STS 19 December 1991 and STS 17 October 1996 cited by Albácar, 709.

[72] STS 13 March 1987 [RA 1987 no.1479] and STS 26 April 1985 [RA 1985 no.1991].

[73] For a broad explanation and quotations: *Díez-Picazo*, Fundamentos, 206.

[74] STS 19 July 1989 cited by *Moreno*, 915.

debt (§ 426 par. 1 sent. 2 BGB, art. 1299 Italian CC and art. 1145 Spanish CC all with parallel wording).

The compensation may also be based on the claim for subrogation. The question of the legal basis for the demand for compensation can be relevant in commercial practice. For instance, in those cases in which any other co-debtor has granted another security for his own debt, subrogation serves to assign this security right to the performing debtor. However, it is only the German Civil Code that expressly grants a right of subrogation to the performing co-debtor in § 426 par. 2 BGB.

In contrast, neither in Italy nor in Spain has such a right been expressly included among the rules of co-debt. However, the general rules of subrogation (art. 1210 no. 3° Spanish CC and art. 1203 no 3° Italian CC) have been declared[75] to be applicable to the situation in which one co-debtor performs. Consequently, the final result is the same in all of these three legal systems. The performing surety shall thus receive compensation from all the other sureties for their respective parts of the total amount.

cc) Solution for a special case. Concurrency of guarantee and other security rights

A special arrangement of a plurality of securities is the concurrency of a guarantee and other security rights. A possible solution that is suggested in order to reduce the unfair consequences of the absence of regulation with regard to the internal relationship among "independent" sureties is to grant the guarantor an advantageous or privileged position. This solution has been extensively discussed in Germany, where this issue has been described as being a "time-honoured matter of dispute" (altehrwürdige Streitfrage[76]) by writers and by the courts[77]. By contrast, in Spain and Italy this alternative has never had such a corresponding resonance[78].

The starting point of this discussion is to consider whether the guarantee itself contains a special factor of risk. In all countries, the surety compels himself with his whole present and future patrimony to secure the debt of another person. The grant of a real security right may imply a greater risk for the surety. Depending on the circumstances of the case, this might be a much higher risk than the one that is assumed by a surety[79]. However, the

---

[75] Case law and explanation in: *De Maria/Franzoni*, 902; *Díez-Picazo*, Fundamentos, 214.

[76] *Reinicke* and *Tiedtke*, 186.

[77] In favour: *Horn/Staudinger* on § 774 no. 65–74. *Contra*: *Lambsdorff* and *Skora*, no. 313.

[78] Guilarte keeps breve notice of these theories in *Guilarte*, 318 ff.

[79] Opinion of the German Supreme Court: BGH 29 June 1986, BGHZ 108, 179; BGH 24 September 1992, NJW 1992, 3228.

latter is liable with regard to his whole future patrimony. Such a form of liability is never present in the case of a real security. This therefore makes a surety worthy of special protection[80]. Hence, the Law grants the surety special legal privileges or protective rules (favor fideiussoris).

For instance, the surety enjoys a right of subrogation that is expressly granted ex lege in art. 1949 Italian CC and 1839 Spanish CC. The proprietary surety is also subrogated into the rights of the creditor upon performance. However, this right is only a presumption that is established in art. 1203 par. 3 Italian CC and 1210 par. 3° Spanish CC. Moreover, according to art. 1852 Spanish CC, the surety is discharged whenever an act of the creditor prevents him from being subrogated into his rights, mortgages and privileges[81]. The German Supreme Court has also considered that other provisions on guarantee such as the benefit of discussion act as evidence that the legislator has taken into account the special risk of the surety and has thus decided to compensate the surety with such provisions[82].

It may be wondered whether these rules are sufficient compensation for the special risk of the guarantor. The guarantor may also deserve a privileged position within the internal relationship. The German Supreme Court holds that the guarantor should not be given a privileged position within the internal relationship. Therefore the guarantor should be treated like every other surety within the internal relationship[83]. However, this is still considered to be a controversial issue by legal scholars, some of whom are not convinced by the reasoning of the Supreme Court[84].

Current banking practice tends to give preference to proprietary security rights. This is due to the fact that they are easily enforceable. In many instances it is the case that proprietary sureties are persons that have a small patrimony. However they may become the owner of a valuable good that is acquired over time or is inherited. Therefore, a person whose solvency would otherwise be insufficient to enable them to grant a guarantee is required to grant a proprietary security over the one unique valuable good. It would therefore be unfair to grant a legal privilege to one of the sureties upon a criterion that is based on the assumed risk, if this criterion does not take into account the risk that is really assumed by each party in relation to their economic situation. The reasons that are cited to support the prefe-

[80] *Reinicke* and *Tiedtke*, 186.

[81] This theory has been considered in Germany regarding § 776–774 BGB; see *Knütel*, 559, 588.

[82] BGH 28 February 1989, BGHZ 107, 92.

[83] BGH 29 June 1989, BGHZ 108, 179; BGH 24 September 1992, NJW 1992, 3228; *Reinicke* and *Tiedtke*, 186.

[84] *Reinicke* and *Tiedtke*, 187; *Guilarte* 1979, 318 ff.

rence in favour of the guarantor are weak and do not seem to provide a fair final result.

V. Concurrency of a contract of guarantee and an assumption of debt

By the assumption of debt a third person enters the obligatory relationship becoming a principal debtor alongside the original one.

1. In general

Co-debtors in Italy are ex lege joint and severally liable. Given the existence of a plurality of debtors and a plurality of guarantees for the debt, the guarantor who performs the debt in the first place has a right of reimbursement against the debtors for the full debt. Moreover, he has a right of reimbursement against each of the guarantors, for their respective parts (art. 1954 Italian CC).

The liability of co-debtors in the Spanish Civil Code is several (mancomunada). Each of the debtors therefore only owes a part of the total debt. If the original debt was secured by a guarantee, this guarantee would be proportionally reduced by virtue of the application of art. 1826 Spanish CC. This provision serves to limit the extent of the guarantee to that of the principal debt. In such a situation the guarantee decreases in its extent and then the new debtor undertakes half of the principal debt.

2. Assumption of debt for security purpose

An assumption of the debt by a new debtor is considered to be a security right if it takes place in order to secure the performance of the debt that is owed by the original debtor. This kind of security right is called an assumption of debt for security purpose.

In order for the assumption to provide security, the liability that is assumed by the new debtor must be joint and several[85].

The problem is mainly how to consider the guarantees created before the adherence to the original debt. According to the rules on co-debt, if the new debtor performs the obligation, he has "a right of refund from his co-obligors for the part corresponding to each, with interest on the sum advanced" (art. 1299 Italian CC and art. 1145 Spanish CC). But in this situation the new person that is assuming the debt is only a surety and therefore he must have the right to be fully refunded by the "real" debtor if he per-

[85] It might be expressly agreed or it might be considered that the liability of the co-debtors is always joint and several in case of assumption of debt for security purpose. *Roca Sastre*, 189.

forms the obligation. Therefore he should not just receive a "corresponding part" of the sum.

The solution to this problem is to consider this "part" as not being per capita in relation to the debtors but rather as being subject to the agreement of the parties. The right to be refunded would therefore be agreed to by them. For example, the new debtor that is assuming the debt for a security purpose would have a 100 % right of refund against the other co-debtor (secured party), while this other co-debtor would have a 0% against the new debtor. If one of them also has a guarantee (or any other kind of security) to ensure his debt, then the right of the other co-debtor to profit from this guarantee will be dependent upon the right of refund that this one has against his co-debtor.

If in our example, the debtor with no right of refund has constituted a joint and several guarantee ensuring his debt, the one that is enjoying a 100% right of refund may require the total payment of the debt from the guarantor. Otherwise, if the guarantor is the first party that is required to make payment by the creditor, the guarantor will not have any right of refund against the co-debtor of his principal if the principal does not refund him.

VI. Concurrency of guarantee contracts and letters of comfort

Legal writers have not clarified the effects of the concurrency of letters of comfort with guarantee contracts. However, according to the variety of the formulations of the letters of comfort, the solutions are dependent on the facts and circumstances of each case and the actual wording of the relevant letter.

Chapter 5

Personal security rights as Credit Risk Mitigators in the Basle II Accord and in the Capital Requirements Directive

Introduction

In terms of risk management, personal security rights play a significant role reducing the credit risk assumed by the creditor, i.e. as credit risk mitigators. Such risk mitigating factor has been recently recognised by the regulators in view of calculating the regulatory capital[1] requirements for financial institutions.

Credit risk, market risk, and operational risk have increased in complexity over the latest years becoming a key concern for banking regulators worldwide and even more after the 2007 financial turmoil. The tools and mechanisms to monitor and measure those risks have also become increasingly sophisticated and more comprehensive than ever before. Moreover, the ability to measure, manage and transfer this kind of risks has improved dramatically as well. The Capital Adequacy Accord[2] published in June 2004 by the Basel Committee on Banking Supervision (commonly known as Basel II) has taken this increased capacity to manage and transfer risk into account for the new capital requirement standards.

The Basel II regulatory framework aims at improving the sensitivity to the risks that banks actually face and offer stronger incentives for im-

---

[1] On regulatory capital, see: *Elizalde* and *Repullo*, Economic and Regulatory Capital in Banking: What is the Difference?, CEMFI and UPNA, July 2006 (ftp://ftp.cemfi.es/pdf/papers/repullo/economic%20capital.pdf).

[2] "International Convergence of Capital Measurement and Capital Standards: A revised Framework", 2004 (http://www.bis.org/publ/bcbs128.htm). This document has been incorporated in the comprehensive version of International Convergence of Capital Measurement and Capital Standards: A Revised Framework, June 2006, including the elements of the 1988 Accord that were not revised during the Basel II process, the 1996 Amendment to the Capital Accord to Incorporate Market Risks, and the 2005 paper on The Application of Basel II to Trading Activities and the Treatment of Double Default Effects.

proved risk management[3]. This goal is achieved by providing an extensive regulatory framework that reflects more accurately the effective underlying risks in the banking sector and takes into account the significant advances in risk management practices, and applied technologies as well as developments in the banking markets since the publication of Basel I in 1988. For this purpose, capital requirements have been more closely aligned to the risk of credit loss and a new capital charge for exposures has been introduced to the risk of loss caused by operational failures. Within this context, Credit Risk Mitigation Techniques (CRM)[4] have been largely considered in the new regulation as a way to reduce the capital requirements for banks.

Within the EU, the new Basel II Accord has been implemented in the form of the so called Capital Requirements Directive (CRD), published in June 2006[5] and implemented then at national level in the EU Member States[6]. The EU Commission published the proposal for the CRD in July 2004. The content of the Directive mainly reflects the letter and spirit of the Basel II Accord[7]. Both texts regulate extensively the use of Credit Risk Mitigation Techniques as methods to effectively reduce credit risk[8]. Under the new regulation, all kinds of lenders (those operating under the Standard

---

[3] For a practical approach towards credit risk under the Basel II Accord see: *Glantz*, Mun, The banker´s handbook on credit risk: implementing Basel II, Burlington, 2008.

Credit Risk Mitigation is also often referred to as Credit Risk Transfer (CRT).

[5] The Capital Requirements Directive, comprising Directive 2006/48/EC and Directive 2006/49/EC, was published in the Official Journal on Friday 30 June.

[6] The CRD has been transposed:

a) In Italy by amendments introduced to the Circolare n.155 18 dicembre 1991 as updated in June 2007) and Circolare n.216 5 agosto 1996 as updated in July 2007). Also see Circolare 263 sets out the compulsory regime for all banks starting from January 1st 2008. See also: Basilea 2 consultants; Il Nuovo Accordo di Basilea e i sistemi di Internal Rating; 1.7 Il ruolo delle garanzie; http://www.basilea2.it/garanzie.pdf;

b) In Spain through the Real Decreto 216/2008, de 15 de febrero, de recursos propios de las entidades financieras complemented by the Circular 3/2008, a las entidades de crédito, sobre determinación y control de los recursos propios mínimos, as approved May 22, 2008;

c) In Germany by amendments introduced to the Banking Act, the Solvabilitätsverordnung and the Mindestanforderung an das Risikomanagement (MaRisk). See Deutsche Bundesbank, Transposing the new Basel capital rules into German Law, monthly report, December 2006. http://www.bundesbank.de/download/volkswirtschaft/mba/2006/200612 mba_en_transposing.pdf.

[7] Within this Part, where the Basel II Accord is mentioned, the same is also valid for the Capital Requirements Directive. Legal references are made to the Capital Requirements Directive.

[8] The explanatory memorandum of the CRD mentions the lack of recognition of effective risk mitigation as one of the shortcomings of the previous regulation and one of the needs for improved European requirements.

Approach and those under IRB)[9] will be allowed to reduce capital requirements through the use of a wide range of security rights (personal and proprietary) and other techniques to mitigate credit risk.

In this Chapter we revise the meaning and structure of the Basel II Accord and the CRD focusing on the regulation of credit risk mitigation techniques and specifically on the treatment of personal security rights as eligible to provide capital relief to the lending (secured) institutions.

A. The New Basel II Accord and the Capital RequirementsDirective

I. A risk sensitive banking regulation for a changing environment

In the last years, risk management practices and technologies have experience a significant evolution and are more generally used within the banking sector.

Also the banking markets have clearly evolved since the adoption of the first Capital Requirement Framework (Basel I) in 1988, which approach towards risk measuring remained rather simple. As way of example, the 1988 Accord sets capital requirements based on broad classes of exposures and does not distinguish between the relative degrees of creditworthiness among individual borrowers. Moreover, there was no explicit recognition of effective risk mitigation, which followed to a generally less accurate consideration of risk.

During the last years, the 1988 Basel Capital Accord has grown more pervasive, being integrated into national regulations in most advanced countries. Meanwhile, the limitations and shortcomings of this rather simple regulation have become progressively more manifest. The existence of a gap between supervisory requirements and risk-based measures of economic capital has led to forms of regulatory arbitrage. Paradoxically, the inability of the 1988 Accord to differentiate between investment grade and junk borrowers might also have made some financial institutions more risk-seeking, instead of helping them control their risks.

The stagnant rules set out in the 1988 Accord have not kept pace with advances in sound risk management practices, the existing capital regulations not reflecting banks' actual business practices.

This drawback was acknowledged by supervisors and addressed by the Basel Committee on Banking Supervision[10], which engaged for several

---

[9] See below under: Chapter 5, A., II. The goal of the Basel II Accord and the tree pillars methodology, 251.

years in a revision process that finally lead to the "International Convergence of Capital Measurement and Capital Standards: a Revised Framework"[11], also known as the New Basel Capital Accord - Basel II (Basel II).

This new framework presents a more sophisticated set of standards for establishing minimum capital requirements for banking organisations, intending to lessen the gap between regulatory capital requirements and real economic risk faced by these organisations.

The Basel II Framework as also reflected in the CRD, hence, sets out the details for adopting more risk-sensitive minimum capital requirements for banking organisations. The new framework reinforces these risk-sensitive requirements by laying out principles for banks to assess the adequacy of their capital and for supervisors to review such assessments to ensure banks have adequate capital to support their risks. It also seeks to strengthen market discipline by enhancing transparency in banks' financial reporting. The Basel Committee, however, intended to maintain broadly the aggregate level of minimum capital requirements set in the 1988 Accord, while providing incentives to adopt the more advanced risk-sensitive approaches of the revised Framework. Basel II combines these minimum capital requirements with supervisory review and market discipline to encourage improvements in risk management.

In this regard, the Committee recognises the need to distinguish between those banks that are able to better assess their risk and those that have less sophisticated tools to do so. In assessing their capital requirements, the first follow the "Internal Rating Based" (IRB) approach which allow them to better identify the actual need for capital requirement according to their real risks. The second type of banks will follow a simplified method to assess their capital requirements, in line with that set up in the Basel Accord of 1988 based on Risk Weightings. This distinction aims at providing incentives for banks to develop better risk assessment tools in order to adapt their capital needs to their real risk.

II. The goal of the Basel II Accord and the three pillars methodology

The global aim of the Basel II Accord is to promote the adequate capitalisation of banks as well as to encourage improvements in risk management, thereby strengthening the stability of the financial system. The Accord is structured in three pillars. The first one is focused on the strengthening of

---

[10] The Basel Committee on banking supervision is a group of central banks and bank supervisory authorities in the G10 countries, which also developed the first standard in 1988.

[11] Find full text in the Bank of International Settlements website: http://www.bis.org/publ/bcbs128.htm

the minimum requirements set out in the 1988 Accord, while the second and third pillars represent innovative additions to capital supervision.

i) In "Pillar 1" the Basel I's guidelines are revised by aligning the minimum capital requirements more closely to each bank's actual risk of economic loss.

Under Basel I, banks need to align 8% of each credit granted independently of the quality of the borrower. Basel II maintains this fixed percentage of 8% but improves the capital framework's sensitivity to the risk categories. Regarding credit risk, higher levels of capital are generally required for those borrowers that present higher levels of credit risk, and vice versa.

In order to calculate their capital requirements, banks may choose among three different approaches, depending on the level of sophistication of their risk management and internal control structures.

Under the "standardised approach" (RSA) to credit risk, banks that engage in less complex forms of lending and credit underwriting and that have simpler control structures may use external measures of credit risk (Risk Weightings) to assess the credit quality of their borrowers for regulatory capital purposes.

Banks that engage in more sophisticated risk-taking and that have developed advanced risk measurement systems may, with the approval of their supervisors, select from one of two "internal ratings-based" ("IRB") approaches to credit risk. Under an IRB approach, banks rely partly on their own measures of a borrowers' credit risk to determine their capital requirements, subject to strict data, validation, and operational requirements. The IRB Approach is based on the estimation by banks of two factors – the PD (Probability of Default) and the LGD (Loss Given Default) – for different kinds of activities using a complex formula established in the Accord to determine risk weightings. Under the IRB Advanced banks determine the risk weightings by adding to the Basel formula multiple internal factors.

Second, the new Framework establishes an explicit capital charge for a bank's exposures to the risk of losses caused by failures in systems, processes, or staff or that are caused by external events, such as natural disasters. Similar to the range of options provided for assessing exposures to credit risk, banks will choose one of three approaches for measuring their exposures to operational risk that they and their supervisors agree reflects the quality and sophistication of their internal controls over this particular risk area.

By aligning capital charges more closely to a bank's own measures of its exposures to credit and operational risk, the Basel II Framework encourages banks to refine those measures. It also provides explicit incentives in the form of lower capital requirements for banks to adopt more comprehensive and accurate measures of risk as well as more effective processes for controlling their exposures to risk.

ii) "Pillar 2", foresees the need of exercising effective supervisory review of the banks' internal assessments of their overall risks in view of ensuring that bank management is exercising sound judgement and has set aside adequate capital for these risks.

Supervisors will evaluate the activities and risk profiles of individual banks to determine whether those organisations should hold higher levels of capital than the minimum requirements in Pillar 1 would specify and to see whether there is any need for remedial actions.

Engaging banks in a dialogue with the supervisor on their internal processes for measuring and managing their risk will likely motivate them to develop sound control structures and to improve those processes.

iii) "Pillar 3" leverages the ability of market discipline to motivate prudent management by enhancing the degree of transparency in banks' public reporting. It sets out the public disclosures which will likely lend greater insight into the adequacy of banks' capitalisation.

The Committee believes that, when marketplace participants have a sufficient understanding of a bank's activities and the controls it has in place to manage its exposures, they are better able to distinguish between banking organisations so that they can reward those that manage their risks prudently and penalise those that do not.

The CRD replicates this scheme for the EU banking context.

B. Recognition of Credit Risk Mitigation Techniques: an achievement of the Basel II Accord

I. Capital relief through the use of Credit Risk Mitigation Techniques (CRM)

CRM techniques are mechanisms aiming at effectively reducing the credit risk of a lender and are commonly used in today's banking practice[12]. One of the new features of the Basel II Accord is the recognition of such risk

[12] However, this effective reduction of risk was not always recognised by regulators and supervisors in terms of minimum capital requirements. It is true that some risk mitigation techniques had partly been recognised in several jurisdictions by the national regulator. That is for instance the case for the use of Mortgage Insurance for high LTV loans in countries like US, Canada or Australia. In these countries the use of MI for loans reduces the risk weighting of high LTV loans from 100 % to 50 %, diminishing so the capital requirements for the lender. However these practices have developed differently in every country and only to a limited extent.

mitigating effect in terms of capital relief. This is in line with the Basel II global approach of adapting capital requirements to real economic risk. In this respect, the principle of using CRMs relies on the fact that no exposure in respect of which credit risk mitigation is obtained shall produce a higher risk-weighted exposure amount or expected loss amount than an otherwise identical exposure in respect of which there is not credit risk mitigation. This principle is also reflected in the CRD[13].

II. The concept of CRM, unfunded credit protection and guarantee

1. The concept of CRM: broad and comprehensive

The number and types of CRMs available to lending institutions has become extensive. In first place, the definition of Credit Risk Mitigation under Basel II and the CRD is unambiguous but broad. According to the new standards, CRM "means a technique used by a credit institution to reduce the credit risk associated with an exposure or exposures which the credit institution continues to hold"[14]. This definition is broad and purely based on risk elements[15].

2. The concept of unfunded credit protection

A basic distinction is made between "funded"[16] and "unfunded" credit protection.

---

[13] Art. 93. 2 CRD, Directive 2006/48/EC: "No exposure in respect of which credit risk mitigation is obtained shall produce a higher risk-weighted exposure amount or expected loss amount than an otherwise identical exposure in respect of which there is no credit risk mitigation."

[14] See art. 4 (30) CRD, Directive 2006/48/EC.

[15] This has facilitated innovation in this field. Several types of CRMs have been developed. The Bank of International Settlements has studied such developments and their impact on financial stability (which appear particularly important considering the 2008 financial crisis). See BIS, Credit Risk Trasfer Developments 2005 to 2007, 2008 and BIS, Credit Risk Transfer, 2003.

[16] According to art. 4 (31) CRD, Directive 2006/48/EC, funded credit protection is a "technique of credit risk mitigation where the reduction of the credit risk on the exposure of a credit institution derives from the right of the credit institution – in the event of the default of the counterparty or on the occurrence of other specified credit events relating to the counterparty – to liquidate, or to obtain transfer or appropriation of, or to replace it with, the amount of the difference between the amount of the exposure and the amount of a claim on the credit institution". Proprietory security rights are funded credit protection in this context. Recognised types of unfunded credit protection are: financial collateral (e.g. collateral in the form of cash or debt securities); additional collateral eligible under the Foundation IRB approach (e.g. collateral in the form of real estate or short-term claims); other funded credit protection (e.g. collateral in the form of deposits held with third-party financial undertakings or life insurance policies); on-balance sheet netting

According to art. 4 (32) CRD, Directive 2006/48/EC, unfunded credit protection means a "technique of credit risk mitigation where the reduction of the credit risk on the exposure of a credit institution derives from the undertaking of a third party to pay an amount in the event of the default of the borrower or on the occurrence of other specified events".

Consequently, any kind of risk mitigation technique can be recognised as unfunded credit protection provided: a) it effectively mitigates the credit risk of a credit institution; b) it is provided by a third party and c) it covers either the case of default of the borrower or any occurrence of other specified events[17].

Certainly, all typical personal security rights meet the definition of unfunded credit protection and may, hence, provide capital relief to the protected borrowers. Third-party guarantees and credit derivatives are explicitly recognised and regulated but any other type of credit protection meeting both the generic definitions and the minimum requirements are eligible for capital relief.

It can be concluded that the personal security rights are subject to be recognised for capital relief purposes are not numerus clausus.

3. *The concept of guarantee under the CRD*

The term "guarantee" is not specifically defined neither in the Basel II Accord nor is it in the CRD. Rather than making reference to a specific type of regulated contract, it intends to cover any type of personal security right with a risk mitigating effect. In this sense, it is indeed true that "there is significant variance from country to country in the legal, contractual and operational characteristics of the guarantees and therefore recognition should be based on the real nature of the guarantee, irrespective of the terminology used. It is essential that any guarantee fulfilling the minimum requirements be recognised as an eligible credit risk mitigant.[18]

---

vis-à-vis the same counterparty, the same customer or group or affiliated entities and master netting agreements covering repurchase transactions and capital market-driven transactions.

[17] This definition opens the possibility for banks to use CRM for risks others than the borrower's default. That is for instance the case of Mortgage Insurance, by which the risk covered by the insurance company is the loss arising from a mortgage loan. This means, the insurance company secures the lender in case a borrower of a mortgage loan defaults and the lender still suffers a loss after foreclosing the collateral, which secures the loan. Under the previous regulation there are no general standards, which follow to the recognition of these kinds of CRMs. Basel II offers hence a wide range of possibilities for the use of existing mechanisms to manage and reduce the credit risk as well as the development of new products.

[18] Cools, Letter of the Ministry of Finance, Financial Supervisory Authority, Bank of Finland, to the European Commission, Letter 1 (26), 23rd October 2003, 13. (http://rahoi-

The term "guarantee" is, hence, to be understood in broad terms and not as a regulated type of contract.

For instance, the Finnish Authorities argued that the types of guarantees found in Finland, where a protection provider guarantees the loss after the lending institution has realised other credit risk mitigation, thus ensuring the exposure, fulfil the requirements imposed on guarantees in the CRD. This approach has been generally accepted within the EU. Contracts such as mortgage insurance have been, as a result, recognised as a "guarantee" in this context and for the purpose of credit risk mitigation.[19]

III. The regulation of CRMs in Basel II and the CRD

1. In general

CRMs are regulated in the Basel II Accord as well as in the CRD (arts. 90–93 as further developed in the annexes[20]). The CRM framework sets requirements on CRM techniques which an institution must meet in order to qualify for a reduction of its capital requirements. The framework also determines how application of CRM techniques affects capital requirements under the Standardised Approach (RSA) and the Internal Ratings Based approaches. If application of credit risk mitigation does not result in reduction of the risk-weighted items, a financial undertaking need not take account of the credit mitigating effect in its calculations.

2. Application of CRMs for capital relief: distinction between IRB and RSA banks

The distinction between those banks following the IRB Approach and those "standard" banks (RSA) also reflects on the regulation applicable to CRMs.

For those banks using the Standard Approach, the reduction of capital by the use of CRMs is based on the substitution principle: the risk weighting for the operation is substituted by that of the guarantor, which will depend on the latter's quality as a guarantor. For instance, lending activities

---

tustarkastus.fi/NR/rdonlyres/D4629E98-37D0-4270-9D23-269F2AE5449C/0/221003.pdf)

[19] See Answers from the Capital Requirements Directive Transposition Group; Area: 2006/48/EC, Annex VIII, Part 1; Issue: Credit risk mitigation – eligibility; Question number: 184; Date of question: 8/12/1006; Publication of answer: 15 January 2007. (http://ec.europa.eu/internal_market/bank/regcapital/transposition_en.htm).

[20] The application of the Lamfalussy (comitology) approach to these annexes will allow more flexible possibilities to amend the text through a system of committees and avoiding hence going through the standard co-decision procedure for EU legislation, which is long-lasting and burdensome.

are risk weighted 100%. This means that banks need to align 8% of each credit granted independently of the quality of the borrower. If the credit is guaranteed, the risk weighting applied to the operation will be that of the guarantor. Supposed the guarantor is a AAA rated company, then the risk weighting is 20%. Accordingly, the capital that the bank needs to keep aside as capital requirement is 20% of 8%, which amounts 1,6% instead of 8%. The benefit for the bank is 6.4%.

IRB banks use more sophisticated risk measuring and management systems. They can calculate the precise impact of the reduction of risk caused by the use of a CRM within their risk management formulas. The use of a CRM normally reduces the Probability of Default (PD) and the Loss Given Default (LGD) and IRB banks are able to calculate this reduction and diminish, as a consequence, also the allocation of capital. The final result depends on the precise combination of elements present and included into the mathematical calculations.

3. *Minimum requirements for CRMs to be recognised for capital relief*

a) Requirements related to the CRM provider

The new regulation sets the type of guarantors that are recognised as valid to provide any type of credit risk mitigants for the purpose of capital relief[21]. These security providers do have an allocated risk weighting which

---

[21] See Annex VIII, Part 2, 2, CRD, Directive 2006/48/EC under 2. "unfunded credit protection:
2.1. Eligibility of protection providers under all approaches:
26. (a) central governments and central banks;
(b) regional governments or local authorities;
(c) multilateral development banks;
(d) international organisations exposures to which a 0 % risk weight under Articles 78 to 83 is assigned;
(e) public sector entities, claims on which are treated by the competent authorities as claims on institutions or central governments under Articles 78 to 83;
(f) institutions; and
(g) (i) have a credit assessment by a recognised ECAI which has been determined by the competent authorities to be associated with credit quality step 2 or above under the rules for the risk weighting of exposures to corporates under Articles 78 to 83; and
(ii) in the case of credit institutions calculating risk-weighted exposure amounts and expected loss amounts under Articles 84 to 89, do not have a credit assessment by a recognised ECAI and are internally rated as having a PD equivalent to that associated with the credit assessments of ECAIs determined by the competent authorities to be associated with credit quality step 2 or above under the rules for the risk weighting of exposures to corporate under Articles 78 to 83.
27. Where risk-weighted exposure amounts and expected loss amounts are calculated under Articles 84 to 89, to be eligible a guarantor must be internally rated by the credit institution in accordance with the provisions of Annex VII, Part 4.

is used to calculate the risk mitigating effect of the guarantee and as a consequence also of the credit. Individual guarantors do not have a risk weighting allocated in the Basel Accord or CRD, so that personal security rights (unfunded credit protection) granted by a private individual (retail) do not provide any capital relief for the bank.

b) Specific minimum requirements for "Guarantees" to qualify as a CRM under RSA approach

Basel II and the CRD foresee a number of specific requirements applicable to "guarantees" in order to be recognised CRMs.

The requirements set in the CRD for guarantees to be eligible are only applicable for banks undergoing the RSA approach, i.e. those with less sophisticated risk management tools[22].

According to the CRD[23], "(…) for the credit protection deriving from a guarantee or credit derivative to be recognised the following conditions shall be met:

(a) the credit protection shall be direct;
(b) the extent of the credit protection shall be clearly defined and incontrovertible;

---

28. By way of derogation from point 26, the Member States may also recognise as eligible providers of unfunded credit protection, other financial institutions authorised and supervised by the competent authorities responsible for the authorisation and supervision of credit institutions and subject to prudential requirements equivalent to those applied to credit institutions.
2.2 Eligibility of protection providers under the IRB Approach which qualify for the treatment set out in Annex VII, Part 1, point 4.
29. – the protection provider has sufficient expertise in providing unfunded credit protection;
– the protection provider is regulated in a manner equivalent to the rules laid down in this Directive, or had, at the time the credit protection was provided, a credit assessment by a recognised ECAI which had been determined by the competent authorities to be associated with credit quality step 3, or above, under the rules for the risk weighting of exposures to corporate under Articles 78 to 83;
– the protection provider had, at the time the credit protection was provided, or for any period of time thereafter, an internal rating with a PD equivalent to or lower than that associated with credit quality step 2 or above under the rules for the risk weighting of exposures to corporates under Articles 78 to 83; and
– the provider has an internal rating with a PD equivalent to or lower than that associated with credit quality step 3 or above under the rules for the risk weighting of exposures to corporates under Articles 78 to 83.
For the purpose of this point, credit protection provided by export credit agencies shall not benefit from any explicit central government counter-guarantee."

[22] See Annex VIII, Part 3, 2.1 CRD, Directive 2006/48/EC.

[23] Annex VIII, Part 3, 2.1, 14, CRD, Directive 2006/48/EC, under "Requirements common to guarantees and credit derivatives".

(c) the credit protection contract shall not contain any clause, the fulfilment of which is outside the direct control of the lender, that:
   (i) would allow the protection provider unilaterally to cancel the protection;
   (ii) would increase the effective cost of protection as a result of deteriorating credit quality of the protected exposure;
   (iii) could prevent the protection provider from being obliged to pay out in a timely manner in the event that the original obligor fails to make any payments due; or
   (iv) could allow the maturity of the credit protection to be reduced by the protection provider; and

(d) it must be legally effective and enforceable in all jurisdictions which are relevant at the time of the conclusion of the credit agreement."

Hence, in order to provide capital relief a "guarantee" under RSA needs to be direct, certain, irrevocable, unconditional and incontrovertible[24].

Beyond, specifically for a guarantee to be recognised under RSA, the following conditions need to be met: "(a) on the qualifying default of and/or non-payment by the counterparty, the lending credit institution shall have the right to pursue, in a timely manner, the guarantor for any monies due under the claim in respect of which the protection is provided. Payment by the guarantor shall not be subject to the lending credit institution first having to pursue the obligor (…); (b) the guarantee shall be an explicitly documented obligation assumed by the guarantor; and (c) subject to the following sentence, the guarantee shall cover all types of payments the obligor is expected to make in respect of the claim. Where certain types of payment are excluded from the guarantee, the recognised value of the guarantee shall be adjusted to reflect the limited coverage."[25]

In terms of operational requirements, the credit institution shall satisfy the competent authority that it has systems in place to manage potential concentration of risk arising from the credit institution's use of guarantees and credit derivatives. The credit institution must be able to demonstrate how its strategy in respect of its use of credit derivatives and guarantees interacts with its management of its overall risk profile.[26]

Finally, specific requirements are also set for a) sovereign and other public sector guarantees[27], b) mutual guarantee schemes[28] and c) for mort-

---

[24] Annex VIII, Part 3, 2.1,14 CRD, Directive 2006/48/EC.

[25] Annex VIII, Part 3, 2.3, 18 CRD, Directive 2006/48/EC, under "Additional requirements for guarantees".

[26] Annex VIII, Part 3, 2.1,15 CRD, Directive 2006/48/EC.

[27] Annex VIII, Part 3, 2.2,16 and 17 CRD, Directive 2006/48/EC: "16. Where an exposure is protected by a guarantee which is counterguaranteed by a central government or central bank, a regional government or local authority, a public sector entity, claims on

gage insurance and similar types of unfunded credit protection for residential mortgage loans[29].

c) Specific minimum requirements for "Guarantees" to qualify as a CRM under IRB approach

Banks following the IRB approach are not subject to the requirements. However, each countries' supervisor will have to approve the risk models developed by each financial institution, including the risk mitigating effect of their CRM. Normally, similar conditions should be deemed necessary in order to approve the use of security rights as CRM for the purpose of capital relief.

---

which are treated as claims on the central government in whose jurisdiction they are established under Articles 78 to 83, a multi-lateral development bank to which a 0 % risk weight is assigned under or by virtue of Articles 78 to 83, or a public sector entity, claims on which are treated as claims on credit institutions under Articles 78 to 83, the exposure may be treated as protected by a guarantee provided by the entity in question, provided the following conditions are satisfied:
(a) the counter guarantee covers all credit risk elements of the claim;
(b) both the original guarantee and the counterguarantee meet the requirements for guarantees set out in points 14, 15 and 18, except that the counterguarantee need not be direct; and
(c) the competent authority is satisfied that the cover is robust and that nothing in the historical evidence suggests that the coverage of the counterguarantee is less than effectively equivalent to that of a direct guarantee by the entity in question.
17. The treatment set out in point 16 also applies to an exposure which is not counter guaranteed by an entity listed in that point if that exposure's counter guarantee is in turn directly guaranteed by one of the listed entities and the conditions listed in that point are satisfied."

[28] Annex VIII, Part 3, 2.2, 19 CRD, Directive 2006/48/EC: "19. In the case of guarantees provided in the context of mutual guarantee schemes recognised for these purposes by the competent authorities or provided by or counter guaranteed by entities referred to in point 16, the requirements in point 18(a) shall be considered to be satisfied where either of the following conditions are met: (a) the lending credit institution has the right to obtain in a timely manner a provisional payment by the guarantor calculated to represent a robust estimate of the amount of the economic loss, including losses resulting from the non payment of interest and other types of payment which the borrower is obliged to make, likely to be incurred by the lending credit institution proportional to the coverage of the guarantee; or (b) the lending credit institution can demonstrate that the loss-protecting effects of the guarantee, including losses resulting from the non-payment of interest and other types of payments which the borrower is obliged to make, justify such treatment."

[29] Annex VIII, Part 3, 2.3, 18 a) in fine CRD, Directive 2006/48/EC under "Additional requirements for guarantees": (…) In the case of unfunded credit protection covering residential mortgage loans, the requirements in point 14(c)(iii) and in the first subparagraph of this point have only to be satisfied within 24 months (…)".

In any case, regarding the current text of the minimum requirements for a guarantee to be eligible, there is a great need for clarification still. National regulators and supervisors should, hence, focus on the final intention of the regulation, diluting any major perceived ambiguity before releasing any capital in the system. Regulators and supervisors need to check every particular CRM and test its ability to provide effective risk mitigation.

4. Possibilities to develop new CRMs under Basel II: scope for innovation?

The new international capital standard – Basel II – needs to remain flexible and able to adapt to emerging practices and risks. Basel II has been conceived as a new framework, which should contribute to a prudent capital requirements regulation but leaving scope to market evolution and innovation. It intends to enhance the development of new instruments and methodologies of risk measurement and management or at least to be able to recognise them when they are effectively used in the practice provided they meet the criteria set from a regulatory perspective for a stable financial system.

In words of Jaime Caruana, former Governor of Bank of Spain and Chairman of the Basel Committee on Banking Supervision, "Basel II is just as much about aligning supervisory practices more closely with the industry's latest advances as it is about promoting improvements in the management of risk within the industry itself. Standard needs to evolve and keep pace with the times, whilst ensuring that new standards are not unduly burdensome and do not hinder firms' abilities to innovate"[30].

At the same time, recent events in the financial markets[31] have proved that an excessive hunger for innovation and the development of new, sophisticated products, of which the real systemic risks are not sufficiently under control, calls for a turn back to supervisory prudence based, among others, on the deep understanding of the instruments used. This is of course the case for those types of financial instruments which aim at managing risk and as a consequence are used to reduce the levels of capital

---

[30] Caruana, Keynote address, 20th Annual General Meeting. ISDA (International Swaps and Derivatives Association), Barcelona, 16 March 2005.

[31] The 2008 financial crisis which has followed to the bankruptcy of important investment Banks such as Lehman Brothers or the State intervention of financial and insurance institutions such as Fortis Bank, has changed the paradigmas of the banking business as well as that of the banking supervision. A worldwide important set of governmental measures had to be adopted to ensure the stability of the financial system. For an overview of the State measures taken to deal with the financial crisis see: Economic Stabilization Advisory Group, Governmental Assistance to the Financial Sector: an Overview of the Global Responses (v2), November 26, 2008.

requirements, such as CRMs. The implementation of Basel II rules is hence a challenge for legislators and supervisors. Financial services providers often compete on their ability to create value by offering new products and services to customers. These instruments are initially tailored to unique sets of circumstances and may involve novel features of risk-taking or risk mitigation. According to the Basel II regulator, "the challenge therefore is to ensure that the rules support and encourage firms in their efforts to improve their ability to manage their businesses while pursuing new opportunities. It is the constant responsibility for legislators, for standards-setters, and for supervisors, to follow the market evolution and adapt the spirit of the regulation to those innovative products and practices offered and used by the industry" [32].

Following this line of thoughts, the New Capital Accord should, in principle, not prevent other risk mitigation techniques to be applicable and reduce the capital requirements for banks. In this case, the current regulation should be interpreted as to be applicable and adapted to other existing and to the new risk mitigation techniques that might be used in the future. This viewpoint was probably the reasoning behind the Annex VIII, Part 1, paragraph 29 CRD, according to which transactions that are "economically effectively similar" to credit derivatives transactions can be recognised as CRMs. Although, there is no corresponding language for products which have a similar economic effect to a guarantee, the same principle could be considered to apply. While this remains true, the 2008 financial crisis has made it clear that the market innovation, when not sufficiently controlled and managed, may also bring a number of unknown or unpredicted risks with potential major impacts in the economy and the financial stability. The importance of ensuring high standards of solvency will likely imply a justified more cautious approach by legislators and supervisors worldwide.

---

[32] Caruana, Keynote address, 20th Annual General Meeting. ISDA (International Swaps and Derivatives Association), Barcelona, 16 March 2005.

Chapter 6

Security rights in the EU context: market implication and harmonisation of EU Private Law

Introduction

In terms of economic impact, the EU market integration is a growing reality, which also reflects on the needs and use of security rights within Europe. *Vice versa*, availability of well functioning security rights also contributes to the economic development of the EU[1]. Policy measures aiming at achieving an integrated financial market do, hence, have an impact on the use of security in this marketplace. Particularly in a context of economic and financial crisis, action envisaged in order to promote the use of credit will also likely reflect on security.

In legal terms, EU legislation complements the national legal regimes applicable to security rights within the EU. Along the pages of this study, the core of EU legislation applicable to personal security[2] has been referred to where and as appropriate in an integrated manner. Now, in view of the current trend towards harmonisation of European Private Law, a final reflection needs to be made on the impact that efforts made in this direction will have on the law and practice of security rights.

Finally, a critical reference is made to the specific work performed in view of harmonising the law applicable to personal security rights.

A. Security rights in the current EU context. Law and Economics

I. EU policy action in view of enhancing credit and its impact on security rights

The positive impact of credit in terms of economic development has also been recognised in the European context by the EU institutions[3]. It has

[1] See under: Chapter 1, C., IV. Security contributes to economic development, 22.

[2] Mainly, EU consumer law as implemented in Italy and Spain.

[3] See among many other documents: Communication for the spring European Council – Driving European recovery, 4.3.2009, COM (2009) 114 final, 2.

been the view of the EU Commission that improving access to credit could generate significant growth in the EU. According to the logic of market integration, and given the transformation of Europe from a cash to a more diversified credit society, a single market in financial services should lead to economies of scale and enhanced conditions for economic growth.

An extensive agenda[4] has been developed in view of achieving the integration of the EU retail financial markets. Within this agenda, specific action attempts to enhance the use of credit, specifically by consumers and Small and Medium Enterprises, across the EU. The action taken or foreseen for the credit market is mainly based on four areas, these being: credit histories, consumer credit, mortgage credit and credit intermediaries[5].

Given the role of security rights in the framework of lending activities[6], the further development of the EU credit market can only be conceived upon a parallel increased use of security rights. Ensuring a strong legal system seems, hence, crucial in this context.

II. The impact of the financial crisis on EU law, credit and security rights

The global financial and economic crisis starting 2008 has made clear the importance that credit markets have for the economy in the EU. Such assessment has been reflected in the policy action taken by the EU institutions these days. As has been recognised by the European Commission[7], action taken in the course of 2008 and 2009 for the stabilisation of the financial markets has not yet fed through to loosen the credit crunch and get lending flowing again to companies and households. It is considered to be time for action to break the cycle of declining confidence and unwillingness to lend. This is also why the EU must keep up the pace of financial sector reform, implementing reforms to regulation, and looking ahead to a supervisory regime more in tune with today's cross-border realities. As long as lending remains scarce, efforts to boost demand and consumer confidence will be held back[8]. Restoring the flow of credit to the real economy is therefore a key priority in order to prevent a further reduction in eco-

---

[4] See: (http://ec.europa.eu/internal_market/finservices-retail/index_en.htm).

[5] See the European Commission's agenda on integration of retail financial markets and specifically the aims regarding credit: (http://ec.europa.eu/internal_market/finser vices-retail/credit/index_en.htm).

[6] See Chapter 1, C. The practiacal functions of security rights: Law, economics and social implications, 14.

[7] Communication for the spring European Council – Driving European recovery, 4.3.2009, COM (2009) 114 final, 2.

[8] Communication for the spring European Council – Driving European recovery, 4.3.2009, COM (2009) 114 final, 2.

nomic growth[9]. This is why the Commission has proposed the ambitious reform of the European financial system[10]. Part of this reform will consist on a number of "measures on responsible lending and borrowing" which will likely be published in Autumn 2009[11].

The reason for these measures is explained by the Commission as part of the need to reinforce the protection of investors, consumers and small companies. As it is explained in the Annex I to the Communication on Driving Europe's recover[12], the interests of European investors, consumers and SMEs, must be at the centre of the reform. Additional measures are needed to reinforce depositor, investor and policy holder protection, covering the overall adequacy and scope of a broad range of existing financial market directives. An effective and comprehensive legal framework[13] for retail financial services needs to be put into place. Among a large number of other measures, the Commission sees the need to act in view of ensuring responsible lending and borrowing, including a reliable framework on credit intermediation[14/15].

Explicit mention is made to the need to examine ways of ensuring that foreclosure procedures are avoided wherever possible, to prevent citizens from losing their homes. A report setting out best practices in this area will be published by the end of 2009[16].

As explained below, many of these policy and legislative actions will likely impact the use and value of security within the EU.

---

[9] Credit flows should therefore be monitored very closely in the coming months to ensure that extensive public intervention in the financial sector really does result in relief for European households and businesses. See: Communication for the spring European Council – Driving European recovery, 4.3.2009, COM (2009) 114 final, 4.

[10] The principles of the reform is partly based on the report commissioned by the EU Commission to the High level group of experts led by Jacques de Larosière (so called, "de Larosière´s report") and furthered developed by the European Commission itself. It is sketched in the Communication of the 4th of March 2009 and particularly in its Annex I.

[11] Communication for the spring European Council – Driving European recovery, 4.3.2009, COM(2009) 114 final, 7.

[12] Communication for the spring European Council – Driving European recovery, 4.3.2009, COM(2009) 114 final.

[13] Besides legislative action, the Commission also sees the need to promote the strengthening of financial education throughout Europe, by continuing to help teachers to incorporate financial matters into the school curriculum, while respecting the competence of Member States in the field of education. See: Communication for the spring European Council – Driving European recovery, 4.3.2009, COM(2009) 114 final, Annex I.

[14] Communication for the spring European Council – Driving European recovery, 4.3.2009, COM(2009) 114 final, Annex I.

[15] A public hearing on responsible lending and borrowing will be organised in July 2009. Follow-up measures will be presented by autumn 2009.

[16] Communication for the spring European Council – Driving European recovery, 4.3.2009, COM(2009) 114 final, Annex I.

B. EU private law and its impact on security rights

I. How are security rights affected by EU private law

Security rights, in particular the guarantee agreement, involves a plurality of parties and competing interests (this reality has been referred to as poli-contextual function[17] of security rights). The balancing of the interests involved can take place at a number of levels and fields of law. Besides the specific regulation, security contracts are affected, for instance by: a) contract law: fraud, duress, mistake, misrepresentation; b) insolvency law: regulation of right of recourse; c) constitutional law: proportionality considerations; d) property law: requiring secured lending or e) family law: protection of family interest, presumption of undue influence[18]. Consequently, security contracts are affected by a plurality of rules. Changes in this legislation will naturally affect the use of security rights. Accordingly, all attempts to modify, complement or harmonise these fields of law need to be assessed from the perspective of their impact on the use of security rights. In the current EU context, such attempts to adapt legislation on the basis of functional needs have been made through a threefold approach: a) through EU legislation, b) through harmonisation of EU law and c) by referring to fundamental rights in view of harmonising private law.

One should also not forget the legal action taken in view of facilitating cross-border lending and in particular the efforts to harmonise international private law provisions.

1. EU Law: The role of Directives and the need to harmonise the acquis communautaire

a) The EU acqui and the particular relevance of consumer protection for sureties

Security rights, as any other type of contract is impacted by changes in general contract law. With the aim of achieving an EU single market, the legislative competences of the EU have been largely used to draft legislation in the field of contract law; giving origin to an extensive *acquis*[19], which partly also applies to security rights[20]. Indeed, most recent changes in this field of law at national level have had their origin in EU legislation.

---

[17] *Kenny*, 183.

[18] *Kenny*, 183.

[19] Over the last two decades, at least nineteen directives on the core of private law have been issued. All of them are based on art. 94 or 95 EC Treaty, hence on the general purpose of establishing the common and internal market, as envisaged in art. 3 EC Treaty. For an economic analysis see: *Smits*, 2006, 7.

[20] *Kennny*, 179, 180.

EU consumer protection legislation appears to be particularly significant in this context.

So far, the specific role of security rights as credit enhancers has been tangentially considered by EU policy makers. Whereas consumer guarantors were included in the Proposal for a Consumer Credit Directive[21], the respective provision was finally removed from the approved text[22]. Security rights as such are not specifically addressed by EU legislation. However, action taken so far by policy-makers in view of promoting the use of credit will certainly affect the application of national legislation on security rights. This action has mainly been oriented towards increasing consumer's trust by enhancing consumer protection. In this regard, it needs to be reminded that as stated by the ECJ, consumer protection legislation only applies to consumer sureties in restricted cases. For instance, in the *Dietzinger* case, the ECJ took the view that guarantee contracts could only be understood to be subject to the Doorstep Selling Directive[23] where the principal contract concerned the supply of goods or services to a consumer[24]. In *Berliner Kindl* ECJ decision, it was held that the 1987 Consumer

[21] The consumer surety was originally included in the Draft Directive, art. 23. This proposal was launched by the European Commission´s Directorate General on Consumer Protection and had a stressed focus on consumer protection. The lobby done by financial institutions all along the legislative procedure changed the final taste of the Directive. One of the key changes in this regard was the deletion of consumer sureties from the scope of the Directive. For an overview on the evolution of the Proposal see: de la Mata, The EU Commission publishes on 28 October the amended version of the Consumer Credit Directive, CEPS/ECRI, January 2005; The EU Commission amends its Proposed Consumer Credit Directive, CEPS/ECRI, European Voice, December 2004/January 2005; Developments in the Consumer Credit Directive, CEPS/ECRI Research Fellow, December 2004.; Waiting for the EU Commission's amended proposal, CEPS/ECRI, October 2004; Two steps further in the Consumer Credit Directive procedure-The European Parliament votes in its first reading on the Consumer Credit Directive and the European Council launches a questionnaire-, CEPS/ECRI, July 2004; The European Parliament to vote at a plenary session on the amendments to the draft Consumer Credit Directive, CEPS/ECRI, April 2004; European Parliament Committees to present an alternative Consumer Credit Directive proposal, CEPS/ECRI, January 2004; The EU Parliament rejects the EU Commission's proposal for the Consumer Credit Directive and requires withdrawal, CEPS/ECRI, September 2003.

[22] Directive 2008/48/EC of the European Parliament and of the Council of 23 April 2008, on credit agreements for consumers and repealing Council Directive 87/102/EEC, OJ 25. 5. 2008.

[23] Directive 85/577/ECC on contracts negotiated away from business premises, OJ 1985 L 372/31.

[24] See Case C–45/96, Bayerische Hypothekenbank v Edgar Dietzinger [1998] ECR 1–1199: "In view of the close link between a credit agreeement and a guarantee securing its perfomrance and the fact that the person guaranteeing repayment of a debt may either asume joint and several liability for payment of the debt or be the guarator of its repay-

Credit Directive did not cover "suretyship" for repayment of credit where neither surety nor principal debtor was acting in the course of his/her trade or profession[25].

As a consequence, the need for broader coherence in the treatment of consumer sureties is evident and has been identified by both the Court of Justice and the Commission[26]. This lack of coherence has not contributed to a more harmonised approach on the protection of consumer sureties within the EU. Currently, very different protection standards can be found for sureties in the EU[27]. From the perspective of the single market, this lack of harmonious approach does not seem to be the only barrier for market integration. Although there is no aggregated data on the cross-border use of security rights, consumer sureties are not likely to be very active across the borders[28] (at least at present times). Even if current increased movement of persons, capital and businesses make it more likely that guarantee agreements 33are taken cross-border, the lack of harmony in legislation is considered to be a barrier together with other rather technical issues (referred to as natural barriers) such as the creditor's ability to assess the guarantor's risk. Hence the reasons to advocate for a common consumer approach in this field may be based on market integration needs on the basis of art. 95 EC Treaty[29/30]

The vast legislative production as well a policy action regarding consumers' rights has already created a shared value around the protection of consumers, as the weaker parties of a contract. In line with this approach

---

ment, it cannot be excluded that the furnishing of a guarantee falls within the scope of the directive".

[25] Case C–208/98, Berliner Kindl Brauerei AG v Andreas Siepert [2000] ECR 1–1741.

[26] *Kenny* 179.

[27] Colombi Ciacchi, 2007.

[28] See under Chapter 1, C. The practical functions of security rights: Law, economics and social implications, 14.

[29] The objective to promote high standards of consumer protection is also explicitly mentioned in this context.

[30] An alternative legal basis would be art. 153. 1 EC Treaty, which foresees that "in order to promote the interests of consumers and to ensure a high level of consumer protection, the Community shall contribute to protecting the health, safety and economic interests of consumers, as well as to promoting their right to information (…)". While this is a valid basis for EU legislation in the referred field, it forces the use of minimum harmonisation in the Directives (as per art. 153. 4 EC Treaty). Current trend for consumer protection Directives is increasingly moving towards either total harmonization or targeted maximum harmonisation (an example being the Consumer Credit Directive). Whereas it remains a controversial matter, the objective of market integration often justifies maximum harmonisation for Directives which deal with consumer protection. See de la Mata/Lannoo. See Chapter 6, C. Should wie attempt to harmonise EU Personal Security Rights?, 279.

and considering the level of risks assumed by consumer sureties as well as the implications that such risk may have for individuals and families, it would be more than advisable to provide an appropriate level of protection to these parties within a coherent framework as it has been done in the Dutch Civil Code (Book VII).

The academic interest on this subject has increased in recent times and specific research projects have been launched[31]. The PECL[32] and the DCFR[33] have developed a set of harmonised rules on personal security rights which include a chapter aiming at protecting consumer guarantors. All this activity around the subject may set the basis for a more harmonised, coherent and also a stronger protection of consumer sureties within the EU.

In general terms, it is to be expected that specific rules of consumer protection nature which apply in the context of credit but not to sureties, will set a protection standard which will serve to bare the protection needs of consumer sureties in the application of national laws by national courts.

b) The need for a more coherent acquis communautaire

The large number of Directives produced in the last years on a sectorial basis, has given origin to a patchwork of fragmented legislation, often lacking coherence. In the context of the "better regulation approach" and in view of improving the *acquis communautaire*, the EU Commission has taken twofold action: on the one hand, a Common Frame of Reference (CRF)[34] is being developed on the basis of the academic work performed by a team of scholars commissioned by the EU institutions. This team has developed the Draft Common Frame of Reference, which should serve the aim of providing EU law with a coherent set of concepts and terminology. On the other hand, specific action has taken place in view of improving the current *acquis* on consumer law[35].

---

[31] Oxford Unversity has launched a special research project on the subject.

[32] As referred, academic work performed in the context of harmonisation of European contract law has taken this need into account. The Study Group on a European Civil Code developed a set of harmonised rules for personal security rights (PECL Personal Security), including a whole chapter on consumer sureties (Chapter IV). See below.

[33] See below: Chapter 6, B., II., 2., b), bb) The Draft Common Frame of Reference (DCFR) and ists predecessors, 277.

[34] See below: Chapter 6, B., II., 2., b), bb) The Draft Common Frame of Reference (DCFR) and ists predecessors, 277.

[35] See below: Chapter 6, B., II., 2., a), aa), (ii) Revising the consumer acquis: Green Paper on the Review of the Consumer Acquis and the Commission's Proposal for a Directive on consumer rights, 273.

II. Further harmonisation of EU private law

Besides existing EU law, specific work on harmonising private law[36] has also taken place within the EU. The idea of creating a unified set of rules which could be applicable within the EU has gained interest in the last years. Several academic projects have pursued this aim. The underlying thought is not always necessarily to substitute national legislation by a uniform private law code but rather offering a coherent, systematic and complete harmonised set of rules (a kind of EU Civil Code for Patrimonial Rights) to which the parties may adhere if they so wish. The EU institutions have conceived this option as a possible 28th regime, to which the parties may opt in.

On a different level, the idea of referring to fundamental rights as a way to find a common basis to unify certain elements of private law, has also been pursuit in academic literature.

The fact that harmonisation of EU law would have an impact on the law of security rights, justifies giving some attention to the recent political and academic initiatives pursuit in this direction.

1. Non-legislative harmonisation of European contract law. Harmonised protection for sureties through the horizontal effect of fundamental rights

Specifically in the context of guarantees, scholars have recently considered the possibility to achieve harmonisation of contract law by striking the effects of fundamental rights, instead as by legislative means[37]. The idea behind such harmonisation is that the European Court of Justice (ECJ) and the European Court of Human Rights need to drive the balance between competing fundamental rights in order to assess the appropriate level of protection for the weaker party[38]. This line of thoughts can be applied in view of achieving harmonisation in the protection of sureties within the EU[39]. German constitutional law has partly served as basis for this attempt[40].

A preliminary consideration of this option, gives raise to two basic concerns. First, the obvious lack of democratic legitimacy of the ECJ to act as community legislator. Besides, constitutional principles appear to be a not

---

[36] The scope is limited to patrimonial law.

[37] On the impact of Human Rights in Private Law in Germany see: *Starck/Friedmann* and *Barack-Erez*, 97.

[38] *Cherednychenko*, 38.

[39] The rights of sureties differ significantly within the EU. For a thorough study on the issue, see: Colombi Ciacchi, 2005.

[40] See Colombi Ciacchi, 2006.

sufficient basis to define a way to protect the weaker party of a contract (in particular the surety)[41].

2. Legislative harmonisation of EU private law

The idea of harmonising EU law by means of unified rules has gained importance in the last years, thanks to specific political action as well as enormous and high quality academic work.

a) Political action

The debate on harmonization of EU private law has been lively followed since the EU Parliament first launched the idea of a European Civil Code in 1989[42]. The vision and approach has changed ever since, in a quite significant manner. The EU Commission issued the first of its three Communications on the subject in 2001[43]. In 2002 the European Parliament proposed an extremely ambitious timescale for the enactment of a European Civil Code by the year 2010[44]. The idea of a Code was though left aside in the Commission's Communication issued in 2003,[45] and then explicitly rejected in 2004[46]. The Council has "welcomed" "the Commission's repeated reassurance that it does not intend to propose a 'European Civil Code' which would harmonise contract laws of Member States and that Member States' differing legal traditions will be fully taken into account"[47].

Obviously, EU institutions are working around the matter of EU private law in the context of the aims and competences given to the EU in the EC Treaty. As things have developed, one could distinguish two main lines of action attempted by the EU Commission today: a) pursuing the improvement of the present and future EU law (the *acquis*) through the creation of the Common Frame of Reference (CFR) and the revision of the *acquis*; and

[41] For a deep analysis on the subject, see: *Cherednychenko*, 38–58.

[42] Resolution A2–157/89, OJ EC 1989, C 158/400.

[43] Communication from the Commission to the European Parliament and the Council, European Contract Law, COM (2001) 398 final, OJ EC 2001, C 255/1.

[44] Resolution of the European Parliament on the approximation of the civil and commercial law of the Member States, OJ C140E/538.

[45] Communication from the Commission to the European Parliament and the Council, 'A More Coherent European Contract Law: An Action Plan', COM (2003) 68 final, OJ EC 2003, C 63/01.

[46] Communication from the Commission to the European Parliament and the Council, 'European Contract Law and the revision of the acquis: the way forward', COM (2004) 651 final, OJ EC 2005, C 14/6 (Communication 2004).

[47] Press release of 28/29 November 2005 – 14155/05 (press 287), 28.

b) working on the idea of an 'optional instrument' which can be referred to as a European Civil Code for the purpose of this study [48].

This line is supported by the European Parliament, which has recently underlined the need for harmonisation of European private law[49] and endorsed the Commission's initiative to prepare a Common Frame of Reference. Member States' views on the further process differ[50].

aa) Improving the acquis communautaire: The Common Frame of Reference and the Green paper on the Review of the Consumer Acquis

As clear as the EU institutions are about the need to improve the *acquis communautaire*, they do not seem to find a definite way of achieving such objective. The first project launched by the Commission in order to achieve a greater level of coherence in the EU acquis was the Common Frame of Reference. As it is explained below, this project is still surrounded by a great political uncertaintly, especially after the European Commission itself published its Proposal for an EU Directive on Consumer Rights. Both projects seem to pursue a common objective while following different paths, scopes and methodologies. Overlap and lack of coherence is the result sofar, while the Draft Consumer Rights Directive will likely catch up in terms of timing.

(i) The Common Frame of Reference (CFR)

The European Commission's initial proposal in the context of harmonising EU private law was to develop a Common Frame of Reference (CFR). This, for lawyers and law practitioners, peculiar concept refers to a legal instrument[51] which should serve a plurality of objectives[52]. Mainly con-

---

[48] In its 'Action Plan on A More Coherent European Contract Law' of January 2003 (Action plan), the European Commission called for comments on three proposed measures: a) increasing the coherence of the acquis communautaire, b) the promotion of the elaboration of EU-wide standard contract terms, and c) further examination of whether there is a need for a measure that is not limited to particular sectors, such as an 'optional instrument.' The elaboration of EU-wide standards is not being taken forward. See Commission of the European Communities. First Progress Report on The Common Frame of Reference, COM (2005), 456 final, 10.

[49] See for a recent statement, resolution 3. September 2008, (www.europarl.europa.eu/sides/getDoc.do?type=TA&reference=P6-TA-2008-0397&language=EN&ring=B6-2008-0374).

[50] See an overview of the Council´s discussions: (http://www.copecl.org/).

[51] The form of adoption is still unclear whereas it will have to be endorsed by the European legislator.

[52] In the 2004 Communication, the Commission proposed that the CFR should provide 'fundamental principles, definitions and model rules' which could assist in the improvement of the existing acquis communautaire, the drafting of new legislation and which

ceived as a tool to develop and interpret the law, it is not supposed to be a unified code for the EU but should rather be used to improve the existing *acquis* and help regulators in their future legislative task (better regulation approach)[53]. As it is supposed to deal with the core of contract law, implications for security rights would be direct.

The political stand of the CFR remains open. Political actors, especially in the European Commission, have been reluctant to formulate clear aims or visions with regard to the nature or the date for its coming into force[54].

(ii) Revising the consumer acquis: Green Paper on the Review of the Consumer Acquis[55] and the Commission's Proposal for a Directive on consumer rights[56]

In the Green Paper on the Review of the Consumer Acquis of February 2007, a second project was announced by the European Commission, besides the CFR-process, to review eight directives in the field of consumer contract law[57].

The Green paper posed other essential questions for the future of one critical part of EU private law, this being consumer legislation. This questions mark the path for future EU legislation which will be of essence for the development of EU credit markets[58] and security rights. One of these questions regards the idea of whether full harmonisation is desirable for

might form the basis of an optional instrument if it were decided to create one. See: Communication 2004, para. 72.

[53] Model rules would form the bulk of the CFR, its main purpose being to serve as a kind of a legislators' guide or 'tool box'. Also the ECJ is supposed to apply it in interpreting the law. See: Communication 2004, para. 3.1.3, p. 11.

[54] Some indication may be obtained from the structure and contents of the text as well as from the Commission's documents on the subject. The CFR should provide three types of provisions. First, it will consist of definitions of legal terms (such as "contract"). It will also include fundamental principles (like "freedom of contract", "binding force" or "good faith"). Finally, it should contain coherent model rules of contract law, drawing on the EC *acquis* and on best solutions found in Member states legal orders' (See: Communication 2004, 12, 16). The structure foreseen, resembles to a large extent what it is known in member states as Civil Codes, which should facilitate its use by legislators, practitioners and law interpreters.

[55] Green Paper on the Review of the Consumer Acquis, COM(2006) 744 final of 8 February 2007 (http://ec.europa.eu/consumers/cons_int/safe_shop/acquis/green-paper_cons_acquis_en.pdf).

[56] Proposal for Directive on consumer rights, Brussels, 8.10.2008, COM(2008) 614 final, 2008/0196 (COD). (http://ec.europa.eu/consumers/rights/docs/COMM_PDF_COM_2008_0614_F_EN_PROPOSITION_DE_DIRECTIVE.pdf).

[57] Directives 85/577, 90/314, 93/13, 94/47, 97/7, 98/6; 98/27, 99/44.

[58] In the field of consumer credit, see: *Lannoo/de la Mata*, 7 ff.

consumer law[59]. Besides, it is also questioned whether there should be a horizontal instrument regulating consumer rights instead of a sectorial fragmented approach. This line has been followed and the Proposal for a Directive on Consumer Rights was published in October 2008.

(iii) Prospects on coming EU law: protecting sureties and consumers of financial products and its impact on market integration

In view of the current activity of the European Commission, probably other Directives will also be revised, for instance those relating to the provision of information to buyers of financial services. In the longer term, there may be proposals for further harmonisation measures in sectors where there still appears to be a need for consumer protection (such as contracts for services or personal security) or where the differences between the laws of the Member States appear to cause difficulties for the internal market (e. g. insurance or security over movable property)[60].

bb) Optional instrument: Opting-in a unified code?

The EU Commission considers the possibility to use the CFR as the basis for an optional instrument to which the parties could adhere. Although it has made it clear that the CFR is not intended to propose a 'European Civil Code' which would harmonise contract laws of Member States'[61], it may be used as a set of rules to which the parties (including consumers) may opt-in. The structure and methodology used in the development of the CFR will favour the different use of this work for the purpose of alternative regulatory body. The European Parliament has recently welcomed this idea[62].

One issue arises with regard to the application of an opt-in instrument. If the instrument contains rules of a mandatory nature[63], such nature is dormant as long as the CFR has no formal legal status. If the CFR may be adopted by a choice of law, the parties may chose partial application of the rules ("dépeçage"). Consequently, even those rules conceived as mandatory (for instance those consumer protective rules) may be left out by choice

---

[59] *Lannoo/de la Mata*, 7 ff. The authors study the use of the total harmonisation approach in EU directives as the method to achieve legal harmonisation.

[60] See Draft Common Frame of Reference, Interim outlined edition (www.law.net.eu). See also critical assessment below.

[61] Communication 2004, 8. See also the Green Paper on the Conversion of the Rome Convention of 1980, 2002, 654 final, 14.

[62] See: Resolution 3. September 2008, (www.europarl.europa.eu/sides/getDoc.do?type=TA&reference=P6-TA-2008-0397&language=EN&ring=B6-2008-0374).

[63] For instance the rules on personal security in the DCFR do contain mandatory provisions. See below.

of the parties[64]. This effect could be avoided by the issuance of an EU regulation in which it is laid down that dépeçage is not allowed, i.e. when the CFR is opted in, it will be entirely applicable, the option being either submitting the relationship to the CFR (including mandatory rules) or not. The new regulations in the area of private international law (Rome I and Rome II) should in the light of these remarks be looked at carefully, as provisions in these regulations might be overridden by the choice of law provision in a future "CFR regulation"[65].

b) *The academic action*

aa) *An overview*

The European Commission's initiative of creating a CFR, actually builds on decades of academic work performed in the field of European private law. In the course of the last 25 years a strong and solid network of highly reputed academics devoted its efforts to the study and development of European private law. Its contribution to the harmonisation of private laws in Europe is uncontested.

Besides the uncountable number of scientific articles and academic discussions on the subject, some specific academic projects have had a significant impact on the evolution of EU private law and are worth being mentioned here.

The *Principles of European Contract Law* were prepared by the *Commission on European Contract Law* ("the Lando Commission")[66]. The work performed by this Lando Commission was continued by the *Study Group on a European Civil Code*. This Group has prepared several volumes of *Principles of European Law* and more volumes are forthcoming[67].

Taking a different approach, the *Acquis Group* "targets a systematic arrangement of existing Community law which will help clarifying the common structures of the emerging Community private law"[68]. Out of this work, a volume on pre-contractual obligations, conclusion of contract and

---

[64] See *van Erp*, 1.

[65] *Van Erp*, 1.

[66] See *Lando/Beale*, Black letter rules in several language versions are available at (http://frontpage.cbs.dk/law/commission_on_european_contract_law/index.html).

[67] Von Bar, Benevolent intervention in another's affairs (PEL Ben. Int.), Munich 2006; Hesselink et al., Commercial agency, franchise and distribution contracts (PEL CAFDC), Munich 2006; Barendrecht et al., Service contracts (PEL SC), Munich 2007; Dobnig, Personal security (PEL Pers. Sec.), Munich 2007; Hondiius, Sales (PEL S), Munich 2008; Lilleholt et al., Lease of goods (PEL LG), Munich 2008. More information at (www.sgecc.net).

[68] See: (www.acquis-group.org).

unfair terms has been published[69]. Also the *Common Core of European Private Law Project* (the so called, Trento Common Core Project) has completed several comparative studies on European private law[70].

Other academic groups have focused on specific fields of private law. Based in Pavia, the *Academy of European Private Lawyers*, ("Gandolfi Project") has published a draft "European Contract Code", inspired by the Italian Civil Code and a draft Contract Code prepared for the Law Commissions of England and Scotland by Harvey McGregor[71]. Besides, while the *European Group on Tort Law* ("Tilburg Group") has drafted *Principles of European Tort Law*[72]*, the Commission on European Family Law* conducts research concerning the harmonisation of family law in Europe[73]. At a different level, the *Unidroit Principles of International Commercial Contracts* are geographically not limited to Europe but its scope is restricted to commercial contracts exclusively[74].

Finally, since the European Institutions started the debate on harmonisation of European Private Law, academic work on the subject has been frenetic. Particularly worth being mentioned in this chapter is the work of the Draft Common Frame of Reference as it is inspiring the political attempt to develop a CFR and has devoted specific attention to security rights.

In the same frame of the EU Commissions efforts on European private law, two French organisations, *Association Henri Capitant des Amis de la Culture Juridique Française* and *Société de Législation Comparée*, also performed scientific research in this context. The result of this contribution was the publication of two books in 2008 one on common contractual principles and the other on common contractual terminology[75].

---

[69] Contract I: pre-contractual obligations, conclusion of contract, unfair terms. Prepared by Research Group on the Existing EC Private Law (Acquis Group), München 2007. Chapter 8 on "remedies" is published in Schulze, Common frame of reference and existing EC contract law, Munich 2008.

[70] This group has been lead by Ugo Mattei and Mauro Bussani. See: (www.jus.unitn.it/dsg/common-core).

[71] Gandolfi/Gatt, Code européen des contrats: avant-projet, Milano 2004. See: (http://www.accademiagiusprivatistieuropei.it).

[72] Principles of European Tort Law: text and commentary, Wien 2005 (www.egtl.org).

[73] See: (www2.law.uu.nl/priv/cefl).

[74] Unidroit principles of international commercial contracts 2004, Rome 2004. See: www.unidroit.org. See also Bonell, An international restatement of contract law: the UNIDROIT Principles of International Commercial Contracts, N.Y., 2005; Bonell, The Unidroit Principles in Practice: Caselaw and Bibliography on the Unidroit Principles of International Commercial Contracts, N.Y., 2006.

[75] *Fauvarque Cosson/Mazeuad*, Projet de cadre commune de référence. Principes contractuels communs, Paris 2008.

bb) The Draft Common Frame of Reference (DCFR) [76] *and its predecessors*

The latest result of this fabulous scientific team work is the recently published Draft Common Frame of Reference (DCFR), as the main academic contribution to the CFR-process.

The DCFR was delivered to the European Commission in December 2008, while a full version with comments and comparative notes has been published in 2009. This is the delivery from the Study Group on a European Civil Code (Study Group) and the Research Group on EC Private Law (Acquis Group) under a frame research contract launched by the European Commission[77].

As it is explained in the introduction to the DCFR, this text is the result of more than 25 years' collaboration of jurists from all jurisdictions of the present Member States within the European Union. It began in 1982 with the constitution of the Commission on European Contract Law (CECL) and was furthered by the establishment of the Study Group in 1998 and the Acquis Group in 2002. From 2005 the Study Group, Acquis Group and Insurance Contract Group formed the so-called "drafting teams" of the CoPECL[78] network.

The DCFR consists of more than 6000 pages, including principles, definitions, rules, comments and comparative notes[79]. The coverage is very broad[80]. Building on the well known Principles on European Contract Law, the result of this joint effort will certainly serve as the key basis for an eventual CFR. Its content, scope and structure would allow its use as an optional instrument[81] to which parties may opt-in. Beyond this possible use, the DCFR do have a much broader meaning as they have built on common principles of EU private law, being possibly used by the EU institutions as a guiding tool for their law-making activities as well as by law practitioners and academics in their work on EU private law.

---

[76] *von Bar*, Principles, Definitions and Model Rules of European Private Law. Draft Common Frame of Reference (DCFR). Outline Edition, Munich, 2009. Find the first (interim) edition of the DCFR under: (http://webh01.ua.ac.be/storme/DCFRInterim.pdf).

[77] More on the contract and the network, http://www.copecl.org/.

[78] See: www.copecl.org.

[79] See: http://www.sellier.de/pages/en/buecher_s_elp/europarecht/643.principles_defi nitions_and_model_rules_of_european_private_law.htm (accessed 21 April 2009).

[80] It includes rules on the formation, validity, interpretation and contents of contracts and, by analogy, other juridical acts, the performance of obligations resulting from them and on the remedies for non-performance of such obligations, but also a series of model rules on so-called "specific contracts" and theights and obligations arising from them.

[81] So was it recently considered by the European Parliament. See for a recent statement, resolution 3. September 2008, (www.europarl.europa.eu/sides/getDoc.do?type= TA&reference=P6-TA-2008-0397&language=EN&ring=B6-2008-0374).

In terms of its impact on security rights, besides general contract law aspects, the DCFR contain a specific part on personal security which is dealt below.

cc) Academic attempt to harmonise the law of security rights: Study Group on a European Contract Law and its integration in the DCFR

The law on security rights has been included in the academic studies attempting to harmonise EU contract law.

It was first included in the Principles of European Contract Law developed by the Study Group. As a result of four years work by a network of EU researchers, an EU-wide harmonised set of rules on personal security rights was published in 2007[82]. This work has been pursuit in the framework of the Draft Common Frame of Reference. On this basis, Book IV of the DCFR (regulating "Specific contracts and the rights and obligations arising from them") included a Part G on "Personal Security"[83]. Coherence between these rules and general contract law as developed within the other Books of the DCFR (in particular Book I to III) has been achieved[84].

The rules make a basic distinction between dependent and independent personal security contracts. Building on the heritage of national law traditions, they attempt to provide a set of useful provisions in view of the needs and uses of modern times. An example of this approach can be found in Chapter 4 of this Part G (Book IV), entitled "special rules for personal security of consumers[85]". Under the frame of an extreme diversity of national regulation of the subject within the EU, this Chapter takes consideration of the special needs of consumer sureties today as well as of the EU law on consumers, providing practical solutions. Given demand for consumer protection in current practice in this field, this Chapter appears to be of particular interest. On one side, it may serve as a point of reference in those jurisdictions with lower protection standards for consumers-sureties. Second, the possible use of the DFCR as an opt-in text may contribute to achieving a greater EU market integration for credit, eliminating legal barriers to it[86/87]. Finally, an alternative use of the referred Chapter

---

[82] *Drobnig* et al., 2007. I had the honour to work four years on the development of this rules and the comments thereto, in the frame of the Max-Planck-Institut für ausländisches und internationales Privatrecht in Hambug. For the fruitful and pleasant work I wish to thank my colleagues at the time.

[83] See Draft Common Frame of Reference, Interim edition, 282 ff.

[84] The version of the rules as developed by the Study Group on a European Civil Code was originally in coherence with the PECL. The relation between the PECLs and the DCFR has been included in the DCFR, 51 (Table of destinations).

[85] Consumer is understood as non-professional.

[86] See the study on private law systems in the EU and the role of discrimination on the grounds of nationality as a justification for a European Civil Code. *v.* Bar (head of

will more likely (or sooner) take place in the context of the foreseeable further developments of the EU *acquis*, in view of a possible future EU law on consumer sureties, eventually as a maximum harmonisation Directive, on the basis of art. 95 EC Treaty.

C. Should we attempt to harmonise EU Personal Security Rights?

In the current crisis context securing lending to the economy has become one key objective of the EU institutions. Given the supporting role that security rights provide to lending activities it is questionable whether harmonising the law applicable to personal security rights within the EU would not provide advantages in this respect.

As previously mentioned, cross-border lending and even more, cross border personal security is still largely underdeveloped within the EU. This is particularly true for securities provided by consumers and SMEs as larger corporations are usually prepared to submit their contracts to one particular legislation (common in practice being English law).

The reasons for the current lack of integration are many fold. On the one hand, as has been largely explained, both lending and securing activities imply the need to assess risks. Obviously, this risk evaluation becomes more difficult when it needs to be performed across the borders. Different credit recording systems or different behavioural patterns in the member states make cross border security riskier and more costly, giving origin to the so called natural barriers to market integration. Another commonly mentioned natural barrier is language differences, especially in the context of business with consumers and SMEs. Besides, legal barriers also create obstacles to market integration[88]; especially, as we have seen above, the very diverse consumer protection rules applicable to consumers in the context of security rights. All these barriers to cross-border business are the reason why financial institutions have so far opted for entering mergers

---

team)/Barendrecht/Basedow/Drobnig/vanGerven/Hondius/Kerameus/Koussoulis/Lando/Loos/Tilmann, The Private Law Systems in the EU: Discrimination on Grounds of Nationality and the Need for a European Civil Code, European Parliament, Directorate General for Research, Working Paper, Legal Affairs Series JURI 103 EN (1999). See specific parts on security by Drobnig and the Hamburg team and *v. Bar/Lando/Swann* loc. cit. (fn. 5 above).

[87] See *Lannoo/de la Mata*, 7 ff.

[88] *de la Mata/Lannoo*, 2–5. Legal barriers as obstacles to market integration are also commonly mentioned in the explanatory notes to Internal Market Directives, such as the Consumer Credit Directive.

and acquisition processes (M&A) [89] with local institutions that know how to proceed in that country remaining competitive and efficient.

In this context, harmonisation of personal security laws in the EU is, if not the only, one important measure towards market harmonisation. The next question is whether complete harmonisation of the law applicable to personal security interest should be attempted or whether efforts should be limited to those core areas that generate greater barriers, this being clearly consumer protection issues[90].

The comparative studies on the law of personal security rights within the EU has shown that the basic commonalities among the different legal systems would allow for a legal harmonisation of the security provisions without unbareable complexity[91]. However, a complete harmonisation of the personal security legislation at EU level should not be necessary at the current stage. Harmonisation could be limited to consumer protection aspects of personal security legislation. Such harmonisation would have a twofold justification. First, it is creating distortions to market integration and consumer protection which would justify issuing a harmonising Directive on the basis of art. 95 EC Treaty. Beyond, attempting to increase the common standards of consumer protection remains within the scope of the EU competencies (art. 4 and art. 151 EC Treaty). In the context of credit, consumers are highly in need of protection[92]. Specially, consumer sureties, often not able to assess the risk they are assuming and contracting under emotional pressure while helping beloved persons or relatives altruistically.

Using art. 95 EC Treaty as the legal basis for consumer protection legislation, is not absent of complexity. Eliminating the legal barrier to market integration often means applying maximum harmonisation approach to the harmonising Directive. Under total/maximum harmonisation, member states may not go beyond the protection level agreed in the Directive when implementing at national level. Maximum harmonisation in the context of consumer protection is often strongly criticised as it prevents higher standards of protection there where it is socially demanded with the consequent elimination of the natural competition among legislations[93]. While this is obviously true, the direct benefits of market integration for consumers in terms of access to credit and better conditions seems to compensate

---

[89] For references on recent M&A in the field of consumer finance, see de *la Mata/ Lannoo*.

[90] The reason is based on the divergent legislations and the application of International Private Law rules. See *de la Mata/Lannoo*, 5.

[91] See PECL and *Drobnig* et al.

[92] As proved in practice and evidenced by the large case law on the subject Europe-wide. See Colombi Ciacchi, 2007, with extensive references.

[93] See Reifner in several publications.

to a certain extent the negative effects of full harmonisation[94]. This has increasingly been the approach taken by the European Commission in latest consumer protection legislation[95] and this trend is expected to continue in the current crisis context[96].

Finally, one can think of a set of harmonised rules on personal security which may be used by the parties as the law applicable to the contract on a voluntary basis (an opt-in text). This is the idea behind the DCFR or the PECL on Personal Security. This option, allows for national differences while eliminating legal barriers exclusively for cross-border business.

D. Final consideration: comparative law of security rights in view of current EU developments

Bringing this comparative law study into the light of the current developments in European private law, gives raise to a final reflection.

In the context of an EU integrated market, promoting the knowledge of private law in the different jurisdictions has gained immense practical importance. Due to increased cross-border business, practitioners explore the sources of their legal obligations. Lawyers and courts increasingly refer to foreign legislation and case law, searching for efficient solutions to their practical needs and using comparative law studies for this purpose.

In terms of law making, comparative law contributes to the approximation of national legislations through a natural evolutionary process[97]. Academic work on European private law has called the attention of Courts[98] and legislators becoming a great source of inspiration both at national and EU level. Even if a broader view of existing private law within Europe shows rather communalities than differences in the final results[99], in technical terms, legal solutions in one jurisdiction might be used in another (this has been referred to as "borrowing" or "transplanting"[100] legal solutions). The present study has brought upon several examples of this nature.

---

[94] *de la Mata/Lannoo*.

[95] For instance, the Consumer Credit Directive was based on targeted maximum harmonization.

[96] See for instance: Communication on Driving Europe's Recovery, 4.4.2009, Annex I, above.

[97] *Watson*, 2001.

[98] DCFR, 7.

[99] "(…) laws may be regarded as regional manifestations of an overall common European legacy". DCFR, 6.

[100] *Watson*, 2000 (http://www.ejcl.org/ejcl/44/44-2.html).

In view of the EU policies aiming at increasing credit market integration, comparative studies on credit and credit related issues might be of particular importance in the near future.

In times of reflection on the needs and benefits of a private law harmonisation in Europe, the reason for efforts endeavoured to comparative law studies gain sense as it may also contribute to a common evolution of certain core values, which will likely be essential the more integrated our markets become. An illustration of this is provided by the impact that the different approaches on consumer rights have had in several European countries, such as Spain. Simply the exposure to the idea of the need to protect the consumer (either on the basis of market integration needs or by even linking it to the idea of fundamental rights) has modified the perception for this need in these jurisdictions. As things evolved the different approaches that currently exist in Europe on the rights of consumer sureties will likely converge facilitating harmonisation of laws and with it the elimination of eventual legal barriers to market integration.

European private law harmonisation can, thus, only be seen as a natural on-going process based on the needs of our current society as it develops. Building up on our common legacy, comparative law contributes so to the further development of a European shared law tradition on the basis of our modern society and our market needs.

Table of Statutes: Italian and Spanish Law

Italy

Codice Civile (Civil Code), Regio Decreto 16 marzo 1942, no. 262, Approvazione del Testo del Codice Civile.

Legge fallimentare, RD 16 March 1942 cited as Legge Fallimentare.

Legge Cambiaria, RD 14 dicembre 1933 no. 1699 (LC) cited as Legge Cambiaria.

Legge 11 febraio 1994 no. 109, Legge quadro in materia di lavori publici, as ammended cited as Legge 109/94 (see art. 30). (http://www.simone.it/appaltipubblici/merloni/art.merloni/art30.htm) and its development through the Regolamento di attuazione DPR 554/1999 (art. 100 to art. 108).

Decreto legge 12 de marzo de 2004 no. 123 cited as Decreto legge 123/2004 (GURI no. 109 del 11.5.2004 Suplemento Ordinario no. 89). (http://www.unipa.it/~cdl/guriall/guri2004/mag04/4dm123.pdf).

Spain

Código de Comercio (Commercial Code), Real Decreto de 22 de agosto de 1885 por el que se publica el Código de Comercio, Gaceta nos. 298 a 328, de 16 de octubre al 24 de noviembre de 1885.

Código Civil (Civil Code), Real Decreto de 24 de julio de 1889, Gaceta nos. 206 a 208, de 25, 26 y 27 de julio de 1889.

Ley Hipotecaria, Texto refundido según Decreto de 8 de febrero de 1946, BOE no. 58 de 27 de febrero de 1946, as amended, cited as Ley Hipotecaria.

Ley 57/1968 de 27 de Julio reguladora de las percepciones de cantidades anticipadas en la construcción y venta de viviendas, BOE no. 181 de 29 de julio de 1968 (Order of 29th November 1968 (BOE 5 December 1968)).

Fuero Nuevo de Navarra, adopted by the Ley 1/1973 of 1 March 1973, BOE de 7 de marzo de 1973, cited as Fuero Nuevo de Navarra.

Ley 50/1980, de 8 de octubre, de Contrato de Seguro (Law on Insurance Contract), (BOE no. 250, de 17 de octubre de 1980), as amended.

Ley 26/1984, de 19 de Julio, General para la Defensa de los Consumidores y Usuarios (General Law on Consumer's Protection), BOE no. 176, de 24 de julio de 1984.

Ley 19/1985, de 16 de Julio, Cambiaria y del Cheque (BOE no. 172, de 19 de July) (LCC) cited as Ley 19/1985, cambiaria y del cheque (LCC).

Ley de Sociedades Anónimas, Texto refundido de la ley de sociedades anónimas, aprobado por Real Decreto Legislativo 1564/1989 de 22 de diciembre (LSA), BOE no. 310 de 27 de diciembre de 1989, cited as Ley de sociedades anónimas (LSA).

Ley 26/1991, de 21 de noviembre, sobre contratos celebrados fuera de los establecimientos mercantiles (Law on doorstep transactions), BOE no. 283, de 26 de noviembre de 1991.

Ley 2/1995, de 23 de marzo, de Sociedades de Responsabilidad Limitada (LSRL) (BOE no. 71 de 24 marzo 1995) cited as Ley 2/1995, de Sociedades de Responsabilidad Limitada (LSRL)).

Ley 7/1995, de 23 de marzo, de Crédito al Consumo, (Consumer Credit Act), BOE no. 72, de 25 de marzo 1995 and corrección de errores en BOE no. 113, de 12 de mayo.

Ley 7/1998, de 13 de abril, sobre Condiciones Generales de la Contratación, (Law on General Trade conditions) BOE no. 89, de 14 de abril de 1998, cited as Ley 7/1998, sobre condiciones generales de la contratación.

Real Decreto 390/1996, de 1 de marzo, de desarrollo parcial de la Ley 13/1995, de 18 de mayo, de contratos de las Administraciones Públicas, BOE no. 70 de 21 de marzo 1996.

Ley 38/1999 de 5 de Noviembre, de Ordenación de la Edificación, (LOE), (BOE no. 266, de 6 Noviembre 1999).

Real Decreto 2486/1998, de 20 de noviembre, por el que se aprueba el Reglamento de ordenación y supervisión de los Seguros Privados, (BOE 282/1998, de 25 de noviembre de 1998), as amended by Real Decreto 1361/2007, de 19 de octubre.

Ley 22/2003, de 9 de julio, concursal, BOE no. 164, de 10 Julio 2003, cited as Ley 22/2003, concursal.

Reglamento General de la Ley de Contratos de las Administraciones Públicas, Real Decreto 1098/2001 de 12 de octubre, BOE no. 257 de 26 de octubre 2001.

Ley 30/2007, de 30 de octubre, de Contratos del Sector Público, BOE 261, de 31 de octubre de 2007 (Ley 30/2007), (amending Ley de Contratos de las Administraciones Públicas (LCAP) Texto Refundido de 21 junio 2000, Real Decreto Legislativo 2/2000 de 16 de junio, BOE no. 148 de 21 junio 2000).

Ley 22/2007, de 11 de julio, sobre comercialización a distancia de servicios financieros destinados a los consumidores, (BOE no. 166 de 12 de julio 2007).

Rules on the Guarantee in Italian Civil Code (Bilingual)[1]

Italian
CAPO XXII: Della fideiussione

SEZIONE I: Disposizioni generali

Art. 1936 Nozione

E' fideiussore colui che, obbligandosi personalmente verso il creditore, garantisce l'adempimento di un'obbligazione altrui. La fideiussione è efficace anche se il debitore non ne ha conoscenza.

Art. 1937 Manifestazione della volontà

La volontà di prestare fideiussione deve essere espressa.

Art. 1938 Fideiussione per obbligazioni future o condizionali

La fideiussione può essere prestata anche per un'obbligazione condizionale o futura, con la previsione in quest'ultimo caso dell'importo massimo garantito.

Art. 1939 Validità della fideiussione

La fideiussione non è valida se non è valida l'obbligazione principale, salvo che sia prestata per un'obbligazione assunta da un incapace.

English
CHAPTER XXII Guarantee

SECTION I General Provisions

Art. 1936. Notion

A guarantor is a person who guarantees the performance of the obligation of another by binding himself personally to the creditor. A guarantee obligation is binding even if the debtor has no knowledge of it.

Art. 1937 Manifestation of intent

The intent to undertake a guarantee must be expressed.

Art. 1938 Guarantee for future or conditional obligations.

A guarantee can be undertaken even for a conditional obligation or for a future obligation indicating, in the latter case, the maximum amount guaranteed.

Art. 1939 Validity of guarantee

A guarantee is not valid unless the primary obligation is valid, except when the guarantee is undertaken for an obligation contracted by a person lacking capacity.

[1] This translation is exclusively intended to facilitate the comparative analysis in the text.

Art. 1940 Fideiussore del fideiussore

La fideiussione può essere prestata così per il debitore principale, come per il suo fideiussore.

Art. 1940 Guarantor of guarantor

A guarantee can be undertaken for the guarantor of a primary debtor just as for the primary debtor himself.

Art. 1941 Limiti della fideiussione

La fideiussione non può eccedere ciò che è dovuto al debitore, né può essere prestata a condizioni più onerose.
Può prestarsi per una parte soltanto del debito o a condizioni meno onerose.
La fideiussione eccedente il debito o contratta a condizioni più onerose è valida nei limiti dell'obbligazione principale.

Art. 1941 Limitations of guarantor

A guarantee cannot be undertaken for a greater amount than that owed by the primary debtor nor under more burdensome conditions.
It can be undertaken for only a portion of the debt or under less burdensome conditions.
Guarantee which is in excess of the debt or which is contracted under more burdensome conditions is valid to the extent of the primary obligation.

Art. 1942 Estensione della fideiussione

Salvo patto contrario, la fideiussione si estende a tutti gli accessori del debito principale, nonché alle spese per la denunzia al fideiussore della causa promossa contro il debitore principale e alle spese successive.

Art. 1942 Scope of guarantee

Unless otherwise agreed, guarantee covers all the incidents of the primary debt,- as well as the expenses incurred in notifying the guarantor of suits instituted against the primary debtor and the subsequent expenses.

Art. 1943 Obbligazione di prestare fideiussione

Il debitore obbligato a dare un fideiussore deve presentare persona capace, che possieda beni sufficienti a garantire l'obbligazione e che abbia o elegga domicilio nella giurisdizione della corte di appello in cui la fideiussione si deve prestare.
Quando il fideiussore e divenuto insolvente, deve esserne dato un altro, tranne che la fideiussione sia stata prestata dalla persona voluta dal creditore.

Art. 1943 Obligation to furnish guarantor

A debtor who is bound to furnish a guarantor shall select a person not lacking capacity who owns sufficient property to guarantee the obligation, and who has or elects a domicile within the jurisdiction of the court of appeals where the guarantee is to be undertaken.
If the guarantor becomes insolvent, another one shall be furnished, unless the guarantor was a person se1ected by the creditor.

SEZIONE II
Dei rapporti tra creditore e fideiussore

SECTION II
Relationship between Creditor and Guarantor

Art. 1944 Obbligazione del fideiussore

Il fideiussore e obbligato in solido col debitore principale al pagamento del debito.

Art. 1944 Obligation of guarantor

A guarantor is bound in solido with the primary debtor for the payment of the debt. However, the parties can agree that the

Le parti però possono convenire che il fideiussore non sia tenuto a pagare prima dell'esclusione del debitore principale. In tal caso il fideiussore, che sia convenuto dal creditore e intenda valersi del beneficio dell'escussione, deve indicare i beni del debitore principale da sottoporre ad esecuzione.
Salvo patto contrario, il fideiussore è tenuto ad anticipare le spese necessarie.

guarantor shall not be bound to pay before remedies against the primary debtor are exhausted. If the guarantor in such case is sued by the creditor and intends to avail himself of the exhaustion of remedies, he shall indicate the assets of the primary debtor on which execution is to be levied.
Unless otherwise agreed, the guarantor is bound to advance sums for necessary expenses.

Art. 1945 Eccezioni opponibili dal fideiussore

Il fideiussore può opporre contro il creditore tutte le eccezioni che spettano al debitore principale, salva quella derivante dall'incapacità.

Art. 1945 Defences of guarantor

A guarantor can set up against the creditor a l l the defences available to the primary debtor, except the defence arising from incapacity.

Art. 1946 Fideiussione prestata da più persone

Se più persone hanno prestato fideiussione per un medesimo debitore e a garanzia di un medesimo debito, ciascuna di esse e obbligata per l'intero debito, salvo che sia stato pattuito il beneficio della divisione.

Art. 1 946 Guarantee undertaken by more than one person

If more than one per- son has undertaken guarantee for the same debtor to guarantee payment of the same debt, each guarantor is liable for the entire debt, unless the benefit of division of the obligation was agreed upon.

Art. 1947 Beneficio della divisione

Se è stato stipulato il beneficio della divisione, ogni fideiussore che sia convenuto per il pagamento dell'intero debito può esigere che il creditore riduca l'azione alla parte da lui dovuta.
Se alcuno dei fideiussori era insolvente al tempo in cui un altro ha fatto valere il beneficio della divisione, questi è obbligato per tale insolvenza in proporzione della sua quota, ma non risponde delle insolvenze sopravvenute.

Art. 1947 Benefit of division

If the benefit of division has been agreed upon, each guarantor sued in an action for payment of the entire debt can demand that the creditor limit the action to the share owed by such guarantor.
If any guarantor was inso l vent at the time when another guarantor enforced his right to the benefit of division, the l atter is l iab l e for such inso l vency in proportion to his share, but is not answerab l e for subsequent insolvencies.

Art. 1948 Obbligazione del fideiussore del fideiussore

Il fideiussore del fideiussore non è obbligato verso il creditore, se non nel caso in cui il debitore principale e tutti i fideiussori di questo siano insolventi, o siano liberati perché incapaci.

Art. 1948 Obligation of guarantor of guarantor

The guarantor of a guarantor is not l iab l e to the creditor except when the primary debtor and all his sureties are inso l vent or are released by reason of incapacity.

SEZIONE III
Dei rapporti tra fideiussore e debitore principale

Art. 1949 Surrogazione del fideiussore nei diritti del creditore

Il fideiussore che ha pagato il debito è surrogato nei diritti che il creditore aveva contro il debitore.

Art. 1950 Regresso contro il debitore principale

Il fideiussore che ha pagato ha regresso contro il debitore principale, benché questi non fosse consapevole della prestata fideiussione.
Il regresso comprende il capitale, gli interessi e le spese che il fideiussore ha fatte dopo che ha denunziato al debitore principale le istanze proposte contro di lui.
Il fideiussore inoltre ha diritto agli interessi legali sulle somme pagate dal giorno del pagamento. Se il debito principale produceva interessi in misura superiore al saggio legale, il fideiussore ha diritto a questi fino al rimborso del capitale.
Se il debitore è incapace, il regresso del fideiussore è ammesso solo nei limiti di ciò che sia stato rivolto a suo vantaggio.

Art. 1951 Regresso contro più debitori principali

Se vi sono più debitori principali obbligati in solido, il fideiussore che ha garantito per tutti ha regresso contro ciascuno per ripetere integralmente ciò che ha pagato.

Art. 1952 Divieto di agire contro il debitore principale

Il fideiussore non ha regresso contro il debitore principale se, per avere omesso di denunziargli il pagamento fatto, il debitore ha pagato ugualmente il debito.
Se il fideiussore ha pagato senza averne dato avviso al debitore principale, questi

SECTION III
Relationships between Guarantor and Primary Debtor

Art. 1949 Guarantor subrogated to rights of creditor

A guarantor who has paid the debt is subrogated to the rights which the creditor had against the debtor.

Art. 1950 Recourse against primary debtor

A guarantor who has paid has a right of recourse against the primary debtor, even if the latter had no knowledge that the guarantee was undertaken.
The right of recourse includes principal, interest, and expenses sustained by the guarantor after notifying the primary debtor of the actions instituted against him.
The guarantor is, moreover, entitled to legal interest on the sums paid by him, from the date of payment. If the primary debt produced interest in excess of the legal rate, the guarantor is entitled to such higher interest until recovery of the principal.
If the debtor lacks capacity, recourse by the guarantor is permissible only to the extent of the benefit that has accrued to such incapacitated debtor.

Art. 1951 Recourse against more than one primary debtor

If there is more than one primary debtor, all liable in solido, the guarantor who acted for all the debtors has a right of recourse against each for the recovery of the whole amount which he has paid.

Art. 1952 Limitations on actions against primary debtor

A guarantor has no recourse against the primary debtor if, due to the failure of the guarantor to notify the debtor of the payment made by him, the debtor also paid the debt.
If the guarantor paid without notifying the

può opporgli le eccezioni che avrebbe potuto opporre al creditore principale all'atto del pagamento.
In entrambi i casi è fatta salva al fideiussore l'azione per la ripetizione contro il creditore.

primary debtor, the latter can set up against the guarantor the defences which he could have set up against the primary creditor at the time of payment.
In either case, the guarantor retains his action for recovery against the creditor.

Art. 1953 Rilievo del fideiussore

Il fideiussore, anche prima di aver pagato, può agire contro il debitore perché questi gli procuri la liberazione o, in mancanza, presti le garanzie necessarie per assicurargli il soddisfacimento delle eventuali ragioni di regresso (1179), nei casi seguenti:
1) quando è convenuto in giudizio per il pagamento;
2) quando il debitore è divenuto insolvente;
3) quando il debitore si è obbligato di liberarlo dalla fideiussione entro un tempo determinato;
4) quando il debito è divenuto esigibile per la scadenza del termine;
5) quando sono decorsi cinque anni, e l'obbligazione principale non ha un termine, purché essa non sia di tal natura da non potersi estinguere prima di un tempo determinato.

Art. 1953 Release of guarantor

In the following cases a guarantor can, even before making payment, bring an action against the debtor either to cause the latter to release him or, failing that, to require him to provide the guarantees necessary (1179) to insure satisfaction of the guarantor's possible claims for recourse:
1) when the guarantor is sued for payment;
2) when the debtor has become insolvent;
3) when the debtor has undertaken to release him as guarantor within a specified time;
4) when the debt has come to maturity because of expiration of the time limit
5) when five years have elapsed and no time limit was established for performance of the primary obligation, unless the obligation is of such character that it could not be extinguished before a specified time.

SEZIONE IV
Dei rapporti fra più fideiussori

Art. 1954 Regresso contro gli altri fideiussori

Se più persone hanno prestato fideiussione per un medesimo debitore e per un medesimo debito, il fideiussore che ha pagato ha regresso contro gli altri fideiussori per la loro rispettiva porzione. Se uno di questi è insolvente, si osserva la disposizione del secondo comma dell'art. 1299.

SECTION IV
Relationships among Co-sureties

Art. 1954 Recourse against co-sureties

If more than one person has acted as guarantors for the same debtor and for the same debt, a guarantor who has paid has recourse against the co-sureties for their respective shares. If one of the co-sureties is insolvent, the provision of the second paragraph of Article 1299.2 applies.

SEZIONE V
Dell'estinzione della fideiussione

Art. 1955 Liberazione del fideiussore per fatto del creditore

La fideiussione si estingue quando, per fatto del creditore, non può avere effetto la surrogazione del fideiussore nei diritti, nel pegno, nelle ipoteche e nei privilegi del creditore.

Art. 1956 Liberazione del fideiussore per obbligazione futura

Il fideiussore per un'obbligazione futura è liberato se il creditore, senza speciale autorizzazione del fideiussore, ha fatto credito al terzo, pur conoscendo che le condizioni patrimoniali di questo erano divenute tali da rendere notevolmente più difficile il soddisfacimento del credito.
Non è valida la preventiva rinuncia del fideiussore ad avvalersi della liberazione.

Art. 1957 Scadenza dell'obbligazione principale

Il fideiussore rimane obbligato anche dopo la scadenza dell'obbligazione principale, purché il creditore entro sei mesi abbia proposto le sue istanze contro il debitore e le abbia con diligenza continuate.
La disposizione si applica anche al caso in cui il fideiussore ha espressamente limitato la sua fideiussione allo stesso termine dell'obbligazione principale.
In questo caso però l'istanza contro il debitore deve essere proposta entro due mesi.
L'istanza proposta contro il debitore interrompe la prescrizione anche nei confronti del fideiussore.

CAPO XXIII Del mandato di credito

Art. 1958 Effetti del mandato di credito

Se una persona si obbliga verso un'altra, che le ha conferito l'incarico, a fare credito a un terzo, in nome e per conto proprio,

SECTION V
Extinguishment of Guarantee

Art. 1955 Release of guarantor caused by creditor

Guarantee is extinguished when subrogation of the guarantor to the rights, pledges, and mortgages and privileges of the creditor has become impossible because of actions of the creditor.

Art. 1956 Release of guarantor for future obligation

The guarantor for a future obligation is released if the creditor, without special authorization from the guarantor, extended credit to the third party knowing that the debtor's financial conditions, have become such as to make satisfaction of the claim considerably more difficult.
A prior waiver by the guarantor to avail himself of the release is not valid.

Art. 1957 Maturity of primary obligation

The liability of a guarantor remains in effect even after the primary obligation has matured, provided that the creditor, within six months, has instituted an action against the debtor and has diligently pursued it.
This provision applies even if the guarantor has expressly limited his guarantee to the same period as that of the primary obligation.
In such case, however, the action against the debtor shall be instituted within two months.
The action instituted against the debtor also interrupts prescription with respect to the guarantor.

CHAPTER XXIII Mandate To Grant Credit

Art. 1958 Effects

If a person directs another to extend credit to a third person in the name and for the account of the person thus directed, and the

quella che ha dato l'incarico risponde come fideiussore di un debito futuro.
Colui che ha accettato l'incarico non può rinunziarvi, ma chi l'ha conferito può revocarlo, salvo l'obbligo di risarcire il danno all'altra parte.

latter binds himself to act accordingly, the person so directing is answerable as a guarantor for a future debt.
The person who has accepted the mandate cannot renounce it, but the principal can revoke it, subject to his duty to compensate the other party for damages.

Art. 1959. Sopravvenuta insolvenza del mandante o del terzo

Se, dopo l'accettazione dell'incarico, le condizioni patrimoniali di colui che lo ha conferito o del terzo sono divenute tali da rendere notevolmente più difficile il soddisfacimento del credito, colui che ha accettato l'incarico non può essere costretto ad eseguirlo.
Si applica inoltre la disposizione dell'art. 1956.

Art. 1959 Supervening insolvency of principal or of third person

If, after acceptance of the mandate, the financial conditions of the principal or of the third person have become such as to render the satisfaction of the claim considerably more difficult, the person who has accepted the mandate cannot be compelled to carry it out.
The provision of Article 1956 also applies.

Rules on the Guarantee in Spanish Civil Code (Bilingual)[1]

Spanish
TÍTULO XIV. De la fianza

CAPÍTULO PRIMERO. De la naturaleza y extensión de la fianza

Art. 1.822

Por la fianza se obliga uno a pagar o cumplir por un tercero, en el caso de no hacerlo éste.
Si el fiador se obligare solidariamente con el deudor principal, se observará lo dispuesto en la sección cuarta, capítulo III, título I de este libro.

Art. 1.823

La fianza puede ser convencional, legal o judicial, gratuita o a título oneroso.
Puede también constituirse no sólo a favor del deudor principal, sino al del otro fiador, consintiéndolo, ignorándolo y aun contradiciéndolo éste.

Art. 1.824

La fianza no puede existir sin una obligación válida.
Puede, no obstante, recaer sobre una obligación cuya nulidad pueda ser reclamada a virtud de una excepción puramente personal del obligado, como la de la menor edad.
Exceptuase de la disposición del párrafo

English
TITLE XIV. About the guarantee

CHAPTER ONE: About the nature and extent of the guarantee

Art. 1822

By guarantee a person binds himself to pay or perform for a third party in case the latter fails to do so. If the guarantor binds himself solidarily with the principal debtor, the provisions of Section Four, Chapter III, Title I of this Book shall be observed.

Art. 1823

The guarantee may be conventional, legal or judicial, gratuitous or under onerous title.
It may be constituted, not only in favour of the principal debtor, but also of another guarantor, whether with the consent of the latter, without his knowledge, or even in spite of his opposition thereto.

Art. 1824

A guarantee cannot exist without a valid obligation.
Nevertheless, an obligation, the nullity of which may be claimed by virtue of a purely personal exception on the part of the obligor, as that of minority, may be the subject of a guarantee.

[1] This translation is exclusively intended to facilitate the comparative analysis in the text.

anterior el caso de préstamo hecho al hijo de familia.

From the provisions of the preceding paragraph, the case of a loan granted to a minor, who is not emancipated, shall be excluded.

Art. 1.825

Puede también prestarse fianza en garantía de deudas futuras, cuyo importe no sea aún conocido; pero no se podrá reclamar contra el fiador hasta que la deuda sea líquida.

Art. 1.825

Guarantee may be given with respect to future debts, the amount of which is not yet known; but no action may be raised against the guarantor until the debt is liquidated.

Art. 1.826

El fiador puede obligarse a menos, pero no a más que el deudor principal, tanto en la cantidad como en lo oneroso de las condiciones.
Si se hubiera obligado a más, se reducirá su obligación a los límites de la del deudor.

Art. 1.826

A guarantor may bind himself to less but not to more than the principal debtor as to quantity, as well as to the burden of the conditions.
If he has bound himself for more, his obligation shall be reduced to the limits of the debtor's obligations.

Art. 1.827

La fianza no se presume: debe ser expresa y no puede extenderse a más de lo contenido en ella.
Si fuere simple o indefinida, comprenderá, no sólo la obligación principal, sino todos sus accesorios, incluso los gastos del juicio, entendiéndose, respecto de éstos, que no responderá sino de los que se hayan devengado después que haya sido requerido el fiador para el pago.

Art. 1.827

Guarantee may not be presumed, it must be express and cannot be extended further than that specified therein. If it is simple and indefinite, the guarantee shall include not only the principal obligation but all its accessories, including the costs of the suit, but with regard to the latter, that the guarantor will only be liable for the costs incurred once a demand for payment has been made on him.

Art. 1.828

El obligado a dar fiador debe presentar persona que tenga capacidad para obligarse y bienes suficientes para responder de la obligación que garantiza. El fiador se entenderá sometido a la jurisdicción del Juez del lugar donde ésta obligación deba cumplirse.

Art. 1.828

A party bound to furnish a guarantor shall present a person having capacity to bind himself, and with sufficient assets to warrant the obligation which he guarantees. The guarantor shall be considered subject to the jurisdiction of the judge of the place where this obligation is to be fulfilled.

Art. 1.829

Si el fiador viniere al estado de insolvencia, puede el acreedor pedir otro que reúna las cualidades exigidas en el artículo anterior. Exceptúase el caso de haber exigido y pactado el acreedor que se le diera por fiador una persona determinada.

Art. 1.829

If the guarantor becomes insolvent, the creditor may demand another guarantor having capacity to bind himself, and with sufficient assets to warrant the obligation which he guarantees. The guarantor shall be considered subject to the jurisdiction of the judge of the place where this obligation is to be fulfilled.

CAPÍTULO SEGUNDO.
De los efectos de la fianza

SECCIÓN PRIMERA. De los efectos de la fianza entre el fiador y el acreedor

Art. 1.830

El fiador no puede ser compelido a pagar al acreedor sin hacerse antes excusión de todos los bienes del deudor.

Art. 1.831

La excusión no tiene lugar:
1º.Cuando el fiador haya renunciado expresamente a ella.
2º. Cuando se haya obligado solidariamente con el deudor.
3º. En el caso de quiebra o concurso del deudor.
4º. Cuando éste no pueda ser demandado judicialmente dentro del Reino.

Art. 1832

Para que el fiador pueda aprovecharse del beneficio de la excusión, debe oponerlo al acreedor luego que éste le requiera para el pago, y señalarle bienes del deudor realizables dentro del territorio español, que sean suficientes para cubrir el importe de la deuda.

Art. 1.833

Cumplidas por el fiador todas las condiciones del artículo anterior, el acreedor negligente en la excusión de los bienes señalados es responsable, hasta donde ellos alcancen, de la insolvencia del deudor que por aquel descuido resulte.

CHAPTER TWO.
Effects of the guarantee.

SECTION ONE. About the effects of the guarantee between guarantor and creditor

Art. 1.830

The guarantor cannot be compelled to pay a creditor until all of the debtor's assets have been subject to discussion.

Art. 1831

A discussion of the debtor's assets is not required:
1° When the guarantor has expressly waived it.
2° When he has bound himself solidarily with the debtor.
3° In case of bankruptcy or insolvency of the debtor.
4° When the debtor cannot be sued within the Kingdom.

Art. 1832

In order for the guarantor to avail himself of the benefit of discussion he must raise it against the creditor after the latter makes a demand for payment from him and he must indicate to him the assets of the debtor that may be seized within the Spanish territory and which are sufficient to cover the amount of the debt.

Art. 1833

When the guarantor has fulfilled all the conditions of the preceding article, the creditor who is negligent in making discussion upon the assets pointed out to him shall be liable, to the extent of the value of said property, for the insolvency of the debtor resulting from such negligence.

Art. 1.834

El acreedor podrá citar al fiador cuando demande al deudor principal, pero quedará siempre a salvo el beneficio de excusión, aunque se dé sentencia contra los dos.

Art. 1.834

A creditor may call upon the guarantor if he institutes a claim against the principal debtor, but the benefit of discussion shall always be reserved, even when a judgment is rendered against both of them.

Art. 1.835

La transacción hecha por el fiador con el acreedor no surte efecto para con el deudor principal.
La hecha por éste tampoco surte efecto para con el fiador, contra su voluntad.

Art. 1.835

Payment made by the guarantor with the creditor shall have no effect with regard to the principal debtor.
That made by the latter shall also have no effect for the guarantor, against his will.

Art. 1.836

El fiador de un fiador goza del beneficio de excusión, tanto respecto del fiador como del deudor principal.

Art. 1.836

The guarantor of a guarantor enjoys the benefit of discussion both with respect to the guarantor and to the principal debtor.

Art. 1.837

Siendo varios los fiadores de un mismo deudor y por una misma deuda, la obligación a responder de ella se divide entre todos. El acreedor no puede reclamar a cada fiador sino la parte que le corresponda satisfacer, a menos que se haya estipulado expresamente la solidaridad.
El beneficio de división contra los cofiadores cesa en los mismos casos y por las mismas causas que el de excusión contra el deudor principal.

Art. 1.837

If there are several guarantors for the same debtor and for the same debt, their liability therefore shall be divided among all of them. The creditor may only claim from each guarantor the part that each may have to pay, unless solidarity has been expressly stipulated. The benefit of division against the co-guarantors shall cease in the same case and for the same reasons as that of the benefit of discussion against the principal debtor.

SECCIÓN SEGUNDA. De los efectos de la fianza entre el deudor y el fiador

SECTION TWO. About the effects of the guarantee between the Debtor and the Guarantor

Art. 1.838

El fiador que paga por el deudor, debe ser indemnizado por éste.
La indemnización comprende:
1º. La cantidad total de la deuda.
2º. Los intereses legales de ella desde que se haya hecho saber el pago al deudor, aunque no los produjese para el acreedor.
3º. Los gastos ocasionados al fiador después de poner éste en conocimiento del deudor que ha sido requerido para el pago.
4º. Los daños y perjuicios, cuando proce-

Art. 1.838

A guarantor who pays on behalf of a debtor shall be indemnified by the latter.
The indemnity consists of:
1º. The total amount of the debt.
2º. The legal interests on the debt from the day on which the payment was communicated to the debtor, even when it did not produce interest for the creditor.
3º. The expenses incurred by the guarantor after the latter has informed the debtor that payment has been demanded from him.

dan.
La disposición de este artículo tiene lugar aunque la fianza se haya dado ignorándolo el deudor.

4°. Losses and damages when appropriate.
The provisions of this article shall be applicable even if the guarantee has been given without the knowledge of the debtor.

Art. 1.839

El fiador se subroga por el pago en todos los derechos que el acreedor tenía contra el deudor. Si ha transigido con el acreedor, no puede pedir al deudor más de lo que realmente haya pagado.

Art. 1.839

By virtue of the payment, the guarantor subrogates to all the rights which the creditor had against the debtor. If he has agreed with the creditor, he cannot demand of the debtor more that the amount he has actually paid to him.

Art. 1.840

Si el fiador paga sin ponerlo en noticia del deudor, podrá éste hacer valer contra él todas las excepciones que hubiera podido oponer al acreedor al tiempo de hacerse el pago.

Art. 1840

If the guarantor pays without notifying debtor, the latter shall have the right to raise against him all the exceptions that he could have raised against the creditor at the time payment was made.

Art. 1.841

Si la deuda era a plazo y el fiador la pagó antes de su vencimiento, no podrá exigir reembolso del deudor hasta que el plazo venza.

Art. 1.841

If the debt was a deferred one and the guarantor paid it before the due date, he cannot require the debtor to reimburse him until the term has expired.

Art. 1.842

Si el fiador ha pagado sin ponerlo en noticia del deudor, y éste, ignorando el pago, lo repite por su parte, no queda al primero recurso alguno contra el segundo, pero sí contra el acreedor.

Art. 1.842

If the guarantor has paid without notifying the debtor, and the latter, not having knowledge of the payment, also pays it, the former has no remedy against the debtor, only against the creditor.

Art. 1.843

El fiador, aun antes de haber pagado, puede proceder contra el deudor principal:
1°. Cuando se ve demandado judicialmente para el pago.
2°. En caso de quiebra, concurso o insolvencia.
3°. Cuando el deudor se ha obligado a relevarle de la fianza en un plazo determinado, y este plazo ha vencido.
4°. Cuando la deuda ha llegado a hacerse exigible, por haber cumplido el plazo en que debe satisfacerse.
5°. Al cabo de diez años, cuando la obliga-

Art. 1.843

The guarantor, even before making payment, may proceed against the principal debtor:
1°. When he is sued for the payment.
2°. In case of bankruptcy or insolvency.
3°. When the debtor has bound himself to relieve him from the guarantee within a specified term, and this term has expired.
4°. When the debt has become due and payable because the term in which it should have been paid has expired.
5°. At the end of ten years, when the principal obligation does not have a fixed term

ción principal no tiene término fijo para su vencimiento, a menos que sea de tal naturaleza que no pueda extinguirse sino en un plazo mayor de los diez años.
En todos estos casos la acción del fiador tiende a obtener relevación de la fianza o una garantía que lo ponga a cubierto de los procedimientos del acreedor y del peligro de insolvencia en el deudor.

for its expiration, unless it is of such nature that it cannot be extinguished except in a period greater ten years.
In all these cases, the action of the guarantor tends to secure his release from the guarantee or to obtain security to protect him from any proceedings of the creditor and from the danger of insolvency of the debtor.

SECCIÓN TERCERA. De los efectos de la fianza entre los cofiadores

SECTION THREE. About the effects of the guarantee with regard to co-guarantors

Art. 1.844

Cuando son dos o más los fiadores de un mismo deudor y por una misma deuda, el que de ellos la haya pagado podrá reclamar de cada uno de los otros la parte que proporcionalmente le corresponda satisfacer.
Si alguno de ellos resultare insolvente, la parte de éste recaerá sobre todos en la misma proporción.
Para que pueda tener lugar la disposición de este artículo, es preciso que se haya hecho el pago en virtud de demanda judicial, o hallándose el deudor principal en estado de concurso o quiebra.

Art. 1.844

When there are two or more guarantors for the same debtor and for the same debt, the one who has paid it may demand of each of the others the part which he or they should proportionately have to pay.
Should any of them be insolvent, his part shall be paid by all in the same proportion.
In order that the provision of this article may be applicable, the payment must have been made following a judicial compliant or when the principal debtor has made an assignment or is insolvent or bankrupt.

Art. 1.845

En el caso del artículo anterior podrán los cofiadores oponer al que pagó las mismas excepciones que habrían correspondido al deudor principal contra el acreedor y que no fueren puramente personales del mismo deudor.

Art. 1.845

In the case of the preceding article, the co-guarantors may raise against the one who paid, the same exceptions which would have been available to the principal debtor against the creditor, and which are not purely personal of the same debtor

Art. 1.846

El subfiador, en caso de insolvencia del fiador por quien se obligó, queda responsable a los cofiadores en los mismos términos que lo estaba el fiador.

Art. 1.846

The sub-guarantor, in case of insolvency of the guarantor for whom he bound himself, remains liable to the co-guarantors in the same terms as the guarantor.

CAPÍTULO TERCERO. De la extinción de la fianza

Art. 1.847

La obligación del fiador se extingue al mismo tiempo que la del deudor, y por las mismas causas que las demás obligaciones.

Art. 1.848

La confusión que se verifica en la persona del deudor y en la del fiador cuando uno de ellos hereda al otro, no extingue la obligación del subfiador.

Art. 1.849

Si el acreedor acepta voluntariamente un inmueble, u otros cualesquiera efectos en pago de la deuda, aunque después los pierda por evicción, queda libre el fiador.

Art. 1.850

La liberación hecha por el acreedor a uno de los fiadores sin el consentimiento de los otros, aprovecha a todos hasta donde alcance la parte del fiador a quien se ha otorgado.

Art. 1.851

La prórroga concedida al deudor por el acreedor sin el consentimiento del fiador extingue la fianza.

Art. 1.852

Los fiadores, aunque sean solidarios, quedan libres de su obligación siempre que por algún hecho del acreedor no puedan quedar subrogados en los derechos, hipotecas y privilegios del mismo.

Art. 1.853

El fiador puede oponer al acreedor todas las excepciones que competan al deudor principal y sean inherentes a la deuda; más no las que sean puramente personales del deudor.

CHAPTER THREE: About the extinction of the guarantee

Art. 1.847

The obligation of the guarantor shall expire at the same time as that of the debtor and for the same causes as all other obligations.

Art. 1.848

The confusion which takes place in the person of the debtor and of the guarantor when one of them inherits from the other, does not extinguish the obligation of the sub-guarantor.

Art. 1.849

If the creditor voluntarily accepts immovable real property or any other goods in payment of the debt, even if he afterwards loses them by way of eviction, the guarantor is released.

Art. 1.850

The release of one of the guarantors made by the creditor without the consent of the guarantor, benefits all of them to the extent of the obligation of the guarantor to whom the release was granted.

Art. 1.851

The extension granted to the debtor by the creditor without the consent of the guarantor, extinguishes the guarantee.

Art. 1.852

The guarantors, even when they are solidarily liable, are released from their obligation whenever by any act of the creditor, they cannot be subrogated to the rights, mortgages and privileges of the same.

Art. 1.853

A guarantor may raise against the creditor all the exceptions that pertain to the principal debtor and that are inherent to the debt but not those which are purely personal to the debtor.

CAPÍTULO FOUR. De la fianza legal y judicial

Art. 1.854

El fiador que haya de darse por disposición de la ley o de providencia judicial, debe tener las cualidades prescritas en el artículo 1.828.

Art. 1.855

Si el obligado a dar fianza en los casos del artículo anterior no la hallase, se le admitirá en su lugar una prenda o hipoteca que se estime bastante para cubrir su obligación.

Art. 1.856

El fiador judicial no puede pedir la excusión de bienes del deudor principal.
El subfiador, en el mismo caso, no puede pedir ni la del deudor ni la del fiador.

CHAPTER FOUR. About the legal and judicial guarantee

Art. 1.854

The guarantor, acting when required by law or by judicial order, must possess the qualifications prescribed in article 1828.

Art. 1.855

If the person who is bound to grant guarantee in the cases of the preceding article, is unable to furnish it, a pledge or mortgage found sufficient to cover his obligation shall be admitted in its place.

Art. 1.856

The judicial guarantor cannot demand the discussion of the assets of the principal debtor.
The sub-guarantor, in the same case, cannot demand that of the debtor nor that of the guarantor.

Rules on the Guarantee in German Civil Code (Bilingual)[1]

German Titel 20
Bürgschaft

§ 765 Vertragstypische Pflichten bei der Bürgschaft

(1) Durch den Bürgschaftsvertrag verpflichtet sich der Bürge gegenüber dem Gläubiger eines Dritten, für die Erfüllung der Verbindlichkeit des Dritten einzustehen.
(2) Die Bürgschaft kann auch für eine künftige oder eine bedingte Verbindlichkeitübernommen werden.

§ 766 Schriftform der Bürgschaftserklärung

Zur Gültigkeit des Bürgschaftsvertrags ist schriftliche Erteilung der Bürgschaftserklärung erforderlich. Die Erteilung der Bürgschaftserklärung in elektronischer Form ist ausgeschlossen. Soweit der Bürge die Hauptverbindlichkeit erfüllt, wird der Mangel der Form geheilt.

§ 767 Umfang der Bürgschaftsschuld

(1) Für die Verpflichtung des Bürgen ist der jeweilige Bestand der Hauptverbindlichkeit maßgebend. Dies gilt insbesondere auch, wenn die Hauptverbindlichkeit durch Verschulden oder Verzug des Hauptschuldners geändert wird. Durch ein Rechtsgeschäft, das der Hauptschuldner

English Title 20
Guarantee

§ 765 Typical contractual duties in guarantee

(1) By a contract of guarantee the surety puts himself under a duty to the creditor of a third party to be responsible for discharging that third party's obligation.
(2) Guarantee may also be assumed for a future or contingent obligation.

§ 766 Written form of the declaration of guarantee

For the contract of guarantee to be valid, the declaration of guarantee must be issued in writing. The declaration of guarantee may not be made in electronic form. If the surety discharges the main obligation, the defect of form is remedied.

§ 767 Extent of the guarantee debt

(1) The currently applicable amount of the main obligation determines the duty of the surety. This applies in particular, without limitation, if the main obligation has been changed through no fault of or default by the principal debtor. The duty of the surety is not extended by a legal transaction that the principal debtor undertakes after as-

[1] This translation is exclusively intended to facilitate the comparative analysis in the text. It is based on the official translation of the German Ministry of Justice as published in http://www.gesetze-im-internet.de/englisch_bgb/englisch_bgb.html.

nach der Übernahme der Bürgschaft vornimmt, wird die Verpflichtung des Bürgen nicht erweitert.
(2) Der Bürge haftet für die dem Gläubiger von dem Hauptschuldner zu ersetzenden Kosten der Kündigung und der Rechtsverfolgung.

sumption of the guarantee.
(2) The surety is liable for the costs of termination and prosecution of rights that are reimbursable by the principal debtor to the creditor.

§ 768 Einreden des Bürgen

(1) Der Bürge kann die dem Hauptschuldner zustehenden Einreden geltend machen. Stirbt der Hauptschuldner, so kann sich der Bürge nicht darauf berufen, dass der Erbe für die Verbindlichkeit nur beschränkt haftet.
(2) Der Bürge verliert eine Einrede nicht dadurch, dass der Hauptschuldner auf sie verzichtet.

§ 768 Defences of surety

(1) The surety may assert the defences to which the principal debtor is entitled. If the principal debtor dies, then the surety may not invoke the fact that the heir has only limited liability for the obligation.
(2) The surety is not deprived of a defence by the fact that the principal debtor waives it.

§ 769 Mitbürgschaft

Verbürgen sich mehrere für dieselbe Verbindlichkeit, so haften sie als Gesamtschuldner, auch wenn sie die Bürgschaft nicht gemeinschaftlich übernehmen.

§ 769 Co-guarantee

Where more than one person enters a guarantee commitment for the same obligation, they are jointly and severally liable even if they do not assume guarantee jointly.

§ 770 Einreden der Anfechtbarkeit und der Aufrechenbarkeit

(1) Der Bürge kann die Befriedigung des Gläubigers verweigern, solange dem Hauptschuldner das Recht zusteht, das seiner Verbindlichkeit zugrunde liegende Rechtsgeschäft anzufechten.
(2) Die gleiche Befugnis hat der Bürge, solange sich der Gläubiger durch Aufrechnung gegen eine fällige Forderung des Hauptschuldners befriedigen kann.

§ 770 Defences of voidability and set-off

(1) The surety may refuse to satisfy the creditor as long as the principal debtor is entitled to avoid the legal transaction on which the obligation is based.
(2) The surety has the same authority as long as the creditor can obtain satisfaction by set-off against a claim of the principal debtor that is due.

§ 771 Einrede der Vorausklage

Der Bürge kann die Befriedigung des Gläubigers verweigern, solange nicht der Gläubiger eine Zwangsvollstreckung gegen den Hauptschuldner ohne Erfolg versucht hat (Einrede der Vorausklage). Erhebt der Bürge die Einrede der Vorausklage, ist die Verjährung des Anspruchs des Gläubigers gegen den Bürgen gehemmt, bis der Gläu-

§ 771 Defence of unexhausted remedies

The surety may refuse to satisfy the creditor as long as the creditor has not attempted without success to obtain execution of judgment against the principal debtor (defence of unexhausted remedies). If the surety raises the defence of unexhausted remedies, the limitation of the claim of the creditor against the surety is suspended

biger eine Zwangsvollstreckung gegen den Hauptschuldner ohne Erfolg versucht hat.

until the creditor has attempted without success to obtain execution of judgment against the principal debtor.

§ 772 Vollstreckungs- und Verwertungspflicht des Gläubigers

(1) Besteht die Bürgschaft für eine Geldforderung, so muss die Zwangsvollstreckung in die beweglichen Sachen des Hauptschuldners an seinem Wohnsitz und, wenn der Hauptschuldner an einem anderen Ort eine gewerbliche Niederlassung hat, auch an diesem Ort, in Ermangelung eines Wohnsitzes und einer gewerblichen Niederlassung an seinem Aufenthaltsort versucht werden.
(2) Steht dem Gläubiger ein Pfandrecht oder ein Zurückbehaltungsrecht an einer beweglichen Sache des Hauptschuldners zu, so muss er auch aus dieser Sache Befriedigung suchen. Steht dem Gläubiger ein solches Recht an der Sache auch für eine andere Forderung zu, so gilt dies nur, wenn beide Forderungen durch den Wert der Sache gedeckt werden.

§ 772 Duty of creditor of enforcement and realisation

(1) If the guarantee applies to a monetary claim, then enforcement of judgment must be attempted against the movable things of the principal debtor at his residence and, if the principal debtor has a business establishment in another locality, at the latter as well, and, in the absence of a residence and a business establishment, at his place of abode.
(2) If the creditor has a pledge over or right of retention to a movable thing of the principal debtor, then he must attempt to satisfy his claim from this thing too. If the creditor has such a right to the thing for another claim as well, then this only applies if both claims are covered by the value of the thing.

§ 773 Ausschluss der Einrede der Vorausklage

(1) Die Einrede der Vorausklage ist ausgeschlossen:
1. wenn der Bürge auf die Einrede verzichtet, insbesondere wenn er sich als Selbstschuldner verbürgt hat,
2. wenn die Rechtsverfolgung gegen den Hauptschuldner infolge einer nach der Übernahme der Bürgschaft eingetretenen Änderung des Wohnsitzes, der gewerblichen Niederlassung oder des Aufenthaltsorts des Hauptschuldners wesentlich erschwert ist,
3. wenn über das Vermögen des Hauptschuldners das Insolvenzverfahren eröffnet ist,
4. wenn anzunehmen ist, dass die Zwangsvollstreckung in das Vermögen des Hauptschuldners nicht zur Befriedigung des Gläubigers führen wird.
(2) In den Fällen der Nummern 3, 4 ist die Einrede insoweit zulässig, als sich der

§ 773 Exclusion of defence of unexhausted remedies

(1) The defence of unexhausted remedies is excluded:
if the surety waives the defence, including without limitation if he has assumed guarantee as principal debtor, if pursuit of rights against the principal debtor is made appreciably more difficult due to a change of residence, of business establishment or of place of abode occurring after assumption of guarantee, if insolvency proceedings have been opened in relation to the assets of the principal debtor, if it must be assumed that enforcement of judgment against the assets of the principal debtor will not result in satisfaction of the claim of the creditor.
(2) In the cases cited in nos. 3 and 4, the defence is admissible to the extent that the creditor may satisfy his claim out of a movable thing of the principal debtor over which he has a security right or of which

Gläubiger aus einer beweglichen Sache des Hauptschuldners befriedigen kann, an der er ein Pfandrecht oder ein Zurückbehaltungsrecht hat; die Vorschrift des § 772 Abs. 2 Satz 2 findet Anwendung.

he has a right of retention; the provisions of § 772 (2) sentence 2 apply.

§ 774 Gesetzlicher Forderungsübergang

(1) Soweit der Bürge den Gläubiger befriedigt, geht die Forderung des Gläubigers gegen den Hauptschuldner auf ihn über. Der Übergang kann nicht zum Nachteil des Gläubigers geltend gemacht werden. Einwendungen des Hauptschuldners aus einem zwischen ihm und dem Bürgen bestehenden Rechtsverhältnis bleiben unberührt.
(2) Mitbürgen haften einander nur nach § 426.

§ 774 Statutory passing of claims

(1) To the extent that the surety satisfies the claims of the creditor, the claim of the creditor against the principal debtor passes to him. The passing of ownership may not be asserted to the disadvantage of the creditor. Objections by the principal debtor under a legal relationship existing between himself and the surety are unaffected.
(2) Co-sureties are only liable to each other under § 426.

§ 775 Anspruch des Bürgen auf Befreiung

(1) Hat sich der Bürge im Auftrag des Hauptschuldners verbürgt oder stehen ihm nach den Vorschriften über die Geschäftsführung ohne Auftrag wegen der Übernahme der Bürgschaft die Rechte eines Beauftragten gegen den Hauptschuldner zu, so kann er von diesem Befreiung von der Bürgschaft verlangen:
1. wenn sich die Vermögensverhältnisse des Hauptschuldners wesentlich verschlechtert haben,
2. wenn die Rechtsverfolgung gegen den Hauptschuldner infolge einer nach der Übernahme der Bürgschaft eingetretenen Änderung des Wohnsitzes, der gewerblichen Niederlassung oder des Aufenthaltsorts des Hauptschuldners wesentlich erschwert ist,
3. wenn der Hauptschuldner mit der Erfüllung seiner Verbindlichkeit im Verzug ist,
4. wenn der Gläubiger gegen den Bürgen ein vollstreckbares Urteil auf Erfüllung erwirkt hat.
(2) Ist die Hauptverbindlichkeit noch nicht fällig, so kann der Hauptschuldner dem Bürgen, statt ihn zu befreien, Sicherheit leisten.

§ 775 Claim to release of the surety

(1) If the surety has provided guarantee on the instructions of the principal debtor, or if he is entitled under the provisions on agency without specific authorisation, as a result of assuming the guarantee, to the rights of a voluntary agent against the principal debtor, then he may demand that the principal debtor releases him from the guarantee if the financial situation of the principal debtor has substantially deteriorated, if pursuit of rights against the principal debtor is made appreciably more difficult due to a change of residence, of business establishment or of place of abode occurring after assumption of guarantee, if the principal debtor is in default of discharging his obligation, if the creditor has obtained an enforceable judgment for discharge against the surety.
(2) If the main obligation has not yet fallen due, then the principal debtor may provide security to the surety instead of releasing him.

§ 776 Aufgabe einer Sicherheit

Gibt der Gläubiger ein mit der Forderung verbundenes Vorzugsrecht, eine für sie bestehende Hypothek oder Schiffshypothek, ein für sie bestehendes Pfandrecht oder das Recht gegen einen Mitbürgen auf, so wird der Bürge insoweit frei, als er aus dem aufgegebenen Recht nach § 774 hätte Ersatz erlangen können. Dies gilt auch dann, wenn das aufgegebene Recht erst nach der Übernahme der Bürgschaft entstanden ist.

§ 776 Waiver of a security

If the creditor waives a preferential right connected with the claim, a mortgage or ship mortgage, a pledge existing for the claim or a right against a co-surety, then the surety is released to the extent that he would have been able to obtain compensation under § 774 from the right waived. This also applies if the right waived only arose after assumption of the guarantee.

§ 777 Bürgschaft auf Zeit

(1) Hat sich der Bürge für eine bestehende Verbindlichkeit auf bestimmte Zeit verbürgt, so wird er nach dem Ablauf der bestimmten Zeit frei, wenn nicht der Gläubiger die Einziehung der Forderung unverzüglich nach Maßgabe des § 772 betreibt, das Verfahren ohne wesentliche Verzögerung fortsetzt und unverzüglich nach der Beendigung des Verfahrens dem Bürgen anzeigt, dass er ihn in Anspruch nehme. Steht dem Bürgen die Einrede der Vorausklage nicht zu, so wird er nach dem Ablauf der bestimmten Zeit frei, wenn nicht der Gläubiger ihm unverzüglich diese Anzeige macht.
(2) Erfolgt die Anzeige rechtzeitig, so beschränkt sich die Haftung des Bürgen im Falle des Absatzes 1 Satz 1 auf den Umfang, den die Hauptverbindlichkeit zur Zeit der Beendigung des Verfahrens hat, im Falle des Absatzes 1 Satz 2 auf den Umfang, den die Hauptverbindlichkeit bei dem Ablauf der bestimmten Zeit hat.

§ 777 Temporary guarantee

(1) If the surety has provided guarantee for an existing obligation for a specified period of time, then at the end of the specified period of time he is released, unless the creditor effects collection of the claim without undue delay under the provisions of § 772, continues the proceedings without any substantial delay and without undue delay after the end of the proceedings notifies the surety that he is claiming payment from him. If the surety is not entitled to the defence of unexhausted remedies, then he is released at the end of a specified period of time, unless the creditor makes this notification to him without undue delay.
(2) If notification has been made in good time, then the liability of the surety in the case of sub§ (1) sentence 1 is limited to the scope the main obligation has at the time when the proceedings ended, or in the case cited in sub§ (1) sentence 2 to the scope the main obligation has at the end of the specified period of time.

§ 778 Kreditauftrag

Wer einen anderen beauftragt, im eigenen Namen und auf eigene Rechnung einem Dritten ein Darlehen oder eine Finanzierungshilfe zu gewähren, haftet dem Beauftragten für die aus dem Darlehen oder der Finanzierungshilfe entstehende Verbindlichkeit des Dritten als Bürge.

§ 778 Credit mandate

A person who instructs another person to grant a third party a loan or financing assistance in his own name and for his own account is liable as surety to the mandatary for the obligation of the third party arising from the loan or the financing assistance.

Charts

Chart 1: Nominal House Price year on year growth rates
(Q4 2005 to Q4 2008)

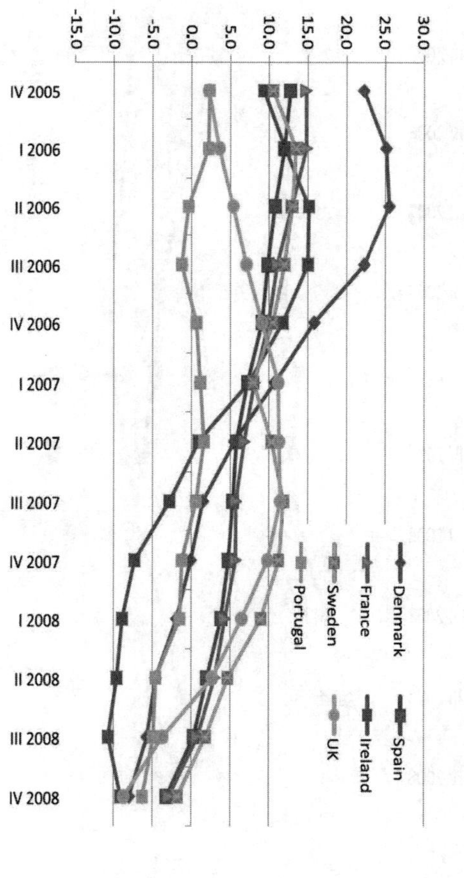

Source: EMF http://www.hypo.org/DocShareNoFrame/docs/2/NNCMCIPDDKOIJNPAJJJLLMFEPDBG9DBYPWTE4Q/EMF/Docs/DLS/2009-00128.pdf

Chart 2: Nominal House Price Index (Q4 2005 0 100%)

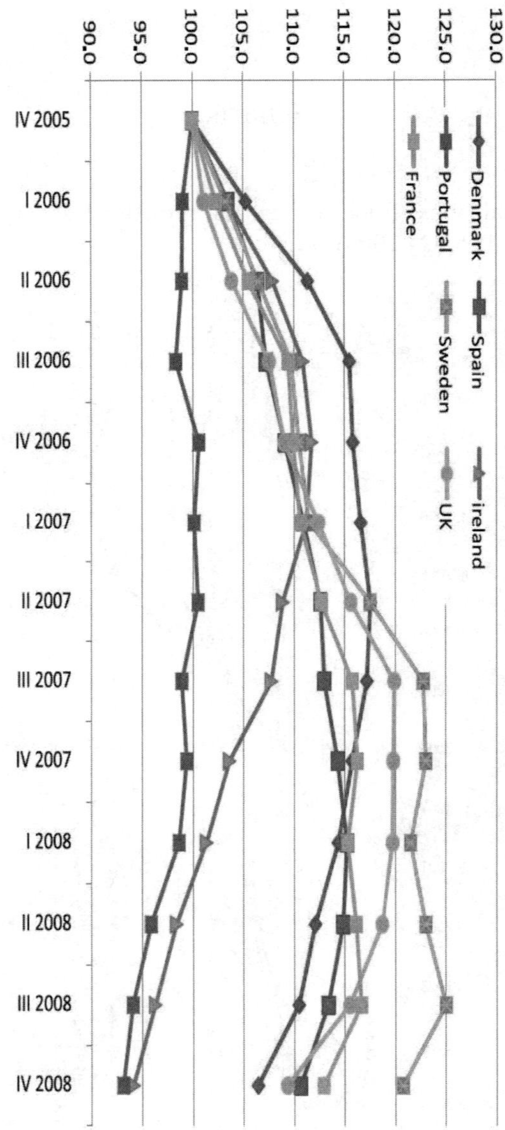

Note: Standardised nominal house price indices on national values
Source: EMF: http://www.hypo.org/DocShareNoFrame/docs/2/NNCMCIPDDKOIJNPAJJJLLMFEPDBG9DBYPWTE4Q/EMF/Docs/DLS/2009-00128.pdf

Chart 3: House Price (national) percentage change

	1998	1999	2000	2001	2002	2003	2004	2005	2006	2007
Belgium	4.8%	6.5%	3.9%	5.1%	7.1%	7.2%	5.5%	16.3%	12.1%	8.1%
Bulgaria	n/a	n/a	n/a	n/a	n/a	n/a	47.6%	36.5%	14.7%	23.2%
Czech Republic	n/a	7.3%	14.4%	6.9%	27.5%	7.0%	0.1%	n/a	n/a	n/a
Denmark	10.6%	8.3%	7.2%	7.9%	5.3%	5.2%	11.7%	17.0%	16.2%	2.0%
Germany	0.0%	0.0%	0.8%	0.0%	-1.6%	-0.8%	-0.8%	-1.7%	-0.9%	1.7%
Estonia	n/a	n/a	n/a	n/a	16.9%	19.7%	42.7%	42.1%	20.9%	7.2%
Greece	14.4%	8.8%	10.6%	14.4%	13.8%	5.4%	2.3%	10.9%	12.2%	3.5%
Spain	5.8%	7.7%	8.6%	9.9%	15.7%	17.6%	17.4%	13.9%	10.4%	5.8%
France	2.9%	7.5%	7.9%	8.1%	9.0%	11.5%	17.6%	14.7%	9.9%	5.7%
Ireland	28.8%	20.4%	15.3%	8.0%	3.6%	14.1%	11.2%	10.6%	13.6%	-7.3%
Italy	2.0%	6.7%	8.6%	7.9%	10.0%	10.7%	n/a	7.3%	8.5%	6.0%
Cyprus	n/a	n/a	n/a	n/a	n/a	n/a	n/a	n/a	10.0%	15.0%
Latvia	n/a	n/a	n/a	n/a	14.0%	17.5%	4.9%	48.6%	n/a	n/a
Lithuania	n/a	n/a	n/a	n/a	n/a	n/a	n/a	n/a	n/a	n/a
Luxembourg	5.2%	6.5%	6.4%	10.4%	9.8%	12.2%	13.6%	11.5%	3.5%	n/a
Hungary	7.8%	30.9%	28.4%	8.6%	-1.1%	n/a	n/a	n/a	n/a	n/a
Malta	8.5%	4.9%	3.2%	5.0%	8.7%	13.3%	20.3%	9.8%	3.5%	1.1%
Netherlands	11.7%	16.2%	16.5%	11.2%	8.5%	5.0%	4.3%	4.3%	4.7%	4.2%
Austria	n/a	n/a	n/a	3.5%	-0.2%	0.4%	-2.8%	4.9%	3.1%	3.7%
Poland	n/a	n/a	7.2%	10.0%	-4.2%	-6.9%	n/a	n/a	n/a	19.3%
Portugal	5.8%	8.6%	8.8%	5.3%	0.7%	1.3%	0.8%	2.7%	2.1%	n/a
Romania	n/a	n/a	n/a	n/a	n/a	n/a	n/a	n/a	n/a	n/a
Slovenia	n/a	n/a	n/a	n/a	n/a	n/a	12.0%	13.4%	15.0%	n/a
Slovakia	n/a	n/a	n/a	n/a	n/a	n/a	n/a	n/a	n/a	24.0%
Finland	10.2%	8.8%	5.9%	-0.9%	7.4%	6.4%	7.1%	6.1%	7.5%	6.0%
Sweden	9.6%	9.2%	11.0%	8.0%	6.3%	6.6%	9.6%	9.6%	11.4%	10.7%
UK	10.9%	11.5%	14.3%	8.4%	17.0%	15.7%	11.8%	5.5%	6.3%	10.9%
Albania	n/a	n/a	n/a	n/a	n/a	n/a	n/a	n/a	n/a	n/a
Iceland	n/a	n/a	n/a	10.6%	4.8%	11.6%	10.5%	28.5%	n/a	14.9%
Norway	8.5%	11.2%	15.7%	7.0%	5.0%	1.7%	10.2%	8.3%	13.1%	12.3%
Russia	n/a	n/a	n/a	n/a	n/a	n/a	n/a	n/a	n/a	n/a
Serbia	n/a	n/a	n/a	n/a	n/a	n/a	n/a	n/a	n/a	n/a
Ukraine	n/a	n/a	n/a	n/a	n/a	n/a	n/a	n/a	n/a	n/a

Source: European Mortgage Federation National Experts, National Statistics Offices

Notes:

n/a: figures not available

Ireland: average price of all residential property approved for mortgage

Source: EMF Hypostat, 2008, p. 66.
http://www.hypo.org/Objects/6/Files/Hypostat%202008%20-%20light%20version.pdf

Chart 4: Credit 2003–2009. Distribution of Credit and expected default

4. ENTIDADES DE CRÉDITO
A) Balance agregado según los estados de supervisión

4.3 Crédito.
Otros sectores residentes.

Millones de euros

	Total (a)	Del cual: A tipo variable	Del cual: En moneda extranjera	Crédito comercial	Deudores con garant. real	Del cual: Con garant. hipotecaria	Otros deudores a plazo: Total	Otros deudores a plazo: Del cual: Adquis. tempor. activos	Otros deudores a plazo: Del cual: Activos financ. híbridos (b)	Deudores a la vista	Arrendamiento financiero	Dudosos (c)	Crédito asumido por el Estado
	1=4+5+7+10+11+12	2	3	4	5	6	7	8	9	10	11	12	13
04	945 697	602 618	7 179	60 249	544 918	531 642	280 811	8 858	...	22 955	29 282	7 484	-
05	R 1 202 617	789 263	8 669	75 361	729 287	709 682	325 290	3 683	33	28 057	34 990	9 631	-
06	1 508 626	1 016 519	11 440	85 376	922 976	883 841	414 589	3 524	14	34 113	40 713	10 859	-
07	1 760 213	1 197 991	15 910	90 842	1 068 372	1 018 785	497 883	6 537	-	40 572	46 293	16 251	-
08	1 869 882	1 248 392	24 896	74 215	1 108 796	1 064 549	529 457	16 070	5	49 128	45 229	63 057	-
09 *Abr*	1 857 844	1 253 196	22 244	58 668	1 104 504	1 060 954	521 951	8 239	5	46 496	42 363	83 862	-
May	1 860 128	1 261 327	21 005	58 451	1 106 115	1 062 838	522 021	11 822	5	45 086	41 720	86 735	-
Jun	1 861 005	1 249 510	20 903	54 653	1 107 918	1 067 288	517 819	18 483	10	54 079	40 938	85 597	-
Jul	1 850 523	1 235 911	20 631	56 290	1 109 868	1 070 078	510 939	13 397	11	45 171	40 260	87 994	-
Ago	1 838 390	1 246 269	20 315	54 106	1 109 196	1 068 976	503 363	14 281	11	41 397	39 443	90 884	-
Sep	1 846 010	1 247 736	19 655	51 109	1 113 100	1 071 398	511 464	23 136	11	41 244	39 358	89 735	-
Oct	1 834 771	1 245 450	19 371	51 329	1 113 842	1 072 314	495 989	12 319	12	43 203	38 885	91 522	-
Nov	1 834 405	1 250 217	18 945	51 054	1 113 978	1 072 585	491 304	12 395	12	47 057	38 422	92 590	-
Dic	1 837 037	1 249 050	17 877	55 263	1 115 828	1 074 976	493 839	23 364	13	40 946	37 833	93 327	-
10 *Ene*	1 816 431	1 246 615	18 539	51 693	1 111 651	1 071 026	476 409	10 774	14	43 191	37 089	96 398	-
Feb	1 818 754	1 247 317	19 021	51 368	1 111 188	1 070 728	480 819	15 354	14	40 758	36 391	98 230	-
Mar	1 827 094	1 249 088	19 296	49 104	1 112 189	1 071 498	494 289	25 226	14	38 062	35 982	97 469	-
Abr	1 818 540	1 248 249	19 442	49 186	1 110 820	1 069 867	484 579	17 471	14	38 541	35 527	99 886	-
May	1 825 044	1 250 975	20 929	48 935	1 111 806	1 071 264	490 370	20 747	14	38 397	35 269	100 266	-
Jun	1 850 230	1 257 912	21 716	49 997	1 115 333	1 075 237	503 494	30 195	14	47 827	34 673	98 906	-
Jul	1 836 403	1 248 714	20 779	51 182	1 112 483	1 072 723	499 437	22 667	14	38 453	34 372	100 475	-
Ago	P 1 825 285	1 249 768	21 437	49 204	1 110 220	1 069 638	493 814	22 055	14	35 716	33 828	102 502	-

Veánse notas al final del capítulo

Source: Banco de España http://www.bde.es/webbde/es/estadis/infoest/a0403.pdf
Column 12 shows those credits expected to default.

Chart 5: Development of total credit to private sector as a percentage of GDP in EU-16 and US

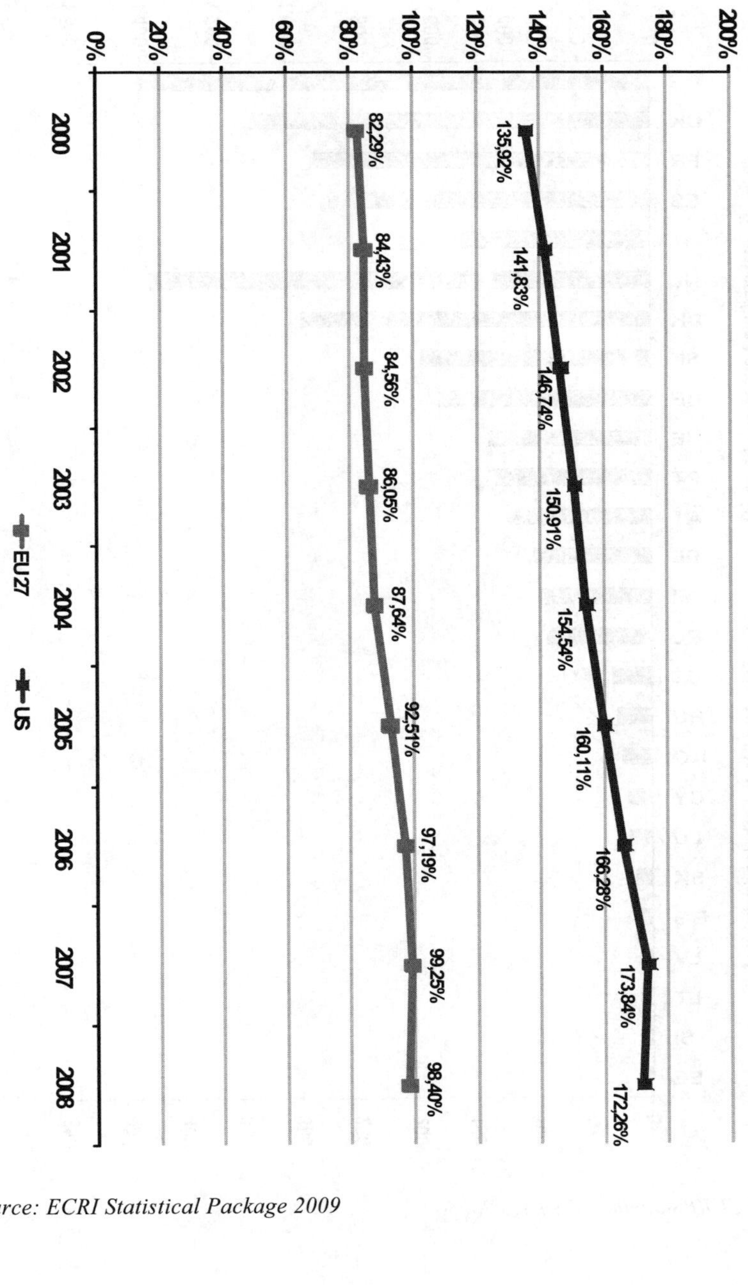

Source: ECRI Statistical Package 2009

Chart 6: Total credit to households in EU-27 in billions of Euro (2007)

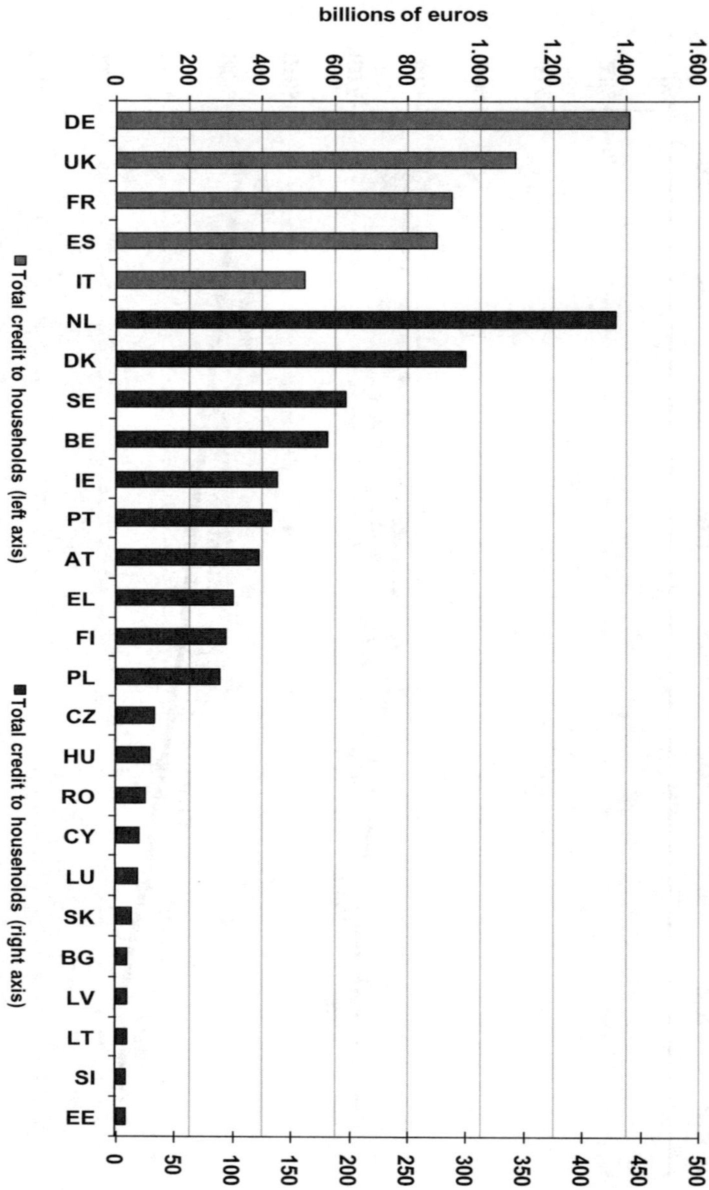

Source: ECRI Statistical Package 2008

Chart 7: Development of total credit to households as a percentage of final consumption expenditure in EU-16 and US

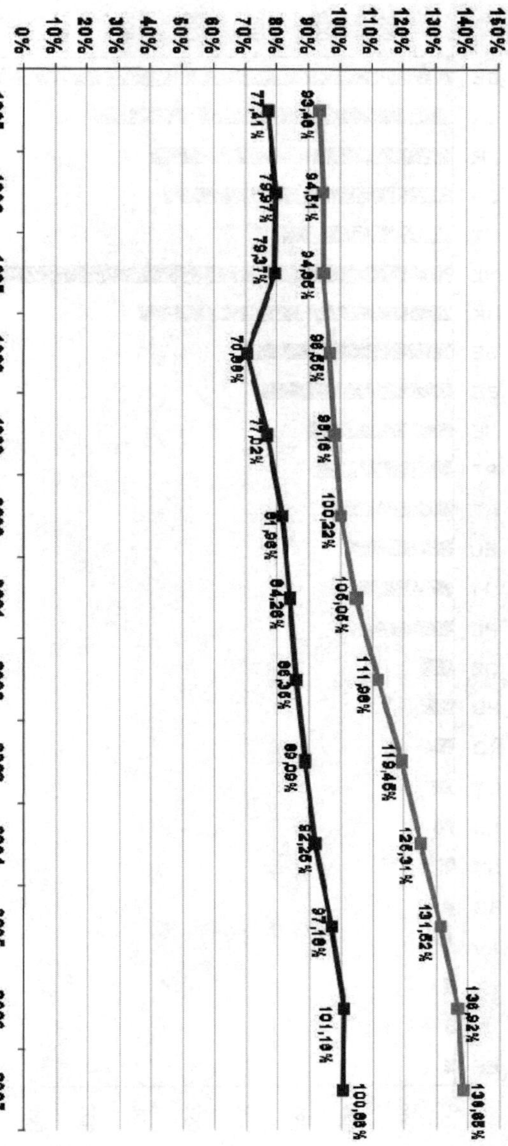

Source: ECRI Statistical Package 2009

Chart 8: Total credit to households in EU-27 in billions of Euro (2008)

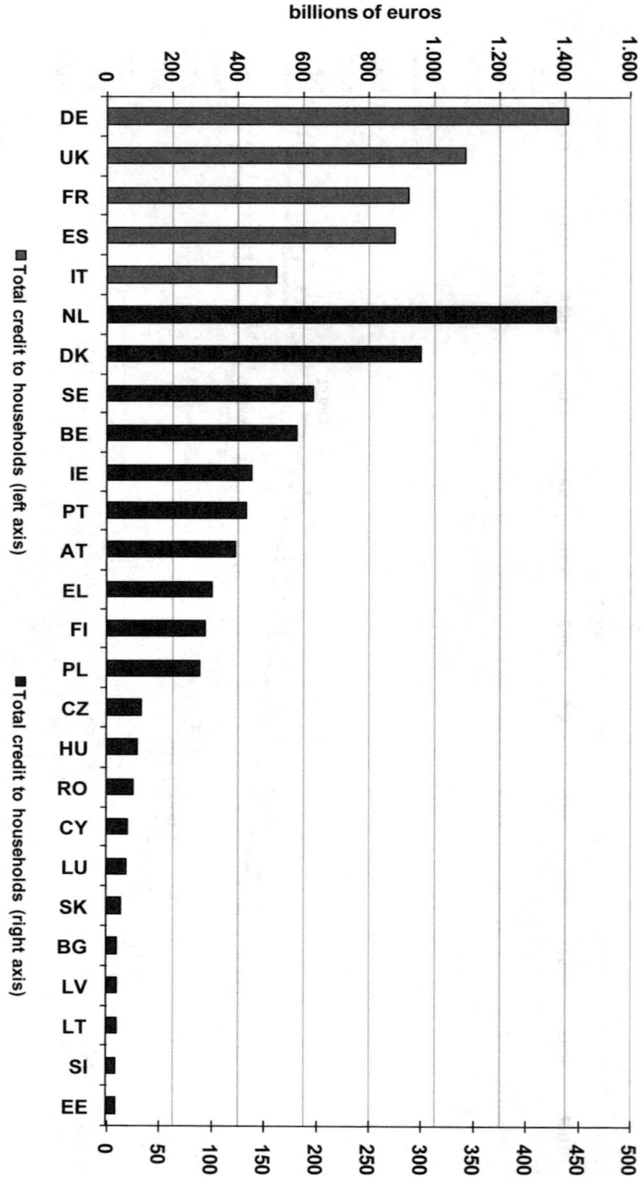

Source: ECRI Statistical Package 2009

Bibliography

Abeyratne, Banking and Debt Recovery in Emerging Markets, Aldershot, 2001.

Abril Campoy, La confusión de derechos, Valencia, 1995.

Adame Martínez, Asunción de deuda en derecho civil, Granada, 1996.

Agostino, Sull'estinzione della fideiussione prevista dall'art. 1956 cc; GI, 1968, I, 1, 334.

ALASECE, Credit insurance and Medium and Small Size Companies in Spain, Boletín /Bulletin No. 7 ALASECE, July 1999 (http://alasece.com/bolentin3.htm).

Albácar, Código Civil, doctrina y jurisprudencia, Madrid, 2000, 709.

Albadalejo, Compendio de derecho civil, Barcelona, 1997.

Alcaro, Fideiussione e garanzie, Rivista di diritto civile, 1983, II, 612 ff.

Alcaro, Il soggetto-banca e la fideiussione omnibus, Rivista di diritto commerciale, 1981, II.

Aletti, Lettere di patronaggio nella pratica bancaria, Università degli Studi dell'Insubria, 2001.

Allara, La fattispecie estintive del rapporto obbligatorio, Torino, 1952.

Almeida Costa, Direito das Obrigações, Coimbra, 1994.

Alonso Sánchez, Protección del fiador en vía de regreso, Madrid, 1993.

Alpa, Istituzione di diritto privato, Torino, 1997.

Alventosa del Rio, La fianza en el ámbito de la responsabilidad, Granada 1988.

Andrews and Millet, Law of guarantees, London, 1992.

Añoveros Trías de Bes, El aval cambiario, Madrid, 1992.

Arcos, El Mandato de Crédito, Pamplona, 1996.

Arija, Notas sobre la eficacia de la cláusula de globalización en los contratos de fianza, Estudios Jurídicos en Homenaje al Profesor Luís Díez-Picazo, t. II., Cívitas, Madrid, 2003.

Aru/D'Amelio e Finzi, Commentario del codice civile II (Della Fideiussione, on art. 1936), Firenze, 1949.

Attanasio/Goldberg/Kyriazidou, Credit Constraints in the Market for Consumer Durables: Evidence from Micro Data on Car Loans, Working Paper 7694, National Bureau of economic research, May 2000 (http://www.nber.org/papers/w7694).

Baldini, La polizza fideiussoria. Escutibilità e clausole vessatorie, Rivista Tidona, April 2001 (http://www. Tidona.com/versionestampa/stampa_aprile01_2.htm).

Ballarín and Cuñat, Estudios sobre jurisprudencia bancaria, esp. Fianza bancaria y suspensión de pagos, Pamplona, 2000.

Barasi, La teoria generale delle obbligazioni, I, Milano, 1948.

Barbero, Sistema Istituzionale del diritto privato italiano, II, Torino, 1958.

Barbiera, Inefficacia parziale della fideiussione omnibus, Rivista di diritto civile, 1991, I.

Barbiera, Autonomia privata e garanzie reali: un rapporto difficile, sclerotizato da chiusure specialistiche e da dogmi tradizionali passivamente accettati, La civilistica

italiana dagli anni '50 ad oggi tra crisi dogmatica e riforme legislative (Congresso dei civilisti italiani, Venezia 23–26 giugno 1989), Padova, 1991.
Basozabal, El contrato de asunción de deuda, Anuario de Derecho Civil, 2000, 83 ff.
Benfatti/Munari, Fideiussione omnibus e buona fede, La deroga agli artt. 1956 e 1957 c.c., Milano, 1992.
Bercovitz, Comentarios al CC y Compilaciones Forales, Pamplona, 2000.
Bianca, Diritto civile, V (La responsabilità), Milano, 1994.
Bigus/Langer/Schiereck, Wie werden Kreditsicherheiten in der Praxis eingesetzt? – Ein Überblick über empirische Befunde. Zeitschrift für Bankrecht und Bankwirtschaft 16, 2004, 465–480.
Big*us/Langer/Schiereck*, Warum gibt es Kreditsicherheiten? Kredit und Kapital 38(4), 2005, 573–617.
Bank of International Settlement, Joint forum, Credit Risk Trasfer Developments 2005 to 2007, 2008.
Bank of International Settlement, Housing finance in the global financial market, CGSF Paper, no. 26, 2006.
Bank of International Settlement, Committee on the global financial system, Credit Risk Transfer, 2003.
Bisconti, Assunzione di debito e garanzia del credito, Napoli, 1993.
Biscontini, Solidarietà fideiussoria e "decadenza", Napoli, 1980.
Biscontini/Perlingieri, Codice civile commentato (Commento art. 1937), Napoli, Bologna, 1991.
Blanco, Aval cambiario y aval como contrato de garantía, Revista de Derecho Bancario y Bursátil, no.7, 1982, 677 ff.
Blanco/Sánchez-Calero and Sánchez-Calero Guilarte, Comentarios a la jurisprudencia de derecho bancario y cambiario v. I (Aval cambiario y aval como contrato de garantía), Madrid, 1993.
Bo, Nuovo Digesto Italiano (voce Fideiussione), Torino, 1937–1940.
Bo, Sulla gratuità del contratto di fideiussione, Diritto Commerciale, 1937, 22 ff.
Bo, Contributto alla dottrina dell'obbligazione fideiussoria, Milano, 1934.
Bo, Note sulla forma della fideiussione, Foro Italiano, 1937, I, 321 ff.
Bonell, The Unidroit Principles in Practice: Caselaw and Bibliography on the Unidroit Principles of International Commercial Contracts, New York 2006.
Bonell, An international restatement of contract law: the UNIDROIT Principles of International Commercial Contracts, N.Y. 2005.
Bonvicini, La responsabilità civile, Milano, 1973, v. III.
Bouza, Las garantías mobiliarias en el comercio internacional, Madrid, 1991.
Bozzi, La fideiussione, Milano, 1995.
Bozzi, L'autonomia negoziale nel sistema delle garanzie personali, Napoli, 1990.
Bozzi, Enciclopedia giuridica, (voce Fideiussione omnibus), XV, Roma, 1993.
Bozzi/Rescigno, Trattato di diritto privato, v. 13, Obbligazioni e contratti, (La fideiussione, le figure affini e l'anticresi), Torino, 1985, 205–294.
Briganti, Rapporti atipici nell'esperienza negoziale (Garanzie personali atipiche), Milano, 1988.
Briganti, Fideiussione e promessa del fatto altrui, Napoli, 1981.
Boetius, Der Garantievertrag, Diss. München, 1966.
Buckland, A Textbook of Roman Law, London, 1963.
Burke, Brussels I regulation (EC) 44/2001: application to financial services under article 5(1)(B), 2004 (http.//ssrn.com/abstract=1159014).

Broekhuizen/Drobnig/Sagel-Grande/Snijders, Neuere Entwicklungen im Recht der persönlichen Kreditsicherheiten in Deutschland und in den Niederlanden (Suretyship and independent guarantees under Dutch law), 2003, 93 ff.

Brink/Bärmann, Recht der Kreditsicherheiten in europäischen Ländern, Teil I: Bundesrepublik Deutschland, Berlin, 1976.

Busccisano, Enciclopedia giuridica, XXI, (voce: Novazione) Roma, 1990.

Bussani, Il modello italiano delle garanzie reali, Contratto e impresa, Milano, 1997, 165 ff.

Cabrillac and Mouly, Droit des Sûretés, Paris, 2002.

Caffarena Laporta, La solidaridad de deudores, Madrid, 1980.

Calderale, Fideiussione e Contratto autonomo di garanzia, Bari, 1989.

Camacho de los Ríos, Comentario a la Sentencia del Tribuna Supremo de 25 de febrero de 1994, La Ley, 30 de septiembre de 1994.

Camacho de los Ríos/Nieto/Bonet, Tratado de garantías en la contratación mercantil, v. 1 (El seguro de caución), Madrid, 1996.

Campogrande, Trattato de la fideiussione nell diritto moderno, Torino, 1902.

Concordato cauzione, credito, Mercato, cauzione e credito in Italia (http://www.concordato.it/ccmerca.htm).

Cano Rico, Manual práctico de la contratación mercantil, v. I, Madrid, 1999.

Cantillo/Munari, Fideiussione omnibus e buona fede, (La buona fede nella fideiussione "omnibus" secondo l'attuale orientamento della Corte di cassazione), Milano, 1992.

Caouette et al., Managing credit risk: the great challenge for global financial markets, Hoboken, New Jersey, 2008.

Caprio/Presti, Le garanzie nel credito alle imprese, Funzione economica, disciplina giuridica ed evidenze empiriche, Torino, 2001.

Carpino/Sauveplan, Real securities over corporeal movables (Italian Law in Security over corporeal movables), Leiden, 1974.

Caruana, Keynote address, 20th Annual General Meeting. ISDA (International Swaps and Derivatives Association), Barcelona, 16 March 2005.

Carrasco, Comentario a la STS de 19 de mayo de 1990, Cuadernos cívitas de jurisprudencia civil, no. 23, 1990.

Carrasco, Fianza, accesoriedad y contrato de garantía, Madrid, 1992 (spec. "Aplicación generalizada de las normas de la fianza", 51–64).

Carrasco, Cordero and González, Derecho de la construcción y la vivienda, Madrid, 2000.

Carrasco, Cordero and González, Comentarios a la Ley de Ordenación de la Edificación, Pamplona, 2001.

Carrasco, Cordero and Marín, Tratado de los derechos de garantía, Pamplona, 2002.

Casanova Mussons, La relación obligatoria de la fianza, Barcelona, 1984.

Castán, Derecho civil español, común y foral, Madrid, v. I, 1969.

Cavatorta, Garanzie fideiussorie e attività assicurative, XV Congresso Regionale della Sezione Piemonte-Val d'Aosta dell Aida, Stressa, 24–25 ottobre 1981, 11 ff.

Cherednychenko, The harmonisaton of contract law in Euorpe by means of the horizontal effect of fundamental rights, (http://ssrn.com/abstract=1026206).

Cian/Trabucchi, Commentario breve al Codice Civile, Padova, 1992.

Cicu, Estinzione di rapporti giuridici per confusione, Sassari, 1908.

Cohan, The form of contract of guarantee in Comparative Law, 54 Law Quarterly Review, 1938, 220 ff.

Colas, Efectos del contrato de fiaza: Relaciones entre Acreedor, Deudor principal y fiador, Cuadernos de Aranzadi Civil, Navarra, 2007.

Colombi Ciacchi, Protection of Non-Professional Sureties in Europe: Formal and Substantive Disparity, 2007.
Colombi Ciacchi, The Constitutionalization of European Contract Law, European Review of Contract Law, no. 2, 2006, 167.
Colombi Ciacchi, Non Legislative harmonisation of private law under European Constitution: the Case of Unfair Suretyship, European Law Review of Private Law, no. 13, 2005, 285 f.
Constadaky, Le mandat du crédit, Paris, 1932.
Cools, Letter of the Ministry of Finance, Financial Supervisory Authority, Bank of Finland, to the European Commission, Letter 1 (26), 23rd October 2003. (http://rahoitustarkastus.fi/NR/rdonlyres/D4629E98-37D0-4270-9D23-269F2AE5449C/0/221003 .pdf)
Cossio, Instituciones de derecho civil, v. I, Madrid, 1975.
Costanza, Fideiussione omnibus: clausole in deroga all'art. 1956 c.c. Invalidità o inefficacia?, Giustizia Civile, 1992, I, 221 ff.
Cristóbal Montes, La cofianza, Madrid, 1993.
Cristóbal Montes, La obligación derivada de la confianza, Revista crítica de derecho inmobiliario, no. 660, 2000, 2257 ff.
Cristóbal Montes, El beneficio de la división en la confianza, Revista crítica de derecho inmobiliario, no. 676, 2003, 887 ff.
Dagot, Les sûretés, Paris, 1981.
Dagot, Sûretés réelles contre sûretés personnelles, Juris-classeur périodique, Edition notariale, 1986, I, 93.
Dam, Credit Markets, Creditors' Rights and Economic Development, The Law School the University of Chicago, February 2006.
D'Amelio and Finzi, Libro delle obbligazioni, I, Firenze, 1948.
Distaso, Enciclopedia di diritto, (voce Beneficio di escussione), V, Milano, 1959.
De Angulo, Panorama de encuadre de las garantías personales atípicas, Revista jurídica del notariado, no. 7, 1993, 9–32.
de la Mata, Un paso más hacia la unificación del derecho privado europeo. Comunicación de la Comisión de 15 de Marzo de 2003 sobre un derecho contractual europeo más coherente, Aranzadi Civil, 2003.
de la Mata, The EU Parliament rejects the EU Commission's proposal for the Consumer Credit Directive and requires withdrawal, CEPS/ECRI, September 2003.
de la Mata, European Parliament Committees to present an alternative Consumer Credit Directive proposal, CEPS/ECRI, January 2004.
de la Mata, The European Parliament to vote at a plenary session on the amendments to the draft Consumer Credit Directive, CEPS/ECRI, April 2004.
de la Mata, Two steps further in the Consumer Credit Directive procedure, CEPS/ECRI, July 2004.
de la Mata, Waiting for the EU Commission's amended proposal, CEPS/ECRI, October 2004.
de la Mata, Developments in the Consumer Credit Directive, CEPS/ECRI Research Fellow, December 2004.
de la Mata/Lanoo, Integration of the EU Consumer Credit Market. Proposal for a More Efficient Regulatory Model, CEPS working paper, no. 214, 2004.
de la Mata, The EU Commission amends its Proposed Consumer Credit Directive, CEPS/ECRI, European Voice, December 2004/January 2005.
de la Mata, The EU Commission publishes on 28 October the amended version of the Consumer Credit Directive, CEPS/ECRI, January 2005.

de la Mata, Household's overindebtedness in the EU today. CEPS Policy Brief, May 2005.

De Marchi, Onerosità e gratuità dell'avallo e delle garanzie personali in generale, Rivista di Diritto Civile, 1958, I, 637 ff.

De Marco and Sparano, La fideiussione bancaria, Milano, 1981.

De Maria/Franzoni, Il Codice Civile commentato con la giurisprudenza, on art. 1269, Bologna, 1999, 868.

De Martini, Obbligazione principale annullabile e fideiussione valida, nota a Cass. 28 febbraio 1944 no. 120, Giur. Compl. Cass. Civile, 1944, 487.

De Martino, Novissimo Digesto Italiano, (Fideiussione (diritto romano)), v. II and VII Torino, 1961, 272.

De Nictolis, Nuove garanzie personali e reali, Padova, 1998.

Deiana, Attribuzioni indirette ed attribuzioni onerose nel contratto di fideiussione, Rivista di Diritto Civile, 1939, 441 ff.

Delgado, Elementos de derecho civil, Madrid, 1979.

Derleder, Die unbegrenzte Kreditbürgschaft, NJW 1986, 97–109.

Diamond, A Review of Security Interests in Property, HMSO, 27th of January, 1999, London.

Di Majo/Munari, Fideiussione omnibus e buona fede (Clausola "omnibus" nella fideiussione e buona fede), Milano, 1992.

Di Sabato, Fideiussione e negozi di assunzione del debito altrui: criteri di interpretazione, Rivista di Diritto Civile, 1969, I, 500.

Di Prisco/Rescigno, Tratatto di dirito privato, Obbligazioni e contratti I (I modi di estinzione delle obbligazioni diversi dall'adempimento), Torino, 1984, 297 ff.

Díez-Picazo, La prescripción en el Código Civil, Barcelona, 1964.

Díez-Picazo, La representación en el Derecho Privado, Madrid, 1979.

Díez-Picazo, Fundamentos de derecho civil patrimonial v. II (Las relaciones obligatorias), Madrid, 1993.

Dolmetta, Sulla vessatorietà della clausola di rinuncia alla decandenza ex art. 1957 cc, Banca borsa e titoli di credito, 1989, II, 412 ff.

Donati, Natura giuridica delle c.d. polizza fideiussorie, Banca borsa e titoli di credito, 1957, I, 75.

Drobnig, Mobiliarsicherheiten – Vielfalt oder Einheit? Vergleichender Generalbericht in: Kreuzer, Mobiliarsicherheiten – Vielfalt oder Einheit?, Baden-Baden, 1999.

Draft Common Frame of Reference (DCFR), Principles, Definitions and Model Rules of European Private Law. Outline Edition, Munich 2009.

Drobnig/Sagel-Grande/Snijders, Neuere Entwicklungen im Recht der persönlichen Kreditsicherheiten in Deutschland und in den Niederlanden (Suretyship and independent guarantees under Dutch law), 2003, 93 ff.

Drobnig et al., Principles of European Law, Study Group on a European Civil Code, Personal Security (PEL Pers.Sec.), 2007.

Dyke, Recent Developments in the Mortgage Industry, 2007 (http://www.cubefarmco.com/pdfs/RecentDev_Clip.pdf).

Economic Stabilization Advisory Group Governmental Assistance to the Financial Sector: an Overview of the Global Responses (v. 3), December 19, 2008.

Economic Stabilization Advisory Group, Governmental Assistance to the Financial Sector: an Overview of the Global Responses (v. 2), November 26, 2008.

Elizalde/Repullo, Economic and Regulatory Capital in Banking: What is the Difference?, CEMFI and UPNA, July 2006.

Embid, El seguro de caución: el régimen jurídico convencional y naturaleza jurídica, La Ley, no. 2954, 6 ff.

Embid/Alonso Ureba/Martínez-Simancas, Instituciones del mercado financiero v. IV, (El seguro de caución), 1999, 1851 ff.

Embid, Commentary to the STS 21 April 1989 [RA 1989 no. 3248], La Ley 1990, II, 198.

Embid, Commentary to the STS 5 June 1992 [RA 1992 no. 5002], Cuadernos cívitas de jurisprudencia civil, 1992, § 776.

European Mortgage Federation (EMF) Hypostat (statistics report) 2008.

Seiler/Erman, Bürgerliches Gesetzbuch: Handkommentar mit AGBG, EGBGB, ErbbauVO, HausratsVO; HausTWG, ProdHaftG, SachenRBerG, SchuldRAnpG, VerbrKrG, Münster/Cologne, 2000.

Espinosa Goedert, Mandato de crédito. „El Mandatum pecunia credendae" en el Derecho Romano, Barcelona, 1994.

EU Commission, Towards a common operational definition of over-indebtedness, February, 2008. (http://Ec.europa.eu/employment_social/spsi).

Fahri de Montalbán, Sociedades de garantía recíproca, Revista electrónica de derecho Societario, no. 1, Abril 2000 (http://www.societario.com/revista/1/doctrina/sgrdiana-i.htm).

Fauvarque Cosson/Mazeauad, Projet de cadre commune de référence. Terminologie contractuelle commune, Paris 2008.

Falaschi, L'art. 1956 cc; Fideiussione e mandato di credito, Foro Italiano, 1958, IV, 187.

Falcón, Exposición de derecho civil común y foral, v. IV, 1889.

Farré, Código Civil comentado y concordado, Barcelona, 2000.

Fernández/Nieto/Bonet, Tratado de Garantías en la contratación mercantil (El mandato de crédito) Madrid, 1996, 832.

Fernández, Commentary to the STS 23 February 2000 [RA 2000 no. 1242], Cuadernos cívitas de jurisprudencia civil 53 [2000] § 1451.

Ferrara, Trattato di diritto civile italiano, I, Roma, 1921.

Ferri, Onerosità delle garanzie prestate successivamente al credito garantito, II, 1975.

Fínez Ratón, La extinción de la fianza como sanción al comportamiento del acreedor (estudio del art. 1852 del Código Civil), Revistra Crítica de Derecho Inmobiliario, no. 614, 1992, 9 ff.

Fínez Ratón, La prórroga forzosa como causa de extinción de la fianza (análisis del art. 1851 CC) RJN, 1993, 94.

Fleisig, The Right to Borrow, in The World Bank: View Point, Note 44, April, 1995 (http://www.worldbank.org/html/fpd/notes/44/44summary.html).

Fleisig, The Power of Collateral, Finance & Development, June 1996 (http://www.worldbank.org/fandd/english/pdfs/0696/0150696.pdf or http://www.worldbank.org/html/fpd/notes/43/43fleisig.html).

Fletcher, The Law of Insolvency, 2. ed. London, 1996.

Font, Comentario a la STS de 16 de febrero de 1983, Cuadernos cívitas de jurisprudencia civil, no. 1, 1983, 243.

Fragali, Fideiussione e assicurazioni, Banca borsa e titoli di credito, 1956, I, 135 ff.

Fragali/Scialoja/Branca, Commentario al Codice Civile (Della Fideiussione on art. 1936 –1959), Bologna-Roma, 1957.

Fragali, Confideiussione e pluralità di fideiussioni autonome, Banca borsa e titoli di credito, 1963, I, 196 ff.

Fragali, L'azione del debitore contro il creditore garantito da fideiussione, Banca borsa e titoli di credito, 1967, I, 508 ff.

Fragali, L'inerzia del creditore nelle fideiussione solidale. Studi in memoria di Tullio Ascarelli. V. II. Milano, 1969, 744.

Francisco, El seguro de caución, 5campus.org, Finanzas, 2000 (http://www.5campus.org/leccion/segucau).

Franzoni, Il Codice Civile commentato con la giurisprudenza, Bologna, 1999.

Friedmann and Barak-Erez, Human Rights in Private Law, Oxford, 2001.

Freitag, Kein Rückzahlungsanspruch des auf erstes Anfordern zahlenden Bürgen bei lediglich geschuldeter unbefristeter selbstschuldnerischer Bürgschaft, BGH 23. 1. 2003 – VII ZR 210/01, EWiR 2003, 699/700.

Freitag, Abgrenzung der gegenständlich beschränkten Bürgschaft von der Zeitbürgschaft, BGH 15. 1. 2004 – IX ZR 152/00, WuB I F. 1 a. Bürgschaft 7.04.

Freitag, Vorzeitige Rückzahlung und Vorfälligkeitsentschädigung nach der Reform der Verbraucherkreditrichtlinie, ZIP 2008, 1102–1110.

Gabrielli, Autonomia privata e diritto comune europeo delle garanzie mobiliari, Rivista Critica Diritto Privato, 1995, 643 ff.

Galbraith, Il nuevo Stato industriale, Torino, 1968.

Galgano, Diritto Civile e Commerciale, II, (Le Obbligazioni e i contratti, 2) Padova, 1993.

Gandolfi/Gatt, Code européen des contrats: avant-projet, Milano 2004.

Gambino, Fideiussione, "fideiussion indemnitatis" e polizza fideiussoria, Rivista di diritto commerciale, 1960, II, 57.

García Cortés/Nieto/Bonet, Tratado de Garantías en la contratación mercantil (El aval cambiario), v. 1, Madrid, 1996, 508 ff.

García Goyena, Concordancias, motivos y comentarios del código civil español, Zaragoza, 1974.

García Medina, La doctrina jurisprudencial del art. 1852 del Código Civil y la extinción de la fianza, Boletín Aranzadi Civil-Mercantil num. 47/2002, 2003.

Garrido, Preferenza e proporzionalità nella tutela del credito, Milano, 1998

Garrido, Garantías reales, privilegios y par condicio, Centro de Estudios Registrales, Madrid, 1999, 25–66.

Geri, Ulteriore osservazioni in temi di assicurazioni cauzionale e loro natura, Assicurazioni, 1969, II, 127 ff.

Girino, Fideiussione e scadenza dell'obbligazione principale, Rivista di Diritto Civile, 1971, I, 544 ff.

Giuliani/Franzoni, Il codice civile commentato con la giurisprudenzia, Bologna, 1999.

Giusti, La fideiussione e il mandato di credito, Milano, 1998.

Glöckner, Ausgleich zwischen mehreren Bürgen bei unterschiedlichen Höchstbetragsbeschränkungen, Zeitschrift für Wirtschaftsrecht, 1999, no. 20, 821.

González Porrai, Commentarios al Código Civil y Compilaciones forales, XVI, 1980.

Gómez-Salvago, Subrogación del cofiador que paga la deuda afianzada, en la preferencia que correspondía al crédito principal frente a los cofiadores. Comentario a la STS de 11 de junio de 2004. Revista de Derecho Procesal, 2005.

Goode, Principles of Corporate Insolvency Law, 2. ed., London, 1997.

Goode, Consumer Credit Law and Practice, 2001, (Binder 1, IC [37.2]/1892).

Gordillo, Comentario al Código civil, Ministerio de Justicia, v. II, Madrid, 1993.

Glantz/Mun, The banker's handbook on credit risk: implementing Basel II, Burlington, 2008.

Grana, Determinabilità de l'oggetto e giudizio di buona fede nella fideiussione omnibus, Contratto e impresa, 1985, 749 ff.

Graziani, Il mandato di credito, Rivista di Diritto Commerciale, 1932, I, 322.

Grossi, Istituzioni di diritto privato e tradizione romanistica, Quaderni Fiorentini, XIII, Milano, 1984, 651 ff.
Grunert, Kreditsicherheiten: eine Umfrage zu deren Häufigkeit, den erzielten Verwertungserlösen und der Bewertungsfrequenz, Zeitschrift für Bankrecht und Bankwirtschaft, 21, 2009, 2, 126–135.
Guilarte, Notas sobre la cofianza y su régimen en el Código civil español, Revista de Derecho Privado, 1975, 891–920.
Guilarte/Albadalejo, Comentarios al Código Civil y Legislaciones Forales, Madrid, 1990.
Guilarte, Comentario del Código Civil, v. II (De la fianza), Ministerio de Justicia. Madrid, 1991.
Gullón, Curso de Derecho Civil (Contratos en especial), Madrid, 1972.
Gullón, Sobre el artículo 1844 del Código Civil, Centenario del Código Civil I, 1990, 1030 ff.
Guide to Credit Scoring, Office of Fair Trading, London, 1993.
Habersack, Münchener Kommentar zum Bürgerlichen Gesetzbuch, 1997, on § 776.
Hémard, Les sûretés personnelles en Europe occidentale au XIX et au XX siècles. Rapport général, in Les sûretés personnelles (Recueils de la société Jean Bodin pour l'histoire comparative des institutions, 30), III, Bruxelles, 1969.
Hermannsdorfer, Seguros privados, Madrid, 1933.
Horn/Staudinger, Kommentar zum Bürgerlichen Gesetzbuch mit Einführungsgesetz und Nebengesetzen, Zweites Buch, Recht der Schuldverhältnisse, §§ 765–778, Berlin, 1997.
Infante, Un equívoco del TS: extinción de la fianza por fusión de la sociedad acreedora beneficiaria. Un inútil arrebato conceptualista: fianza y aval son contratos diferentes, Revista de Derecho Patrimonial, num. 5/2000, Navarra 2000.
Infante, Commentary on the STS 23 February 2000 [RA 2000 no. 1242], Revista de Derecho Privado, June, 2001, 201 ff.
Ippolito, Assicurazione di responsabilità e polizza c.d. fideiussoria, Assicurazioni, 1985, 94.
Jahn, Bills of Exchange. A guide to legislation in European Countries, International Chamber of Commerce, 1990.
Jahn, Wechselrecht Europa, 2. ed., Köln, 1993.
Jestaz, Cautionnement, Répertoire de Droit Civil, Dalloz, II, Paris, 1971.
Jimenez Mancha, La compensación de créditos, Madrid, 1999.
Jones, Roman law bases of suretyship in Some Modern Civil Codes, Tulane Law Review no. 52, 1977, 129–155.
Kaser, Das römische Privatrecht, München, 1960.
Katz, An economic analysis of the guaranty contract, University of Chicago Law Review, 1999, 47–116.
Knütel, Festschrift für Flume, 1978, I, 559 ff.
Lacruz, Elementos de derecho civil II, Barcelona, 1986.
Lalaguna, Curso de derecho civil II, Derecho de obligaciones, Valencia, 1999.
Lambsdorff and Skora, Handbuch des Bürgschaftsrechts, München, 1994.
Lando et al., eds., Principles of European Contract Law. Part III, The Hague 2003.
Lando/Beale, eds., Principles of European Contract Law. Parts I and II Revised, The Hague 2000; Black letter rules in several language versions are available at http://frontpage.cbs.dk/law/commission_on_european_contract_law/index.html.
Lanno/de la Mata, Integration of the EU Consumer Credit Market. Proposal for a More Efficient Regulatory Model, CEPS working paper, no. 214, 2004.

Lanzillo, Regole del mercato e congruità dello scambio contrattuale, Contratto e impresa, 1985, 341 f.

Lasarte, Principios de derecho civil, v. III, Madrid, 1994, 398.

León, El Mandato de crédito, Revista de Derecho Privado, 1982, 1077–1083.

Lehmbecker, The Quality of Eligible Collateral and Monetary Stability: An Empirical Analysis, Europäische Hochschulschriften, Reihe 5: Volks- und Betriebswirtschaft, Vol. 3300, 2008.

Lepach, Die persönliche Kreditsicherheiten unter besonderer Berücksichtigung der Bürgschaft im deutschen und spanischen Recht, Hamburg, 1987.

Levitzky, SME Guarantee Schemes: A summary, The financier, Vol. 4, no. 1&2 February/May 1997 (http://www.the-financier.com).

Llebot, Las garantías en los procedimientos concursales, Madrid, 2000.

Luminoso, Enciclopedia Giuridica, XXVI, (voce Remissione del debito) Roma, 1991.

Machauer/Weber, Bank Behavior based on internal credit ratings of borrowers, CFS Working Paper No. 98/98, 2008.

Magee/Serbein, Property and Liability Insurance, 4. ed., Homewood, 1967.

Mankowski/Magnus, European Commentary on Brussels I Regulation, Hamburg, 2007

Malaury and Aynès, Droit civil – Les sûretés, Paris, 1994.

Manresa, Comentarios al Código Civil, XII, Madrid, 1970.

Mastropaolo, I contratti autonomi di garanzia, Torino, 1989.

Mariconda, Fideiussione "omnibus" e principio di buona fede: la Cassazione a confronto, Foro Italiano, 1989, I, 3102 ff.

Marty and Reynaud, Droit Civil III, 1, Les sûretés. La publicité foncière, Paris, 1971.

Mather, Securities Acceptable to the Lending Banker, London, 1960.

Mazza/Franzoni, Il Codice Civile commentato con la giurisprudenza, Bologna, 1999, 1430.

Mc Guiness, Law of guarantees, Toronto, 1986.

Medina, Nuevas y especiales formas de garantía en el comercio, Madrid, 2009.

Mellado/Nieto/Bonet, Tratado de garantías en la contratación mercantil, v. 1 (La fianza en el derecho foral español), Madrid, 1996, 186.

Messineo, Manuale di diritto civile, v. III, Milano, 1972.

Miccio, Commentario al Codice Civile, IV, (Della fideiussione, on art. 1944, Torino, 1966, 527.

Molle, I titoli di credito bancari, Milano, 1972, 187.

Molle/Cicu/Messineo, Trattato di diritto civile e commerciale (I contratti bancari), Milano, 1981.

Montés/Valpuesa, Derecho de obligaciones y contratos, Valencia, 1994.

Moralejo, Accesoriedad y subsidiariedad en las garantías a primer requerimiento. (A propósito de la SRS de 17 de febrero de 2000), Revista de Derecho Mercantil no. 240, Abril/Junio, Madrid, 2001, esp. 685–687.

Morales, Creditism: World Credit Economy, Paper presented at the annual meeting of the American Sociological Association, Hilton San Francisco & Renaissance Parc 55 Hotel, San Francisco, CA, Aug 14, 2004 (http://www.allacademic.com/meta/p110123_index.html)

Moreno, Código civil y jurisprudencia concordada, Madrid, 1996, 915.

Moretti/Nicita/Visalli, Giurisprudenza sistematica civile e commerciale fondata da Bigiavi (Sequestro convenzionale. Fideiussione, Mandato di credito. Anticresi. Transazione. Cessione dei beni ai creditori), Torino, 1980, 82 ff.

Moscati, Lo Stato fideiussore, Rivista di Diritto Civile, 1981, I, 94 ff.

Mouillart, Hypothèque ou caution (de la garantie à la réassurance), Banque, 1989, 906.

Mouly, Droit des Sûretés, Paris, 2001.
Mungari, L'assicurazione dei rischi finanziari (garanzie creditizie e fideiussorie: disciplina e prospettive di reforma), Assicurazione, 1983, 654 ff.
Muñoz de Dios, El fraude en la compraventa de viviendas futuras y posibles soluciones preventivas, Revista de Derecho Privado, 1981, 1067.
Nappi, Fideiussione temporalmente delimitata (Zeitbürgschaft) ed art. 1957 cc., Banca borsa e titoli di credito, 1995, II, 564 ss.
Nieto/Bonet, Tratado de garantías en la contratación mercantil, v. 1, Madrid, 1996.
Norman, European Community law: the national law of the member states. 4. Netherlands; Institute of Advanced Legal Studies Library: Collection Development, 2001 (http://ials.sas.ac.uk/library/guides/research/res_neth.htm). Also published in IALS Bulletin Issue 9 Autumn 1991.
Nuñez Zorrilla, La problemática actual de las denominadas garantías independientes o autónomas, Madrid, 2001.
Phillips and O'Donovan, The Modern Contract of Guarantee, 2. ed., Sydney, 1992.
Phillipson, Development of the roman law of debt security, Stanford Law Review, no. 20, 1968, 1230.
Pellegrini/D'Amelio e Finzi, Commentario al codice civile, Libro delle obbligazioni, I, (Dei modi di estinzione delle obbligazioni diversi dall'adempimento), Firenze, 1948, 142 ff.
Perlingieri, Manuale di diritto civile, Napoli, 1997.
Pérez Alvarez, Solidaridad en la fianza, Pamplona, 2. ed., 1985
Perlingieri/Sialoja/Branca, Commentario del codice civile (Dei modi di estinzione delle obbligazioni diversi dall'adempimento (art. 1230–1259)), Bologna-Roma, 1975, 438 ff.
Petit-Dutaillis and Bernard, Les crédit et les banques, Paris, 1964.
Petti, La fideiussione e le garanzie personali del credito, Padova, 2000.
Piazza, Enciclopedia giuridica, XIV, (voce Garanzia), Roma, 1989, 1.
Puig Peña, Tratado de Derecho Civil Español, v. IV, 2, Madrid, 1946.
Polo, Commentary to the STS 22 Dec. 1941 [RA 1941 no. 1400] Revista de Derecho Privado, 1942, 414 ff.
Principles of European Contract Law: von Bar, Benevolent intervention in another's affairs (PEL Ben. Int.), Munich 2006; Hesselink et al., Commercial agency, franchise and distribution contracts (PEL CAFDC), Munich 2006; Barendrecht et al., Service contracts (PEL SC), Munich 2007; Dobnig, Personal security (PEL Pers. Sec.), Munich 2007; Hondius, Sales (PEL S), Munich 2008; Lilleholt et al., Lease of goods (PEL LG), Munich 2008. More information at www.sgecc.net.
Ramón, La distinción entre cofianza y pluralidad de fianzas independientes, Revista internauta de práctica jurídica, no.5, May–June, 2000, (http://www.uv.es/~ripj/5cof .htm).
Rapone, Note to the Supreme Court decision: Cass. 9 April 1990, no. 2965, Giurisprudenzia Italiana, 1991, I, 1.
Ravazzoni, La fideiussione, Milano, 1957, 146 ff.
Ravazzoni, Fideiussione in luogo de cauzione, Assicurazioni, 1959, I, 266.
Ravazzoni, Novissimo Digesto Italiano, (Fideiussione (dir. civ.)), VII, 1961, 274–293.
Ravazzoni, Nuove riflessioni sulle cauzione fideiussorie, Assicurazioni, 1973, 553 ff.
Ravazzoni, La fideiussione generale, Banca borsa e titoli di credito, 1980, I, 257.
Ravazzoni, Le garanzie dell'obbligazione, Parma, 1993, 165.
Recueils de la société Jean Bodin pour l'histoire comparative des institutions, Les Sûretés Personnelles (Troisième partie, période contemporaine), Bruxelles, 1969.

Reinicke and Tiedtke, Bürgschaftsrecht, Luchterhand, 2. ed., 1995.
Reinicke and Tiedtke, Kreditsicherung, Luchterhand, 4. ed., 2000.
Rescigno, Studi sull'accollo, Milano, 1958.
Rescigno, Novissimo Digesto Italiano, V, (voce Debito (successione nel)), Torino, 1960, 193.
Rescigno, Il problema della validità delle fideiussioni c. d. omnibus, Banca borsa e titoli di credito, 1972, II, 25 ff.
Rescigno, Obbligazioni e contratti, I, Torino, 1984.
Reyes, Fianza y nuevas modalidades de garantía, Valencia, 1996.
Reyes, Algunas consideraciones sobre los arts. 1838 y 1839 del Código Civil, Anuario de Derecho Civil, 1988, 220.
Rivolta, Le nuove disposizioni sulla fideiussione, Rivista di Diritto Civile, 1992, II, 675 ff.
Robles, El mandato de crédito, Revista Crítica de Derecho Inmobiliario, 1948, 541 ff.
Roca/Nieto/Bonet, Tratado de garantías en la contratación mercantil, v.1 (Rasgos básicos de la regulación española en materia de negocios de garantía), Madrid, 1996, 138–162.
Roca Puig, Responsabilidad por débito ajeno, Estudios de Derecho Privado, Madrid, 1948, I, 188 ff.
Rojo, Las garantías mobiliarias (Fundamentos del Derecho de garantías Mobiliarias a la luz de la experiencia de los Estados Unidos de América), Anuario de Derecho Civil, 1989, 718–811.
Rojo/Menendez, Estudios sobre la ley cambiaria y del cheque (El aval, Derecho cambiario) Madrid, 1986, 549.
Rothemberg, Der Kreditauftrag, Archiv für die zivilistische Praxis 1891, 223 ff.
Rubino/Scialoja e Branca, Commentario al codice civile (Obbligazioni alternative. Obbligazioni in solido, Obbligazioni divisibili ed indivisibili) Bologna, Roma, 1957, 134–136.
Rubio Garrido/Paquau Liaño, Jurisprudencia civil comentada, (on arts. 1821–1856), Granada, 2000.
Rubio Torrano, El mandato de crédito (a propósito de la ley 526 de la Compilación navarra), Revista jurídica de Navarra, no. 4, julio-diciembre, 1987, 101 ff .
Robles Alvarez de Sotomayor, El mandato de crédito, Revista Crítica de Derecho Inmobiliario, 1948, 531 ff.
Salanitro, Le fideiussioni bancarie, Banca borsa e titoli di credito, 1984, I, 135 ff.
Salvestroni, La solidarietà fideiussoria, Padova, 1977.
Sánchez Guilarte, Valor jurídico de las cartas de garantía o cartas de patrocinio, Revista de Derecho Bancario y Bursátil, 1985, 871 ff., and 1986, 219 ff.
Sánchez-Calero/Tirado/Motos/Albadalejo, Comentarios al Código de Comercio y legislación mercantil especial, v. XXIV, 2, Madrid, 1990.
Sánchez Calero Guilarte, El aval de letra de cambio, Revista de Derecho Bancario y Bursátil, no. 46, 1992, 331 ff.
Sánchez Calero, Instituciones de derecho mercantil, II, Madrid, 1996, 80 ff.
Sánchez-Calero Guilarte/Sánchez-Calero Guilarte, Comentarios a la jurisprudencia de derecho bancario y cambiario, v. I (Letra de cambio incompleta: transformación del aval cambiario en una „garantía personal atípica"), Madrid, 1993.
Sánchez Hernández, Comentario a la Sentencia de 13 de julio de 2007 [RA 2007 no. 4864], Cuadernos Cívital de Jurisprudencia Civil no. 76/2008, Madrid, 2008.
Sánchez Román, Estudios de derecho civil, v. IV, Madrid, 1889.

Sandulli, Le nozioni giuridiche di onerosità e di gratuità, Banca borsa e titoli di credito, 1973, I, 339 ff.

Santamaría, Comentarios al Código Civil II, Madrid, 1958.

Saunders, Financial institutions management: a modern perspective, 2nd ed, Chicago, 1997.

Schlesinger, Il "primato" del credito, in La civilistica italiana dagli anni '50 ad oggi tra crisi dogmatica e riforme legislative (Congresso dei civilisti italiani; Venezia 23–26 giugno 1989), Padova, 1991, 485 ff.

Sesta, Enciclopedia giuridica, VIII, (voce Confusione), Roma, 1988, 2 ff.

Sesta/Cendon, Commentario al Codice Civile, Torino, 1991, 1769 ff.

Segré, Mandato, Mandato di Crédito e fideiussione, Temi Emiliana, 1925, 102.

Sierra and Gullón, Comentario del Código Civil, v. IV, Barcelona, 2000.

Siddiqi, Credit risk scorecards: developing and implementing intelligent credit scoring, Hoboken, New Jersey: John Wiley & Sons., 2006.

Sicchero, Regresso e surrogazione legale, Contratto e impresa, 1996.

Simler, Cautionnement et garanties autonomes, 3. ed., Paris, 2000.

Simoneto, Novissimo Digesto Italiano (Il Mandato di Credito), Torino, 1957, 150–151.

Simonetto, La fideiussione prestata da privati, Padova, 1985.

Simone, Dizionario Simone, „Polizza fideiussoria" (http:www.simone.it/cgi?local/ Dizionari/newdiz.cgi?voce,5,4155).

Simonetto, La fideiussione prestata da privati, Padova, 1985.

Simpson/Rover/Norton/Andenas, Emerging Financial Markets and Secured transactions (General Principles of a Modern Secured Transactions Law), London, 1998, 143, 144.

Starck, Human Rights and Private Law in German Constitutional Development and in the jurisdiction of the Federal Constitutional Court, in: Friedmann and Barak-Erez, Human Rights in Private Law, Oxford, 2001.

Stoll, Vertrauensschutz bei einseitigen Leistungsversprechen, Festschrift Flume I, 1978, 760 ff.

Stolfi, In tema di fideiussione per debiti futuri, Rivista di Diritto Commerciale, 1971, 225.

Stolfi, In tema di fideiussione generale, Rivista di Diritto Civile, 1972, I, 529 ff.

Simonetto, La natura della fideiussione e la nullità della clausola c. d. omnibus, Rivista trimestrale di diritto processuale civile, 1987, 544 ff.

Smits, European Private Law: A Plea for a Spontanous Legal Order, Maastricht, 2006 (http://ssrn.com/abstract=897478).

Suso Vidal, El derecho de regreso entre coavalistas de créditos bancarios: especial consideración del supuesto de pago voluntario al acreedor por parte de uno de ellos, Revista de Derecho Mercantil, no. 157.158, 1980, 519 ff.

Swartzt, Security interests and bankruptcy priorities: a review of current theories, Legal Studies, 1981, 1–37; 14–21.

Talamanca, Enciclopedia di Diritto, v. XVII, (Fideiussione (Storia)), Milano, 1968, 331.

Tamburrino, Appunti sulla natura e sulla disciplina cosidetta assicurazione fideiussoria, Assicurazioni, 1970 I, 525.

Tendler, Les Sûretés, Paris, 1983.

Thietz-Bartram, Die Bankgarantie im italienischen Recht, Berlin, 1989.

Terranova, Validità ed effetti della fideiussione generale, Rivista di Diritto Commerciale, 1987, II, 148 ff.

Tilocca, Novissimo Digesto Italiano, XV, (voce Remissione del debito) Torino, 1968, 412.

Tirado/Motos/Albadalejo, Comentarios al Código de Comercio y legislación mercantil especial, v. XXIV, 2., (Ley del Contrato de Seguros), Madrid, 1990.
Tirado, Seguro de caución. Pignoración de pólizas de seguro, Contratos Bancarios, Madrid, 1992.
Torrente, Manuale di diritto privato, Milano, 1960.
Torres Mateos, Contratos de garantía, Navarra, 2006.
Trabucchi, Diritti di obbligazione, Padova, 1988.
Trabucchi/Cian, Commentario breve al Codice Civile, Padova, 1992 (art. 1933–1964).
Tucci, Tutela del credito e validità della fideiussione omnibus, Foro Italiano, 1988, I, 118.
Univelex, dir. Di Brina, La copertura assicurativa, Assicurazione del credito (http://univelex.unive.it/diritto-commerciale/menu/mf400000.htm).
Valcavi, Sulla inderogabilità dell'art. 1957 cc, Giustizia Italiana, 1990, I, 1, 460.
Valcalvi, Sulla fideiussione bancaria ed i suoi limiti, Foro Italiano, 1990, I, 558 ff.
Valcavi, Sulla ineguatezza del principio di buona fede a proteggere il fideiussore, Giustizia Italiana, 1990, I, 1, 622 ff.
Valcavi, Sulla nullità "ope legis" delle fideussioni "omnibus" e sulle relative conseguenze, Foro Italiano, 1992, I, 791 ff.
Valignani, Fideiussione bancarie e buona fede, Giustizia Italiana, 1990, I, 1, 1137 ff.
Valenzuela/Nieto/Bonet, Tratado de garantías de la contratación mercantil (El contrato de fianza: una síntesis de sus problemas actuales), Madrid, 1996, 439 ff.
Vaz Serra, Fiança e figuras analogas, Boletim do Ministério da Justiça, no. 71, Portugal, 1957, 287 ff.
Viale, Fideiussione omnibus, Contratto e impresa, 1990, 276 ff.
Vicent, Compendio Crítico de Derecho Mercantil, v. II, Barcelona, 1990.
Vicent/Nieto/Bonet, Tratado de garantías en la contratación mercantil (Las garantías en el ordenamiento jurídico), v. I, Madrid, 1996, 383 ff.
Villani, „Fatto del creditore" ed estinzione della fideiussione, Rivista trimestrale di diritto processuale civile, 1971, 309 ss; spec. 311.
Villiers, The Spanish Legal Tradition, Aldershot, 1999.
Von Bar, Principles, Definitions and Model Rules of European Private Law. Draft Common Frame of Reference (DCFR). Outline Edition, Munich 2009.
Von Bar/Barendrecht/Basedow/Drobnig/van Gerven/Hondius/Kerameus/Koussoulis/Land o/ Loos/Tilmann, The Private Law Systems in the EU: Discrimination on Grounds of Nationality and the Need for a European Civil Code, European Parliament, Directorate General for Research, Working Paper, Legal Affairs Series JURI 103 EN (1999).
Watson, The evolution of Western Private Law, expanded ed., Baltimore, 2001.
Watson, Legal Transplants and European Private Law, vol 4.4 Electronic journal of comparative law, December 2000, (http://www.ejcl.org/ejcl/44/44-2.html).
Weerasooria, Banking Law and the Financial Systems in Australia, Sydney, 1993.
Weth, Bürgschaft und Garantie auf erstes Anfordern, Archiv für die Zivilistische Praxis, 1989, 303 ff.
Wood, Comparative Law of Security and Guarantees, London, 1995.
Zuddas, Enciclopedia Giuridica, VII (voce Compensazione) Roma, 1988, 6.
Zuliani, Assicurazioni del credito e delle cauzioni, Trieste, 1958.

Index

Studien zum ausländischen und internationalen Privatrecht

Alphabetical Index

Brockmeier, Dirk: Punitive damages, multiple damages und deutscher ordre public. 1999. *Vol. 70.*

Brokamp, Arno: Das Europäische Verfahren für geringfügige Forderungen. 2008. *Vol. 207.*

Brückner, Bettina: Unterhaltsregreß im internationalen Privat- und Verfahrensrecht. 1994. *Vol. 37.*

Buchner, Benedikt: Kläger- und Beklagtenschutz im Recht der internationalen Zuständigkeit. 1998. *Vol. 60.*

Budzikiewicz, Christine: Materielle Statuseinheit und kollisionsrechtliche Statusverbesserung. 2007. *Vol. 185.*

Büttner, Benjamin: Umfang und Grenzen der Dritthaftung von Experten. 2006. *Vol. 169.*

Burkei, Felix: Internationale Handelsschiedsgerichtsbarkeit in Japan. 2008. *Vol. 213.*

Busse, Daniel: Internationales Bereicherungsrecht. 1998. *Vol. 66.*

Dawe, Christian: Der Sonderkonkurs des deutschen Internationalen Insolvenzrechts. 2005. *Vol. 159.*

Dernauer, Marc: Verbraucherschutz und Vertragsfreiheit im japanischen Recht. 2006. *Vol. 164.*

Dilger, Jörg: Die Regelungen zur internationalen Zuständigkeit in Ehesachen in der Verordnung (EG) Nr. 2201/2003. 2004. *Vol. 116.*

Döse-Digenopoulos, Annegret: Der arbeitsrechtliche Kündigungsschutz in England. 1982. *Vol. 6.*

Dohrn, Heike: Die Kompetenzen der Europäischen Gemeinschaft im Internationalen Privatrecht. 2004. *Vol. 133.*

Dopffel, Peter (Ed.): Ehelichkeitsanfechtung durch das Kind. 1990. *Vol. 23.*

– (Ed.): Kindschaftsrecht im Wandel. 1994. *Vol. 40.*

–, *Ulrich Drobnig* und *Kurt Siehr* (Ed.): Reform des deutschen internationalen Privatrechts. 1980. *Vol. 2.*

Dornblüth, Susanne: Die europäische Regelung der Anerkennung und Vollstreckbarerklärung von Ehe- und Kindschaftsentscheidungen. 2003. *Vol. 107.*

Drappatz, Thomas: Die Überführung des internationalen Zivilverfahrensrechts in eine Gemeinschaftskompetenz nach Art. 65 EGV. 2002. *Vol. 95.*

Drobnig, Ulrich: see *Dopffel, Peter.*

Dutta, Anatol: Die Durchsetzung öffentlichrechtlicher Forderungen ausländischer Staaten durch deutsche Gerichte. 2006. *Vol. 172.*

Eckl, Christian: Treu und Glauben im spanischen Vertragsrecht. 2007. *Vol. 183.*

Eichholz, Stephanie: Die US-amerikanische Class Action und ihre deutschen Funktionsäquivalente. 2002. *Vol. 90.*

Eisele, Ursula S.: Holdinggesellschaften in Japan. 2004. *Vol. 121.*

Eisenhauer, Martin: Moderne Entwicklungen im englischen Grundstücksrecht. 1997. *Vol. 59.*

Ernst, Ulrich: Mobiliarsicherheiten in Deutschland und Polen. 2005. *Vol. 148.*

Eschbach, Sigrid: Die nichteheliche Kindschaft im IPR – Geltendes Recht und Reform. 1997. *Vol. 56.*

Faust, Florian: Die Vorhersehbarkeit des Schadens gemäß Art. 74 Satz 2 UN-Kaufrecht (CISG). 1996. *Vol. 50.*

Fenge, Anja: Selbstbestimmung im Alter. 2002. *Vol. 88.*

Festner, Stephan: Interessenkonflikte im deutschen und englischen Vertretungsrecht. 2006. *Vol. 177.*

Fetsch, Johannes: Eingriffsnormen und EG-Vertrag. 2002. *Vol. 91.*

Fischer-Zernin, Cornelius: Der Rechtsangleichungserfolg der Ersten gesellschaftsrechtlichen Richtlinie der EWG. 1986. *Vol. 15.*
Förster, Christian: Die Dimension des Unternehmens. 2003. *Vol. 101.*
Forkert, Meinhard: Eingetragene Lebenspartnerschaften im deutschen IPR: Art. 17b EGBGB. 2003. *Vol. 118.*
Freitag, Robert: Der Einfluß des Europäischen Gemeinschaftsrechts auf das Internationale Produkthaftungsrecht. 2000. *Vol. 83.*
Fricke, Martin: Die autonome Anerkennungszuständigkeitsregel im deutschen Recht des 19. Jahrhunderts. 1993. *Vol. 32.*
Fricke, Verena: Der Unterlassungsanspruch gegen Presseunternehmen zum Schutze des Persönlichkeitsrechts im internationalen Privatrecht. 2003. *Vol. 110.*
Fröschle, Tobias: Die Entwicklung der gesetzlichen Rechte des überlebenden Ehegatten. 1996. *Vol. 49.*
Fromholzer, Ferdinand: Consideration. 1997. *Vol. 57.*
Fuglinszky, Ádám: Mangelfolgeschäden im deutschen und ungarischen Recht. 2007. *Vol. 188.*
Funken, Katja: Das Anerkennungsprinzip im internationalen Privatrecht. 2009. *Vol. 218.*
Gärtner, Veronika: Die Privatscheidung im deutschen und gemeinschaftsrechtlichen Internationalen Privat- und Verfahrensrecht. 2008. *Vol. 208.*
Gal,Jens: Die Haftung des Schiedsrichters in der internationalen Handelsschiedsgerichtsbarkeit. 2009. *Vol. 215.*
Ganssauge, Niklas: Internationale Zuständigkeit und anwendbares Recht bei Verbraucherverträgen im Internet. 2004. *Vol. 126.*
Gerasimchuk, Eleonora: Die Urteilsanerkennung im deutsch-russischen Rechtsverkehr. 2007. *Vol. 181.*
Giesen, Reinhard: Die Anknüpfung des Personalstatuts im norwegischen und deutschen internationalen Privatrecht. 2010. *Vol. 235.*
Gilfrich, Stephanie Uta: Schiedsverfahren im Scheidungsrecht. 2007. *Vol. 189.*
Godl, Gabriele: Notarhaftung im Vergleich. 2001. *Vol. 85.*
Gößl, Ulrich: Die Satzung der Europäischen Aktiengesellschaft (SE) mit Sitz in Deutschland. 2010. *Vol. 239.*
Gottwald, Walther: Streitbeilegung ohne Urteil. 1981. *Vol. 5.*
Graf, Ulrike: Die Anerkennung ausländischer Insolvenzentscheidungen. 2003. *Vol. 113.*
Grigera Naón, Horacio A.: Choice of Law Problems in International Commercial Arbitration. 1992. *Vol. 28.*
Grolimund, Pascal: Drittstaatenproblematik des europäischen Zivilverfahrensrechts. 2000. *Vol. 80.*
Häcker, Birke: Consequences of Impaired Consent Transfers. 2009. *Vol. 223.*
Hahn, H. u.a.: Die Wertsicherung der Young-Anleihe. 1984. *Vol. 10.*
Handorn, Boris: Das Sonderkollisionsrecht der deutschen internationalen Schiedsgerichtsbarkeit. 2005. *Vol. 141.*
Hartenstein, Olaf: Die Privatautonomie im Internationalen Privatrecht als Störung des europäischen Entscheidungseinklangs. 2000. *Vol. 81.*
Hartnick, Susanne: Kontrollprobleme bei Spendenorganisationen. 2007. *Vol. 186.*
Hawellek, Jeronimo: Die persönliche Surrogation. 2010. *Vol. 248.*
Hein, Jan von: Das Günstigkeitsprinzip im Internationalen Deliktsrecht. 1999. *Vol. 69.*

Heinze, Christian A.: Einstweiliger Rechtsschutz im europäischen Immaterialgüterrecht. 2007. *Vol. 195.*
Heiss, Helmut (Ed.): Zivilrechtsreform im Baltikum. 2006. *Vol. 161.*
Hellmich, Stefanie: Kreditsicherungsrechte in der spanischen Mehrrechtsordnung. 2000. *Vol. 84.*
Hellwege, Phillip: Die Rückabwicklung gegenseitiger Verträge als einheitliches Problem. 2004. *Vol. 130.*
Henke, Johannes: Effektivität der Kontrollmechanismen gegenüber dem Unternehmensinsolvenzverwalter. 2009. *Vol. 229.*
Henke, Matthias F.: Enthält die Liste des Anhangs der Klauselrichtlinie 93/13/EWG Grundregeln des Europäischen Vertragsrechts? 2010. *Vol. 247.*
Henninger, Thomas: Europäisches Privatrecht und Methode. 2009. *Vol. 224.*
Herb, Anja: Europäisches Gemeinschaftsrecht und nationaler Zivilprozess. 2007. *Vol. 187.*
Hettenbach, Dieter: Das Übereinkommen der Vereinten Nationen über die Verwendung elektronischer Mitteilungen bei internationalen Verträgen. 2008. *Vol. 212.*
Hinden, Michael von: Persönlichkeitsverletzungen im Internet. 1999. *Vol. 74.*
Hippel, Thomas von: Der Ombudsmann im Bank- und Versichungswesen. 2000. *Vol. 78.*
Hirse, Thomas: Die Ausweichklausel im Internationalen Privatrecht. 2006. *Vol. 175.*
Hoffmann, Nadja: Die Koordination des Vertrags- und Deliktsrechts in Europa. 2006. *Vol. 168.*
Hotz, Sandra: Japanische, deutsche und schweizerische Irrtumsregelungen. 2006. *Vol. 176.*
Huber, Stefan: Entwicklung transnationaler Modellregeln für Zivilverfahren. 2008. *Vol. 197.*
Hutner, Armin: Das internationale Privat- und Verfahrensrecht der Wirtschaftsmediation. 2005. *Vol. 156.*
Hye-Knudsen, Rebekka: Marken-, Patent- und Urheberrechtsverletzungen im europäischen Internationalen Zivilprozessrecht. 2005. *Vol. 149.*
Janköster, Jens Peter: Fluggastrechte im internationalen Luftverkehr. 2009. *Vol. 227.*
Janssen, Helmut: Die Übertragung von Rechtsvorstellungen auf fremde Kulturen am Beispiel des englischen Kolonialrechts. 2000. *Vol. 79.*
Jeremias, Christoph: Internationale Insolvenzaufrechnung. 2005. *Vol. 150.*
Jung, Holger: Ägyptisches internationales Vertragsrecht. 1999. *Vol. 77.*
Junge, Ulf: Staatshaftung in Argentinien. 2002. *Vol. 100.*
Kadner, Daniel: Das internationale Privatrecht von Ecuador. 1999. *Vol. 76.*
Kannengießer, Matthias N.: Die Aufrechnung im internationalen Privat- und Verfahrensrecht. 1998. *Vol. 63.*
Kapnopoulou, Elissavet N.: Das Recht der mißbräuchlichen Klauseln in der Europäischen Union. 1997. *Vol. 53.*
Karl, Anna-Maria: Die Anerkennung von Entscheidungen in Spanien. 1993. *Vol. 33.*
Karl, Matthias: see *Veelken, Winfried.*
Kern, Christoph: Die Sicherheit gedeckter Wertpapiere. 2004. *Vol. 135.*
Kircher, Wolfgang: Die Voraussetzungen der Sachmängelhaftung beim Warenkauf. 1998. *Vol. 65.*

Klauer, Stefan: Das europäische Kollisionsrecht der Verbraucherverträge zwischen Römer EVÜ und EG-Richtlinien. 2002. *Vol. 99.*

Klein, Jean-Philippe: Die Unwirksamkeit von Verträgen nach französischem Recht. 2010. *Vol. 245.*

Kleinschmidt, Jens: Der Verzicht im Schuldrecht. 2004. *Vol. 117.*

Kliesow, Olaf: Aktionärsrechte und Aktionärsklagen in Japan. 2001. *Vol. 87.*

Klingel, Katharina: Die Principles of European Law on Personal Security als neutrales Recht für internationale Bürgschaftsverträge. 2009. *Vol. 222.*

Klüber, Rüdiger: Persönlichkeitsschutz und Kommerzialisierung. 2007. *Vol. 178.*

Köhler, Martin: Die Haftung nach UN-Kaufrecht im Spannungsverhältnis zwischen Vertrag und Delikt. 2003. *Vol. 111.*

Koerner, Dörthe: Fakultatives Kollisionsrecht in Frankreich und Deutschland. 1995. *Vol. 44.*

Kopp, Beate: Probleme der Nachlaßabwicklung bei kollisionsrechtlicher Nachlaßspaltung. 1997. *Vol. 55.*

Kronke, Herbert: Rechtstatsachen, kollisionsrechtliche Methodenentfaltung und Arbeitnehmerschutz im internationalen Arbeitsrecht. 1980. *Vol. 1.*

Kroymann, Benjamin: Das Kapitalgesellschaftsrecht der VR China. 2009. *Vol. 217.*

Kuckein, Mathias: Die ‚Berücksichtigung' von Eingriffsnormen im deutschen und englischen internationalen Vertragsrecht. 2008. *Vol. 198.*

Laimer, Simon: Durchführung und Rechtsfolgen der Vertragsaufhebung bei nachträglichen Erfüllungsstörungen. 2009. *Vol. 219.*

Landfermann, Hans-Georg: Gesetzliche Sicherungen des vorleistenden Verkäufers. 1987. *Vol. 18.*

Leifeld, Janis: Das Anerkennungsprinzip im Kollisionsrechtssystem des internationalen Privatrechts. 2010. *Vol. 241.*

Lenhard, Anselm: Die Vorschläge zur Reform des englischen Mobiliarkreditsicherungsrechts. 2010. *Vol. 233.*

Leicht, Steffen: Die Qualifikation der Haftung von Angehörigen rechts- und wirtschaftsberatender Berufe im grenzüberschreitenden Dienstleistungsverkehr. 2002. *Vol. 82.*

Linhart, Karin: Internationales Einheitsrecht und einheitliche Auslegung. 2005. *Vol. 147.*

Linker, Anja Celina: Zur Neubestimmung der Ordnungsaufgaben im Erbrecht in rechtsvergleichender Sicht. 1999. *Vol. 75.*

Lohmann, Arnd: Parteiautonomie und UN-Kaufrecht. 2005. *Vol. 119.*

Lorenz, Verena: Annexverfahren bei Internationalen Insolvenzen. 2005. *Vol. 140.*

Lüke, Stephan: Punitive Damages in der Schiedsgerichtsbarkeit. 2003. *Vol. 105.*

Lüttringhaus, Jan D.: Grenzüberschreitender Diskriminierungsschutz – Das internationale Privatrecht der Antidiskriminierung. 2010. *Vol. 234.*

Maesch, Petja: Kodifikation und Anpassung des bulgarischen IPR an das Europäische Recht. 2010. *Vol. 252.*

Magnus, Dorothea: Medizinische Forschung an Kindern. 2006. *Vol. 170.*

Magnus, Robert: Das Anwaltsprivileg und sein zivilprozessualer Schutz. 2010. *Vol. 238.*

Martens, Sebastian: Durch Dritte verursachte Willensmängel. 2007. *Vol. 190.*

Mata Muñoz, Almudena de la: Typical Personal Security Rights in the EU. 2010. *Vol. 253.*

Maurer, Tobias: Schuldübernahme. 2010. *Vol. 236.*

Meckel, Verena: Die Corporate Governance im neuen japanischen Gesellschaftsrecht. 2010. *Vol. 242.*
Meier, Sonja: Irrtum und Zweckverfehlung. 1999. *Vol. 68.*
Melin, Patrick: Gesetzesauslegung in den USA und in Deutschland. 2004. *Vol. 137.*
Minuth, Klaus: Besitzfunktionen beim gutgläubigen Mobiliarerwerb im deutschen und französischen Recht. 1990. *Vol. 24.*
Mistelis, Loukas A.: Charakterisierungen und Qualifikation im internationalen Privatrecht. 1999. *Vol. 73.*
Mitzkait, Anika: Leistungsstörung und Haftungsbefreiung. 2008. *Vol. 205.*
Mörsdorf-Schulte, Juliana: Funktion und Dogmatik US-amerikanischer punitive damages. 1999. *Vol. 67.*
Monleón, Nicole: Das neue internationale Privatrecht von Venezuela. 2008. *Vol. 204.*
Morawitz, Gabriele: Das internationale Wechselrecht. 1991. *Vol. 27.*
Moser, Dominik: Die Offenkundigkeit der Stellvertretung. *Vol. 246.*
Mülhens, Jörg: Der sogenannte Haftungsdurchgriff im deutschen und englischen Recht. 2006. *Vol. 174.*
Müller, Achim: Grenzüberschreitende Beweisaufnahme im Europäischen Justizraum. 2004. *Vol. 125.*
Müller, Carsten: International zwingende Normen des deutschen Arbeitsrechts. 2005. *Vol. 157.*
Naumann, Ingrid: Englische anti-suit injunctions zur Durchsetzung von Schiedsvereinbarungen. 2008. *Vol. 202.*
Němec, Jiří: Ausländische Direktinvestitionen in der Tschechischen Republik. 1997. *Vol. 54.*
Neumann, Nils: Bedenkzeit vor und nach Vertragsabschluß. 2005. *Vol. 142.*
Neunhoeffer, Friederike: Das Presseprivileg im Datenschutzrecht. 2005. *Vol. 146.*
Niklas, Isabella Maria: Die europäische Zuständigkeitsordnung in Ehe- und Kind -schaftsverfahren. 2003. *Vol. 106.*
Nojack, Jana: Exklusivnormen im IPR. 2005. *Vol. 152.*
Nordmeier, Carl F.: Zulässigkeit und Bindungswirkung gemeinschaftlicher Testamente im Internationalen Privatrecht. 2008. *Vol. 201.*
Oertel, Christoph: Objektive Haftung in Europa. 2010. *Vol. 249.*
Pattloch, Thomas: Das IPR des geistigen Eigentums in der VR China. 2003. *Vol. 103.*
Peinze, Alexander: Internationales Urheberrecht in Deutschland und England. 2002. *Vol. 92.*
Pfeil-Kammerer, Christa: Deutsch-amerikanischer Rechtshilfeverkehr in Zivilsachen. 1987. *Vol. 17.*
Plett, K. und *K.A. Ziegert* (Ed.): Empirische Rechtsforschung zwischen Wissenschaft und Politik. 1984. *Vol. 11.*
Pißler, Knut B.: Chinesisches Kapitalmarktrecht. 2004. *Vol. 127.*
–: Gläubigeranfechtung in China. 2008. *Vol. 203.*
Primaczenko, Vladimir: Treuhänderische Vermögensverwaltung nach russischem Recht. 2010. *Vol. 244.*
Reichert-Facilides, Daniel: Fakultatives und zwingendes Kollisionsrecht. 1995. *Vol. 46.*

Reiter, Christian: Vertrag und Geschäftsgrundlage im deutschen und italienischen Recht. 2002. *Vol. 89.*
Richter, Stefan: see *Veelken, Winfried.*
Ringe, Georg: Die Sitzverlegung der Europäischen Aktiengesellschaft. 2006. *Vol. 171.*
Rogoz, Thomas: Ausländisches Recht im deutschen und englischen Zivilprozess. 2008. *Vol. 200.*
Rohde, Kerstin: Haftung und Kompensation bei Straßenverkehrsunfällen. 2009. *Vol. 232.*
Rohe, Mathias: Zu den Geltungsgründen des Deliktsstatus. 1994. *Vol. 43.*
Rothoeft, Daniel D.: Rückstellungen nach § 249 HGB und ihre Entsprechungen in den US-GAAP und IAS. 2004. *Vol. 122.*
Rühl, Giesela: Obliegenheiten im Versicherungsvertragsrecht. 2004. *Vol. 123.*
Rusch, Konrad: Gewinnhaftung bei Verletzung von Treuepflichten. 2003. *Vol. 109.*
Sachse, Kathrin: Der Verbrauchervertrag im Internationalen Privat- und Prozeßrecht. 2006. *Vol. 166.*
Sachsen Gessaphe, Karl August Prinz von: Das Konkubinat in den mexikanischen Zivilrechtsordnungen. 1990. *Vol. 22.*
Sandrock, Andrea: Vertragswidrigkeit der Sachleistung. 2003. *Vol. 104.*
Schacherreiter, Judith: Das Franchise-Paradox. 2006. *Vol. 167.*
Schärtl, Christoph: Das Spiegelbildprinzip im Rechtsverkehr mit ausländischen Staatenverbindungen. 2005. *Vol. 145.*
Schepke, Jan: Das Erfolgshonorar des Rechtsanwalts. 1998. *Vol. 62.*
Scherpe, Jens M.: Außergerichtliche Streitbeilegung in Verbrauchersachen. 2002. *Vol. 96.*
–: see *Basedow, J.*
Schilf, Sven: Allgemeine Vertragsgrundregeln als Vertragsstatut. 2005. *Vol. 138.*
Schimansky, Annika: Der Franchisevertrag nach deutschem und niederländischem Recht. 2003. *Vol. 112.*
Schindler, Thomas: Rechtsgeschäftliche Entscheidungsfreiheit und Drohung. 2005. *Vol. 139.*
Schlichte, Johannes: Die Grundlage der Zwangsvollstreckung im polnischen Recht. 2005. *Vol. 144.*
Schmidt, Claudia: Der Haftungsdurchgriff und seine Umkehrung im internationalen Privatrecht. 1993. *Vol. 31.*
Schmidt, Jan Peter: Zivilrechtskodifikation in Brasilien. 2009. *Vol. 226.*
Schmidt-Ahrendts, Nils: Das Verhältnis von Erfüllung, Schadensersatz und Vertragsaufhebung im CISG. 2007. *Vol. 193.*
Schmidt-Parzefall, Thomas: Die Auslegung des Parallelübereinkommens von Lugano. 1995. *Vol. 47.*
Schneider, Winfried-Thomas: Abkehr vom Verschuldensprinzip? 2007. *Vol. 179.*
Schnyder, Anton K.: Internationale Versicherungsaufsicht zwischen Wirtschaftsrecht und Kollisionsrecht. 1989. *Vol. 20.*
Scholz, Ingo: Das Problem der autonomen Auslegung des EuGVÜ. 1998. *Vol. 61.*
Schreier, Michael: Schutz vor willkürlichen und diskriminierenden Entlassungen. 2009. *Vol. 230.*
Schröder, Vincent: Die Verweisung auf Mehrrechtsstaaten im deutschen Internationalen Privatrecht. 2007. *Vol. 192.*

Schubel, Joanna: Gestaltungsfreiheit und Gestaltungsgrenzen im polnischen Vertragskonzernrecht. 2010. *Vol. 250.*
Schütze, Elisabeth: Zession und Einheitsrecht. 2005. *Vol. 155.*
Schurr, Francesco A.: Geschäftsimmanente Abstandnahme. 2006. *Vol. 165.*
Seibl, Maximilian: Die Beweislast bei Kollisionsnormen. 2009. *Band 231.*
Seibt, Christoph H.: Zivilrechtlicher Ausgleich ökologischer Schäden. 1994. *Vol. 42.*
Seif, Ulrike: Der Bestandsschutz besitzloser Mobiliarsicherheiten. 1997. *Vol. 52.*
Selbig, Sabine: Förderung und Finanzkontrolle gemeinnütziger Organisationen in Großbritannien und Deutschland. 2006. *Vol. 173.*
Sieghörtner, Robert: Internationales Straßenverkehrsunfallrecht. 2002. *Vol. 93.*
Siehr, Kurt: see *Dopffel, Peter.*
Söhngen, Martin: Das internationale Privatrecht von Peru. 2006. *Vol. 162.*
Solomon, Dennis: Der Bereicherungsausgleich in Anweisungsfällen. 2004. *Vol. 124.*
Sonnentag, Michael: Der Renvoi im Internationalen Privatrecht. 2001. *Vol. 86.*
Spahlinger, Andreas: Sekundäre Insolvenzverfahren bei grenzüberschreitenden Insolvenzen. 1998. *Vol. 64.*
Spelsberg-Korspeter, Ullrich: Anspruchskonkurrenz im internationalen Privatrecht. 2009. *Vol. 225.*
Sprenger, Carsten: Internationale Expertenhaftung. 2008. *Vol. 199.*
Stegmann, Oliver: Tatsachenbehauptung und Werturteil in der deutschen und französischen Presse. 2004. *Vol. 120.*
Stehl, Kolja: Die Überwindung der Inkohärenz des Internationalen Privatrechts der Bank- und Versicherungsverträge. 2008. *Vol. 211.*
Steinbrück, Ben: Die Unterstützung ausländischer Schiedsverfahren durch staatliche Gerichte. 2009. *Vol. 221.*
Stiller, Dietrich F.R.: Das internationale Zivilprozeßrecht der Republik Korea. 1989. *Vol. 19.*
Stringari, Katerina: Die Haftung des Verkäufers für mangelbedingte Schäden. 2007. *Vol. 184.*
Sujecki, Bartosz: Das elektronische Mahnverfahren. 2008. *Vol. 206.*
Takahashi, Eiji: Konzern und Unternehmensgruppe in Japan – Regelung nach deutschem Modell? 1994. *Vol. 38.*
Tassikas, Apostolos: Dispositives Recht und Rechtswahlfreiheit als Ausnahmebereiche der EG-Grundfreiheiten. 2004. *Vol. 114.*
Thiele, Christian: Die zivilrechtliche Haftung der Tabakindustrie. 2003. *Vol. 115.*
Thoma, Ionna: Die Europäisierung und die Vergemeinschaftung des nationalen ordre public. 2007. *Vol. 182.*
Thoms, Cordula: Einzelstatut bricht Gesamtstatut. 1996. *Vol. 51.*
Tiedemann, Andrea: Internationales Erbrecht in Deutschland und Lateinamerika. 1993. *Vol. 34.*
Tiedemann, Stefan: Die Haftung aus Vermögensübernahme im internationalen Recht. 1995. *Vol. 45.*
Tochtermann, Peter: Die Unabhängigkeit und Unparteilichkeit des Mediators. 2008. *Vol. 210.*
Trillmich, Philip: Klauselkontrolle nach spanischem Recht im Vergleich mit der Klauselrichtlinie 93/13/EWG. 2009. *Vol. 216.*
Trulsen, Marion: Pflichtteilsrecht und englische family provision im Vergleich. 2004. *Vol. 129.*

Veelken, Winfried, Matthias Karl, Stefan Richter: Die Europäische Fusionskontrolle. 1992. *Vol. 30.*
Verse, Dirk A.: Verwendungen im Eigentümer-Besitzer-Verhältnis. 1999. *Vol. 72.*
Waehler, Jan P. (Ed.): Deutsch-polnisches Kolloquium über Wirtschaftsrecht und das Recht des Persönlichkeitsschutzes. 1985. *Vol. 12.*
– (Ed.): Deutsches und sowjetisches Wirtschaftsrecht. Vol. 1. 1981. *Vol. 4.*
– Vol. 2. 1983. *Vol. 9.*
– Vol. 3. 1990. *Vol. 25.*
– Vol. 4. 1990. *Vol. 26.*
– Vol. 5. 1991. *Vol. 28.*
Wang, Xiaoye: Monopole und Wettbewerb in der chinesischen Wirtschaft. 1993. *Vol. 35.*
Kai Wantzen: Unternehmenshaftung und Enterprise Liability. 2007. *Vol. 191.*
Wazlawik, Thomas: Die Konzernhaftung der deutschen Muttergesellschaft für die Schulden ihrer US-amerikanischen Tochtergesellschaft. 2004. *Vol. 131.*
Weidt, Heinz: Antizipierter Vertragsbruch. 2007. *Vol. 194.*
Weinert, Mirko: Vollstreckungsbegleitender einstweiliger Rechtsschutz. 2007. *Vol. 180.*
Weishaupt, Axel: Die vermögensrechtlichen Beziehungen der Ehegatten im brasilianischen Sach- und Kollisionsrecht. 1981. *Vol. 3.*
Weller, Matthias: Ordre-public-Kontrolle internationaler Gerichtsstandsvereinbarungen im autonomen Zuständigkeitsrecht. 2005. *Vol. 143.*
Weppner, Simon: Der gesellschaftsrechtliche Minderheitenschutz bei grenzüberschreitender Verschmelzung von Kapitalgesellschaften. 2010. *Vol. 251.*
Wesch, Susanne: Die Produzentenhaftung im internationalen Rechtsvergleich. 1994. *Vol. 39.*
Weyde, Daniel: Anerkennung und Vollstreckung deutscher Entscheidungen in Polen. 1997. *Vol. 58.*
Wiese, Volker: Der Einfluß des Europäischen Rechts auf das Internationale Sachenrecht der Kulturgüter. 2006. *Vol. 160.*
Willemer, Charlotte: Vis attractiva concursus und die Europäische Insolvenzverordnung. 2006. *Vol. 163.*
Witzleb, Normann: Geldansprüche bei Persönlichkeitsverletzungen durch Medien. 2002. *Vol. 94.*
Wu, Jiin Yu: Der Einfluß des Herstellers auf die Verbraucherpreise nach deutschem und taiwanesischem Recht. 1999. *Vol. 71.*
Wurmnest, Wolfgang: Grundzüge eines europäischen Haftungsrechts. 2003. *Vol. 102.*
–: see *Basedow, J.*
Zeeck, Sebastian: Das Internationale Anfechtungsrecht in der Insolvenz. 2003. *Vol. 108.*
Ziegert, K.A.: see *Plett, K.*
Zobel, Petra: Schiedsgerichtsbarkeit und Gemeinschaftsrecht. 2005. *Vol. 154.*

For a complete catalogue please write to the publisher
Mohr Siebeck • P.O. Box 2030 • D–72010 Tübingen/Germany
Up-to-date information on the internet at www.mohr.de